INDONESIA FREE:
A POLITICAL BIOGRAPHY OF MOHAMMAD HATTA

MAVIS ROSE

INDONESIA FREE:
A POLITICAL BIOGRAPHY OF
MOHAMMAD HATTA

EQUINOX
PUBLISHING
JAKARTA KUALA LUMPUR

EQUINOX PUBLISHING (ASIA) PTE LTD
No 3. Shenton Way
#10-05 Shenton House
Singapore 068805

www.EquinoxPublishing.com

Indonesia Free:
A Political Biography of Mohammad Hatta
by Mavis Rose

ISBN 978-602-8397-24-7

First Equinox Edition 2010

Printed in the United States

1 3 5 7 9 10 8 6 4 2

Table of Contents

ILLUSTRATIONS

INTRODUCTION

Generally speaking, biographies are only written for idolising a hero. The more inferior the biography is, the greater will be the idolisation of the great man the biography describes....So far as I am concerned, I am more likely to hear or read statements showing my failures and my shame rather than praise and eulogy.

Mohammad Hatta, "On Character,"
in *Portrait of a Patriot*

Mohammad Hatta, the first Vice-President and joint proclaimer of the Republic of Indonesia, was a man who devoted almost his entire life to an ideal. From his early years until his death in 1980, the issue of Indonesian freedom overshadowed all other aspects of his life. Hatta's biography depicts the dogged determination, courage, and optimism, required by an Indonesian leader if he were to confront a colonial power and win his country's independence. His life history also portrays the disillusionment and frustration a leader experiences when his life-long democratic ideal is shattered and the new nation reverts to a type of government similar to the one he had dedicated his life to transforming.

Indonesian freedom meant more to Hatta than the attainment of national sovereignty; it also demanded an element of social reform. Freedom for Indonesia must also ensure the people's participation in their country's government. Independence must not bring to birth a nation in which the majority of the people would be powerless, as in the colonial period. Hatta's concept of democratic government and social and economic betterment for the people he named *kedaulatan rakyat*, people's sovereignty.

Hatta's revolutionary activism began in West Sumatra in a society with a traditional form of government which was unusually egalitarian. The culture, philosophies, process of modernization, and spirit of revolt of his Minangkabau ethnic group all played a part in shaping his concepts of freedom. By the time of Hatta's birth, the tradition of democracy in the Minangkabau, where the local clans governed the *nagari* or village states, had almost crumbled, and had been replaced by an autocratic system of rule centered on Batavia. The authority of the *penghulu* (or family heads) had been transferred into the hands of Dutch officials and their salaried assistants.

Why did a quiet, studious young man like Mohammad Hatta enter the stressful, hazardous, cloak-and-dagger milieu in which a purposeful revolutionary must operate? Clearly his motivation was sufficiently compelling to overcome any natural aversion to such a lifestyle. Hatta also grew up in an unsettling epoch, a period of accelerated technological change, Asian renaissance, global warfare, colonial unrest, and class struggle. Reverberations from these upheavals impinged on him, converting general dissatisfaction into open revolt.

There was a deep-seated religious element in Hatta's activism, a conviction that his struggle for *kedaulatan rakyat* constituted a divine commissioning. He was as much a religious as a revolutionary ascetic. Hatta was an eclectic Muslim -- Modernist, Sufist, and Wahhabist -- while his Dutch schooling had drawn him philosophically closer to the West than the Middle East. Hatta, like many of his Minangkabau fellow nationalists, was also fascinated by Marx, responding to his call for social justice and intrigued by his economic theories.

Hatta's mercantile background made him very conscious of the economic factors influencing social transformation and the colonial system. He was always a strong supporter of cooperative systems, which he saw as a practical means of strengthening the weakest Indonesian sectors, and at the same time developing a spirit of independence and self-reliance. The Soviet Union's collectivist system, in Hatta's opinion, dampened initiative and contravened Islamic law by discouraging private enterprise.

Hatta rose to prominence as a leader through his organizational abilities, his drive, his creative thinking and provocative writings. He laid great stress on political education through the use of cadres and party newspapers. Hatta himself was not always an effective classroom teacher;

he was more successful as the provider of ideas and material. The academic way in which he expressed his concepts made it difficult for many people to understand him. He tended to be more eloquent with his pen than with his voice, being too reserved and inhibited to use dramatic effect in his public speaking or to unleash his passions before an audience.

It was during the Japanese Occupation and the Revolution that Hatta gained widest acceptance as a national leader. In these critical periods, his cool levelheadedness and his ability to plan carefully and act shrewdly impressed his fellows. Hatta would have liked to step into the role of national leader in periods of crisis in the post-Dutch period. That he had no opportunity to do so was a source of frustration to him, as he saw the parliamentary system lose credibility through mismanagement and irresponsible behavior on the part of the rival parties.

Hatta's relationship with Sukarno provided the major drama in his political life, affecting his close ties with his ally, Sjahrir. For a man like Hatta, dedicated to steering Indonesia away from the Javanese/ colonial hierarchical system of government in the direction of *kedaulatan rakyat*, his dependence on Sukarno's patronage to gain acceptance on Java was an anathema. It also proved to be his Achilles heel. His resignation from the vice-presidency in 1956 combined elements of anger and relief. Hatta had a tendency to be ambivalent in his statements about Sukarno, being at times protective and affectionate, on other occasions pouring out bitterness and condemnation on Sukarno's head. Hatta saw Sukarno, along with the Communists, as responsible for thwarting the advancement of his social and economic goals.

Yet the two leaders achieved much when they worked in partnership, together proclaiming independence and successfully warding off serious challenges within and without the Republic of Indonesia during the Revolution. There was wide support and loyalty for the *Dwi Tunggal* throughout the archipelago, with a recognition that the two men complemented each other. Hatta needed Sukarno's charm and ability to communicate with the Javanese masses. Sukarno benefitted from Hatta's discipline, integrity, and economic sense.

When Hatta resigned from the vice-presidency, his political impact weakened and he never regained the power he had possessed as a member of the *Dwi Tunggal*. Likewise, without Hatta's steadying influence and dedication to a principle rather than to personal ambition, Sukarno's political performance deteriorated, and his regime ended in political and economic disaster.

To remain at the apex of power, Hatta would have had to modify his ideals. This he was not prepared to do, believing that, within the framework of *kedaulatan rakyat*, both the Old and New Orders were counter-revolutionary. From 1960 to the end of his life, Hatta's political activism reverted to being covert. His efforts to regain a leadership position in the New Order regime were thwarted by Suharto's decision to ban the Islamic socialist party which Hatta formed to replace the banned Masjumi and PSI parties.

Although Hatta never achieved the same degree of international recognition as Sukarno, he did play a major and significant role in the founding of Indonesia and in drawing attention to the needs and oppression of its people. He was undoubtedly a statesman of the highest caliber, prepared to sacrifice ambition, wealth, and high office for his ideals. His leadership role must be assessed as much for its ethical qualities as for its attainment of political power.

Writing Hatta's biography has been for me an immensely satisfying experience. Since reading his anthology *Portrait of a Patriot* as a first-year undergraduate, my curiosity to discover more about Hatta has compelled me to research the life of this complex leader who walked in Sukarno's shadow but yet was a "powerhouse" in his own right. I have been aware that it was impossible to discover the whole truth about Hatta, for only a fraction of his life could be uncovered and recorded. There are also formidable barriers dividing me from Hatta, as I am neither an Indonesian nor a Muslim. I have tried to break down some of these obstacles by interaction with Indonesian people, by extensive reading of Indonesian texts, and by a study of Islam. Fortunately Hatta and I have perspectives in common which acted as bridges. I regret very much that I never had the privilege of meeting him, as he died just at the time I commenced my research. My other disappointment is that I was not allowed access to his private papers.

In conclusion, I would like to express my thanks to the staff of Cornell University's Modern Indonesia Project for accepting my script for publication. My thanks go too to Dr. James Walter, Dr. Colin Brown, and Dr. Doliar Noer of Griffith University, Brisbane, who acted as my supervisors while I researched Hatta's life as a Master of Philosophy thesis.

My two Indonesian language teachers, Mrs. Margaret Bocquet-Siek and Mrs. Christina Whittington, were also most supportive, lending me materials from their private collections. Last but not least I would like to express my deep appreciation to those generous and wonderfully helpful people who allowed me to interview them and who spoke so unstintingly to me about their remembrances and impressions of Hatta.

Mavis Rose
School of Modern Asian Studies
Griffith University, Brisbane

Mohammad Hatta

PROLOGUE

October 1927. For Mohammad Hatta and the three fellow students detained with him in the Cassius-Straat prison in The Hague, a month of gloom -- but also of challenge. Winter in Europe was always a daunting prospect, contrasting sharply with the warmth and color of their equatorial homeland. This winter they could expect no homely comforts to ease the damp chill, only the starkness of a cell.

As chairman of the Perhimpunan Indonesia [Indonesian Association], Mohammad Hatta was regarded by the Dutch authorities as the ringleader of a Marxist-inspired student activist group which was plotting to oust the Dutch from their most prestigious colony, the Dutch East Indies. The charges against Hatta and his fellow students were that they were involved in revolution and in incitement against the Dutch Crown.[1] The powerful Ministry of Colonies was demanding a harsh sentence; it seemed that these prison walls might enclose them for many years to come.

While accepting an offer of legal aid from the social Democratische Arbeiders Partij [Social Democratic Workers' Party],[2] Hatta was also determined to conduct his own defense.[3] No Dutchman could adequately explain the factors which had contributed to his deep conviction that he must dedicate his life to freeing his country from colonial rule. He must establish that he and the three other students arrested were not attacking the Dutch Crown *per se*, but only trying to redress the wrongs perpetrated on the indigenous peoples of the Dutch East Indies, which the students

---

1   A description of the events surrounding the detention of Mohammad Hatta and his three fellow students is to be found in chap. 3 below.
2   The Social Democratic Workers' Party or SDAP was the main opposition party in the Tweede Kamer [Second Chamber] of the Dutch Parliament. For details of Hatta's acceptance of the offer of legal aid, see Mohammad Hatta, *Memoir* (Jakarta: Tintamas, 1979), p. 219.
3   Ibid., pp. 219-20.

now referred to as "Indonesia." He must explain why intrinsically law-abiding, studious young men such as himself were advocating the overthrow of the colonial power.

Hatta did not have the appearance of a violent insurrectionist. He was a small, slim young man with thoughtful brown eyes and a grave expression. He was an introspective person, quiet and self-contained, who seldom allowed his emotions to show on the surface. Even in anger he remained cool. Only the knitting of his eyebrows and the sting of his comments revealed his displeasure. His solemnity sometimes made him appear morose, yet this was deceptive. Under his reserve lurked a warm, gentle, and compassionate nature. When Hatta smiled, the transformation was remarkable, softening his stern features with an attractive, boyish grin, bringing a sparkle to his somber eyes.

Hatta was the most effective and dedicated leader the Perhimpunan Indonesia had had to date, and the depth of economic and political analysis in his writings had brought prestige to the student group, upgrading the association from a social club to a major force in the Indonesian nationalist movement.[4] Now his pen must assist him to prepare a defense speech which would convince a Netherlands court of the justice of the struggle for independence, so that the Dutch people might realize how adversely colonial policies had affected the lives of the majority of Indonesian people, both materially and spiritually.

Hatta began by explaining why Indonesian students could not be as relaxed about issues of government as their European counterparts:

My Lord Chairman! I would first of all put up a question for discussion which is related to the general psychological factor: why Indonesian student youth takes an *active* part in politics. Because in the Western countries this is regarded as something abnormal, as a morbid symptom.[5]

Hatta was no doubt visualizing his European fellow students at the

---

4 See chaps. 2 and 3 below for details of Hatta's activities as leader of the Perhimpunan Indonesia prior to his detention.
5 Mohammad Hatta, "Indonesia Free," speech presented to the Dutch Court on March 9, 1929, in *Portrait of a Patriot: Selected Writings by Mohammad Hatta* (The Hague: Mouton, 1972), p. 206.

Rotterdam School of Commerce or at the University of Leiden as they ardently bandied about the socialist ideas which the 1917 Revolution in Russia had stimulated. There was a general wave of disaffection with the European "Establishment" in the aftermath of World War I. Hatta tried to explain that, even before he reached Europe for his tertiary education, he had already become involved in a revolutionary movement:

> In Europe the best part of academic youth shows a warm interest in the great social questions, not in an active way, however, but only in the *abstract*. In the *West*, intellectual youth is *preparing* itself in the universities for political and social activities. In *Indonesia*, it *takes part* in it already while it is still at school.... In a colonial society youth very quickly learns the hard truth; it sees with its own eyes the distress and the misery of the oppressed mass.... It feels and understands the anguish and the misery of its people....[6]

For Hatta, the independence struggle had begun in West Sumatra, in the *Alam Minangkabau*.[7] It was in that fertile, productive region that he first became aware that he belonged to a politically subjugated people. In the *Alam Minangkabau*, the concept of freedom was closely associated with the permanent removal of the Dutch and their system of rule, which had destroyed traditional democracy and economic prosperity.

6 Ibid., p. 207.
7 *Alam Minangkabau* literally means the natural world of the Minangkabau people, the region they define as their homeland.

C H A P T E R   O N E
THE ALAM MINANGKABAU

In politics, there may be differences of opinion but national sentiment must be tied to one's Native Land, which is united and which desires freedom. Much time is devoted to propagating unity so that Bataks lose their Batakness, Minangkabau lose their Minangkabauness, and so that Sundanese and Javanese and Madurese dispense with their narrow national feelings.... There are still many among us who call themselves Indonesian nationalists but whose social intercourse and spirit are still very much bound to their region and place of birth.[1]

At the time of Mohammad Hatta's birth on August 12, 1902, in the Minangkabau region of West Sumatra, Indonesia did not exist as a political entity. The international world recognized the series of islands stretching from Sumatra to West New Guinea as Netherlands India or the Dutch East Indies. To the indigenous people, ties of loyalty to their region and ethnic group were paramount.

Hatta had reason to be proud of the Minangkabau who had gained the reputation of being among the most intellectual and entrepreneurial ethnic groups in the archipelago.[2] Their name was believed to derive from the words *menang kerbau* meaning the "Victory of the Buffalo." These words related to a legendary tale of a Minangkabau defeat of the Javanese by the cunning ploy of using a buffalo calf with steel blades hidden in

---

1 Mohammad Hatta, "Di Atas Segala Lapangan Tanah Air Aku Hidup Aku Gembira," *Daulat Ra'jat*, January 20, 1934.
2 See Elizabeth E. Graves, *The Minangkabau Response to Dutch Colonial Rule in the Nineteenth Century* (Ithaca: Cornell Modern Indonesia Project, 1981), p. 1.

its horns to vie against the large bull buffalo fielded by the Javanese.[3] The Minangkabau traditionally harbor deep respect for the buffalo, reflected in the architectural styling of their houses and their traditional headdresses.

A second interpretation of the word "Minangkabau" claims that it derived from *pinang kabhu* meaning "original home,"[4] the mountainous heartland with its fertile plateaus stretching from the west coast of Central Sumatra across the Bukit Barisan range. The three core regions of settlement or *luhak* which formed the "original home" -- Agam, Tanah Datar, and Lima Puluh Kota -- were separated from each other by high mountains and deep gullies. Two different systems of customary law or *adat* evolved in the *Alam Minangkabau*: the *Koto-Piliang* and *Bodi-Caniago*. The clans or *suku* identifying with the *Koto-Piliang* tradition were mainly situated in the *luhak* of Tanah Datar and to a lesser extent in Lima Puluh Kota. Politically, this system supported a monarchy and a hierarchical system of village government.[5] The Agam *luhak*, where Hatta's maternal and paternal families had their roots, adhered to the *Bodi-Caniago* tradition, which had an egalitarian style of political organization.[6] Under both systems most Minangkabau villages or *nagari* were essentially autonomous, their councils being led by the *penghulu* or *suku* chieftains.[7]

Islam was firmly established in the *Alam Minangkabau*, where its religious centers or *surau* had gained considerable prestige because of their high standard of scholarship, being especially renowned for studies of Islamic law.[8] The mystical Sufist form of Islam which took root in the Minangkabau about the twelfth century AD was remarkably tolerant regarding local customs which, strictly speaking, did not accord with

---

3   Drs. D. Darwis Datuk Rajo Malano, *Filsafat Adat Minangkabau: Sebagai Pembina Budi Luhur* (Padang: Yayasan Lembaga Studi Minangkabau, n.d.), p. 63.

4   See P. E. de Josselin de Jong, *Minangkabau and Negri Sembilan: Socio-Political Structure in Indonesia* (Jakarta: Bhratara, 1960), p. 7.

5   Christine Dobbin, *Islamic Revivalism in a Changing Peasant Economy: Central Sumatra, 1784-1847,* Scandinavian Institute of Asian Studies, Monograph Series No. 47 (London and Malmo: Curzon Press, 1983), p. 62. In practice, however, the monarch wielded little power. See Graves, *Minangkabau Response*, p. 37.

6   Dobbin, *Islamic Revivalism*, p. 62, and de Josselin de Jong, *Minangkabau and Negri Sembilan*, pp. 12-13, and 74-76.

7   Graves, *Minangkabau Response*, p. 37.

8   Dobbin, *Islamic Revivalism*, p. 124.

Islamic tenets.[9] During the late eighteenth century, international demand for coffee drew more foreign traders to Sumatran ports, creating an economic boom for the Minangkabau but also unsettling traditional society. The most ardent opposition to this societal change came from the Islamic leaders.

In response to what was seen as a fall in moral standards, together with fear of Western influences, an Islamic revival took place in the early nineteenth century, led by a group of pilgrims recently returned from Mecca. While in the Holy City, the pilgrims had come under the influence of the fundamentalist Wahhabis of Arabia,[10] a militant and puritanical group whose insistence on a stricter adherence to the Islamic behavioral code was making a deep impression in the Middle East, a region disturbed by Europe's revolutionary and Enlightenment trends. On their return to Sumatra in 1803, the pilgrims, known as the Padri, were fired to emulate the Wahhabi movement in the Minangkabau. Their extremism and militancy, however, led to civil war rather than political stability. The monarchy and those villages which supported it became the particular target of Padri attack, several members of the royal family being slain.

Faced with a tide of religious fanaticism, the surviving princes appealed to the Dutch for military assistance in return for territorial concessions. The Dutch accepted the offer, hoping to gain access to the economic wealth of the Minangkabau. On February 10, 1821, the Dutch signed a treaty with the Minangkabau monarch's nephew which ceded to the Netherlands three royal villages "together with the remaining lands of the State of Maninkabo,"[11] land which was not the royal prerogative to give away. The Padri's fanaticism had left the *Alam Minangkabau* vulnerable

---

9 The point most at issue was female inheritance of property. This matter was usually accommodated by making a differentiation between *harta pusaka* or collective family property, which was subject to *adat*, and *harta pencarian* or personal property which was subject to Islamic law. See Buya Hamka, "Tanya Jawab Agama: Harta Pusaka Minangkabau," in *Panji Masyarakat*, September 15, 1979, pp. 35-38.

10 Dobbin, *Islamic Revivalism*, p. 128. See also Deliar Noer, *The Modernist Muslim Movement in Indonesia, 1900-1942*, 2nd ed. (Kuala Lumpur: Oxford University Press, 1978), p. 86. Wahhabis take their name from Muhammad bin Abd al Wahab (1703-87). They do not accept innovations in and accretions to Islamic doctrine but emphasize the basic scriptures, the Qu'ran and Hadits.

11 Christine Dobbin, "Economic Change in Minangkabau as a Factor in the Rise of the Padri Movement, 1784-1830," *Indonesia 23* (April 1977): 10.

to a foreign take-over. As Hatta commented with some asperity in his memoirs: "the Padri forgot that the highest law in Islam is peace."[12]

The seriousness of the Dutch threat and the internal divisions within their homeland alerted the Minangkabau people to the need for unity. Foregoing civil war, most of them united their resources under the moderate Padri leader, Tuanku Imam Bonjol, who organized a dogged campaign to hold back the intruders. Not having anticipated such a fierce counteraction, the Dutch in 1833 issued a conciliatory statement, referred to as the *Plakat Pandjang* [Long Declaration]. In this they tried to entice the Minangkabau to give up the struggle, assuring the people that they would remain under the rule of their own leaders and that no taxes would be levied.[13] Minangkabau forces, however, did not give in until 1837 when Dutch technological advantage finally broke the resistance, leading to the capture and exile of Tuanku Imam Bonjol.

At the time of Hatta's birth in 1902, the region had experienced more than half a century of Dutch rule, during which the Dutch had made it a major coffee-producing area, introducing the *cultuurstelsel* or system of forced cultivation of crops for the government.[14] The people of the region were reluctant to enslave themselves to a system which was aimed at the enrichment of the colonial power to the detriment of the local producers, especially when it also involved corvée service for building the infrastructure needed to serve the coffee trade. Yet the administrative job opportunities opened up by the colonial power were tempting to the Minangkabau, providing both the lure of an assured salary and a new system of social mobility.[15] From their experience in Java, the Dutch realized that they must have local cooperation to gain maximum benefit. Rather than impose direct rule on the local people, Dutch policy was slowly to build up a bureaucratic elite whose fortunes were tied to Dutch interests. As Minister of Colonies J. C. Baud wrote in 1841, the rule of

---

12 Hatta, *Memoir*, p. 2.

13 The *Plakat Pandjang* [Long Declaration] was issued by the Dutch High Commissioners in 1833. It assured the Minangkabau that the Dutch would come as friends and partners, and promised that no direct taxes would be imposed. For a complete text, see H. J. J. L. Ridder de Stuers, *De Vestiging en uitbreiding van Nederlanders ter Westkust van Sumatra*, vol. 2 (Amsterdam: Van Kampen, 1850), pp. 87-89.

14 See Graves, *Minangkabau Response*, pp. 60-73.

15 Ibid., p. 47.

non-interference "must be scrupulously followed until the *democratic* principle which is the reigning one practically everywhere in the Padang highlands, has been supplanted by the *aristocratic* principle."[16] The scheme worked. With the introduction of salaried officials, traditional challenges for the position of *penghulu* or head of the *suku* declined and "Javanization" became a reality in many villages.[17] In spite of this stifling of village democracy, protest continued against the imposition of foreign rule in the *Alam Minangkabau*, increasingly embodying an element of nostalgia for the lost democratic ideal. From the time of his birth, Hatta was surrounded by these strong currents of unrest.

Mohammad Hatta was born in the town of Bukit Tinggi, once a Padri stronghold, but by the beginning of the twentieth century a Dutch administrative center and military outpost, referred to as Fort de Kock. Bukit Tinggi remained a focal point of Minangkabau life, in spite of the strong Dutch presence in the town. Ethnic and Islamic influences impinged strongly upon young Hatta, deterring him from forming close ties with his European schoolmates at the local school.

The Minangkabau people responded favorably to the Western-type education offered in the colonial schools, which increased in number under the Ethical Policy launched by the Dutch in the first decade of the twentieth century. Although arising from social concern for the deteriorating welfare of the local peoples, the policy was not entirely altruistic. Education policies were geared to train indigenous civil servants and to back up the "association policy" of forging closer links between the white and brown peoples of the Indies. The latter policy smacked too strongly of Dutch self-interest and paternalism to gain widespread acceptance in the Minangkabau. As Hatta commented many years later: "Here arose a theory which said that the *inlander* [native] was considered to be a younger brother who did not know how to set up and run his own household, therefore must be led and educated by his experienced older brother."[18]

The decision as to whether Hatta should be educated in the traditional

---

16 Baud to Merkus [Government Commissioner], 1 Sept. 1841, 363/W Zeer Geh., Kabinet des Konings 4140, as cited in Dobbin, *Islamic Revivalism*, p. 233, n. 34.

17 Dobbin, *Islamic Revivalism*, p. 233.

18 Mohammad Hatta, "Associatie-Politiek Lagi," *Daulat Ra'jat*, October 20, 1933.

surau or in the modern Dutch system reflected a dilemma faced by many Minangkabau parents in this period. In Hatta's case, the problem was further complicated in that he was expected to carry on the religious tradition of his paternal family. Hatta's grandfather had established a *surau* at Batu Hampar, a village about fifteen miles from Bukit Tinggi. The Batu Hampar *surau* was in itself a religious community, a Sufist *tarekat*, the initial aim of which was to guide its followers along the pathway to a closer understanding of God.[19] The *surau* in practice also served to counter Western influences, and prevent Dutch-supported Christian social and educational institutions from undermining Islam's position in the region.

Hatta's father, Haji Djamil, also a religious scholar, assisted in the work of the *surau*. Hatta's mother was Haji Djamil's fourth wife. In the Minangkabau it was not unusual for a man to have several wives, particularly when he was constantly traveling as a trader between the hinterland and the coast. Haji Djamil combined trade with his religious duties, for an *ulama* was expected to be self-sufficient. In the matri-lineal social structure of the Minangkabau, a man is most at home in his sister's house. In his wife's house, among her mother's relatives, he is more like a visitor making overnight stays. Minangkabau children traditionally look for guidance more to their maternal uncle or *mamak* than to their father, because their mother's older brother is the figure of authority in their mother's household.

Hatta was his mother's second child but first son, his older sister, Rafi'ah, having been born two years previously. The baby boy was named Attar, meaning perfume, also the name of a renowned Persian poet, a distinguished Sufist tarekat leader, Fariduddin Al Aththar. The Minangkabau speech pattern altered the sound of the boy's name, and it was as Hatta that Haji Djamil's son was known all his life.

Hatta never had an opportunity to get to know his father, who died just eight months after his son's birth. Recalling family references to the

---

19 The word "sufi" is said to derive from the Arabic word for wool, *suf*, associated with the woolen garb worn by Eastern ascetics. The principal occupation of a Sufist is meditation on the Unity of God and the progressive advancement in the *tarekat* or journey of life so as to attain unification with God. See T. P. Hughes, *A Dictionary of Islam*, rev. ed. (Lahore: Premier Book House, 1965), pp. 608-22.

striking resemblance between him and his late father, Hatta commented: "When I was a child, there was a belief among people in the Minangkabau that, if a son resembled his father, one of them would yield to the other and quickly die."[20] Undoubtedly the fact that he was the son of an *ulama* and the grandson of a famed *tarekat* leader was to remain a significant influence in Hatta's life, instilling in him a sense of obligation to uphold the family religious tradition.

Nevertheless, his father's death drew Hatta away from the influence of the *tarekat* community and into the modern urban environment of Bukit Tinggi, where his maternal family lived and worked. His mother remarried, this time to Haji Ning, a business acquaintance of Hatta's maternal grandfather. Haji Ning's trade interests were centered in Padang on the coast, but he commuted regularly to Bukit Tinggi to obtain goods for export. Hatta expressed deep affection for his stepfather, commenting in his memoirs that Haji Ning treated him so well that at first he did not realize that he was not his natural father.[21]

Hatta's maternal family were well-to-do business people, engaged in a variety of enterprises, including timber exports, a transport business, and a government postal contract. Hatta therefore grew up in a family environment where commercial matters were a major concern. Hatta's grandmother, it was said, played an important role in his upbringing. She was very much the traditional Minangkabau matriarch, keeping a tight rein not only on domestic affairs but on the family business as well. She was, by all accounts, a woman of exceptional strength of will. In her youth, she had supported the Padri movement, retaining the black robe and white headdress adopted by women devotees. Her fearlessness and determination were legendary, including the story of how she had brandished a pistol before a Dutch official in his office, demanding redress for the loss of thirty of her horses shot by Dutch soldiers.[22]

It was generally acknowledged among his family that Hatta came closest to matching his grandmother's model of perfection, as she perhaps

---

20 Hatta, *Memoir*, p. 14.
21 Ibid., p. 6.
22 Julinar Idris Koestano, "Bung Hatta: Pembimbing Rakyat dan Keluarga Kami," in *Bung Hatta: Pribadinya dalam Kenangan*, ed. Meutia F. Swasono (Jakarta: Sinar Harapan and University of Indonesia, 1980), p. 11. The writer is Hatta's cousin, son of his Uncle Saleh.

recognized in him a reflection of her own strength and determination. Yet in his memoirs Hatta was not particularly complimentary about his grandmother, whose dominating personality obviously irked him. It was she who was over-protective, restricting such schoolboy delights as swimming in the river, tree climbing, and participating in team football.

As the only son among the six children born to his mother in her two marriages, Hatta certainly had an important role in the family as a potential future *penghulu* and as the maternal uncle to his sisters' children, though naturally at this time this was less important to him than the freedom to engage in childhood pursuits. Hatta was also critical of his grandmother's interference in the business affairs of her eldest son, his *mamak* Saleh. "She was a woman who was strict, tenacious, and exact in her work, always insisting on neatness," commented Hatta, "wanting to control my uncle's work in the same way that she handled her household duties."[23] The result of this close supervision, he pointed out, was that his uncle was unable to develop his own initiative.

The characteristics of his grandmother were strikingly similar to those attributed to Hatta by his staff in later years, although Hatta did make a determined effort to temper his perfectionism by adhering to democratic principles and by delegating authority.[24] This trait Hatta may have acquired from his maternal grandfather. In his comments about this grandparent, Hatta was warmer, contending that "he treated all his workers, even his stablemen, as equals."[25] Perhaps the democracy espoused by Minangkabau *penghulu* was a reaction to the autocratic ways of their women folk!

Commercial families had been among the first to take advantage of the European education system, seeing it as an avenue to new professions, as well as a means of acquiring Western monetary techniques.[26] However, Hatta's education in the Dutch elementary school in Bukit Tinggi did not please his paternal family. The Dutch system did not provide the skills and knowledge required by a budding *ulama*, and was moreover unlikely to foster Islamic values. It was akin to exposing the child to the foreign

---

23 Hatta, *Memoir*, p. 9.
24 According to Nyonya Maria Ullfah Soebadio in interview (February 22, 1982), Hatta placed almost too much trust in his staff. She said that, as his prime ministerial secretary, she had personally felt a great weight of responsibility, knowing that Hatta trusted her implicitly.
25 Hatta, *Memoir*, p. 8.
26 Graves, *Minangkabau Response,* p. 106.

influences which the *surau* had been established to offset.

From the age of seven, Hatta had been spending short periods at the Batu Hampar *surau*, where his uncle, Syekh Arsyad, assumed the leadership on the death of Hatta's grandfather. Syekh Arsyad urged Hatta's mother to allow her son to follow in his father's footsteps and undertake religious studies at Mecca, later proceeding to university in Cairo. As Hatta's maternal grandfather was about to undertake his *haj* to Mecca, he could take the boy with him. Hatta's uncle, one of his late father's younger brothers, was a student in Mecca and could assume responsibility for the boy. Hatta's mother and her brother Saleh totally rejected the proposal. The most they would concede was that Hatta should receive further instruction in Arabic in case he should wish to undertake religious studies in the future.

Hatta's religious teacher in Bukit Tinggi, Syekh M. Jamil Jambek, had a different perspective on Western education from Syekh Arsyad. He was one of the pioneers of a new trend in Islam referred to as Modernist Reform.[27] The Modernists encouraged Muslims to learn from the West in order to mount a challenge to European domination, especially in the fields of science and technology. The fresh, stimulating approach of the Modernists appealed to Muslim youth and suited the aspirations of Hatta's maternal family. Yet for Hatta personally there was an element of conflict in the Modernist viewpoint. The Modernists suspected that the guidance provided by the Sufist *tarekat* leader contravened the Islamic law that a man should have a direct relationship with Allah. But Hatta, as the member of a family renowned for its spiritual guidance to the *surau* community, could not easily condemn the *tarekat* leader. This religious dilemma may have influenced his decision to become involved in nationalist rather than Islamic brotherhoods and may explain his reluctance to identify fully with Modernist Islamic political parties in the future, remaining most of his life religiously neutral in politics.

In his memoirs, written in old age, Hatta seemed to identify his ideal of a religious leader with his uncle, Sjekh Arsyad, as if to indicate that the educated traditionalist would have more understanding of the

---

27 For information on Syekh Jambek, details of the Modernist Reform movement, and an outline of its origins, see Noer, *Modernist Muslim Movement*, p. 32 and pp. 35-39, and H. A. R. Gibb, *Modern Trends in Islam* (Chicago: University of Chicago Press, 1947).

needs of the people than the urban Modernist. Through the words of this prestigious *tarekat* leader, Hatta seemed to be presenting his own religious viewpoint, defending his conviction that socialism was a basic principle in Islam. Hatta asserted that it was Syekh Arsyad who taught him to be socially aware and to minister to the needs of his own people, stressing that "as God loved us, so we must love one another."[28] Hatta may have been trying to convince his fellow Muslims that his socialism did not just develop from Marx. Hatta's description of his uncle presents an Islamic leader who was puritanical and ascetic, but also considerate, balanced, and humane, a man of peace rather than a religious fanatic leading a *jihad*. Another interesting facet of Syekh Arsyad was that he did not support the concept of an Islamic state, citing the Ottoman Empire as an example of political decline which discredited Islam.[29]

In spite of his respect and obvious affection for Syekh Arsyad and the Batu Hampar community, Hatta was too strongly influenced by his modern urban environment and by a family moving away from traditional ways to be satisfied with the narrower type of education offered by the *surau*. Yet his entry into the Dutch elementary school did expose him to racial conflict, his memoirs recording an incident of harassment when the Minangkabau students were baited by European and Eurasian children for supporting the Turks in the Balkans War of 1912.[30] In his 1929 defense speech, Hatta recalled that from primary school age he was conscious of "the sharp conflict between *white* and *brown*, between *ruler* and *ruled*."[31] Hatta appears to have been on amicable terms with his Dutch teachers. Yet these teachers, merely by expressing the patronizing attitudes prevalent among the European population, often unconsciously wounded their Indonesian pupils.

Hatta pointed out to the court how humiliated an Indonesian felt when it was assumed that he was second-rate:

Yes, my Lord Chairman, *ad nauseum* must we hear and read... that "the native is lazy, dirty, untrustworthy, dishonest, ungrateful,

---

28 Hatta, *Memoir*, p. 20.
29 Ibid., pp. 27-28.
30 Ibid., p. 27.
31 Mohammad Hatta, "Indonesia Free," in *Portrait of a Patriot*, p. 209.

careless, improvident," and that he lacks energy, thrift, economic awareness and so on.... Every day we are specially reminded in this way that we belong to an unfree and therefore inferior people, with whom those in the colony can take any kind of liberty.[32]

Perhaps the most galling and unacceptable part of the Dutch school curriculum was that the indigenous children were forced to condemn as rebels their freedom fighters -- heroes such as the Minangkabau leader, Tuanku Imam Bonjol. Hatta hotly defended these champions of the people, claiming that "they too were national heroes just as were William of Orange, William Tell, Mazzini, and Garibaldi."[33] That was the irony of the situation. The Dutch exalted the deeds of European nationalists; they were immensely proud of their own fight for freedom against Spanish domination; yet they were unwilling to accept that their Eastern subjects might resent the rule of a foreign power.

Anti-Dutch resentment smoldered into open defiance in the *Alam Minangkabau* in 1908 at the small village of Kamang near Bukit Tinggi in protest against unlawful taxes which contravened the *Plakat Pandjang*. Hatta was only six years old at the time of the Kamang uprising, but it etched an impression of Dutch tyranny on his memory because it caused the deaths of almost one hundred Minangkabau. An incident which further incensed Hatta's family was the arrest of his Great-Uncle Rais on suspicion of being involved in the insurrection. When released from detention, Rais was expelled from the Minangkabau hinterland, not only a heavy sentence but a serious economic blow to a prosperous trader. Hatta's family blamed this harsh decision on the Dutch Assistant-Resident, Westenenck, who had also been the colonial official accompanying the Dutch forces during the Kamang incident.[34] Although in his spare time, a scholar of some repute with a particular interest in the Minangkabau region, Westenenck was not a popular administrator. He was suspected of exacting a personal revenge on Rais, who had made disparaging remarks

---

32 Ibid.
33 Ibid., pp. 209-10.
34 For a detailed Dutch account of this incident, see B. J. D. Schrieke, "De Nacht van Kamang -- Een Les Uit Indies' Krijg-Geschiedenis," *Het Nieuws van Den Dag*, July 18, 1933.

about the Assistant-Resident's sexual exploits with local women.[35] Westenenck was later to become the man most responsible for Hatta's own detention in a Dutch jail.

In spite of his Dutch schooling and urban environment, Hatta was raised according to Minangkabau concepts. Great emphasis was placed on his general education; and it was his maternal relatives' decisions which prevailed in family disputes. Traditionally, a young Minangkabau man must prove his self-reliance by leaving home in early adulthood to *merantau* (leave for abroad). There was no concept in Minangkabau society of sitting back and living off the spoils of one's forebears, and any income earned must not be used solely for the young man's self-enrichment but a substantial amount must be returned to the family's coffers to enhance its prestige. Even in a democratic village society, wealth added to a *suku's* power and status in the community.[36]

Hatta's maternal family were ambitious people, with sufficient wealth to ensure that he had access to whatever additional educational opportunities were available, such as private lessons in French and English. Combined with Arabic classes and general religious instruction, the study regimen he followed left the small boy with little time for recreation. He learned to use every moment of the day as effectively as possible, a lesson he followed throughout his life.

Hatta was a natural student, a pensive boy, neat and orderly in his dress.[37] He was a child who could live within a thought-world of his own, often preferring to walk home by himself on a separate track rather than accompany his schoolmates. Indeed, this self-containment worked to Hatta's advantage in later years when he was isolated in prison cells. He was not pugilistic, avoiding the rougher fist fights, although enjoying a friendly tussle. His close friend, Bahder Djohan, recalling their first meeting, related that Hatta had deliberately mounted the narrow ricefield dike along which Bahder Djohan was walking, knowing that there would be a confrontation when they met, with the likelihood of one of them

35 See Bahder Djohan, *Bahder Djohan Pengabdi Kemanusiaan, Bagian 1: Otobiografi* (Jakarta: Gunung Agung, 1980), pp. 10-11.
36 For a discussion of *merantau*, see Mochtar Naim, "Perantauan Masyarakat Minang dan Kaitannya dengan Masalah Kewiraswastaan," *Prisma*, October 9, 1978, pp. 30-38.
37 See St. Rais Alamsjah, ed., *10 Orang Indonesia Terbesar Sekarang* (Jakarta: Bintang Mas, 1952), pp. 32-34.

ending up in the muddy water below. "When close to me, he cleverly dodged by so that neither of us fell," commented Bahder Djohan. He added: "I turned around and gave him a piece of my mind -- and that is how we became acquainted."[38]

Hatta completed his elementary schooling in the European school in Padang, which only accepted a handful of Minangkabau students -- an indication of Hatta's scholastic ability and his family's status. At first, Hatta resided with his grandfather in Padang, then in 1915 moved to live elsewhere in the port city, this time with his mother and stepfather, Haji Ning. "Although I was not a blood relation," Hatta remarked, "I was considered to be a part of the family and many people in Padang called me Haji Ning's son."[39]

Hatta graduated from the primary school with sufficiently good results to proceed directly to a Hoogere Burger School [HBS] or senior high school in Batavia, the colonial capital on Java. To his disappointment, his mother insisted that he was too young to live apart from his family in a city of such ill-repute and should first attend the MULO or junior high school in Padang.[40] Hatta admitted that he rebelled against his mother's decision and that her ultimatum sparked off a personal crisis. "Because I was confused and dejected. I wanted to give up school and begin to earn a living," he confessed in his memoirs.[41] He applied and was accepted for a job as a postal assistant, but finally yielded to the pleas of his mother and Uncle Saleh that he try the MULO school for three years.

It was a wise decision, for his years at the MULO proved to be a time of interest and national awakening. With a slackening of the pressure of academic competition, he was able to participate much more in extracurricular activities, moving in a wider circle of companions, because the student body was predominantly Minangkabau. He was even able to play competitive football, serving as his club's treasurer, his first executive position. "Hatta played as a center forward," recalled Bahder Djohan.[42]

---

38 Bahder Djohan, *Bahder Djohan Pengabdi Kamanusiaan*, p. 13.
39 Hatta, *Memoir*, p. 31.
40 Ibid., p. 34. MULO is an abbreviation for Meer Uitgebreid Lager Onderwijs [Extended Lower Education].
41 Ibid.
42 Bahder Djohan, "Mengenang Seorang Teman di Masa Ramaja," in *Bung Hatta: Pribadinya dalam Kenangan*, p. 223.

1916 was a momentous year in the development of a nationalist movement within the Dutch East Indies because of the phenomenal growth of Sarikat Islam, an organization which had originated in Java in 1912 as a Muslim traders' association, predominantly Modernist in outlook, but which had increasingly become politicized. The surge of nationalist spirit in the Indies at this time stimulated the formation of politically active youth groups, the first being Jong Java in 1915. Hatta attended a rally of students in Padang in December 1917 at which a young Minangkabau high school student, Nazir Pamontjak, introduced the Jong Sumatranen Bond, which had been recently formed in Batavia. Both Hatta and Bahder Djohan, as treasurer and secretary respectively, became leading activists in the Padang branch. Jong Sumatranen Bond received considerable moral and financial support from within the local community, in particular from a young but dynamic Modernist *ulama*, Haji Abdullah Ahmad, and from Engku Taher Marah Sutan, the leader of a local traders' group, Sarekat Usaha, which followed closely the model set by Sarikat Islam.

In September 1918 Abdul Muis, one of the foremost Sarikat Islam leaders and a native of Bukit Tinggi, visited Padang. Muis and the Javanese leader of Sarikat Islam, Tjokroaminoto, had recently been nominated by the colonial government to the newly established advisory council, the Volksraad. Although having no legislative powers, this council was the Dutch government's response to Indonesian demands for a parliament for the Indies.

As an executive member of the Jong Sumatranen Bond, Hatta participated in many of the welcoming celebrations for Abdul Muis. In his memoirs, Hatta recalled that, from remarks made here, he gained the impression that activist students such as himself were regarded as the "hope of the nation,"[43] the generation which must bear the brunt of the anticolonial struggle. Later, in his defense speech, Hatta tried to explain to the court how seriously he took the challenges to educated youth such as himself to use their new knowledge for the welfare of their own people, that "the consciousness of their calling to lead their own people from darkness into light arouse[s] in many Indonesians studying here in this

---

43 Hatta, *Memoir*, p. 50.

country the readiness to set aside their own interests."[44]

Following Muis' visit, Hatta made even greater efforts to keep himself informed about current affairs, making a point of reading reports of debates in the Volksraad. When a left-wing coup was attempted in the Netherlands in November 1918, just as the war in Europe was grinding to a halt, the Governor-General of the colony, J. P. van Limburg Stirum, made the surprise announcement that, in the event of the overthrow of the government in the Netherlands, the Volksraad would assume the authority exercised by the minister of the colonies and the Dutch government in regard to the Indies. In other words, the Volksraad would become a real parliament.

The response from Indonesians was euphoric, but their joy was shortlived. The coup in the Netherlands failed and, as if to balance the socialist threat, power passed quickly into the hands of the Anti-Revolutionary Party, an extremely right-wing group. Its leader, Dr. H. Colijn, a former colonial officer, was one of the members of the Dutch parliament who had been ardently opposed to the establishment of the Volksraad. Colijn contended that the native was too weak economically to have political responsibility. There was no acknowledgment that the weakness of the native economy was a direct result of colonial policies.

Hatta was beginning to endorse Colijn's viewpoint that to advance politically, the people must be economically strong. For Hatta, this required that foreign economic dominance be broken. Indeed, many years later one of Hatta's contemporaries was to remark on the similarity of personality between Hatta and Calvinist Colijn.[45] On the other hand, one could say that there was a marked resemblance in general between the Dutch and the puritanical Minangkabau Muslims. Their work ethic was similar. They were both astute traders with a strong entrepreneurial spirit, and both encouraged their sons to go abroad with the ideal of enriching their homeland, preventing overpopulation and underemployment.

When reviewing the history of this period in his defense speech, Hatta described the immense disillusionment felt by Indonesians in the wake of the retraction of the Governor-General's "November Promise" that

---

44 Hatta, "Indonesia Free," p. 215.
45 A comment made by Soebadio Sastrosatomo in an interview, February 22, 1982.

the Volksraad would assume executive powers. From this time onwards, the more radical nationalists began to dissociate themselves from the Volksraad, seeing the council as of no consequence in achieving self-government.

In May 1919, Hatta passed his MULO finals. He was now almost seventeen years old, an age when traditionally a Minangkabau youth would have left the security of his home environment to go to the *rantua*. This time his mother raised no objections to his further education in Batavia. Hatta decided to apply for entry to the Prins Hendrikschool, a senior high school with a special emphasis on commercial subjects. In his memoirs, he asserts that this choice was not made for personal commercial interests but to further the nationalist cause. According to Hatta, he became increasingly aware at this time of the economic loss suffered by his people because of the colonial intrusion into the *Alam Minangkabau*.[46]

That Hatta had a natural flair for financial matters was recognized by his associates for, on arrival in Java, he was once again asked to serve as treasurer, this time to the Central Branch of the Jong Sumatranen Bond in Batavia. In its short period of existence, the branch had managed to accumulate a debt of f.1,000 to the printers of its journal, *Jong Sumatra*.[47] Hatta was ruthless in extracting subscriptions from members, embarrassing defaulters by placing their names on a black list. He also solicited donations from Sumatran residents of Batavia, encouraging them to sponsor the youth group. His efforts, although considered draconian by some of his fellows, paid off. By the end of his first year in office, Hatta had succeeded in lifting the group's bank balance out of the "red," as well as settling the publisher's debt. As Bahder Djohan, then a student at the medical college STOVIA, commented: "By his action the JSB in that year closed its accounts with more than f.700 in hand, a considerable sum at that time."[48] Hatta was establishing his reputation as an efficient organizer, unafraid of unpopularity.

An advantage of being on the executive of the Jong Sumatranen Bond in Batavia was that it allowed Hatta direct access to the Minangkabau

---

46 Hatta, *Memoir*, p. 34.
47 Ibid., p. 80.
48 Bahder Djohan, *Bahder Djohan Pengabdi Kemanusiaan*, p. 32.

leaders of Sarikat Islam, Abdul Muis and Haji Agus Salim. Hatta remained a lifelong admirer of Haji Agus Salim, known affectionately in the nationalist movement as the "Grand Old Man," although he would later disagree with him on many issues. According to Hatta's memoirs, their first meeting took place in February 1920 at Haji Agus Salim's home, where he often held open house for discussion of the nation's problems and political goals.[49]

Haji Salim had played an active role in promoting a labor movement, which brought him into conflict with the Marxist group within Sarikat Islam. When in 1920 the Marxists changed their name from the Social Democratic Association to the Perserikatan Komunis Indonesia [Indonesian Communist Union -- PKI], Haji Agus Salim became even more reluctant to accommodate the group within Sarikat Islam, whose leaders feared they were being deliberately inched out of power by subversive tactics.

Fascinating as it was to be at the hub of nationalist activities, Hatta realized that his priority must be his study program. He had already restricted his social activities to a minimum, although at the time he had won the heart of an outstandingly beautiful girl called Anni, the spirited daughter of Tengku Nurdin, an Acehnese government translator.[50] Tengku Nurdin had been a particular favorite of the Islamic scholar, Snouck Hurgronje, and was now working for Hazeu, Snouck Hurgronje's successor in the Bureau of Native Affairs.[51] The romance did not reach the stage of a formal marriage contract, for Hatta had become one of a small group who believed that they should remain single until the independence of Indonesia had been achieved. Anni, also an ardent nationalist and a campaigner for women's rights, clearly respected Hatta's viewpoint. She and her future husband, Rusli Rachim, maintained a close association with Hatta, fully supporting him in his activism.[52]

---

49 Hatta, *Memoir*, pp. 84-85.
50 An Indonesian close to the Hatta family suggests that Hatta and Anni were engaged. Other friends of the family believe that it was nationalist zeal rather than romantic love that drew the two together.
51 According to Ny. Maria Ullfah Soebadio, Tengku Nurdin was a well-known personality in Batavian circles because of the distinctive Acehnese hat which he insisted on wearing. Interview, February 22, 1982.
52 See Maskun Sumadiredja, "Mengenang Bung Hatta," in *Bung Hatta: Pribadinya dalam Kenangan*, p. 402. The writer states that Hatta used Rachim's name as a means of corresponding secretly with

The inconsistency of dividing the nationalist young people of the Indies into ethnic groups such as Jong Java, Jong Minahasa, Jong Ambon, and, of course, the Jong Sumatranen Bond, became more apparent in Batavia, alerting Hatta and Bahder Djohan to the divisiveness of regionalism. They mulled over ways of opening up these tight ethnic compartments, deciding to try to publish an archipelago-wide magazine in the Malay language, the *lingua franca* of the Indies. It was a more democratic language than Javanese because different social levels were not built into it. "Between us we divided our responsibility," recorded Hatta, "Bahder Djohan would be the editor and I would concentrate on organizing the finance for the printer."[53] The project remained a pipe-dream -- both young men were too heavily involved in studies and other activities to bring the idea to fruition.

Although living in lodgings while in Batavia, Hatta came under the wing of his Uncle Ayub Rais, the son of Great-Uncle Rais who had been forced out of Minangkabau following the Kamang uprising. Ayub Rais was just as spirited an anticolonialist as his father, throwing his energies into the Batavian business world, at that time dominated by European and Chinese entrepreneurs. Rais was determined to prove that the indigenous businessman could compete with the foreign, a spirit of economic challenge which immediately caught Hatta's attention and won his admiration. Rais' attitude accorded with his own desire to win back the wealth of the country for its native peoples. Rais also encouraged Hatta to think seriously about continuing his commercial studies at the recently established Rotterdam Handelshogeschool or School of Commerce on graduation from Prins Hendrikschool, offering to finance his courses there, an offer which Hatta gratefully accepted.

Ayub Rais was a philanthropist as well as a merchant, deeply concerned about the poverty of the mass of people on Java. He encouraged Hatta to study the history of socialism, purchasing for him six volumes of H. P. Quack's *De Socialisten*. Hatta admitted that Quack's work was ponderous, but slowly its contents captured his interest, especially the author's analysis of Greek socialism. "I had, up till then, been under the

---

Sukarno in Bandung.
53 Hatta, *Memoir*, p. 74.

impression that socialism only emerged in the eighteenth century," Hatta admitted. "Quack opened my eyes to the fact that a type of socialism had been in existence centuries ago, even before Christ, and although the views on socialism in ancient times were different from those put forward in the eighteenth century, there was much that was basically the same, especially in regard to the problem of the rich and the poor, the 'haves' and the 'have nots' in society."[54]

Although Hatta qualified for entry to the Rotterdam Handelshogeschool, his plans were thrown into confusion because of a financial setback suffered by his uncle. As he could not meet his creditors' demands Ayub Rais was sentenced to a short jail term. It was too late for Hatta to apply for a government scholarship. He seriously considered accepting a job as a shipping clerk to help his uncle out of his difficulties. Rais, however, was unimpressed, and urged Hatta not to alter his plans but instead try to obtain a private scholarship. Hatta did want to go to Europe and accepted his uncle's advice. His good scholastic record gained him the assurance of a privately funded scholarship to come into effect when he reached the Netherlands. The thrifty, abstemious Hatta had managed to save a sufficient sum from his allowance to pay his own passage to Rotterdam and to support himself until his scholarship was finalized.

Before leaving for Europe, Hatta spent a month in the *Alam Minangkabau*, saying farewell to his family and friends. His uncle, Syekh Arsyad, was clearly disappointed that Hatta was to take an economics degree in Europe rather than pursue religious studies in Cairo. He had already chided Hatta for choosing the Prins Hendrikschool, warning his nephew that he was directing his life along "too worldly" a path.[55] "I could see that my Uncle Arsyad was unhappy that I was leaving for the Netherlands," Hatta recalled. "When we said farewell, I felt his tears flowing," adding, as if to emphasize how out of character was this display of emotion, "I'd never seen that happen before!"[56]

For Syekh Arsyad, Hatta's decision meant the loss of someone who combined a brilliant mind with a genuinely devout nature, two ingredients which could have sustained the eminence of the *surau*. It was evident that

54 Hatta, *Memoir,* p. 70.
55 Ibid., p. 55.
56 Ibid., p. 99.

Islamic scholarship had not the same attraction for Hatta as the struggle to outwit the Dutch and restore his people's prosperity and freedom. Perhaps the aging Syekh Arsyad also had a premonition that this would be their final meeting. He died before Hatta returned home.

Hatta (R) holding reins outside his home in Bukit Tinggi

Early teens

Members of the Perhimpunan Indonesia
(Standing L to R: Djunaedi, Hatta, Ichsan, Dahlan Abdullah;
sitting L to R: Subardjo, Sukiman, Nasir Pamontjak)

At Mont Blanc, 1924

On Praesidium of League against Colonialism Congress, 1927

Four Students on Trial
(Standing L to R: Ali Sastroamidjojo,
Abdul Madjid, Nazir Pamontjak)

The New PNI Group at Boven Digul
(Standing: second from L Sjahrir; second from R Hatta.
Bondan seated)

Exiles on Banda Neira
(Standing from L: Iwa Kusuma Sumantri, Hatta, Dr. Tjipto;
far right: Sjahrir)

CHAPTER TWO
THE IRRESISTIBLE CHALLENGE

*The sweet eternal urge for freedom in man began to reveal itself
again in the hearts of twentieth-century Indonesians. A soft glimmer
broke through the dark night of serfdom. Then finally, after decades
of servitude and resignation, there was the beginning of movement
in the political life of Indonesian society. The concept of national
freedom settled in the head and heart of every young Indonesian.
No power could nip this bud; it was there, never to die again. It was
destined to grow and it will grow into a national tree of liberty.*[1]

On August 3, 1921, just nine days before his nineteenth birthday,
Hatta sailed from Teluk Bayur, then known as Emmahaven, the port
of Padang. Not only his relatives came to bid him farewell but also a
contingent from the Jong Sumatranen Bond. He traveled second-class
aboard the Rotterdamse Lloyd ship "Tambora," sharing a cabin with
a Dutch sergeant-major, and with as companions three Indonesian
students bound for the University of Leiden.[2] Apart from an initial bout
of seasickness, Hatta found the voyage both enjoyable and interesting. At
Marseilles, where his ship made a brief call, he had his first opportunity
to step on to European soil. He expressed satisfaction in his memoirs
that he was sufficiently competent in the French language to assist fellow
passengers.[3] On September 5, the ship steamed into the mouth of the
River Maas, moving up towards Rotterdam, where Hatta got his first

---

1   Mohammad Hatta, "National Claims," in *Portrait of a Patriot,* p. 310. First published in *Indonesia
    Merdeka,* 1924-25.
2   See Hatta, *Memoir,* pp. 101-4, for details of the voyage.
3   Ibid., p. 103.

glimpse of the port city where his next educational experience would be enacted.

Hatta's recollections of his first weeks in the Netherlands suggest that he adjusted remarkably well to his new environment. The Dutch orientation in his education in the Indies may have cushioned him from culture shock, and he was not socially isolated. He was welcomed and housed overnight on arrival by a Dutch family, friends of a colonial official, Van Leeuwen, whom Hatta had known while a student in Batavia.[4] Although declining Van Leeuwen's invitation to join the Theosophical Society in Batavia, a religious meeting ground for Dutch and Indonesians, Hatta did become a member of the Orde der Dienaren van Indie [Order of Servers of the Indies], which had as its aims "unity, mutual assistance, and brotherhood."[5] He may have felt it was expedient to do so as he was dependent on Dutch financial aid for his studies.

Hatta never regretted the fact that he chose Europe rather than the Middle East for his *rantau*. In a letter to a Minangkabau friend written a few years later, he admitted that "it is good for Indonesians... to mix with the white people whom they confront in their homeland."[6] One of the pleasing differences between life in the colony and residence in Europe was the lowering of the racial barrier. Hatta later described to the court how this situation boosted an Indonesian's morale:

> My Lord Chairman! A stay in this country is of great value to Indonesian youth! Because by learning to know the Dutch society itself it learns at the same time to reduce the so-called superiority of the white race, so inflatedly presented in Indonesia as a psychological injection to the oppressed people, to its true proportions.[7]

The freer association of the races also had psychological *dis*advantages for students dedicated to removing the colonial power. It was possible

---

4   Ibid., p. 104.
5   Ibid., p. 150. Hatta claims to have only attended one meeting of the Order on the eve of his departure for West Sumatra.
6   Cited in M. Rasjid Manggis Dt. Radjo Panghoeloe, "Bung Hatta Sepanjang yang Saya Kenal Sampai Menjelang Remaja," in *Bung Hatta: Pribadinya dalam Kenangan*, p. 211.
7   Hatta, "Indonesia Free," in *Portrait of a Patriot*, p. 212.

to feel an empathy with Europeans, thus dissipating the hostile feelings which fueled anticolonial sentiments. Hatta relished the knowledge that in the Netherlands he was entitled to as much legal protection and as many civil rights as any European, that there was no dual system of law operating as in the Indies. He later tried to explain to the court how much the democratic institutions of the Netherlands highlighted the faults in the colonial system:

> It is as if another sky is arching out over their heads. They become aware here of the feeling of freedom; they feel relieved of the narrow and suffocating atmosphere of colonial society.... The truth is that we have been set free from the colonial hypnosis.... From here we can see the *colonial* truth clearly.[8]

Yet the colonial atmosphere was not entirely absent from Hatta's environment. On his second day in Holland, he transferred to a hostel which had been established in The Hague by the Ministry of Colonies to house overseas students.[9] For Hatta, it was a short-term arrangement. Apart from being inconveniently far from Rotterdam, the adviser for overseas students attached to the ministry was none other than Westenenck, the former Assistant-Resident in Bukit Tinggi. Westenenck had recently retired from active colonial service, after rising to the office of governor. As adviser, his job was not just to counsel the overseas students but, more importantly, to monitor their activities while in Europe, especially their links with left-wing socialist groups. Hatta had no intention of living in Westenenck's shadow. He moved to lodgings within walking distance of the Rotterdamse Handelshogeschool. Indeed, Hatta's future close association with Marxist groups, although motivated by nationalist aims, also allowed him the personal satisfaction of provoking Westenenck.

Hatta recalled that one of the first Minangkabau to make contact with him was Nazir Pamontjak, the student who had inspired the establishment of the Padang branch of the Jong Sumatranen Bond, who was now studying law at Leiden University.[10] Nazir Pamontjak urged Hatta to

8 Ibid., pp. 211-12.
9 Hatta, *Memoir*, pp. 104-5.
10 Ibid., p. 105.

join the overseas students' association, the Indische Vereeniging [Indies Association], which was now viewed as an extension of the regional youth groups but without their ethnic divisions. In his defense speech, Hatta drew attention to the *"community feeling* of Indonesians studying in the Netherlands."[11] In the midst of a cosmopolitan society, ethnicity lost its importance; one identified with a nation rather than with a regional group. However, to belong to a nation which was called the *Dutch* East Indies was to admit one's subordination to a Western power. Hatta recalled that at their first meeting in the student hostel, Nazir Pamontjak had stressed: "In the Netherlands, we are called 'Indonesians.'" He warned Hatta never to use the derogatory term *"inlander."*[12]

The name "Indonesia" had evolved from the Indology course offered by the University of Leiden, where it denoted the Indian islands, a term used to describe the Southeast Asian archipelago. The Javanese students argued that there was an historical precedent for uniting the peoples of the archipelago in that Netherlands India roughly corresponded to a major section of the ancient kingdom of Majapahit, although Majapahit was never an integrated power structure such as the Dutch East Indies. For Hatta, a neo-Majapahit did not have the same appeal, for it smacked of Javanese hegemony over the rest of the archipelago. Most Minangkabau preferred the idea of Indonesia as a new twentieth-century nation.

The concept of a "nation state" with borders defined by international treaty had assumed great importance in Europe, a concept further strengthened after World War I. As Hatta commented: "The decisions of Versailles could only bring about new sentiments of nationalism."[13] Undoubtedly Hatta's own nationalism was stimulated by living in Europe, where he often felt forced to subordinate his academic work to his nationalist activities. However, he was determined to gain at least a *doctorandus.*[14] Most Dutch politicians were men of academic standing. For Hatta, it was important that Indonesians be no less well qualified.

---

11 Hatta, "Indonesia Free," p. 217.

12 Hatta, *Memoir*, p. 105. The term *inlander* means "native" or "indigenous."

13 Mohammad Hatta, "The Inheritance of Versailles," in *Portrait of a Patriot*, p. 453. First published in *Pandji Islam*, 1939.

14 In the Dutch tertiary education system, a *doctorandus* signifies the completion of doctorate course work and is roughly equivalent to a master's degree. To obtain a full doctorate, a thesis must be submitted.

The continent of Europe was still reverberating from the shock waves of World War I and the Russian Revolution, with society in a state of unusual disarray and flux. The flame of revolt against Europe's established order warmed the Indonesian students with its glow, adding momentum to their desire to throw off the Dutch mantle just as the Bolsheviks had that of the Tsarist regime and as Turkey, under its dynamic leader, Mustapha Kemal Pasha, was struggling to extricate itself from the impotent wreck of the Ottoman Empire. In 1918 Lloyd George, representative of the most extensive colonial power of all, was prepared to admit that "the principle of self-determination was as applicable to colonies as it was to occupied European territories,"[15] and India, Britain's most prestigious colony, was promised the gradual development of institutions of self-government. Prime Minister Colijn was not so conciliatory; Hatta and his fellow nationalists were aware that they faced an uphill battle for independence.

In the climate prevailing in Europe in 1921, most students had to come to terms with Marxism/Leninism, especially if they were seriously contemplating social and political change. Marx's confidence that a just and humane society would evolve through the mass effort of economically exploited people appealed to Hatta, because these sentiments accorded with his own ideals. "Wealth acquired through the energy of another is the greatest cause of decadence and demoralization,"[16] wrote Hatta -- one of the reasons young Minangkabau men were encouraged to venture out to the *rantau*. It also echoed Marx's contention: "It is true that labor produces for the rich wonderful things -- but for the worker it produces privation. It produces palaces -- but for the worker hovels."[17] For the average Dutch colonist, cheap Indies labor produced a much more comfortable lifestyle.

Hatta, commenting on the low wages paid by Dutch enterprises to their native employees, wrote: "The Marxist theory of surplus value applied

---

15 See G. Barraclough, *An Introduction to Contemporary History* (Harmondsworth: Penguin Books, 1967), p. 156.

16 Mohammad Hatta, "Indonesia and Her Independence Problem," in *Portrait of a Patriot*, p. 170. Lecture given during the international holiday course organized by the International League of Women for Peace and Freedom during August and September 1927 in Gland.

17 See P. Walton and A. Gamble, *From Alienation to Surplus Value* (London: Sheed and Ward, 1972), p. 24.

here completely: the price of labor is for the most part misappropriated by the European exploiter."[18] For Hatta, the alienation and dialectics of labor, when applied to the Indonesian situation, produced a racial factor: the European colonizer in conflict with his Indonesian employees, not just laborers but all sectors of the indigenous workforce.[19] Hatta was always to view the colonial struggle in terms of white exploitation of colored peoples.

When Hatta arrived in Europe in 1921, Lenin's standing in socialist circles was very high. The Indonesian students were encouraged by Lenin's resolve to assist the fight against imperialism in Asia. Hatta concurred with Lenin's emphasis on organization and discipline, because they were qualities which from an early age Hatta had been taught to respect and emulate. Lenin's cell system and general methodology for undermining the "establishment" prior to revolution also impressed Hatta. It was a format which he would adapt to his political purposes throughout his life.

Hatta's reading of Quack's *De Socialisten* had given him a broad base from which to assess the socialist trends around him and to trace their origins. Certainly Marx's concepts had to be adapted to fit a peasant society like the Indies. The urban proletariat was small as a result of colonial policies of not developing major secondary industry but of exporting raw materials to the machines of Europe. Nor was class structure identical in all Indonesian ethnic groups. In the Agam plateau of West Sumatra social standing was achieved more than inherited, depending on a man's position in the *suku* or clan. Prestige was also related to one's religious position and academic standing. It was not unusual for Minangkabau to be both farmers and businessmen, peasant and bourgeois at the same time. Hatta was aware of a symbiotic relationship between the rural and urban areas in his own society, an interdependency. "As long as there is a balance between town and village," he was later to write, "there is harmony in economic life."[20] In Java there was a wider social gap between the elite

---

18 Mohammad Hatta, "Drainage," in *Portrait of a Patriot*, p. 32. First published in *Hindia Poetra*, No. 6, 1923.

19 See Mohammad Hatta, "Kedudukan Buruh di Indonesia," *Daulat Ra'jat*, No. 68, July 30, 1933.

20 Mohammad Hatta, "Some Main Features of the World Economy," in *Portrait of a Patriot*, p. 64. First published in *Sin Tit Po*, 1938, Nos. 6, 7, 8, and 9.

and the lower classes and a feudal system was more evident. Indeed, the feudal order had become more inflexible and less responsible by being propped up by Dutch military might.

Hatta made use of his first vacation period to explore areas of Europe outside the Netherlands. On Christmas Day 1921 he dined in Hamburg at the home of Le Febvre, a former Resident of West Sumatra. Le Febvre had been prematurely retired from colonial service allegedly because he protected the Minangkabau from rice speculators during a period of food shortages. Although his actions cost him his job, they earned him the epithet of a "government representative whom the people loved."[21] Le Febvre had also been one of the few colonial officials to support formation of the Jong Sumatranen Bond.

From his memoirs, it appears that Hatta valued the friendship of the Le Febvre family, and he returned to Hamburg in subsequent vacation periods to visit them. Again, such instances of kindness and understanding, although appreciated, created a dilemma. The spontaneous warmth and friendliness shown by Dutch people to the Indonesian students made it more difficult for them to view the colonizer as an enemy, dissolving to a degree the dichotomy which existed in the Indies. Students such as Hatta had to make a clear distinction. It was not the white people *per se* whom they hated, only their system of colonial exploitation with its emphasis on race.

The student association, its title changed in 1922 to Indonesische Vereeniging to reflect the students' perception of the archipelago, played an important role in offsetting pro-European influences, keeping the reality of the situation in the colony alive. The association was important for Hatta personally, as most Indies students were pursuing law degrees at the University of Leiden, few taking commercial studies at the Handelshogeschool. Without the student association, Hatta might well have been isolated.

The capacious Leiden flat of law student Subardjo was a favorite meeting place for the students, and Hatta frequently stayed there at weekends, rather than commuting to and from Rotterdam. On the wall hung a large red and white flag, on which was centered a buffalo's head.

---

21 See Danau Totok, "Apalagi pada Masa Kelaparan Ini," *Oetoesan Melajoe*, No. 102, June 2, 1919.

Subardjo has claimed that he suggested the red and white colors because of their historical association with the ancient kingdom of Majapahit, the red symbolizing bravery and the white holiness.[22] The buffalo's head was regarded as a symbol of the patience, determination, and courage of the Indonesian people, the gentleness and docility of the buffalo belying a hidden strength. Indonesian students were encouraged to stand and meditate momentarily before the flag prior to sitting an examination to remind them that they must pass for the sake of Indonesia.

In February 1922, Hatta was again asked to assume the office of treasurer. As a member of the executive committee, he was also expected to serve on the editorial board of the group's journal. This was no hardship. Hatta was discovering that he had a natural flair for political comment. As treasurer, he also had to raise sufficient funds to finance a journal. Formerly the paper had been funded by the Indonesische Verbond van Studenten [Indonesian Students' League], a federation of Dutch, Chinese, and Indonesian students with interests in the Indies. Now that the new emphasis was on independence, the students had withdrawn from the league, and taken responsibility for financing their own journal. The journal's former name, *Hindia Poetra* [Sons of the Indies] was changed to *Indonesia Merdeka* [Free Indonesia] to accord with the students' insistence on non-cooperation with the Dutch and complete independence for the Indies.

Hatta became an ardent supporter of the concept of "non-cooperation," a policy adopted by freedom movements in several other countries, including Turkey and India. Hatta pointed out in his defense speech that "cooperation is only possible between two groups that have the *same rights* and *obligations* and, furthermore, *common interest*."[23] He argued: "When this condition is not fulfilled, cooperation merely means that the strong party bullies the weaker, using the latter as an instrument to support its own interests."[24] Non-cooperation helped to weaken the bonds created by "association." "It sharpens the colonial antithesis, marks the division between ruler and ruled, outwardly serving as a repellent and inwardly as

---

22 A. Subardjo Djoyoadisuryo, *Kesadaran National* (Jakarta: Gunung Agung: 1978), p. 116.
23 Hatta, "Indonesia Free," p. 246.
24 Ibid.

a unifier," asserted Hatta.[25]

As Hatta's personal commitment to the nationalist cause deepened, his writings became more fiery and challenging. He himself changed, conforming much more to the model of a totally dedicated revolutionary.[26] He disciplined himself to suppress his natural passions and emotions, concentrating his whole being on the achievement of Indonesian freedom. His puritan upbringing acted as a prop, giving him the moral support for his revolutionary asceticism. The wild oats a Minangkabau traditionally sows in the *rantau* became the seeds of revolution.

It was not really surprising that Hatta's life should take this course. From early childhood he had moved in circles where patriotism and religion went hand in hand, hotly united in condemning the injustices and indignities which followed in the wake of the Dutch intrusion into the Minangkabau heartland, the deliberate undermining of traditional democracy. While a member of the Jong Sumatranen Bond Hatta sensed the expectation that activist young people like himself should be prepared to forego personal ambition for the sake of the nationalist struggle. Hatta was also aware that Syekh Arsyad expected him to emulate his father's role of service to Allah by moral leadership in the community and by continuing to defend Islam from Western domination. Service was being demanded of him from many sides: from his God, his family, and his people. By submitting his life to the Independence of Indonesia, Hatta could try to fulfill these onerous expectations and duties. One might say that the future course of his life had been so clearly mapped out for him that there was really no way in which he could turn aside without losing self-respect.

Although the majority of his fellows were genuinely concerned to foster the aims of the nationalist cause, few had that touch of religious zeal which added depth to Hatta's commitment. They were light-hearted students, keen to sample the somewhat frenzied social life of continental

---

25 Mohammad Hatta, "Non-Cooperation," in *Portrait of a Patriot*, p. 341. First published in *Indonesia Merdeka*, No. 4, July 1930.

26 According to Bakunin and Nechaev's *Revolutionary Catechism*, a revolutionary should be: "Hard with himself, he must be hard towards others. All the tender feelings of family life, of friendship, love, gratitude and even honor must be stifled in him by a single, cold passion for the revolutionary cause." As cited in B. Mazlish, *The Revolutionary Ascetic: Evolution of a Political Type* (New York: Basic Books, 1976), p. 106.

Europe in the 1920s. Most of them were also Javanese, with a religious outlook less puritanical than Hatta's. Just as many Minangkabau in the early nineteenth century had chafed under the zealous Padri curtailment of their traditional leisure-time activities, so there were students who balked at Hatta's homilies, nicknaming him "the pastor."[27]

Subardjo recalled that "Hatta's personality was marked by an exacting nature and a strong sense of self-discipline, which flowed from his puritanical Islamic outlook";[28] that Hatta "could not easily conceal his disapproval of the bohemian way of conduct of many members of the Indonesian Association, who were neglecting their patriotic duties as well as their studies."[29] Subardjo was more typical of the average student, a *bon vivant* rather than a puritan. Normally conversation centered on social topics -- dances, girl friends, the casual exchange of young men -- but when Hatta appeared in the room, the level of discourse altered. Light-hearted banter switched to deeper, more academic discussion.[30]

Hatta made no apologies for his strait-laced behavior. In his defense speech, he contended that, while European students could devote themselves to the "silly-sweet pleasures of youth," the Indonesian must prepare himself for the task of releasing his people from distress and misery.[31] He tried to explain to the court the sacrificial nature of his nationalist activities:

> The hard struggle for independence which it [Indonesian youth] sees looming before it, puts it in a serious mood and perhaps makes it old for its age.... For the national ideal all selfish motives and personal considerations must give way.[32]

As the students grew accustomed to Hatta's ways, they accepted his asceticism and tendency to preach. He was basically a gregarious person,

---

27 St. Rais Alamsjah, ed., *10 Orang Indonesia Terbesar*, p. 42.

28 A. Subardjo Djoyoadisuryo, "Inside Story," manuscript partly published in *Djakarta Times*, July 1970, cited in C. L. M. Penders, *The Life and Times of Sukarno* (London: Sidgwick and Jackson, 1974), p. 28.

29 Ibid.

30 Sunario, "Bung Hatta dan Kepribadinya," in *Bung Hatta: Pribadinya dalam Kenangan*, p. 248.

31 Hatta, "Indonesia Free," p. 207.

32 Ibid., pp. 207-8.

who enjoyed the many *selamatan* or festive meals which the expatriate Indonesians arranged among themselves. His memoirs indicate that Hatta appreciated good food, although he observed strictly the Islamic rules in regard to alcohol. And in spite of his asperity, he was a generous friend to those in need. According to law student Ichsan, "student friends who had problems always came to Hatta to work out a solition."[33] Ali Sastroamidjojo, a Javanese law student who worked closely with Hatta, confirmed that he was not as dour as he appeared on first acquaintance:

> He appeared rather stiff in socializing with fellow students. But this was just a superficial image because for those who came to know Hatta more intimately, that first impression disappeared. They came to realize that his serious nature and behavior were a result of his dedication to the aims of freeing his native land, Indonesia. His dedication was so complete and integral a part of him that he entirely disregarded his own enjoyment and *joie de vivre* as a student.[34]

It was not surprising that, in adopting the demeanor of a paragon of virtue, Hatta should from time to time have had to endure teasing from his friends, who doubtless felt challenged to break through the sanctimonious exterior to unleash the human frailty beneath. When on a vacation course a personable young Polish student admitted that she was attracted to Hatta, his student friends urged her to try to win his affection, promising to keep well out of the way so that Hatta would be left alone in her company as much as possible. A few days later they questioned her to find out how the romance was progressing. Total failure, she was forced to admit![35]

Hatta did not always succeed in achieving his goals. He often neglected his studies, devoting too much time to the student association and to his nationalistic writings. This resulted in personal dilemmas, as when

33 Ichsan, "Kenang-Kenangan dengan Bung Hatta," in *Bung Hatta: Pribadinya dalam Kenangan*, p. 258.
34 Ali Sastroamidjojo, "Pengalaman-Pengalaman Saja dengan Bung Hatta," in *Bung Hatta Mengabdi pada Tjita-Tjita Perdjoangan Bangsa* (Jakarta: Panitia Peringatan Ulang Tahun Bung Hatta Ke-70, 1972), pp. 389-90.
35 Ichsan, "Kenangan-Kenangan," pp. 259-60.

he failed a unit in his diploma examination and lost his scholarship as a result. Although he was permitted to repeat the failed subject, Hatta was temporarily shaken; he needed a scholarship to finance his stay in Europe. He was obliged to "associate" and seek assistance from his Dutch friend, Van Leeuwen, then on home leave. Van Leeuwen arranged a loan for him from a private fund, the stipulation being that it be repaid with interest once Hatta began to earn a living.[36]

* * * *

The Comintern had already established links with the Indonesian students, one of its agents being a Minangkabau Communist, Tan Malaka, whom Hatta had met in Subardjo's flat in Leiden. Hatta recalled that while revisiting Hamburg and the Le Febvre family in the summer of 1922, he was contacted by Darsono, the exiled Vice-President of the Indonesian Communist Party, the PKI. Darsono was then working in the headquarters of the German Communist Party in Berlin, one of the most powerful Communist groups outside Russia and closely linked with the Communist Party of Holland [CPH]. Indonesia was clearly considered to be an important area of influence, the Russian leader Bukharin in 1926 describing it as "the bridge between Europe and Asia."[37] It was logical that the Comintern should seek to establish links with activist overseas students who were recognized as potential leaders of Indonesia's struggle for independence. Both Darsono and the exiled chairman of the PKI, Semaun, were to work very closely with the student association, obtaining funding on its behalf.

Prior to their exile, both Semaun and Tan Malaka had rejected Haji Agus Salim's insistence at the Sixth National Congress of Sarikat Islam in 1921 that members have only one party affiliation. Preferring to withdraw from Sarikat Islam than obey the ruling, the PKI established opposition Sarekat Rakyat [People's Unions]. The separation of the PKI from the main nationalist parties was a decision which Hatta would try hard to

---

36 See Hatta, *Memoir*, p. 160. It was not until 1950, following a reminder from Van Leeuwen, that Hatta actually settled the debt (with interest) in Indonesian currency.

37 See George McT. Kahin, *Nationalism and Revolution in Indonesia* (Ithaca: Cornell University Press, 1952), p. 78.

reverse four years later.

While Hatta established a close working relationship with Semaun and Darsono, winning their support, he and his fellow Minangkabau, Tan Malaka, remained basically opposed on the issues which tend to separate social democrats and Communists. Hatta favored parliamentary democracy while Tan Malaka supported the one-party system. Where he and Tan Malaka agreed most, according to Hatta's memoirs, was on their mutual dislike of and refusal to bow to Stalin.[38]

A significant event for Hatta in the summer of 1922 was the news that Turkey under the leadership of Mustapha Kemal Pasha had defeated the Greek Army on August 26. This, remarked Hatta with a note of satisfaction, "stirred up the air in Europe." "In the hearts of every Asian, Ankara became regarded as a Mecca of the new nationalism which teaches as its basic principle a belief in one's own capability."[39] It was a strong statement. Mecca was the most sacred place on earth to a Muslim.

Hatta was also impressed by the establishment of a parliament in Ankara "based on the principle of People's Sovereignty," a principle which Hatta believed accorded with the democratic ideal of the Minangkabau, and one which he would promote for Indonesia for the rest of his life. Later events in Turkey forced Hatta to modify his opinion of Mustapha Kemal Pasha and admit that "from the beginning of 1926 Turkey was again governed by a dictatorship."[40] although this time a secular one.

From 1923 onwards, Hatta became the leading propagandist of the Indonesian Student's League, whose name had now changed to the Perhimpunan Indonesia or PI. He established a reputation for hard-hitting journalism, using his newly acquired economic expertise to highlight the flaws in the theories put forward by Dutch colonial economists, even highly respected academics such as Dr. Boeke. "I began to query whether J. H. Boeke was correct in the statements he put forward in his dissertation *Tropisch Koloniale Staathuiskunde* [Tropical Colonial Political Economics] published in 1910," Hatta recalled, "which suggested that economic laws valid in the West are not valid for the native peoples of the Netherlands

38 Hatta, *Memoir*, p. 137.
39 Hatta, "Objectives and Policy of the National Movement in Indonesia," p. 113.
40 Mohammad Hatta, "Riwajat Pendek Tentang Perdjuangan Politik di Negeri Turki," in Mohammad Hatta, *Kumpulan Karangan*, vol. 2 (Jakarta: Penerbitan dan Balai Buku Indonesia, 1953), p. 95.

East Indies."[41] Boeke considered that there was a basic difference in the outlook of East and West. The average Eastern peasant had simple and limited wants, while in the West there was a more acquisitive instinct with unlimited desires. The average Easterner did not possess the ability to organize and did not form large-scale corporations, generally lacking the profiteering nature of the Westerner.[42] Boeke's statement implied that the Easterner lacked drive and entrepreneurial spirit.

Hatta's own family's record of enterprise and efficiency negated these economic theories. The Minangkabau economy had been buoyant and well-balanced until the Westerner had entered the region. Hatta pointed out that the returns to foreign investors in the Indies were high because of the considerable effort expended by the Indonesian peasant which left him too exhausted to look after his own interests.[43] Hatta also contended that the Javanese peasant had been betrayed by the willingness of his ruling class to cooperate with the Dutch for personal enrichment, citing as an example the abuse of Javanese "coolies" in the East Sumatran plantations. "And to whom could the masses complain?" Hatta queried, adding: "They knew nobody but their oppressors."[44]

Hatta reiterated this theme in his defense speech: "People were punished daily, they were beaten with rattan, deprived of their freedom, undressed and tarred, threatened with death to prevent them from telling about the maltreatment," he alleged.[45] Hatta protested against the statement by a member of the Netherlands Indies judiciary that "this punishment was indispensable in the Dutch colonies for the time being."[46] "We are absolutely fed up with this kind of 'Dutch civilization,' demonstrated in such a 'brave' way by those who call themselves exponents of Dutch culture."[47]

Apart from using its paper, *Indonesia Merdeka*, as a medium for

---

41 Hatta, *Memoir*, p. 129.

42 For a general summary of Boeke's theories, including a translation of part of his works, see W. F. Wertheim, ed., *Indonesian Economics: The Concept of Dualism in Theory and Policy* (The Hague: van Hoeve, 1966).

43 Hatta, "Drainage," p. 31.

44 Hatta, "National Claims," p. 311.

45 Mohammad Hatta, "Indonesia Free," p. 241, citing from *Nieuwe Rotterdamse Courant,* November 7 and 24, 1926.

46 Hatta, "Indonesia Free," p. 242, citing from *De Telegraaf,* December 20, 1925.

47 Hatta, "Indonesia Free," p. 242.

protest, the PI in 1925 also published a *Gedenkboek*, a commemoration of the student association's first fifteen years of existence. The authors laid emphasis on the "non-cooperation" principle and the replacement of the political entity "Dutch East Indies" by "Indonesia." Hatta's two contributions: "Indonesia in the Middle of the Asian Revolution" and "Indonesia in the World Community" confidently asserted the infectiousness of Asian renaissance, bolstered by Japanese and Turkish successes and the growing strength of the Indian nationalist movement under Gandhi's leadership.

To the students' immense satisfaction, the emergence of the *Gedenkboek* raised a storm of protest both within the Netherlands and from the colonial government. Subardjo graphically recalled the reaction: "Dutch public opinion was in uproar, dumbfounded, astonished and variable."[48] For Hatta, there was the added gratification that Westenenck came under attack from the Ministry of Colonies for not perceiving the extent of radicalism building up within the student group. Subardjo recalled that Westenenck's admonition to the Indies students was: "It is no use thinking that Dutch power will be easily overthrown because it is as immovable and strong as the mountains of Sumatra and Java."[49]

A Ministry of Colonies circular was issued warning students against participating in political or trade union activities on penalty of being denied employment in the Indies civil service and withdrawal of government scholarships. In the colony, parents were advised against sending their sons to the "contaminating atmosphere of Europe."[50] It was suggested that a suitable deterrent to dissident sons might be to discontinue parental allowances. As Hatta pointed out in his defense speech, "to the sons is left the choice... to imitate the fathers in their dull routine, comfortably and willingly and slavishly carrying out orders from above, renouncing the promotion of any ideals and only thinking of a career,"[51] or to join the nationalist cause.

Westenenck was instructed to intensify his surveillance of the students'

---

48 Subardjo Djoyoadisuryo, *Kesadaran Nasional*, p. 126.
49 Cited in ibid., p. 126.
50 See John Ingleson, *Perhimpunan Indonesia and the Indonesian Nationalist Movement 1923-1928* (Clayton, Vic: Monash University Centre of Southeast Asian Studies, 1975), p. 50.
51 Hatta, "Indonesia Free," p. 208.

activities, as they were undoubtedly maintaining a close association with left-wing groups. Not only had the exiled PKI leader, Semaun, established an office in Amsterdam but both he and a former PI chairman, Iwa Kusuma Sumantri, represented the Perhimpunan Indonesia on the Comintern executive. Western education had not produced the type of cultural bonding the Dutch had anticipated between brown and white.

Van Leeuwen assured Hatta that his loan funding would continue irrespective of his student activism. Hatta did, however, receive a letter informing him that the change in direction of the Perhimpunan Indonesia did not accord with the precepts of the Orde der Dienaren van Indie and that he must either resign from the PI or leave the Order.[52] It was not a difficult choice. His increasing involvement in PI activities was steering Hatta away from "association" with the Dutch. For him, being a "server of the Indies" meant attending to the needs of the indigenous people, which he believed entailed ousting the colonial power. Perhaps a more hurtful consequence was that his Minangkabau roommate, Zainuddin, was ordered by his father, a respected Padang businessman, to dissociate from Hatta and return home.[53] It was disconcerting to be regarded as a "contaminating influence" by a member of one's own ethnic group.

At the end of 1925 Hatta was nominated for the chairmanship of the Perhimpunan Indonesia, a tribute to his untiring efforts to promote the association. Hatta accepted the position, drawing on to his executive as secretary a radical Javanese student, Abdul Madjid, a choice he may later have regretted. For his treasurer, he chose a fellow student from the Handelshogeschool, Abutari. A decision which must have given Westenenck cause for concern was the inclusion on the PI executive of the PKI leader, Darsono, now closely linked to Moscow. In his memoirs, Hatta set down the qualities he was looking for in his committee:

> I thought the number of members should not exceed five. Among those who sat on the executive, as many as possible must be members who worked for the Association or wrote essays for *Indonesia Merdeka*, or who carried out propaganda for *Perhimpunan*

---

52 Hatta, *Memoir.*, p. 160.
53 Ibid., pp. 159-60.

Indonesia by correspondence with friends at home, discussing the various problems faced by the nationalist movement. In this way, the activities of Ministry of Colonies advisers, such as the former governor of North Sumatra, Mr. Westenenck, could be prevented from claiming victims.[54]

The last sentence suggested that Hatta had deliberately chosen a committee capable of outwitting Westenenck. 1926 was also the year when PKI activities both in Java and Sumatra were reaching crisis point. With the decline of Sarikat Islam, the PKI had become the dominant dissident group in the colony. As the PI was an overseas wing of the nationalist movement, Hatta needed to remain close to the PKI, monitoring its activities, which he could do most effectively by liaising with Darsono and Semaun.

Hatta's inaugural address as chairman took the form of an analysis of the economic roots of colonialism, which he entitled "The Economic World Structure and the Conflict of Power."[55] Hatta quoted the theory of Hegel on which Marx had drawn, that the "existence of conflict is the first requirement for development."[56] (He did not mention that, according to Minangkabau adat, conflict was believed to produce *Kemajuan* or progress, and that in the Minangkabau world view "history moves towards the attainment of harmony of individual and society."[57] He might not have been conscious of the likelihood that his cultural outlook had conditioned him, and also Tan Malaka, to feel drawn to Marx's dialectical philosophies because of their compatibility with the Minangkabau world view.)

Hatta stressed that the main cause for conflict in Indonesian society was the colonial racial situation, the *"antithesis between ruler and ruled,"* "between white and colored races."[58] Giving expression to the spirit of revolt

---

54 Ibid., p. 190.
55 For full text see Mohammad Hatta, "The Economic World Structure and the Conflict of Power," in *Portrait of a Patriot*, pp. 36-56.
56 Ibid., p. 38.
57 See Taufik Abdullah, "Modernization in the Minangkabau World: West Sumatra in the Early Decades of the Twentieth Century," in *Culture and Politics in Indonesia*, ed. Claire Holt et al. (Ithaca: Cornell University Press, 1972), pp. 188-89.
58 Hatta, "Economic World Structure," p. 38.

now reaching a crescendo in the nationalist movement, he aggressively asserted: "There will be no freedom without force, because it is in the interest of the ruler for the colony to be retained at all costs."[59] It was a statement which would be brought against him at his trial, compelling him to defend himself from accusations of issuing a call to arms.

Dismissing the various Western theories on the causes of colonialism, Hatta maintained that fear of competition and the desire to establish a monopoly over resources were the real motives. He stressed that colonialism had "not the slightest connection with the fundamental concept of right," and was nothing but a "power usurpation euphemistically called right, practised by a nation that has got the power and the desire for it." Because of the European Entente which sanctioned hegemony over the colored races, subjugated nations had to create "under their own steam" the right to national existence.[60]

Hatta, in recalling European economic history, pointed to its dependency on tropical products to provide for Western needs. "This dependence is the Achilles heel of modern Europe," he contended. "Europe tries to protect this vulnerable spot by conducting an imperialistic policy." It would be economically disadvantageous for the colonizer to release a colony voluntarily. "Conflict manifests itself here in its full force," he continued, "because it is the very basic needs of the two peoples that are opposed here in the situation of ruler and ruled."[61]

Hatta mapped out a future strategy for the nationalist movement. The non-cooperation policy would be implemented by formation of a "state within a state," following examples set in Turkey and by the Sinn Fein movement in Ireland. Indonesians must create their own organizations, their own institutions -- in other words, return to managing their own affairs. The trade union movement must be strengthened to resist colonial exploitation, because a cheap labor supply was vital to the colonizer. Cooperative societies must be established to compete with overseas corporations in order to "bring the colonial machine to a standstill."[62] During his 1925 summer vacation, Hatta had toured Sweden, Norway,

---

59 Ibid., p. 39.
60 Ibid., p. 44.
61 Ibid., p. 50.
62 Ibid., p. 53.

and Denmark and had become a dedicated supporter of cooperatives, seeing them as a means of building up the weak peasant or small trader into an economic force strong enough to resist the domination of large corporations. The Minangkabau nationalists may have observed correlations between cooperatives and the family enterprises of their region, for Tan Malaka, too, had written in 1920 on the suitability of cooperatives as a means of combating excessive profits made by middlemen.[63]

Hatta's speech essentially advocated an attack which was aimed predominantly at Dutch economic and institutional targets rather than an armed uprising. Indonesians had economic power, if they only realized how to exploit it.

He concluded with a remarkably accurate prediction:

Although the emphasis of our struggle lies on the destruction of Dutch imperialism, we must not forget for one moment that our struggle is irrevocably connected with the general Pacific problem. As the border land of this great expanse which is presently called the Pacific, our country will naturally be involved in the drama to come. We know that this will be the ultimate solution of the racial conflict.[64]

---

63 See H. A. Poeze, *Tan Malaka: Strijder Voor Indonesie's Vrijheid, Levensloop van 1897 tot 1945* (The Hague: Nijhoff, 1976), p. 85, n. 47. Tan Malaka's article "Verbruiks-cooperaties voor het Javaansche proletariat," was published in *Het Vrije Woord*, May 15, 1920.
64 Hatta, "Economic World Structure," p. 55.

CHAPTER THREE
PROVOCATION AND REPRISAL

As sons of the country themselves, the Indonesians studying here in this country feel themselves to be the real repositories of the task, to which they feel called. In them the people will place more trust, and from them it will seek its protection. They feel how beautiful is the task of the intellectual sons of a country over which a foreign nation of another race wields the sceptre. Their first calling must be to make their people see its humiliation at an intolerable evil, to ignite the urge for freedom in it and thus truly to value the greatest possession of humanity: national freedom.[1]

By the time Hatta was elected chairman of the Perhimpunan Indonesia, he recognized that the group was no longer a social organization but had become "an advance post of the Indonesian national movement," a radical political band whose members had resolved that, on their return to the Indies, they would "go to the masses and struggle with the masses."[2]

In Hatta's opinion, the PI graduates were more adequately equipped for national leadership than the party leaders in the Indies because they had lived in a democratic society free of colonial rule. This point he reiterated in his defense speech:

As the mountaineer, at the top of a hill, has better view of the landscape than the people who live in that landscape, so the Indonesian students in Holland are in a better position to take a

---

1 Hatta, "Indonesia Free," in *Portrait of Patriot*, pp. 214-15.
2 Ibid., p. 216.

view of the colonial situation than their countrymen, who lived under the colonial hypnosis.[3]

Certainly the overseas students had learned to subordinate their religious and ethnic differences to the ideal of an integrated modern nation, Indonesia. In the colony, there were still deep divisions among the local nationalists. The Partai Sarikat Islam had failed in 1924 to persuade the PKI and the veteran Javanese party, Budi Utomo, to join with it in forming a front of radical nationalists.[4] Hatta visualized the PI graduates as a cohesive factor who, by infiltrating the existing parties, could encourage the local nationalists to disregard parochial issues in the wider interests of the independence struggle. Without such cohesion, the "state within a state" concept outlined by Hatta in his inaugural speech as chairman of the PI would be difficult to implement.

The infiltration process was more difficult than Hatta had anticipated. Returning graduates found that their exposure to Western cultural patterns and concepts had alienated them from their compatriots more than they had anticipated. They began to congregate in their own study groups rather than joining existing parties. The two most effective study clubs were in Surabaya and Bandung, the former led by an ex-PI chairman and medical graduate, Dr. Sutomo, and the latter formed by a group of Leiden law graduates.

1926 was a year of mounting tensions in the nationalist movement. Hatta urged the returned graduates to move closer to the Communists, knowing that the PKI was split and in need of strong guidance. In a letter of June 2, to an ex-PI colleague, Sudjadi, now working as a clerk in the colony's Department of Finance, Hatta reproved the Bandung Study Club for closing its group to PKI members: "Cooperation with the communists does no harm," Hatta insisted, "provided we do not lose sight of our principles, [it] strengthens the creation of a national bloc."[5] As he further explained, through Sudjadi, the exiled PKI leaders in Europe were more prepared to cooperate with the Indonesian nationalists than with fellow

---

3 Ibid., p. 244.
4 Kahin, *Nationalism and Revolution*, p. 78.
5 See John Ingleson, *Road to Exile: The Indonesian Nationalist Movement 1927-1934* (Singapore: Heinemann Educational Books [Asia], 1979), p. 16.

Communists:

> He [Semaun] does not trust his Dutch comrades but gives us his
> full trust. He advises us to refuse all cooperation with the Dutch
> communists. Is this then communism? He will never tolerate the
> leadership of the Indonesian workers' movement coming into
> the hands of a Dutch communist. Therefore I see no reason in
> relation to our national unity not to cooperate with the Indonesian
> communists.[6]

The Bandung Study Club's ostracism of the PKI was matched by
a similar coolness on the part of the local Communists. Since its split
with Sarikat Islam, the PKI had preferred to work alone, for which it had
earned a rebuke from Stalin in May 1925 for not observing the Comintern
directive to work within a nationalist group, being accused of "Leftist
deviation."[7] The PKI was internally divided. When the central committee
ordered its rural Sarekat Rakyat to disband, suspicious that they contained
too many reactionary elements, such as peasant landowners, the conflict
within the party heightened. Tan Malaka, now working as a Comintern
agent in Southeast Asia, protested strongly against this PKI directive. He
also advised the PKI leaders not to consider staging a *putsch* without the
full support of the people.[8]

The important role now played by the Comintern in the nationalist
movement had clearly begun to trouble Hatta. He was also aware that his
close liaison with Semaun and Darsono might antagonize the Partai Sarikat
Islam and Haji Agus Salim, for Semaun had been particularly influential
in weakening Sarikat Islam's influence in the trade union movement.
The dilemma for Hatta and the Perhimpunan Indonesia was that the
Comintern was useful, both in terms of financial and moral support and
through its sponsorship of international freedom movements. It was
really only in extreme left-wing circles that the concept of "Indonesia"

---

6   Ibid., p. 17.
7   See Kahin, *Nationalism and Revolution*, p. 76.
8   See Poeze, *Tan Malaka*, pp. 335-40. Tan Malaka issued a booklet, *Massa Actie* to support his views
    regarding precipitate revolutionary action, which was first published in Singapore in 1927, and
    reprinted in Jakarta in 1947.

was taken seriously and promoted. The moderates and conservatives in Western society believed that the Netherlands had a right, through long historical association, to govern the East Indies.

It was clear from reports passed on by Sudjadi that the returned graduates saw the need for a new party based on nationalism to play a leadership role in the colony. Such a party would have the advantage of attracting ex-PI members who were reluctant to integrate into the existing nationalist groups. Hatta strongly supported the proposal, seeing the new party as an extension of the Perhimpunan Indonesia, with the same goals and with a nationalist ideology which would, he hoped, override the factionalism in Indonesian society. In this way, the political momentum gained by the PI would not be dissipated, but its dynamism transferred to the colony.

It was agreed that the Bandung Study Club should serve as the nucleus for the new party. It was a very enthusiastic and responsive group, in spite of its refusal to work with the PKI. It also benefitted from the support of the two radical leaders of the early Indische Partij, Dr. Tjipto Mangunkusumo and Douwes Dekker. Hatta proposed that the new party be named the Sarekat Rakyat Nasional Indonesia [Indonesian National People's Union],[9] as if to indicate a new Sarekat Rakyat based on nationalism rather than communism, at the same time encouraging the PKI's discarded and aggrieved Sarekat Rakyat to link up with the new party.

Once again, events proved that returned PI graduates did not automatically assume a leading role in nationalist affairs of the colony, even within a group like the Bandung Study Club which was tightly linked to the Perhimpunan Indonesia. The dominant member in the Study Club appeared to be a Javanese graduate in architecture from the Bandung Institute of Technology, named Sukarno. As a high school student, Sukarno had boarded with the Sarikat Islam leader, Tjokroaminoto. Thus, like Hatta, he had had a long exposure to radical nationalism, participating in Jong Java while a schoolboy. Sukarno was just one year older than Hatta. He had completed his education in Dutch schools but

---

9   Hatta used the Dutch equivalent, Indonesische Nationalistische Volkspartij, when putting forward
    the program of the new party on November 23, 1926. Notes of PI Executive Meetings, 1925-26, as
    cited in Ingleson, *Perhimpunan Indonesia*, p. 39.

had not had the opportunity to undertake overseas study. Nevertheless, he read widely, was interested in international trends, and reportedly also was an admirer of Hatta's writings.[10]

While it was Hatta's intellectual brilliance and total dedication to the independence struggle which had brought him to the fore as a leader, it was Sukarno's vibrant and dominating personality, accompanied by charm and humor, which drew people to him. He was an eloquent speaker, just as was his mentor Tjokroaminoto, with the same deft use of language and idiom which made the Sarikat Islam leader appear like a messianic figure or *Ratu Adil* to the underprivileged Javanese masses.[11] Sukarno was not prepared to accept that the overseas graduates had a preferential right to leadership of the nationalist movement; in fact he was always to view Hatta's goals as too Western rather than shaped by his own culture. Sukarno had begun to mount his first challenge to Hatta's leadership, a contest which would have an immense impact on Indonesia's independence struggle.

Hatta was not fully aware of Sukarno's challenge in mid-1926. He was too occupied with devising ways to improve the PI's effectiveness as a nationalist spearhead. He continued the policy of advertising the concept of "Indonesia" as widely as possible, delegating a fellow-students Arnold Mononutu, to represent the Perhimpunan Indonesia in Paris, where his room in the Hotel du Progres doubled as a PI branch office. A center of revolt against the Establishment, the Left Bank offered many opportunities for young Indonesian nationalists to win a sympathetic hearing for their cause.

Hatta also spent part of the summer vacation in France, representing the PI at an International Democratic Congress for Peace held at Bierville in August under the *aegis* of the French Communist, Mark Sangnier. Hatta admitted that he went to Bierville "with a little scepticism,"[12] but the gathering turned out to be more rewarding than he had anticipated.

---

10 See P. M. Noor, "Inspirasi-inspirasi yang timbul selama pergaulan saja dengan Bung Hatta," in *Bung Hatta Mengabdi pada Tjita-Tjita Perdjoangan Bangsa,* p. 301.

11 In times of socioeconomic depression or when foreign influences disturb traditional patterns of life, the Javanese long for a messianic leader, a *Ratu Adil* or Just Prince, to rescue them from their misery.

12 M. Hatta, "Propaganda," in *Portrait of a Patriot,* p. 156. First published in *Indonesia Merdeka,* 1926.

There he had an opportunity to liaise closely with other Asian nationalists, especially with the Indian delegate, K. M. Pannikar. He joined fellow Asians in drawing up a manifesto which attempted to analyze the colonial problem in Asia, which the group considered to center around Britain's position in India.[13]

In his own addresses to the congress, Hatta stressed that, although the concept of "brotherhood in peace" appealed to Indonesians, the inequality and lack of freedom existing in the Indies meant that peace was difficult to achieve. He concluded: "Our struggle for freedom is at the same time a struggle for democracy and for humanity."[14] Hatta would always see the achievement of democracy and humanity as the main goals in the independence struggle, rather than a mere transfer of power from the Dutch to the local people.

The strong currents of unrest and dissatisfaction which Tan Malaka had warned the local PKI leaders to control flared up into open revolt in West Java two months after Hatta returned to the Netherlands for the new academic year. The revolts were followed by similar sporadic uprisings in the Minangkabau in January 1927.[15] Some 13,000 Indonesians were arrested, of whom 823 were later dispatched to a new penal settlement established in the furthermost region of the colony, West New Guinea.[16] Hatta, in his defense speech, was later to blame Dutch provocation for the uprisings, quoting from an article written by his friend, ex-Resident Le Febvre, which claimed that colonial officers were deliberately stirring up trouble to gain recognition and honors.[17]

The outbreak of the rebellion in November 1926 made Hatta feel the urgent need for a new party to replace the banned PKI. He believed that in such a new party, religion and foreign ideology must be subordinate to Indonesian nationalism. It was to ensure the supremacy of nationalism, according to Hatta, that on December 5, 1926, he entered into a

---

13 Ibid., p. 151.

14 Ibid., p. 157.

15 For a detailed account of the local factors associated with the uprisings in Batavia, Bantam, and West Sumatra, including Marxist and Islamic fervor, disaffection with the Dutch, and the leadership conflict between Tan Malaka and local leaders such as Alimin and Musso, see H. J. Benda and R. T. McVey, ed., *The Communist uprisings of 1926-1927 in Indonesia: Key Documents*, 2nd ed. (Ithaca, N.Y.: Cornell Modern Indonesia Project, 1969).

16 Cited in Kahin, *Nationalism and Revolution*, p. 86.

17 Hatta, "Indonesia Free," p. 243.

"Convention" with the exiled PKI leader, Semaun, informing only a few PI members about his strategy.[18] Hatta knew that he must be cautious; colonial agitation was at fever pitch in the aftermath of the scattered uprisings, and the existence of an agreement between the Perhimpunan Indonesia and the now illegal Partai Komunis Indonesia would undoubtedly be misconstrued by the Dutch government.

Under the terms of the Convention, Semaun, on behalf of the PKI, recognized that the Perhimpunan Indonesia should assume the direction of the nationalist movement in Indonesia; he assured it of full PKI support and agreed that Indonesian Communists would not oppose PI policies as long as they were directed towards the goal of Indonesian independence. The PKI agreed to allow the PI the use of its printing presses.[19] It was a neat package deal; it allowed the students the material benefits of Comintern association without Communist domination of the independence struggle.

The Convention did not receive approval from the Comintern and Semaun was instructed to terminate it on December 19. The rejection was an indication of Comintern exasperation with nationalist groups which accepted its aid but refused to bow to its authority, and a year later a new Comintern directive was issued to Communist parties that they must dissociate from nationalist groups. As Hatta commented in his later years: "Stalin was a genuine Russian, his country to him was number one."[20] Communist parties represented Moscow's interests, nationalist parties did not.

Hatta had already held discussions with PI members during the year concerning the format and policies of a new nationalist party. On November 23, 1926, he presented an outline of his proposals to a general meeting of the Perhimpunan Indonesia, where they were accepted as official PI policy.[21] On December 20, Hatta received word via Sudjadi that

---

18 Hatta stated that he informed his secretary, Abdul Madjid, about the Convention. See Hatta, *Memoir*, p. 207.

19 For a translation of the text of the Convention between Semaun and Mohammad Hatta, see Ingleson, *Perhimpunan Indonesia*, pp. 85-86.

20 Mohammad Hatta, *Bung Hatta Menjawab*, (Jakarta: Gunung Agung, 1979), p. 8. Strictly speaking, Stalin was a Georgian.

21 See Ingleson, *Perhimpunan Indonesia*, p. 39.

the Bandung Study Club was ready to take the initiative.[22]

In his outline, Hatta proposed that the party should aim at establishing an Indonesian government with "a purely democratic basis, with the village community as the central element."[23] Hatta was determined to restore the democracy of the *Bodi-Caniago* system, the traditional type of government in the Agam region of West Sumatra before the colonial intrusion. He looked to the institutions of the West to give form to his democratic ideal, suggesting a parliament based on universal suffrage, a replacement for the impotent Volksraad. Hatta also included provision for the protection of civil rights, the rights enjoyed by the students in Europe but increasingly denied to Indonesians in the colony. To ensure that the new nation rejected the autocracy of the Governor-General and the Javanese ruler, Hatta dispensed with the concept of "exorbitant rights."

Hatta's inaugural speech as chairman had highlighted the economic motives behind colonialism. A necessary element of building a "state within a state" was, then, to break the dominance of European private enterprise. In the economic goals of the new party, Hatta promoted cooperatives as a practical means of enabling Indonesians to fight against the power of the foreign corporation. Hatta would always be a firm believer in cooperatives. To counteract abuse of indigenous labor, he called for the introduction of an eight-hour working day in line with the policies of the international labor movement.

In the social aims of the party, Hatta proposed the "promotion of national education." He called for the elimination of usury, which was not only consistent with his religious beliefs but also an attempt to relieve the pressures of the Indonesian peasant's chronic indebtedness. Finally, his plan called for an overall improvement in health facilities.

Although Hatta's concepts for a new party were endorsed by his colleagues in the Perhimpunan Indonesia, the Bandung Study Club was more critical, presenting Hatta with his first inkling that the PI might not remain the new party's moving spirit and that the nationalists in the Indies wanted to take the initiative themselves.[24] When interrogated in prison

---

22 Ibid., p. 44.
23 Hatta, "Indonesia Free," p. 277.
24 See Ingleson, *Perhimpunan Indonesia*, p. 45.

on why his plan for a new party had been rejected, Hatta answered:

> I suppose that Sudjadi had objections against this programme
> because it contained the demand for universal suffrage, which in
> his opinion was probably in conflict with the principle of non-
> cooperation, in the sense that perhaps Indonesia for the sake of
> receiving universal suffrage could come to accept seats in the
> Volksraad.[25]

For Hatta, the Volksraad was a symbol of colonial hypocrisy. His vision
was of a national parliament developing separately through the convening
of national congresses.

In a letter of March 9, 1927, to a recently returned PI friend, Gatot
Mangkupradja, Hatta defended his program as "the basis of the forming
of a state within a state." He informed Gatot that Semaun, the PKI leader,
fully supported his plans, agreeing with Hatta that they were the only
ones which would "receive the support of the people."[26] He omitted to
mention that Semaun had originally drawn up a much more radical
program which Hatta had declined to submit to the PI's general meeting
in November 1926, sensing that armed revolution needed to be played
down in favor of more subtle economic strategies. Yet at his trial Hatta
would find it difficult to convince the court that Semaun's fiery plan was
not the blueprint for the new party. Hatta would remain, in colonial eyes,
a Communist revolutionary.

Hatta's personal dilemma in early 1927 was whether to return to
the colony to assist with the establishment and direction of the new
party. According to his memoirs, he was persuaded to remain on as PI
chairman, continuing his successful propaganda activities in Europe.[27] It
was not hard for Hatta to yield to this option, for he knew that in the
Indies he would be restricted by the provisions of the new Penal Clauses.
The Bandung Study Club's rebuff may also have warned him that he could
exert more influence as a nationalist leader overseas, acting as a watchdog
not only on the Dutch government but on the progress of the nationalist

---

25 Ibid.
26 Ibid.
27 Hatta, *Memoir*, p. 208.

movement in the Indies.

The Ministry of Colonies was now mounting a very strict surveillance on student activities, on Westenenck's advice continuing to exert pressure on the attorney-general to take preventive action against the PI. The ministry issued dire warnings that "the agitators' activities in the Netherlands may lead to a bloody collision," insisting that "they may no longer be exempt from punishment in one part of the State while involved in conspiracy to undermine Netherlands' sovereignty in another part."[28] Thus Hatta felt forced to appoint two PI executive committees in 1927, one acting as a screen for the other, to prevent scholarship holders from being victimized by the Dutch authorities.

He did, however, disregard Westenenck's admonitions to students to dissociate from left-wing groups. A new organization, the League against Imperialism, against Colonial Oppression and for National Independence, had just been formed, which, he believed, could be used to gain wider international recognition for Indonesia. Its name alone embodied so much of what the nationalists were fighting for. The league, organized by the German Communist Party under its leader, Willi Munzenberg, was scheduled to hold its first congress in Brussels in February 1927. The Perhimpunan Indonesia was invited to send a delegation, an invitation Hatta accepted.

The congress was attended by a strange medley of international socialists -- Communists, social democrats, Fabians, trade unionists, pacifists, together with nationalists from a wide selection of countries. The Soviet Union remained aloof.[29] Subardjo, Nazir Pamontjak, and a third student, Gatot Tarumihardja, accompanied Hatta. Semaun attended separately, representing the Sarekat Rakyat. Under Hatta's plan for a new party, the Sarekat Rakyat in its title was representative of the Indonesian Communists working in close association with Indonesian nationalists, giving them a sense of continuing identity. The size of the Indonesian contingent attending a radically anticolonial congress clearly disturbed the Dutch authorities, who were further aggravated by the fact that both Hatta and Semaun were elected to the Presidium of the congress. Coming

---

28 See Ingleson, *Perhimpunan Indonesia*, p. 55.
29 See Sarvepalli Gopal, *Jawaharlal Nehru: A Biography, 1889-1947*, vol. I (London: Cape, 1975), p. 100.

immediately in the wake of two Communist revolts in the Indies, the involvement of Hatta and Semaun in the League's management committee appeared to present further evidence of continuing subversive activity.

It was on this Presidium that Hatta first worked alongside Jawaharlal Nehru of India, whose viewpoint and general outlook he found to accord with his own and with whom he was to form a lasting friendship, which was to gain special significance during Indonesia's struggle for independence. As a point of interest, Nehru's biographer has suggested that this congress was a turning point in his subject's mental development because for the first time Nehru articulated a consciousness of the interlinking of economics and politics, a linkage which Hatta had recognized as a schoolboy in Padang. "For the first time, instead of merely condemning British imperialism, Jawaharlal had tried to understand the motives, manner and methods of its functioning."[30] Perhaps Hatta's emphasis on the economic roots of colonialism helped to awaken Nehru's consciousness, since they were thrown closely together through meetings of the Presidium.

Like Hatta, Nehru, without committing himself to communism, was enthused by Marxist/Leninist revolutionary fervor and its underlying call for social justice. Both men supported "non-cooperation" and "non-violence." Both had a high regard for their respective colonizers as people and as technologists, but both could see that colonialism had had a corrupting effect on the colonizer when he wielded despotic power in his colony, rather than permitting the same degree of democracy as was practiced in his metropole. Both Hatta and Nehru were, to some extent, struggling against the cultural stranglehold which their Western education had imposed on them. They were both determined not to allow their cultural bonds to deter them from achieving a restoration of sovereignty and dignity for their people.

The congress opened up further propagandist opportunities for Hatta, including an invitation from the International Women's League for Peace and Freedom to lecture to their holiday course to be held at Gland near Lake Geneva during August and September 1927, a gathering to which Nehru was also invited. The League against Colonialism became an established organization, with headquarters in Paris. Hatta was appointed

30 Ibid., p. 101.

to represent Indonesia, which allowed him further opportunities to maintain close links with influential international radical socialists, not just Communists. It was also decided to establish local branches of the League against Colonialism, the PI being assigned to organize the Dutch branch. This was to have its own journal, *Recht en Vrijheid* [Justice and Freedom], through which Hatta could continue to attack colonial policies.

Although for Hatta the congress had proved to be a stimulating experience, it had also been very demanding in terms of energy and physical endurance. On his return to the Netherlands he collapsed and was forced to rest for two weeks in Subardjo's flat, attributing his illness to the fact that he had been skipping lunch and existing on endless cups of coffee.[31] Nehru, too, complained of fatigue. "I am dead tired after eight or nine days of the Congress here," he wrote from Brussels. "I have not had a good night's sleep and hardly a decent meal since I came here."[32]

For the next months until the end of the academic year, Hatta was forced to devote more time to studying, for he had to pass the *tentamen* [initial examination] in his new stream, Constitutional Law, if he were to be allowed to continue his studies. At the beginning of the summer vacation, he had to travel to Switzerland to tend to a PI colleague, Sumadi, dying of tuberculosis in a sanitorium. While reading a German newspaper in a cafe there, Hatta's eyes alighted on a news report that Dutch police had searched the residence of the Perhimpunan Indonesia. Westenenck had finally convinced the attorney-general that warrants for house searches should be issued,[33] and obviously the Dutch authorities saw Hatta's absence abroad as an opportune time to strike.

Raids were made on the residences of the most active PI members, including Hatta, Subardjo, Abdul Madjid, Darsono, and Ali Sastroamidjojo. In his autobiography, Ali describes the chaos and fear caused by the arrival of the Dutch police, "with pistols drawn": "They went through the house, room by room, cupboard by cupboard, searching very thoroughly for something until everything was turned inside-out and our belongings

---

31 Hatta, *Memoir*, p. 213.
32 Gopal, *Jawaharlal Nehru*, p. 101.
33 See Ingleson, *Perhimpunan Indonesia*, pp. 55-56.

were scattered everywhere."[34] Ali explained that he only discovered later that the Dutch police were searching for copies of the Hatta-Semaun agreement.

Yet the summer drew to a close without any further police harassment. In August and September, Hatta returned to Switzerland, this time as the guest of the International League of Women for Peace and Freedom. He had over the years attended vacation courses in France to try to polish up his fluency in French and now felt confident enough to address the assembly in this language. He chose as his subject "Indonesia and Her Independence Problem."

Hatta was aware that his audience was not wholly sympathetic to his viewpoint, that he was in fact being monitored by Dutch agents. Responding to the challenge, he declared confidently: "The name 'Indonesia' for us is a sacred symbol of a country which in the future will be free. It is to achieve this ideal that today we are struggling against Dutch imperialism and sacrificing our personal interests."[35] Hatta traced the course of Dutch colonization of the archipelago up to the present time, producing statistics to indicate the huge dividends paid by most European corporations operating in Indonesia. Alongside these details, he produced figures of the "starvation wages" paid to native labor, giving the details of the inequitable land rents paid to peasants for the use of their ricelands. Hatta tried to back up his address as much as possible with data based on Dutch sources, including the works of the tropical economist Boeke. He concluded on a defiant note, as if to provoke the Dutch antagonists in his audience: "As for us Indonesian nationalists, we would rather see Indonesia sink to the bottom of the sea than have it subjugated by any other nation whatsoever to permanent slavery."[36] It was a phrase he would use again in the future.

While Hatta was pouring out his defiance before left-wing gatherings, a "Committee of Experts" set up by the Dutch government on the advice of the Ministry of Colonies was examining and assessing the materials seized during the raids on PI headquarters in June, together with accumulated copies of PI members' mail. In the conclusion of its report to the minister

34 Ali Sastroamidjojo, *Milestones on My Journey*, p. 30.
35 Mohammad Hatta, "Indonesia and Her Independence Problem," p. 165.
36 Ibid., p. 183.

of colonies, the committee made the following condemnatory statement:

> Perhimpunan Indonesia appears to be an extraordinarily dangerous
> organization for the State, an organization which, contrary to its
> statutes which states its aim as the "separation of the Netherlands
> Indies from the Netherlands State" by all legal means at its disposal,
> in fact at the same time propagates the use of all sorts of illegal
> means (e.g., violence, underground action, arousal of racial hatred,
> etc.).[37]

The committee, then, saw Semaun's plan for revolution, rather than
Hatta's more moderate program, as the real intent of the student group.
The report was considered sufficiently damning for a case amounting
almost to treason to be made against the PI executive. Preventive action
was not confined to the Netherlands. In the Indies, the veteran nationalist,
Dr. Tjipto Mangunkusumo, was condemned as the moving force behind
the Bandung Study Club and its establishment of a new party closely
associated with the PI and the PKI. He was again sent into exile, this time
to the Moluccan island of Banda Neira.

Hatta sprang to Dr. Tjipto's defense, writing an indignant article in
Recht en Vrijheid, the journal of the League against Colonialism, at the
same time displaying his own deep admiration for the man:

> His stubbornness, his unselfishness, his high spiritedness,
> his uncompromising honesty, his indestructible idealism, his
> indomitable revolutionary sentiment -- these all have inspired and
> worked upon the builders of the Indonesian Nation, which is now
> in the making.[38]

It is interesting to note that these were the same adjectives that many
Indonesians later used to portray the character of Hatta himself, an
indication that they were traits he admired and sought to emulate.

Hatta's article was published in *Recht en Vrijheid* on September 24,

---

37 See Ingleson, *Perhimpunan Indonesia*, p. 56.
38 Ibid., p. 10, n. 4.

1927, but he himself was no longer a free man when it appeared. The previous day, shortly after his return from Switzerland, two Dutch policemen arrived at his home bearing an order for his arrest. On arrival at Cassiusstraat prison, he found that he was not alone; Nazir Pamontjak, Ali Sastroamidjojo, and Abdul Madjid had also been detained. There were warrants out for the arrest of Subardjo, Gatot Tarumihardjo, and Arnold Mononutu but, as they were outside the Netherlands, no action could be taken. The charge laid against them was that the Perhimpunan Indonesia was plotting the violent overthrow of the Netherlands State.

Hatta's cell measured approximately two meters by three. It was sparsely furnished: just a table and chair with a bed which folded onto the wall, the hard surface relieved by a straw palliasse. The four students were in solitary confinement, but each was permitted two thirty-minute exercise periods a day, morning and evening.[39]

The day following his arrest, Hatta received two unexpected visitors from the Dutch Socialist Workers' Party, Dr. J. E. W. Duys and his associate, Mr. Mobach. Duys was a member of the Dutch Parliament as well as being a lawyer. Both men offered to defend the students free of charge, explaining that they were convinced that the police action taken against them was unjust and unlawful. The Dutch socialists had always taken an interest in the Indonesian students, and Hatta, since his growing disaffection with the Comintern, was beginning to regard the party in a warmer light. Previously the reluctance of the Dutch socialists to support absolute independence, their strong support for continuing "association," had always been the stumbling block. The Dutch socialists were no doubt aware of Hatta's change of attitude towards Moscow and were anxious to encourage it. Nevertheless, Hatta was reluctant to hand over his defense completely to them. He had to present the Indonesian side of the independence struggle. As a propagandist, he felt the need to take advantage of the public interest which the case had raised in order to explain just how much damage, both materially and spiritually, the colonial system had done to Indonesia.

The four students were subjected to intense interrogation over the next three months. Hatta, as PI chairman, had to face eight sessions of

---

39 Sastroamidjojo, *Milestones on My Journey*, p. 31.

questioning between September 23 and December 14. It was clear that his Convention with Semaun was considered the most damaging piece of evidence against the students, because it established beyond doubt that the PI and the PKI were in partnership and that the PI would take over the struggle in the Indies where the banned PKI had involuntarily ended its operations. The next most incriminating document was considered to be Semaun's draft plan of action for the new party.

The wide press coverage given to the Hatta-Semaun Convention was an embarrassment to Moscow. It came at a time when, influenced by the rift between the Kuomintang and the Chinese Communist Party in April 1927, Comintern policies towards nationalist groups were under review. At such a time, the agreement of a Communist party to subordinate itself to a nationalist group in Indonesia was unpalatable. The Comintern insisted that Semaun issue a press statement averring that he was confused when he signed the Convention and that his action was contrary to Communist principles. Semaun was expelled from the Comintern executive.[40]

These events worked to Hatta's advantage. They meant that the prosecution could no longer claim that he was a Communist agent. Moscow's heated rejection of the Convention suggested, on the contrary, that he had been trying to curb Communist influences within the nationalist movement. Suddenly the most damaging piece of evidence against the Perhimpunan Indonesia had become a damp squib.

An issue on which Hatta was questioned persistently was whether he incited people to violence in his speeches and writings. Apart from rejecting Semaun's party program, Hatta made it clear that in principle he personally was opposed to violence, stating:

> I reject in the strongest possible terms the suggestion that I have ever advocated violence. My conviction is that a people's freedom is never obtained by the advocacy of violence because such advocacy only provokes the situation and of necessity leads to its own undoing.[41]

---

40 See Hatta, *Memoir*, p. 220.
41 See Ingleson, *Perhimpunan Indonesia*, p. 17.

Yet Hatta had stated in his writings and addresses that he considered that violence was almost inevitable if the colonial ruler did not concede a colony the right to self-determination. In his inaugural address to the PI, he had declared that "the only means that nations have at their disposal for the defense of their national rights is as it was for the primitive peoples: violence, which is now called war."[42] This was not a direct incitement to violence but rather a statement of its inevitability if political injustice prevailed, in which case the colonial power must accept the major responsibility. It was on this delicate nuance that Hatta's case rested.

Perhaps for Hatta the most embarrassing interrogations were those concerning Comintern funding of PI activities, which revealed how thoroughly PI communications had been monitored by the Dutch. Comintern money obtained through Semaun and Darsono had clearly been used to boost PI funds and to assist students disadvantaged by their refusal to withdraw from the student association. The authorities had intercepted several letters written in code regarding Comintern funding. Hatta admitted that "*Kijai*" referred either to the Comintern or to Darsono, an interesting word choice, as a *kiyai* is a religious teacher. Hatta also acknowledged that "1.5 pages" referred to a remittance of $1,500 to Subardjo in Paris from Moscow, $1,250 to be used to fund a delegation to the national congress in Indonesia for the inauguration of the new nationalist party and the remainder to be used for general expenses.[43] Hatta admitted that he had talked to Semaun about assistance for Arnold Mononutu and Subardjo, both of whom were working in the PI's office in the Hotel du Progres in Paris. He stressed that he personally did not accept money from the Comintern and had placed any donations he received in the "national fund."[44] Nevertheless, Hatta would have benefitted indirectly from funds allocated to the PI, through payment of his travel expenses and other administration costs.

After three months of interrogations, Hatta submitted a "Final Explanation" dated December 1, 1927, in which he summed up what he

42 Mohammad Hatta, "The Economic World Structure and the Conflict of Power," in *Portrait of a Patriot*, p. 43.
43 Abdurrachman Surjomihardjo, "'Pandang Remaja' Mohammad Hatta," in *Kompas*, August 14, 1972.
44 Ibid.

had been trying to convey to his interrogators, much of which would also be included in his defense speech. He reiterated the aims and principles of the PI, assuring the prosecution that violence was not a part of the PI's program, because "violence is an act of recklessness which leads only to self-destruction."[45] Certainly he could back up this statement by pointing to the PKI revolts, which had resulted in the liquidation of the party. He stressed his hopes that a solution to the colonial problem would "be achieved peacefully" but, because of Holland's continuing exploitation of Indonesia, he feared that "freedom can only be achieved through violence."[46] Again he was indicating that the Netherlands, not the Indonesian nationalists, must shoulder the responsibility for future violence.

Hatta emphasized that the PI did not regard Indonesian Communists in the same light as their European counterparts, but more as "disguised nationalists" who allied with Communists to "obtain international support in their struggle." Again, showing an acute perception of future historical developments in the Southeast Asian region, he predicted that "because of Indonesia's economic-geographic situation, the Western imperialist powers will never tolerate a communist Indonesia," so it would not be to Indonesia's advantage to aim at establishing a Communist state. Hatta defended the humanitarian aspect of the PI's activities. "Perhimpunan Indonesia demonstrates the deep poverty and proletarianization of the Indonesian masses under Dutch domination," he contended, "and at the same time draws the attention of Western public opinion to the Indonesian national freedom movement."[47]

The arrests of the four PI students drew expressions of sympathy both from the Netherlands and from the nationalist movement in the Indies. Protest meetings were organized by nationalist groups, including the conservative Budi Utomo. Political groups and newspapers launched appeals to raise funds to support the Indonesian students and to pay any costs relating to their defense. In fact, the newly formed nationalist party, the Perserikatan Nasional Indonesia [Indonesian National Union] or PNI

---

45 A translation of the full text of Hatta's "Final Explanation" appears in Ingleson, *Perhimpunan Indonesia*, pp. 75-79.
46 Ibid., p. 77.
47 Ibid., pp. 77-78.

was able to use the "student martyrs" as publicity for its inauguration. (The Bandung Study Club had omitted the word "*rakyat*" or "people" from the party's name, confirming Hatta's fears that the Javanese elite in the group could not stomach the degree of popular participation he envisaged. This would constitute a cultural problem which would plague Hatta for the rest of his life.)

Sukarno, now assuming leadership of the new party, also took advantage of the nationalist sentiment aroused by the student arrests to try to form the nationalist front suggested by Hatta as a basis for a "state within a state," the foundation for a parliament. Because of his close association with Tjokroaminoto, Sukarno was invited to attend the Islamic Association's congress in October 1927 where he explained the need to form a federation of all groups seeking independence for Indonesia. His persuasive appeal met with success, and a national front was formed on December 17, 1927.

Sukarno used the concept put forward by Hatta in his program that the "village community" should be at the center of Indonesian government. He named the new front the Permufakatan Perhimpunan Politik Kebangsaan Indonesia [Consultative Group of Indonesian National Political Associations] or PPPKI, incorporating the village concept of *mufakat*, consensus, which is reached after *musyawarah*, deliberation. Yet Hatta was later to criticize Sukarno for overdoing traditionalist sentiment in insisting on decision making by consensus rather than by majority vote. Hatta argued that villages had sufficient interests in common to achieve *mufakat* and did not need to make decisions in a hurry in normal circumstances, but modern governments, especially when representative of diverse ethnic groups, had to act more swiftly and faced more difficulties in reaching consensus. In such a situation, Hatta was always to stress that a decision should be taken on a majority vote. This issue was to remain a bone of contention between him and Sukarno.

There was another major difference between Sukarno and Hatta with regard to their concepts of village democracy. The democracy of the Javanese village was largely confined to social and agricultural concerns. It was not an independent, self-governing political unit as was the Bodi-Caniago village, but rather was subservient to the ruling aristocracy.

The formation of a nationalist front hard on the heels of a new radical party was viewed with disquiet by the European sector in the colony. The more moderate Governor-General, A. C. D. de Graeff, who had taken office shortly before the 1926-27 uprising, was genuinely concerned at the rift which had developed between brown and white. He was an Ethicist, a believer in "association," who now felt himself trapped in a hostile racial situation. This, he informed his friend, former Governor-General van Limburg Stirum, in a letter of October 16, 1927, "fills me with the greatest concern." He described his own dilemma:

> On one side I am decreed as a traitor while on the other the notion gains that, although the government means well, it is useless to back her up -- because the Europeans have made it clear that there do not exist thinking natives, that all of them are only inferior beings one can approach only with the utmost suspicion and that it is all-important to keep them down.[48]

The sentiments of the Dutch colonial community regarding the need to keep the native down were reiterated by the prosecution when the students' trial opened on March 8, 1928. The courtroom was packed with interested spectators, many of them legal pundits. Political trials on what amounted almost to treason charges were not common in the Netherlands.

The presiding judge opened the proceedings by stating that, from the official report of the investigation, the accused admitted that they were responsible for articles in the magazine *Indonesia Merdeka* but denied that the writings constituted an incitement to rebellion against the government.[49] The public prosecutor also argued that the PI was closely associated with the Comintern and had been implicated in the uprisings in the Indies. He demanded that the four accused should be held responsible for the Perhimpunan Indonesia's actions. As he drew his address to a close, he suggested that Hatta be sentenced to a term of three years' imprisonment, Nazir Pamontjak and Ali Sastroamidjojo each to a term of two and one half years, and Abdul Madjid Djojoadiningrat to

48 See E. M. J. Schmutzer, *Dutch Colonial Policy and the Search for Identity in Indonesia* (Leiden: Brill, 1977), p. 72.
49 Sastroamidjojo, *Milestones on My Journey*, p. 37.

two years' imprisonment.[50] Hatta's heart must have sunk. Three years in a Dutch prison was a grim prospect!

It was then the turn of the defense counsel. In itself the participation of Duys in the trial aroused general interest, because he was better known as a socialist parliamentarian than as a lawyer. Duys contended that the case was not a criminal but a political affair, therefore Section 131 of the Dutch Criminal Law should not be applied to the accused. He attributed the students' revolutionary rhetoric to youthful enthusiasm and their frustration at the colonial situation. Such indiscretions did not warrant their detention for over five months.[51] He attacked the colonial system which had allowed such frustration to build up in young Indonesians, pointing out to the court: "Naturally your verdict will be completely meaningless in terms of encouraging or discouraging a revolution."[52] He suggested, however, that a lenient verdict might help to alleviate tensions.

In view of the length of Hatta's speech -- estimated at three and a half hours -- the court requested him to summarize it and submit the full text to the panel of judges for perusal.[53] The theme of injustice towards and exploitation of Indonesia and its people permeated the speech, which stressed the adverse psychological effects of the people's being downgraded and humiliated. Despite his situation, Hatta was not afraid to lash out at the Dutch, describing them as "petty and bourgeois, small minded and mean,"[54] with an appetite for "hopeless sectarianism." Having cited many instances of abuses and cruelties perpetrated against his people, Hatta appealed to the sense of justice of the judges themselves:

To you, as the servants of law and justice, I put my question as to whether you wish to sanction the illegal deed of the Netherlands Government against the defenceless Indonesian students of

50 See Ingleson, *Perhimpunan Indonesia*, p. 58.
51 Ibid., p. 59. In his defense speech, Hatta drew attention to offensive remarks made by a Dutch journalist, Wybrandts, about Governor-General de Graeff. "Let an Indonesian allow himself a similar remark, and the judicature is immediately ready to pronounce on him or her the well-deserved (or rather undeserved) sentence. And a severe one too!" See Hatta, "Indonesia Free," p. 235.
52 See Ingleson, *Perhimpunan Indonesia*, p. 59.
53 Hatta, *Memoir*, p. 227.
54 Hatta, "Indonesia Free," p. 212, quoting remarks made by Henri Polak about the Dutch.

Perhimpoenan Indonesia. We have been persecuted for years in this country by all possible means. We thought that we would enjoy, in the land of Grotius, where people boast of the basic rights of the free citizen, the same elementary rights.[55]

Duys requested that the students be released until the next session of the court, a request which was granted. Hatta recalled that the decision was greeted with warm applause, and that he and his fellow-students were surrounded by a crowd of delighted well-wishers.[56] The four students were treated to a celebratory dinner by their three defense counsels. Ali Sastroamidjojo confessed that they were all longing for a rice dish but none was included on the menu. "People don't realize what an Indonesian stomach is like if it has not had rice for six months."[57]

During the next two weeks the students savored their freedom, still uncertain if the verdict would be unfavorable. On the evening before the court was scheduled to reassemble, they gathered for a *galgenmaal*, the final meal of the condemned man, staying up late into the night in case this was to be their last experience of freedom for several years.[58]

They need not have worried. In the judgment of the court, while it was admitted that violent language and discussion of violence had been part of the writings of the accused, there was no evidence that they had been actively involved in an attempt to overthrow the State. The Netherlands Penal Code only applied to violence against the Netherlands State in Europe and not to the Indies. All four were acquitted.[59]

The acquittals were celebrated both by the PI and by nationalist groups in the Indies, being seen as a triumph for the independence movement. Hatta's defense speech became standard reading for youth groups and study clubs in the Indies. What particularly satisfied Hatta was that Westenenck was forced to resign as student adviser, as if in some slight way the Kamang uprising and the exile of Great Uncle Rais had been avenged.

---

55 Ibid., p. 292.
56 Hatta, *Memoir*, p. 227.
57 Sastroamidjojo, *Milestones on My Journey*, p. 38.
58 Ibid., p. 39.
59 See Ingleson, *Perhimpunan Indonesia*, p. 61.

The judgment of the court made a profound impression on Hatta personally. He had not expected to be acquitted, in view of the mass arrests in the Indies on much lesser offenses. That a court of law had resisted any attempt to be swayed by one of the country's most powerful ministries and that a European pressure group had failed against a handful of insignificant Indonesian students was astonishing. Certainly, from the Dutch point of view, the verdict was also a victory for the socialists against the ruling conservatives.

If Hatta were to be accused in the future of favoring the Dutch parliamentary system which protected an independent judiciary, it is likely such attitudes stemmed from his fair and just trial in the Netherlands.

CHAPTER FOUR
DIVERSITY WITHOUT UNITY

I say this to all Indonesian young people who are already really aware that they are called upon to go back to their own society and who know how they can release their spirits from the influence of colonialism, who are prepared to leave aside the way of life of Netherlands Indies... and are prepared to adjust their lives to fit in with the lives of their own people... I say to them, throw may from your backs any civil burdens or burdens originating in class differences and differences of origin and in this way you will come right back into Indonesian society.... If the Indonesian youth with western education know how to find the way home to their own people, they will find a release from the crisis of sadness and violence which is shaking them psychologically at the present time.[1]

While the court's acquittal of the four students boosted the morale of Indonesian nationalists, it also further hardened attitudes in the Dutch government. Their defense counsel, Duys, alerted the students to a statement made by the minister of colonies which warned that, should they participate in illegal activities on their return to the Indies, their fate could be arrest or exile to the Boven Digul penal settlement in New Guinea.

The minister's threat no doubt influenced Hatta's decision to remain in Europe, dragging out his studies while he acted as a propagandist for the Indonesian cause. He was aware that the Dutch regarded him as one

---

1 Mohammad Hatta, "Youth in Crisis," in *Portrait of a Patriot*, p. 420. First published in *Daulat Ra'jat*, No. 7, October 30, 1933.

of the most dangerous and radical of the nationalists. Having just served a term of detention, he valued his freedom more than ever, and the strong possibility of being dispatched to an isolated patch of rainforest to rot away physically was not an enchanting prospect.

Yet the longer he remained abroad, the more difficult it became for Hatta to influence decision making in the new party. He did not know Sukarno personally, so did not have the same rapport with him as with his ex-PI colleagues. Nevertheless, the day-to-day organization of the party was largely in the hands of the PI group; Sukarno had no taste for such details. Through regular correspondence with Sudjadi and with PNI executive members such as Sartono and Ali Sastroamidjojo (now back in the Indies), Hatta could monitor the PNI's progress, although admittedly second-hand accounts had limitations and contained biases, and correspondence between the Indies and Europe moved slowly.

Undoubtedly the PNI had made progress during Hatta's period of detention. With Sukarno's natural flair for attracting mass audiences, PNI meetings were both colorful and exciting. In his speeches, Sukarno reiterated many of the themes and points of view which had emanated from the Perhimpunan Indonesia and the Study Clubs, often concepts originally formulated by Hatta. Through the skillful use of Javanese idiom and traditional folklore, especially through use of *wayang* stories and characters, Sukarno could translate the aims and strategies of the nationalist movement into a form understandable to the largely illiterate Javanese masses.

Hatta would never elicit the same ecstatic response from a Javanese crowd as did Sukarno. But occasionally an issue would become so overriding that it broke through his reserve, revealing momentarily the hidden fires of his nationalism. At these times Hatta could relate better to a mass audience, becoming more emotional, human, and warm. Under normal circumstances, however, Hatta was too inhibited by fears of exhibitionism and cultism to allow his emotions free play, preferring to present his speeches in a quiet, down-to-earth manner, as if to emphasize the subject matter rather than draw attention to himself. In an academic gathering, the lack of color in his oratory did not detract so much from his impact, as he could capture his audience's attention by the depth of his subject matter. Frequently his critical comments were sufficiently stinging to make an educated audience sit up and take notice.

Hatta's tendency to assume the mien of a headmaster addressing a school assembly when launching into his admonishments and diatribes evoked an audience response more of abashment than ecstasy. Having made his point, he would soften his severity by relaxing into a sudden grin, which his colleagues referred to as the "*senyum Nabi*" [Prophet's smile].[2]

Hatta was not lacking in sentiment or emotion. But as an introvert, he preferred to keep his love for his country and his revolutionary fervor hidden from public view. It was with his pen that he allowed himself most expression, portraying through the written word the depth of his feelings. It was with his pen that he now hoped to maintain his influence in the nationalist movement.

Two months after Hatta's acquittal, in May 1928, the PNI held its first congress at Surabaya in East Java. Its name was once more changed, this time to the Partai Nasional Indonesia, retaining the same initials. It was clear from the plan of action put forward at the PNI congress that Hatta's original program had not been discarded, merely reworded. The PNI program was just as moderate, with no suggestion that the colonial government would be violently overthrown. In the social welfare section, more detailed goals were listed, such as the improvement of the status of women, transmigration programs, attacks on the evils of liquor and opium, and the promotion of monogamy. PI influence was evident in the aim to "build lasting relations between Asian nations."[3]

Again the concept of "universal suffrage," the right of the ordinary person to a strong voice in government so central to Minangkabau *adat*, was missing. Without this concept, there would be no firm basis for a breakdown of the "aristocratic" principle, so strongly entrenched in Java. Hatta also expressed concern that in the education section the emphasis was on literacy rather than political education. As he had pointed out in his defense speech:

Indonesia cannot and will not wait until the last farmer from the last

---

2 See Burhanuddin, "Bung Hatta Sebagai Kawan dan Guru," in *Bung Hatta: Pribadinya dalam Kenangan*, p. 306, and Hamka, "Memimpin Perdjuangan Revolusi dari Bukit Tinggi," in *Bung Hatta Mengabdi pada Tjita-Tjita Perdjoangan Bangsa*, p. 172. According to Hamka, Hatta seldom laughed uproariously, he usually expressed amusement in a quiet way.

3 For details of the PNI program, see Ingleson, *Road to Exile*, pp. 55-56.

village can wield a pen to regain his freedom. The mass education of Perhimpoenan Indonesia must aim at the character-formation of the masses. For the capacity of a people is not determined in the first place by the number of literates, but by the character of its people.[4]

Yet undeniably there was a fresh surge of nationalist spirit in the Indies in 1928. Local youth were at last aware of the need for unity and solidarity. Largely on the initiative of the Perhimpunan Pelajar-Pelajar Indonesia [Indonesian Students' Association -- PPPI] and with the support of the PNI, a Second Indonesian Youth Congress was held in October 1928 at which the youth took a solemn oath of loyalty to the concept of "one nation, one people and one language," the Malay *lingua franca*, now known as the Indonesian language. At this congress, a young Indonesian composer, Supratman, first played what was to become the Indonesian national anthem, *Indonesia Raya* [Greater Indonesia], which from then on was played at all PNI public meetings.

The PNI did not attract all ex-PI members into its fold. Some preferred to remain in the parties they had joined or formed on their return. Dr. Sutomo's Study Club in Surabaya declined to integrate into the new party because many of the club's members were civil servants who feared colonial government reprisal. Other organizations, like Budi Utomo, did not fully support the principle of "non-cooperation," seeing the Volksraad as a valuable forum in spite of its lack of legislative power.

The Partai Sarikat Islam had not welcomed the formation of the Partai Nasional Indonesia, resenting the fact that, like the outlawed PKI, the new party would compete with it for influence in the trade union movement. The PNI was also attracting away from the Islamic party a number of its fringe members. Haji Agus Salim had already indicated in an article written in the Bandung Study Club's paper, *Indonesia Muda* [Young Indonesia], in early 1927 that he was not entirely happy about the attitudes of the returned PI members. He admonished:

They *must* learn and see and acknowledge that the People of the

---

4   Hatta, "Indonesia Free," p. 264.

people's movement arrived at a state of consciousness before they, "the intellectuals," did. They *must* shake off the suggestion of their education -- namely that they are the natural leaders of their people.... They *must* accept their place in the leadership of the people's movement as *equals* alongside their intellectually less educated colleagues.[5]

Haji Agus Salim seemed to question what Hatta had stressed in his defense speech, that it was the task of Perhimpunan Indonesia members to lead the nationalist movement. On the contrary, Haji Salim was implying that ex-PI members were not practicing the egalitarian principles they had espoused in Europe, but instead appeared to be continuing the elite's role of standing above the masses. Certainly Hatta had never intended returning PI members to remain aloof; he had urged them to "struggle with the masses." In Hatta's opinion the ex-PI members' qualifications for leadership related to their expertise and wider experience rather than to their "elitism." In the Minangkabau, one became an educator on return from the *rantau*, passing on the new knowledge one had acquired outside the home environment. Hatta viewed ex-PI members as educators as well as leaders, the emphasis being on "political education" rather than literacy. Yet Sukarno's rise to the top leadership position in the PNI in some ways negated Haji Agus Salim's criticisms. Sukarno had not been educated abroad and was not from the higher ranks of the Javanese nobility.

Hatta continued to act as a watchdog on the PNI's progress, reprimanding the party leaders when he believed this was necessary. In the PNI journal, *Persatoean Indonesia* [Indonesian Unity], between January and April 1929, he wrote a series of articles entitled "Buah Pikiran Politik [Political Thought]."[6] Acknowledging the fact that his views were those of a far-distant observer rather than an on-the-spot participant in the activities of the PNI, he commented that he believed that the new party was still in a "demonstration stage" and must move on to a higher form of organization. Hatta criticized the way the PNI had restricted its membership to a select few. Yet this comment displayed a certain degree

5   See Ingleson, *Road to Exile*, pp. 48-49.
6   Ibid., pp. 82-83.

of ambivalence on his part as he himself had advocated a slow build-up of politically aware cadres. Hatta was really attacking the elitism of the PNI, its failure to open up membership opportunities to the lower classes and to train second echelon leaders who had risen from among the non-elite.

The PNI's dependence on Sukarno's popular appeal worried Hatta. He urged the party to train alternative leaders to take Sukarno's place should he fall victim to colonial government retribution. Hatta asserted: "It is not enough if there is only one Sukarno, but rather there must be thousands and later millions of Sukarnos." In this way, he stressed, "there will be new power and a new large party."

Hatta suggested that the party structure be decentralized, with district councils formed to supervise and guide party branches, while at the same time maintaining close links with the central executive. He advocated the holding of annual congresses attended by branch representatives, a party "parliament." Between the annual PNI congresses, the central executive would be supervised by a party council, a type of politburo of 50 to 75 members elected from district councils and party members. Hatta also reemphasized that cadres should be trained to carry out political education among the masses. His system had strong elements of Minangkabau local autonomy and Leninist organization.

Hatta was proposing a plan of action which Charles van der Plas of the Office of the Adviser for Native Affairs had, in a secret report in October 1928 to the Governor-General, described as being potentially dangerous if it should ever occur. Like Hatta and Haji Agus Salim, van der Plas observed that the party was based on "the aristocratic-intellectual spirit of the westernised leaders, who stand a long way from the people," and warned: "There would be imminent danger if the party was able to form cadres."[7]

Within the PPPKI (the national front which Sukarno had formed while Hatta was in prison) there was obvious tension between the non-cooperating Partai Sarikat Islam and the cooperating parties. Sutomo's Study Club had expressed criticism of Islamic nationalism, as a result antagonizing Haji Agus Salim. Although Hatta identified with the

7   Ibid., p. 79.

"secular" nationalists, he was personally a nationalist inspired by his religious beliefs, and thus understood the Partai Sarikat Islam's concern that Islam was being relegated to the sidelines of the nationalist movement. Yet the Partai Sarikat Islam too had its deficiencies. Hatta's ex-PI friend, Sukiman, who had opted to join the Islamic party, was later to be expelled for exposing malpractices within it.[8]

As Sukarno's popularity soared, he became more daring in his political statements, evoking a warning that unless he moderated his speeches, the colonial government would be forced to take punitive action against him. In February 1929, Hatta wrote him suggesting that he "withdraw from the frontline of leadership" if only to thwart the colonial government, or else spend a short period in Europe, his expenses being paid by the PI's national fund.[9] Sukarno did not act on Hatta's invitation, but whether by choice is unclear. The PI's break with the Comintern in 1929 undoubtedly reduced its resources. By 1929, Darsono, too, had deserted the Comintern, so he was no longer in position to offer the financial assistance he had in the past.

In Holland Hatta was free to-provoke the colonial government because he was protected by a system which allowed freedom of speech, but he could see that it was time in the Indies to employ more subtle tactics than open defiance. The problem was that Sukarno was not a secretive person: he gained personal satisfaction from shouting out his protests before mass audiences. Sukarno's theatrical nature demanded the spotlight, not the wings.

PI membership had begun to decline in 1928 due to Dutch policies to upgrade the tertiary institutions in the Indies and to discourage Indonesians from studying in Europe. Hatta retained his position as chairman of the PI in 1929, although many of those Indonesian students with whom he had built up the student association into an activist group -- Ali Sastroamidjojo, Iwa Kusuma Sumantri, Sukiman, Arnold Mononutu, and so on -- had returned home.

While attending the second congress of the League against Colonialism

---

8 See Noer, *Modernist Muslim Movement*, pp. 139-40. Sukiman was expelled at the Partai Sarikat Islam Indonesia's congress of March 1933 for "violating PSII ethics," in exposing mismanagement of the pawnshop employees' union.

9 See Ingleson, *Road to Exile*, pp. 85-86.

at Frankfurt in July 1929, Hatta sensed the mounting tension between the social democrats and the Communists. It was evident that the latter wanted to oust the social democratic League chairman, James Maxton of the English Independent Labour Party.[10] Hatta allied himself with a group attempting to preserve the initial cooperative spirit of the League, a group which, according to Hatta, was not just composed of social democrats but also had the sympathetic support of the German Communist leader, Willi Munzenberg.[11]

In writing up an account of this congress in *Indonesia Merdeka*, Hatta made it clear that the League had not lived up to its initial expectations, "the ideal of close cooperation to achieve the freedom of suppressed nations." On the contrary, this second congress in Frankfurt merely demonstrated that "never before in the League has the difference between communists and non-communists come to the foreground so sharply."[12] He declared defiantly: "History of the last decade has clearly indicated that the suppressed nations are prepared to use Moscow when necessary, but in return are not prepared to be used by Moscow."[13] Hatta was demanding that Comintern aid be altruistic, that the Soviet Union should abide by its initial promise to assist all people under colonial oppression without demanding total surrender to Moscow. Hatta's article and his withdrawal of the PI from the Holland branch of the League were to have immense repercussions on his future political life, making him from now on a target for Comintern attack.

Nor was Hatta necessarily lenient with the social democrats. He lashed out, too, at the Second International, criticizing the colonial resolutions formulated at its congress in August 1928, in which Indonesia was categorized as a colony unready for Independence, which had to be "content with the extent of self-government which the population itself demands." Hatta contended that the resolution was "contrary to the

---

10 See Hatta, *Memoir*, pp. 231-32. Emile Burns, "The World Congress of the League against Imperialism," in *Labour Monthly* [London], vol. 11, September 1929, pp. 559-63. The main criticism of Maxton was that he supported the MacDonald Labour Government which was seen as "the most dangerous enemy of the colonial peoples."
11 Hatta, *Memoir*, p. 231.
12 Mohammad Hatta, "A Retrospective Account of the Second Congress of the League against Imperialism and for National Independence Held in Frankfurt," in *Portrait of a Patriot*, p. 200. First published in *Indonesia Merdeka*, 1929.
13 Hatta, "Retrospective Account," p. 203.

socialist principle of self-determination and equality for all nations." He continued: "It is of great importance to establish here that it is precisely for *exploitation* of colonies such as India, Indonesia and others which annually yield hundreds of millions in gold to the respective mother countries that it will not propose Independence."[14] Hatta was making it abundantly clear that national interest was taking precedence over ideology in the Second International's policy making.

Not surprisingly, the Dutch socialists took offense at Hatta's article, written only six months after they had secured the release of the four PI students. Hatta was accused of "substituting his own wish for reality," as those seeking the immediate Independence of Indonesia "cannot be equated with 'Indonesia' at all."[15] In terms of the nationalist groups, the Dutch socialists did have a point; the groups' registered membership was a drop in the ocean compared with the total Indonesian population. But Hatta was convinced he represented the sentiments of his people. He was aware that throughout Java and Sumatra in particular there was a growing wave of anti-Dutch resentment which could not be accurately recorded. He slammed back at his critics:

> Apparently they are so uninformed about the Indonesian national movement, that they do not even know that this claim for independence... has been postulated for years by the big nationalist organisations like the P.K.I. and the Sarikat Rajat of the time, the present Partai Sarikat Islam and the now leading Partai Nasional Indonesia; even the "right wing" Boedi Oetomo's strongest desire is that the oppressors pack their bags today rather than tomorrow.[16]

As 1929 drew to a close, Hatta stressed that he would no longer stand as chairman of the PI, suggesting an Ambonese law student as his successor.[17] A recently arrived Minangkabau student, Sutan Sjahrir,

---

14 Mohammad Hatta, "The Second International and the Oppressed Peoples," in *Portrait of a Patriot*, pp. 358-60. First published in *De Socialist*, specimen copy, September 15, 1928.

15 Mohammad Hatta, "Indonesia's Demand for Immediate Independence," in *Portrait of a Patriot*, p. 373. First published in *De Socialist*, No. 1, October 6, 1928. According to Hatta, this accusation against him was contained in *Het Volk*, September 14, 1928.

16 Hatta, "Indonesia's Demand for Immediate Independence," p. 374.

17 Hatta, *Memoir*, p. 228. The student's name was Abdullah Sjukur.

had also captured Hatta's attention as having PI leadership potential. Sjahrir had been very active in the PNI's youth wing, Pemuda Indonesia, in Bandung, at the same time establishing and teaching in a "people's college." He had already met Sukarno, had even crossed swords with him, reportedly embarrassing Sukarno by requesting him to keep to the point and to refrain from lapsing into the Dutch language when addressing a nationalist meeting.[18] Sjahrir would be one of the few Indonesians immune to Sukarno's charm. His directness would tend to undermine Sukarno's confidence in later years, creating animosity.

In Sjahrir, Hatta detected a political outlook similar to his own, a total dedication to freeing Indonesia from its feudal trappings and restoring democracy. He was impressed by Sjahrir's brilliant mind and his ability to grasp and analyze political realities. Sjahrir was even more independent than Hatta and as outspoken, with as little patience for the elitism evident in the new nationalist party.

Yet Sjahrir was no mere reflection of Hatta; there was a distinct difference of personality. Sjahrir was as mercurial and flamboyant as Hatta was reserved and staid. Sjahrir had thrown off the puritanism of his Islamic Minangkabau background. His vocation, unlike Hatta's, was not religiously inspired but fired by idealism based on Marx and other social theorists who envisaged that the exploited peoples of the world would attain a just society. Sjahrir had grown up in Medan, conscious of the iniquities perpetrated on Javanese imported labor in the nearby Dutch plantations.

Sjahrir had left the Indies just as Governor-General de Graeff was yielding to pressures to take action against Sukarno. On December 19, 1929, a search of houses and offices of PNI branch leaders was ordered; Sukarno and three other PNI leaders, Gatot Mangkupradja, Maskun, and Supriadinata were arrested.

Hatta took up his pen in Sukarno's defense in an article published in *De Socialist*. He criticized the slender evidence on which the arrests had been based, querying: "Do they really expect to strangle the P.N.I. in this manner? In its short period of existence it has already managed to create

---

18 Burhanuddin, "Sjahrir yang Saya Kenal," in *Mengenang Sjahrir*, ed. H. Rosihan Anwar (Jakarta: Gramedia, 1980), p. 49.

such a strong social, economic and political base that it cannot be torn out of the Indonesian soil, which it fertilises with its wonderful ideals."[19] How mistaken he was!

The new PNI leadership of Sartono and Anwari did not live up to Hatta's expectations that new leaders would "arise to continue the work of their predecessors."[20] He was bitterly disappointed when they directed branches to obey the Dutch directive to refrain from political activity, concentrating instead on the economic and social aims of the party. To Hatta, this was the type of subservience to colonial government dictates against which he was trying to fight. In an article entitled "PNI Mendapat Pertjobaan" [The PNI Faces a Test], he urged the nationalists to maintain their spirit. "There is only one remedy which will satisfy the hearts of the leaders who have been sacrificed for the movement, and that is for them to see their friends continue the movement."[21] Hatta's rally cry had little impact. 1930 proved to be a year of inactivity in the nationalist movement, with a resultant loss of momentum. Hatta had assessed the situation correctly. The PNI did depend heavily on Sukarno's vibrant personality; his removal from the political arena highlighted the timidity and self-interest of the majority of PNI leaders.

The vacuum left by the PNI's withdrawal to the sidelines encouraged other groups to vie for leadership of the nationalist movement. One of the main contenders was Sutomo's Study Club in Surabaya, which in November 1930 transformed itself into a recognizable political party, the Persatuan Bangsa Indonesia [Union of the Indonesian People]. The emergence of moderate, cooperating parties to lead the nationalist movement was gratifying to the Governor-General and his staff. Colijn too encouraged the colonial government to show understanding towards those nationalists who sought a harmonious cooperation with, rather than the total destruction of, Dutch rule, as advocated by "the Communists, radical nationalists and Mohammadans."[22]

By late 1930, Hatta had become completely frustrated by the inability

---

19 Mohammad Hatta, "The Raid on the Partai Nasional Indonesia," in *Portrait of a Patriot*, p. 405.

20 Ibid.

21 Mohammad Hatta, "PNI Mendapat Pertjobaan," in *Kumpulan Karangan*, vol. 1 (Jakarta: Bulan Bintang, 1953 and 1976), p. 312. First published in *Persatuan Indonesia*, April 10, 1930.

22 See Schmutzer, *Dutch Colonial Policy*, p. 127.

of either the PNI or the PPPKI to provide strong leadership for the independence struggle. In October of that year, he published an article in *Indonesia Merdeka* entitled "The Crisis of the PPPKI," where he reiterated that the PPPKI had been formed as a "body of defense and reconstruction" after the 1926-27 revolts. He continued: "Of course we never fostered any illusion about the possibility of the melting together of all political parties into one great organisation." In other words, the PPPKI was not to be a one-party organization but the nucleus of a parliament. He again stressed: "The Indonesian concept of freedom has nothing to do with unity of political thought."[23] The PPPKI was "deluded" by the concept of "unity" in everything, attempting to "suppress all criticism, instead of recognizing the constructive power of it." In the Minangkabau, harmony was achieved by facing up to rather than avoiding conflict. "We are supporters of Indonesian unity," stated Hatta, "even of a contained unity, but not of a unity at all costs, at the expense of the basic principles."[24] He censured the PPPKI for its failure to protest when the PNI was under attack and for its failure to take decisive action by majority vote when consensus could not be achieved. He also admonished Budi Utomo and Sutomo's PBI for not withdrawing their members from the Volksraad, following Patel's example in India when Gandhi was arrested. He spoke out strongly against Sutomo's strategies to entice the PNI to amalgamate with his party, thus robbing the PNI of its full commitment to the principle of non-cooperation.

Hatta's acid comments at least stirred the nationalist movement out of its lethargy, ex-law student Singg1h observing that it was all too easy for people like Hatta, secure in the Netherlands, to criticize the nationalists operating in the hazardous colonial situation.[25] sukiman of the Partai Sarikat Islam supported Hatta's criticisms of the PPPKI.[26] Like Hatta, he was worried by the insidious influence of the cooperators, convinced that independence could only be achieved by drawing away from the Dutch, with a parallel growth of Indonesian institutions.

---

23 Mohammad Hatta, "The Crisis of the P.P.P.K.I.," in *Portrait of a Patriot*, p. 334. First published in *Indonesia Merdeka*, 1930.
24 Ibid., pp. 336-37.
25 See Ingleson, *Road to Exile*, p. 135.
26 Ibid., p. 136.

The year 1930 ended with the trial and sentencing of Sukarno and the three other detainees. Following Hatta's example, Sukarno spoke in his own defense, a marathon speech which lasted for two days. The format resembled Hatta's, with a condemnation of colonialism and a portrayal of its dire effects on the Indonesian people. In spite of the weakness of the evidence presented by the prosecution, a verdict of guilty was handed down on December 22, 1930, with a sentence of four years' imprisonment for Sukarno. Not only was the nationalist movement shocked, but Dutch legal experts joined in the protest, claiming that the sentence constituted an affront to the principles and tradition of Dutch law.[27]

Hatta too expressed his disgust at the verdict, urging the Indonesian nationalists to stage a major protest to "show the world that you refuse to accept any tyranny."[28] The new PNI leader, law graduate Sartono, responded cautiously to Hatta's challenge. In February 1931 he organized a conference of PNI leaders in Yogyakarta, at which it was proposed that, if the appeals were upheld, then the PNI would resume its activities. If the judgment of the court were ratified, then the PNI would be dissolved and an alternative party formed. The appeals were rejected and Sartono's suggestion was put into practice. On April 25 the Partai Indonesia or Partindo replaced the PNI.

Hatta was outraged at this cavalier treatment of the party which had been in essence so much his creation. Partindo, to Hatta, became the symbol of capitulation to the Dutch. He was angered that Sartono, Ali Sastroamidjojo, and other PI colleagues had yielded to a court decision which even Dutch legal experts admitted was unjust. In an article in *Bintang Timur* of August 3, he gibed at his colleagues from the Leiden law faculty, "Although I am no lawyer, I am of the opinion that the fortunes of a political party do *not* rest in the hands of a low-level judge."[29]

Hatta not only attacked the lack of democracy shown by the PNI branch leaders in their decision to disband the PNI but also extended his criticism to Sukarno, who used the people as an audience for his oratorical

---

27 Ibid., p. 138.

28 Mohammad Hatta, "The Verdict of the District Court of Bandung," in *Portrait of a Patriot* p. 428. First published in *Persatoean Indonesia*, No. 75 (January 30, 1931).

29 See Ingleson, *Road to Exile*, pp. 146-47. The article was also published in *Daulat Ra'jat* of September 30, 1931.

prowess without offering them any voice in the party's organization. He accused:

> The word "democracy" is always on our leaders' lips. But it does not appear in practice. The people are regarded as a mat on which to wipe one's feet; they are considered necessary in order that there will be applause when a leader makes a fine speech. But they are not taught to take on responsibility or duties themselves.[30]

Hatta announced cryptically that he would engage in "social pedagogy" on his return to the Indies, a term which he defined as "the education of the people in politics, economics and social matters, so that they can become fully aware of their rights and their own worth."[31] He was informing the nationalist movement that he was not prepared to allow his vision of an egalitarian society to become eroded by the Javanese aristocracy, His stance was supported by several factions within the PNI and by Sudjadi, all disapproving of Sartono's disbandment of the party without consulting the mass membership. These Golongan Merdeka [Independent Groups], as they called themselves, also rejected proposals that the PNI amalgamate with Sutomo's PBI, a party not fully committed to the principle of non-cooperation. Hatta's statement, backed strongly by Sjahrir, now vice-chairman and secretary of the PI, gave hope to the Golongan Merdeka that Hatta might join them in forming a party to replace the PNI that was less elitist and more dedicated to Hatta's original insistence on involving the masses in party organization.

In Sjahrir's opinion, the PPPKI, which had a heavy weighting of cooperating parties within it, was exerting too much influence on the direction of the nationalist movement and had guided the PNI astray "onto a path which has led to its grave, for it made the PNI into an institute providing a political vehicle for vain and ambitious intellectuals."[32] It was a strong condemnation of Hatta's former PI colleagues, a group which Sjahrir would always regard as opportunist.

Sjahrir, more than Hatta, separated the Indonesian elite and the

---

30 Ingleson, *Road to Exile*, p. 147.
31 Ibid.
32 See ibid., pp. 148-49.

indigenous entrepreneur from the "exploited classes," seeing the nationalist struggle in more purely Marxian terms than Hatta, with less emphasis on race. In Sjahrir's view, "the people's movement is the movement for the emancipation of the Indonesian people, that is, of the millions of landless who do not aspire to be capitalists, of the farmers, labourers, Kromos and Marhaens."[33]

Marhaen was a Sundanese name, first used by Sarikat Islam, although Sukarno was to claim credit for coining the term.[34] As Sukarno explained in his speeches, the Marxist term "proletariat" did not fit the Indonesian situation because the masses were predominantly rural.[35] Hatta did not use the term *marhaen* as frequently as did Sukarno and Sjahrir and, when he did, he usually denoted all Indonesians, regardless of status or profession.

Hatta advised the Golongan Merdeka, now consolidating under the name Club Pendidikan Nasional Indonesia [Indonesian National Education Club], to publish a journal which would project the concept of "people's" rather than "elite's" sovereignty. The title suggested was *Daulat Ra'jat* meaning literally "People's Sovereignty." In its first issue of September 20, 1931, Hatta explained that the paper's object was to defend the basis of democracy in everything, in politics, economics, and in social intercourse.[36] *Daulat Ra'jat* also contained a clear statement that the Golongan Merdeka intended to form a rival party to Partindo. The task of counteracting the strength of the "aristocratic principle" had begun. Hatta's swing away from his PNI group had brought attacks from many sides, so he defended his stance by way of an "Open Letter" published in this opening issue of *Daulat Ra'jat*. He declared:

My attitudes grow out of a deep belief.... It is true that I am far from my native land and cannot know all that takes place but in the midst of all that happens there are realities which are clearly visible which all people can understand, no matter how far removed

33 Ibid., pp. 149-50.
34 See Cindy Adams, *Sukarno: An Autobiography as Told to Cindy Adams* (New York: Bobbs-Merrill, 1965), pp. 61-62.
35 See Sukarno, "Marhaen and Proletariat," in *under the Banner of the Revolution*, vol. 1 (Jakarta: Publication Committee, 1966), p. 241.
36 *Daulat Ra'jat*, September 20, 1931.

from Indonesia. Two realities I comprehend in depth, which have become very important to me. First, the disbandment of the PNI and the way the PNI was disbanded.[37]

Hatta's rejection of Partindo and the intended establishment of a rival party stirred up considerable local debate. Dr. Rival, a well-known Minangkabau journalist and the editor of *Bintang Timoer*, expressed doubts that Hatta would succeed as a leader on Java, commenting: "In my opinion Javanese nationalism has not reached the stage to give life to Indonesian nationalism." His advice to Hatta was to "live in Sumatra to be elected a Volksraad leader by the people" if he wanted to carry out political work.[38] Hatta reacted angrily, stating that "since 1928 [Dr. Rival] wanted me to retire from political circles because I am a Sumatran while the centre of the political system is in Java." He denied that he would ever "earn wages from the government" as a cooperator.[39] Hatta knew that he had to work with his Javanese fellow students to convince them that democracy such as they had experienced in Europe must be the standard for free Indonesia. Yet there was a ring of truth in Rival's words, as Hatta was to discover over the years.

Hatta's decision to support the formation of a new party enabled the Communist Party of Holland to perceive the chink in his armor which it needed to deliver a wounding thrust. The Dutch Communists had already begun to undermine Hatta's prestige, making use of students who were members of the Communist party as well as of the PI. Hatta's successor had been ousted from office mid-year to be replaced by Rustam Effendi, a Minangkabau Communist. The Comintern paper, *Inprecor*, of August 8, 1931, had already announced that Jawaharlal Nehru, Edo Fimmen, Maxton, and Hatta had all been expelled from the League aqainst Colonialism, the accusation being that they were social reformers.[40] Sjahrir was aware of the Communist cell building up in the student association. He advised Hatta to resign, as he himself was going to do.

---

37 Mohammad Hatta, "Open Letter," *Daulat Ra'jat*, September 20, 1931.
38 Parada Harahap, *Riwajat Dr. A. Rivai* (Medan: Handel Mij. Indische Drukkerij, 1939), p. 146.
39 Mohammad Hatta, "Defense against Dr. Rival's Lies," *Daulat Ra'jat*, December 20, 1931.
40 See Hatta, *Memoir*, p. 243, and as cited in S. Sjahrir, "'Schorsing' -- Mohammad Hatta" [Mohammad Hatta's "Suspension"], *Daulat Ra'jat*, December 10, 1931.

On November 9, 1931, the PI executive moved that both Hatta and Sjahrir should be expelled from Perhimpunan Indonesia on the charge that they were splitting the nationalist movement by supporting the breakaway Golongan Merdeka. The decision portrayed the Comintern's determination to reverse the Hatta-Semaun Convention by bringing the PI firmly under Communist control. The student group was to remain strongly allied with Moscow for the rest of the prewar period.

Sol Tas, a Dutch socialist close to both Sjahrir and Hatta, recalled that Sjahrir accepted the PI decision with nonchalance. "What difference does it make?" he queried. "Last week Hatta and I resigned from the PI; we didn't want to have anything more to do with a Communist organization. You can't kick out someone one who's already left."[41] Tas noticed that Hatta was much more dejected, that the Communist assault and the CPH's domination of the PI had cut much deeper. For Hatta, establishing a reputation had not just been a matter of personal pride, it was his key to ensuring a leadership position in the independence struggle. The new party in process of formation would require Hatta's prestige to mount a challenge to Partindo and the charismatic Sukarno. As Rivai had pointed out, Hatta, as a Sumatran, had a cultural and ethnic disadvantage on Java. If he returned to the Indies as an outcast from the Perhimpunan Indonesia, his task would be even more Herculean. He would have lost the political force which often surrounds the unpolluted martyr.

Apart from the effects on his political future, Hatta hated to leave the PI in such an ignominious manner, thrown out by his fellow students for trying to defend the masses from the feudalistic attitudes of his former associates. The Communists should have been applauding him instead of ruining his reputation. It was anathema to Hatta to see the Perhimpunan Indonesia, which meant so much to him, become subservient to the Comintern and to know that potential leaders might return to the Indies as Communist cadres. Hatta was to find it very difficult to forgive his fellow Minangkabau, Rustam Effendi, for engineering his expulsion. What also rankled was that Abdul Madjid, the student who had worked so closely with him and shared his prison experience, had also joined the

---

41 Sol Tas, "Souvenirs of Sjahrir," trans. Ruth T. McVey, *Indonesia* 8 (October 1969): 135-54 at p. 142.

Communists, voting against him.

Sjahrir tried to repair any damage done to Hatta's reputation by writing in his defense in *Daulat Ra'jat*. He reminded fellow nationalists of Hatta's past record of service to the nationalist movement:

> In Indonesia the name Hatta has become very well known because he has been the most prominent leader in *Perhimpunan Indonesia* and also because of his defence speech, "*Indonesia Vrij*," which explains the meaning of our national movement. He has become famed as the mastermind of the "radical" direction in the national movement and his name is coupled with that of Sukarno.[42]

Sjahrir pointed out that the contents of *Indonesia Merdeka* had served as a torchbearer for the PNI. He defended Hatta's action in withdrawing the PI from the League against Colonialism, describing the policies of the current PI committee as stupid and their action towards Hatta as reactionary.

The editorial board of *Daulat Ra'jat* led by Sudjadi also supported Hatta's stance, on November 20, 1931 publishing an article entitled "P.I. and Hatta," which claimed that "Mohammad Hatta had become a 'victim' in carrying out the duty of following and defending the policies of the general public."[43]

Another wound for Hatta was that his former PI colleagues, now leaders in Partai Indonesia, applauded the action taken by the PI executive, informing him by telegram that they supported his expulsion.[44] Hatta replied by letter to Sartono on November 10 that he regretted that Partindo "did not take a more principled attitude" towards him. "Perhimpunan Indonesia is now used by the Partai Indonesia as a banner to oppose me," he commented grimly. "I send greetings to you with a sincere heart that you have achieved friendly relations between the P.I. and the P.I., and I pray that those links are eternally pleasing." Hatta concluded:

> But I have one hope for my fortunate opponent! I trust that Mr.

42 Sjahrir, "'Schorsing' -- Mohammad Hatta."
43 "PI and Hatta," Editorial, *Daulat Ra'jat*, November 23, 1931.
44 Letter from Hatta to Sartono, November 10, 1931, as cited in *Daulat Ra'jat*, November 30, 1931.

Sartono, the liquidator of the PNI, does not subsequently become the liquidator of the Union of PI-PI also, that the hand which is extended by Perhimpunan Indonesia, which he shakes so enthusiastically, does not feel too hot for him. Because if he does so, people will laugh at him and his brightness as a leader will dim.[45]

In other words, take care in any dealings with an organization under Comintern control because those that oppose its policies receive rough treatment. Hatta spoke from bitter experience.

Hatta was now isolated from the majority of student associates with whom he had worked so closely in the past. He had become the "opposition leader" in the radical nationalist movement, identifying as far as was possible with the mass of the people rather than with the elite. A mountainous task lay ahead -- the democratization of a society which had forgotten that democratic government was not an alien element, a mere Western import, but did have native roots in the archipelago.

---

45 Ibid.

CHAPTER FIVE
THE NEW PNI

Through education the common people will become aware that it is not just the leader who carries responsibility but everyone else as well. It is not just the leader who must struggle, the people also must participate. There is a factor which is often forgotten, the independence of Indonesia cannot be achieved by the leaders only but by the efforts and convictions of the masses. The fate of the Indonesian people is clutched in the hands of the people themselves.[1]

The nationalist press in the Indies devoted considerable space to commentary on Hatta's expulsion from the Perhimpunan Indonesia. In view of the sharp criticisms issuing from Hatta's pen in the past, it was not surprising that those who had suffered were out for vengeance.

Writing in response, Hatta denied that he had violated "discipline" and the "collectivist principles" of PI by supporting the formation of a new nationalist party. He argued:

I myself like discipline but what the PI calls discipline means "censorship." Whoever wants to express an opinion must have the permission of the Executive Committee first. But the committee itself has power to speak out widely without the inspection of members. This is called "collectivism."[2]

Hatta gibed: "This sort of discipline is good for the new leadership which

1 Hatta, *Memoir*, p. 261. Hatta is quoting from his essay on "Education" which appeared in *Daulat Ra'jat*, September 20, 1932.
2 Mohammad Hatta, "Perhimpoenan Indonesia dan Saja," *Daulat Ra'jat*, January 30, 1932.

does not yet really understand the basis of the PI," adding with the *sang-froid* of a veteran: "A person who for years has 'worked himself to the bone and shattered his brain1 to strengthen the PI's principles for his country's sake is not easily censored by 'newcomers.'"[3]

Hatta dismissed the "collectivism" of the present PI committee, seeing it as representative of subservience to Moscow: "In the name of collectivism, the Committee can carry out policies as they wish, especially as most of the leaders only know how to '*membebek*' [act like ducklings following the mother duck] outside the Committee." The "mother duck" was the Communist Party of Holland. Hatta also drew attention to the autocracy of the PI executive, commenting: "More than 75% of the leaders have a feudalistic and bourgeois spirit which resembles *Budi utomo*."[4]

Hatta realized that his days in the Netherlands were numbered. As an outcast from the Perhimpunan Indonesia, he no longer had any mandate to act as its propagandist. He was also aware that the Golongan Merdeka were depending on his support to organize the new party. Yet he was reluctant to leave for the Indies immediately, as he did not want to return after an eleven-year absence without at least achieving a doctorandus degree. To sit his finals, he must wait until the end of the academic year in June 1932.

Hatta sought Sjahrir's help, knowing that the young man had not progressed far in his law course, and that a temporary hiatus would not cause a major academic setback. Sjahrir was a leader. He was personable, and already had a following in Bandung from his days as chairman of Pemuda Indonesia. In Europe he had gained trade union experience by working part-time with Edo Fimmen in the International Transport Workers' Union Secretariat. He and Hatta had established a rapport through their commitment to social as well as political change for Indonesia.

There was an added urgency in establishing the party. In September 1931 De Graeff, on the eve of his retirement from office, had announced the remittance of part of the PNI prisoners' sentences, explaining that, although Sukarno and his associates had committed a crime, their motives

3 Ibid.
4 Ibid.

were good.[5] Sukarno was due for release at the end of the year. Under any circumstances the creation of a new party made up of independent splinter groups from the old PNI would be difficult. If the party's inauguration took place in the atmosphere of euphoria which would probably attend Sukarno's emergence from prison, it would be even more difficult to prevent members from returning to Sukarno's side.

Sjahrir accepted Hatta's commission, although he realized that going back to the Indies was akin to entering "a danger zone."[6] The birth of another nationalist party which was radically socialist would certainly displease the new Governor-General, B. C. De Jonge. The thirties were to be a tough, uneasy period, with the economic recession leading to cuts in the colonial budget.

Prior to his expulsion from the PI, Hatta had written an article criticizing De Jonge's first speech to the Volksraad. He directed his remarks to both the colonial authorities and Indonesian cooperators, reminding them that Karl Marx's theories, which once had been dismissed as Utopian, nowadays "have become a force which is manifest, real, which cannot be belittled any more because yesterday's workers have become today's prime ministers of the capitalist world." Hatta continued:

> These realities provide evidence for Jhr. de Jonge when he opposes Indonesian nationalism!... The Indonesian nationalists, especially the non-cooperators, are not stupid enough to think that their aims will be fulfilled by a self-interested government. They struggle on, developing their aims, with the inward *conviction* that gradually they will conquer and their theories will bring to fruition a Free Indonesia.[7]

Hatta would later defend himself from accusations of being "Marxist," differentiating between Marx and Marxism, and stressing that he did not admire the adulterated versions of Marx put forward by the Communist

5   See R. C. Kwantes, *De Ontwikkeling van de Nationalistische Beweging en Nederlandsch-Indie* (Groningen: Wolters-Noordhof, 1981), pp. 580-81.
6   Tas, "Souvenirs of Sjahrir," p. 145.
7   Mohammad Hatta, "Sedikit Pemandangan tentang Pidato G.G. Baroe di Moeka Volksraad," *Daulat Ra'jat*, September 30, 1931.

Party of Holland.[8]

At a conference held from December 25 to 27, 1931 in Yogyakarta, the Pendidikan Nasional Indonesia (Indonesian National Education) was established. The omission of the word "*Partai*" might have been a ploy; an educational group could evade colonial harassment, just as Sarikat Islam had survived through being an Islamic traders' group in its initial formation. In later years, Hatta seemed to suggest that the Pendidikan Nasional Indonesia was as much a political philosophy as an organized group.[9] His preferred title was Partai Daulat Rakyat, again stressing the sovereignty of the people, but the Golongan Merdeka were anxious to retain the initials "PNI." To distinguish the group from the disbanded PNI, the Pendidikan Nasional Indonesia became known as the New PNI. No one, including the colonial government, saw it as anything but a political group.

On January 1, 1932, at an Indonesia Raya Congress organized by the PPPKI to celebrate his release from prison, Sukarno expressed his disappointment that the old PNI had been replaced by two separate parties during his enforced absence. He assured his audience that this was a "mere misunderstanding," and that the two would soon be reunited.[10] Sukarno did not analyze the basic differences between the old and new PNI, nor explain that the New PNI had isolated itself from Partindo on the principle that confrontation between brown and white was not the only issue involved in the independence struggle but that it was also necessary for the masses to be guaranteed a role in future government.

As if to stress the nativism of the New PNI's stance, Hatta contended that the "democracy" which he envisaged for Indonesia was not the Western concept of *Volkssouvereiniteit*. He insisted: "We want to organize our household in Free Indonesia on the basis of the indigenous democracy found in Indonesian communities," although he admitted that traditional forms of government would require some modernization:

We realize that times have changed, that the forms of the past are

8 See Mohammad Hatta, "Marxisme of Epigonenwijsheid," in his *Verspreide Geschriften* (Jakarta: van der Peet, 1952), p. 121. First published in *Nationale Commentaren*, Nos. 10-14, 1940.
9 See Mohammad Hatta, *Pendidikan Nasional Indonesia* (Bogor: Melati, 1968), p. 8.
10 Ingleson, *Road to Exile*, p. 161.

not sufficient for a Free Indonesia based on democracy. Those original principles must be adapted to the present, raised to a sufficiently high level.[11]

Hatta rejected the use of the term *demokrasi asli* [indigenous democracy] in case it was used by "backward-looking aristocrats to maintain their feudalistic system (of a slavish nature) in Indonesia, using Indonesia's past as an example." Hatta was warning against Java's "aristocratic principle" intruding too deeply into nationalist ideals. He explained: "In short, *Daulat Tuanku* [sovereignty of the master] must be replaced by *Daulat Ra'jat*, that is the basis of people's government, the basis of genuine democracy, the intention of all '*demokrasi asli*,' whether it be in Athens, Rome or in the traditional Indonesian village, in the clan systems, etc."[12]

Sjahrir, on his return to Java, tried to avoid direct confrontation with Sukarno. He acknowledged in a letter to Sol Tas's wife, Maria, herself an ardent revolutionary and feminist, that it would be advantageous for the nationalist movement if Hatta and Sukarno were to work together. In view of Sukarno's following on Java, such association could be essential for Hatta's political survival.[13] Sjahrir avoided committing the New PNI to an alliance with Partindo, the elitist group whose influence he wanted to undermine. He was also aware that Sukarno was toying with the idea of setting up yet another party into which to absorb both Partindo and the New PNI. Sjahrir gloomily admitted:

I expect Sukarno will follow the old line.... Still we are not able to let him go without some effort. He has fascinated the people for two years and will do so again, and he remains for the time being a dominant political factor. He belongs to the revolutionary camp in spite of his opportunism.[14]

11 Mohammad Hatta, "Demokrasi Asli Indonesia dan Kedaulatan Ra'jat," *Daulat Ra'jat*, January 16, 1932.
12 Ibid.
13 Letter from Sjahrir to Maria Duchateau Tas, January 4, 1932, a copy of which was sent by the attorney-general to Governor-General, August 19, 1933. Cited in Ingleson, *Road to Exile*, p. 171.
14 Ibid.

Sukarno may have underestimated the strength of the Golongan Merdeka's rejection of the Partindo leaders and its dedication to Hatta's democratic principle. The New PNI did hold its factions together, few deserting the new party to join Sukarno. Sjahrir's relative and close associate, Djohan Sjahruzah, another personable and hard-working young nationalist, had also made contacts with the Tan Malaka and ex-PKI groups in Surabaya, now harassed and drifting since a colonial clamp-down in 1930.[15] The emphasis on social revolution in the New PNI made the party seem a more attractive alternative than Partindo.

Sukarno, too, was not yet committed to Partindo. It was from the PPPKI that he had received the most support since his release from jail, and he set about restoring its credibility as a nationalist front. At the same time, however, he ignored the guidelines suggested by Sjahrir of confining the front to "non-cooperators," bringing an immediate critical response from Hatta. Although now cramming hard for his finals in quiet lodgings in Rotterdam, Hatta was unable to resist the urge to correct Sukarno's methods of resuscitating the PPPKI. He caustically entitled his article "Persatoean Ditjari, Per-saté-an jang Ada" [Unity is sought but the reality is a hotch-potch], a play on the word *satu* meaning "one" and *saté*, a dish made up of small pieces of meat skewered together. Hatta made the accusation that the nationalist movement was "drunk with unity," when "what is considered to be unity is in actual fact *saté*." He contended:

> Buffalo meat, beef and goat's meat can be skewered together but the view of the people and the concepts of the aristocracy cannot be united. Uniting all these groups just means each one of them sacrificing its principles. Because of that, the *Daulat Ra'jat* group cannot become one with the culture nationalists without each sacrificing its principles.[16]

By using the term "culture nationalists," Hatta seemed to be condemning his fellow nationalists who refused to discard the Javanese "cooperating"

---

15 Djohan Sjahruzah was a contact man for Tan Malaka's Pari. See B. R. O'G. Anderson, *Java in a Time of Revolution: Occupation and Resistance, 1944-1946* (Ithaca: Cornell University Press, 1972), p. 418.

16 Mohammad Hatta, "Persatoean Ditjari, Per-saté-an jang Ada," *Daulat Ra'jat*, April 20, 1932.

and "exploitive of the people" attitudes which had allowed the Dutch to reap such benefits from the masses. For Hatta, also a culture nationalist, Indonesian nationalism must be based on the ideals of the *Alam Minangkabau* because it was one of the regions in the archipelago which had evolved its own socialist system. By pointing to the class system in Java, Hatta was also viewing the nationalist struggle in purer Marxian terms, seeing it not just in terms of racial conflict. He asserted that the people must no longer be regarded as "work horses," and gave his opinion that the PPPKI in its present form was only useful in "raising the standard of the cooperators," the people being used merely as "ladders for the bourgeoisie to rise to the top."[17]

Hatta's repudiation of the PPPKI as a body which was not dedicated to non-cooperation obviously had an influence on Sukarno, for he too lashed out at its performance to date, reiterating Hatta's earlier comments that the PPPKI was in a state of crisis.[18] Sutomo, indignant at thrusts from both Hatta and Sukarno, resigned his chairmanship in protest, his position being filled by Husni Thamrin, a close friend of Sukarno and the leader of a small nationalist group, Kaum Batawi [The Batavians]. But Thamrin was also a member of the Volksraad and thus a cooperator, although a strong defender of the nationalist movement in that forum.

On July 20, 1932, Hatta departed by train from Rotterdam, traveling via Paris to Genoa, where he boarded the German ship, *Saarbrucken*, bound for Singapore. He had successfully passed his doctoral examination, but without the desired "*cuw laude*."[19] His anticipated five years in Europe had stretched out to eleven. The youth of nineteen who had sailed from Teluk Bayur was on the brink of thirty years of age.

Before leaving the Netherlands, Hatta had yielded reluctantly to pressures from a Minangkabau friend, Rashid Manggis, to be interviewed on behalf of *Daulat Ra'jat*. In the interview Hatta carefully avoided questions relating to his future relations with Sukarno, being equally reticent about his own political plans. (It was only on disembarkation

---

17 Ibid.
18 See Ingleson, *Road to Exile*, p. 164.
19 See Hatta, *Memoir*, pp. 249-52. Hatta believed that he was discriminated against by one of his examiners, a Professor de Vries, who asked him irrelevant questions about military service and library research and seemed determined to humiliate and discredit him.

at Singapore than he officially announced that he was joining the New PNI.)[20] He denied rumors that he had been asked to become editor of *Adil*, the journal of the Modernist Islamic Association, Muhammadiyah, remarking: "As a non-cooperating politician, it would be impossible for me to head a non-political newspaper issued by a group which is dependent on the government," a veiled criticism of this prestigious group for adopting a cooperating stance, in contrast with the Partai Sarikat Islam.[21] Whether this remark led to Muhammadiyah's reported exclusion of Hatta is uncertain.[22] Hatta was to have an uneven relationship with Modernist Islamic groups, sometimes close, sometimes at odds, for most of his life.

When interviewed about *swadeshi*, the Indian nationalist policy now adopted by Partindo, Hatta not only rejected it on economic grounds as unsuitable for Indonesia but gave his opinion that *swadeshi* encouraged provincialism rather than breaking down ethnic barriers. He contended:

> *Swadeshi* instructs people to wear their own costumes.... Minangkabau will wear Minangkabau clothes, Palembang people the Palembang style, Central Javanese the styles of Central Java. This will unintentionally revive a spirit of "provincialism" while it is our purpose to encourage Indonesian unity and crush provincialism.[23]

Before he left the Netherlands Hatta had also to bid farewell to his Dutch acquaintances. The main Dutch socialist party, the SDAP, had just split, a splinter left-wing group forming, the Onafhankelijke Sosialistische Partij [Independent Socialist Party] or OSP. It was with the Independent Socialists that Hatta how felt most at ease, because they espoused radical socialism without allegiance to the Soviet Union and also supported the concept of full Indonesian independence. In the party were people whom he admired, such as the trade union leader, Edo Fimmen, and the poetess, Henriette Roland Hoist. The OSP chairman was a young Dutch

---

20 See Bermawy Latief, "Bung Hatta Menganjurkan Menyediakan Diri untuk Berkorban demi Kemerdekaan," in *Bung Hatta: Pribadinya dalam Kenangan*, p. 296.
21 Mohammad Rasjid, "Interview -- Mohammad Hatta," in *Daulat Ra'jat*, August 20, 1932.
22 Hatta was reported to have been expelled from Muhammadiyah Hindia Timur in the paper *Tjahaja Sumatra*, as cited in *Daulat Ra'jat*, December 20, 1932.
23 Rasjid, "Interview -- Mohammad Hatta."

writer, Jacques de Kadt, while on the Committee were Sol Tas and Jef Last, both close friends of Hatta and Sjahrir. Hatta had been asked by Jef Last if he would consider nomination as an OSP candidate for the Tweede Kamer.[24] He replied that, in principle, he would be prepared to sit in a democratically elected parliament as a spokesman for the Indonesian cause, but declined to make any firm decision until he had consulted his associates in case his candidature might be viewed as a breach of the "non-cooperating" principle.[25] Yet it was a tempting proposition. Hatta knew that he would not have the same degree of freedom in the Indies which he had enjoyed in Europe. As a member of the Dutch Parliament, he could continue to hammer away at his colonial opponents without suffering retribution. It would also be a way of resolving the confrontation with Sukarno which he knew he must face up to in the Indies.

Hatta had a four-week sea voyage during which to try to sort out his future nationalist campaign. On disembarkation at Singapore, he took advantage of a two-day stopover to renew acquaintanceships with old friends from the Minangkabau. Since the Communist uprisings, Singapore had become a haven for Indonesian dissidents escaping from the colonial police crack-downs. Hatta tried to arrange an interview with Djamaluddin Tamin, Tan Malaka's representative in Singapore and the secretary of his party, Pari, but Tamin, realizing that Hatta would be under close surveillance by the British authorities, dared not risk a rendezvous.[26] Hatta did not record his attempts to contact Tamin, merely commenting that while in Singapore he "felt again the colonial atmosphere," that "everywhere I went, I was forever followed by secret police."[27]

Hatta received a warm welcome from his family and friends when he arrived at Tanjung Priok, the port of Batavia. Most of the New PNI contingent which greeted him were viewing for the first time the man

---

24 Hatta, *Memoir*, p. 253.

25 Ibid., p. 253, and pp. 276-77.

26 See Poeze, *Tan Malaka*, p. 413. During the *Saarbrucken's* port call at Belawan in East Sumatra, Hatta had slipped into Medan before finally disembarking at Singapore. See *Sinar Deli*, August 22, 1932.

27 Hatta, *Memoir*, p. 253. Hatta's belongings were inspected by the authorities on his arrival and a full set of *Indonesia Merdeka* confiscated. This Hatta had anticipated and had already arranged for an oil man on a Rotterdamse-Lloyd ship to smuggle his personal set into the colony. Dr. Mohamad Roem, then a young law student, recalled helping Hatta to unpack his books. which included a work on "Celibacy." Interview Mohamad Roem, February 2, 1982.

whose policies they had opted to follow. His former PI colleagues were conspicuously absent, although Sartono dud send a note of welcome.[28] A former Minangkabau friend, Hazairin, remarked that, apart from being plumper, Hatta appeared to be just the same.[29] Yet Sjahrir seemed to suggest that Hatta had acquired a Western veneer, commenting in 1934: "Hafil belongs undoubtedly to our most Europeanized intellectuals."[30] Dr. Rivai too suggested that Hatta had moved away from his own culture while in Europe, commenting: "Mohammad Hatta left the Netherlands Indies when he was still very young. Therefore he cannot know now to socialize with an *inlander*."[31]

Sjahrir, who had been elected chairman of the New PNI at its first congress held from June 23 to 26 in Bandung, decided to delay his return to Europe. He had been joined by Maria Tas, who had left her husband, but her stay was short-lived due to colonial refusal to grant her residency.[32] Yet, according to Burhanuddin, a member of the party's executive, although Sjahrir was officially chairman of the New PNI "in the eyes of the members it was Bung Hatta who was the 'Guiding Spirit' of the new party."[33]

Before Hatta reached the Indies, Sukarno had made his decision: he would join Partindo. Discussions with Sjahrir had not been satisfactory; indeed Sjahrir would never be a person with whom Sukarno felt comfortable, sensing the hint of mockery which lurked behind the young man's laughter. Sukarno had consented to address the New PNI's first congress. He adapted his speech to the perceived ideology of the new party, declaring: "I am a Nationalist Marxist," an echo of Tan Malaka's stance. Sukarno assured the New PNI that he "would work to defend the

---

28 See Sunario, "Bung Hatta dan Kepribadinya," in *Bung Hatta: Pribadnya dalam Kenangan*, p. 252, and S. M. Rasjid, "Bung Hatta, Orang Besar Tanah Air," in *Bung Hatta Mengabdi pada Tjita-Tjita*, p. 358.

29 Hazairin, "Kenang-Kenangan tentang Pak Hatta," in ibid., p. 191.

30 Sutan Sjahrir, *Out of Exile* (New York: Day, 1949), p. 4. Sjahrir used the pseudonym "Hafil" for Hatta in this work.

31 As cited in Sutan Sjahrir, "Kaoem Intellectueel dalam Doenia Politik Indonesia," *Daulat Ra'jat*, November 10, 1931. According to Sjahrir, Dr. Rivai's comments were published in *Vaderland* [The Hague], August 30, 1931.

32 Maria Tas and Sjahrir were married in a Muslim ceremony in East Sumatra. The marriage was later annulled by a local Islamic Council. See *Sinar Deli*, February 27, 1934.

33 Burhanuddin, "Bung Hatta Sebagai Kawan dan Guru," in *Bung Hatta: Pribadinya dalam Kenangan*, p. 305.

Marhaen,[34] although again avoiding the issue of "people's sovereignty."

In his memoirs Hatta touched very lightly on his first meeting with Sukarno, which took place two weeks after his arrival in Java. He recalled that a friend, Haji Usman, offered to drive him to Bandung, advising that "although you belong to different parties, it is best if you get to know him."[35] Hatta must have been aware that initial contacts might be strained. A river of dissent flowed between them before they had even seen each other in the flesh.

"About nine o'clock in the evening, Sukarno met us in our hotel," recalled Hatta, a meeting which it appeared was not entirely fruitful. "It seemed that, because of Haji Usman's presence, Sukarno did not want to discuss the problems of Partai Indonesia and the New PNI and, since he did not bring up the subject, neither did I touch upon it."[36]

Sukarno did not in his autobiography record this first meeting with Hatta in Bandung, but instead described his impressions of Hatta following discussions between Partindo and the New PNI several weeks later. As his autobiography was dictated in a period when relations between the two men were at a particularly low ebb, Sukarno's remarks were, not surprisingly, lacking in warmth. He averred that Hatta was a "man totally opposite to me in nature," "an economist by trade and disposition," "careful, unemotional, pedantic." He continued: "a graduate of the Rotterdam Faculty of Economics, he was still walking around mentally with those books under his arm, trying to apply inflexible scientific formulas to a revolution."[37]

Yet Hatta was always to react quickly against contentions that the Partindo and New PNI confrontation was just a personal dispute between him and Sukarno, and always stressed that political obstacles first and foremost divided the New PNI and Partindo. "While Partai Indonesia rejects the basis of People's Sovereignty, which is the flesh and blood of the PNI members, there exists no similarity."[38]

34 As cited in *Daulat Ra'jat*, July 10, 1933.
35 Hatta, *Memoir*, p. 258. Hatta may have been referring to Mohammad Haji Usman, the elderly former Sultan of Ternate, who had been exiled to Java after a rebellion against the Dutch on the island of Halmahera in 1914.
36 Ibid., p. 259.
37 Adams, *Sukarno*, p. 117.
38 Mohammad Hatta, "Pendirian Kita," *Daulat Ra'jat*, September 10, 1932.

Hatta lost no time in organizing cadre training, acknowledging that it required "devotion, conviction, patience, and a strong will." He stressed that he considered cadre education to be more effective than mass rallies, because: "Our people have for too long been 'educated' with general aims, with chants of 'unity,' which leave them confused about what basis is to be adopted." Hatta claimed that, through education, "the masses will be convinced that it is not just the leaders who must know their responsibilities but also the people."[39]

As a basis for instruction, Hatta concentrated on international affairs and Indonesian history, teaching the factors underlying imperialism, and pointing out the exploitive nature of the colonial system. Young rural laborers drawn to the cities to earn a living were viewed as excellent cadre material for the New PNI because of their continuing links with their home villages. Student teachers, too, were valuable as potential leaders, as they had influence in the village community and among the youth. It was now practically impossible for nationalist leaders to gain direct access to the rural population because of obstruction by colonial officials and local rulers who served as civil servants, known as the *pangreh praja.*

So involved was he in party affairs that it was not until October 1932 that Hatta had an opportunity to return to the *Alam Minangkabau*, to a joyful reunion with his family, although to a mixed reception from his compatriots. Hatta carried with him a stigma of Marxism, in spite of his acknowledged devotion to Islam. The heavy police surveillance which overshadowed all his movements deterred many people from associating with him. The uprising in the Minangkabau in January 1927 had resulted in a particularly harsh retaliatory campaign by the colonial government.

A radical Islamic party, Persatuan Muslimin Indonesia [Indonesian Muslim Union], known as Permi or the PMI, had been formed in 1930, reaching an agreement with the old PNI and with Partindo not to compete on each other's territory. In Minangkabau fashion, the party preferred to organize itself independently of Java. Likewise the PSII in West Sumatra worked fairly independently of its central headquarters in Java. Hatta's party aimed to break down such ethnic barriers and it was

---

39 Mohammad Hatta, "Pendidikan: Perloe Kita Tahoe Bekerdja dengan Teratoer: Dari Agitatie ke Organisatie!" *Daulat Ra'jat*, September 20, 1932.

also not specifically Islamic.

An editorial in *Daulat Ra'jat* of December 20, 1932 revealed that Hatta's return to the Minangkabau had not been well-received by the two major parties operating in West Sumatra, which suspected that his intention was to attract away their members to the New PNI. The fact that the two leading figures in the New PNI were Minangkabau and one of them the prestigious Hatta, clearly posed a threat. Already four New PNI branches had formed spontaneously in the region. A particularly malicious attack on Hatta suggested that the new party should be named the "Persatuan Royeeran Indonesia" or "Union of Indonesian Expellees," as one of its members was the "only national leader to return to Indonesia having been expelled from the League and Perhimpunan Indonesia in Holland, from PMI, and finally from Muhammadijah Hindia Timur."[40]

As if acting as a mouthpiece for Hatta, a *Daulat Ra'jat* editorial tried to allay Minangkabau fears, stating: "We did not at any time disparage the existing parties in the Minangkabau, such as the PSII and PMI, but we have a right to choose our own movement according to our own opinion." The editorial continued: "Without denigrating or despising the basis of PSII, i.e., Islam, or the bases of the P.M.I., i.e. Islam and nationalism, we are convinced and hold firm to our basis of Nationalism and People's Sovereignty." The editorial denied that the New PNI was trying to hinder the Islamic parties, explaining the new party's religious stance: "We are based on Nationalism, which means we do not bring religion into the political struggle.... We do not ignore our religion, and our organization does not force its members to abandon their religion."[41]

In this atmosphere of party rivalry and police omnipresence, Hatta could not make as much capital out of his return as he would have wished. He laid low in his mother's house, devoting his energies to preparing a political manifesto for the New PNI, which he entitled "Ke Arah Indonesia Merdeka" [Towards Independent Indonesia], known as the KIM, which from then on served as the party's manual for cadre training.[42] Not to be outdone, Sukarno produced a Partindo manifesto

---

40 As cited in Editorial, *Daulat Ra'jat*, December 20, 1932, under title "Sedikit Djawaban tentang Pendidikan Nasional Indonesia di Minangkabau sambil Memperkenalkan Diri."
41 Ibid.
42 For full text of "Ke Arah Indonesia Merdeka," see Hatta, *Kumpulan Karangan*, 1: 61-81.

several months later, which he entitled "Mencapai Indonesia Merdeka" [Achieving Independent Indonesia], abbreviated to MIM.

In his manifesto, Hatta pointed out that there were three alternatives open to Indonesia in its choice of a future government: rule by aristocracy, rule by intellectuals, and rule by the people. He reminded his readers that the Indonesian aristocracy had predominantly supported the Dutch and would seek to retain their prominent position. The intellectuals considered that their expertise gave them the right to rule independent Indonesia. The New PNI aimed towards a People's Nation and People's Sovereignty. He explained that political democracy was linked to economic democracy. In Indonesia, people traditionally worked collectively and therefore had a good basis for achieving social and economic democracy. Independent Indonesia must foster this cooperative spirit. Hatta had begun his campaign to promote cooperative movements to try to build up Indonesian commercial enterprise to the level where it could compete with the international corporation.

While residing in the Bukit Tinggi area, Hatta visited his Batu Hampar family. He had, no doubt, anticipated that the atmosphere would be different without that special warmth engendered by Syekh Arsyad's presence, but it came as a shock to feel unwelcome. He sensed that his cousin, Syekh Arifin, Syekh Arsyad's eldest son, was uneasy, conscious that Hatta's presence at the *surau* was not approved by the local Assistant-Resident.

In Padang, Hatta again received sympathetic support from his friend, Taher Marah Sutan, the secretary of Sarekat Usaha, whose enthusiasm had so inspired the Jong Sumatranen Bond. Taher Marah Sutan allowed Hatta the use of his home as a meeting place. Public addresses were clearly out of the question in the atmosphere of hostility and harassment surrounding Hatta's return. As it was driving out of Padang, Hatta's car was forced off the road by an unidentified vehicle. Whether the accident was contrived or not remained a mystery but it left Hatta bruised and shaken, with a minor head injury and sprained hand.[43] While recuperating from the accident in his mother's house, Hatta was summoned to the office of the Assistant-Resident, who informed him that he must leave Sumatra

---

43 Hatta, *Memoir*, pp. 268-69.

immediately, as he had been declared a prohibited person in the region.[44] It was the same fate as had befallen Great Uncle Rais many years ago. Hatta was beginning to experience at first hand just how difficult it was to be a radical nationalist in the colonial setting.

The prohibition order warned Hatta to proceed with even greater caution. His party, too, was suffering colonial harassment. In January 1933, the Surabaya branch executive was arrested for issuing a circular including the words: "The Indonesian people must have a revolutionary spirit -- from slavery to freedom."[45] Yet the party was progressing. Six months following Hatta's return, its twelve branches had expanded to sixty-six.[46] As New PNI member and later Hatta's private secretary, Wangsa Widjaja, remarked: "Both Hatta and Sjahrir were dynamic leaders, but with the arrival of Bung Hatta cadre training intensified."[47]

It was clear that Sjahrir's fears that Sukarno's choice of Partindo might mean "political death" for Hatta were unfounded. Hatta was too shrewd, effective, hard-working, and dedicated a leader to crumble easily. He was absolutely convinced that the emphasis on "people" in his party must be maintained. He tried to ensure that the party's executive was not too elitist, although he and Sjahrir gave direction and were the dominant leaders. In the branches, the majority of leaders were low-level civil servants or sons of village officials.[48] Nevertheless, organizing a party made up of separate branches was not easy. Hatta began to understand the disparity between ideals and reality, as he himself confronted the difficulties, frustrations, and obstacles which had beset the old PNI leaders.

Sukarno, back at the head of a nationalist party, having accepted the leadership of Partindo, was determined to keep its membership ahead of the New PNI. Partindo held mass rallies in the Bandung region and accepted new members without prior testing. Hatta's warnings on the unsuitability of mass "agitation" merely spurred on Sukarno to prove that his method was as radical and revolutionary as the New PNI's cell system.

---

44 Ibid., p. 271.
45 As cited in *Daulat Ra'jat*, January 20, 1933.
46 Ingleson, *Road to Exile*, p. 178.
47 Interview with I. Wangsa Widjaja, February 18, 1982.
48 Ingleson, *Road to Exile*, p. 181.

Sukarno had an opportunity to retaliate against Hatta's gibes, when on December 8, 1932, the Onafhankelijke Socialistische Partij in the Netherlands wired Hatta an offer of candidature for the Tweede Kamer. *Aneta*, the Indies news agency, erroneously reported that Hatta had accepted the offer. Sukarno and Partindo wasted no time in using the report to attack Hatta, *Persatoean Indonesia* blazing the headline across its front page: "Drs. Mohammad Hatta is Unmasked! The PNI leader wants to sit in the Second Chamber! Beware, Indonesian People!"[49]

Hatta had warned the OSP that the local nationalists might consider his candidature for the Tweede Kamer to be a violation of the non-cooperation principle. Now he experienced the local reaction in a way which was acutely painful and embarrassing, especially when the *Persatoean Indonesia* article continued: "Here it can be seen that the champion of 'non-cooperation' already wishes to join a body representative of the Dutch imperialists, where he will sit alongside the oil and sugar groups among others. It appears that this PNI leader will support his country's needs in an Imperialist Dutch body."[50]

Hatta defended himself hotly, explaining not only that he had rejected the OSP's offer as soon as the telegram arrived, but also his reasons for seriously contemplating accepting. He replied to his critics:

> I have never taught that non-cooperation is anti-parliamentarianism.... Non-cooperation means not wanting to cooperate with the *colonial government*; in a colonized country a non-cooperator rejects a false parliament which has been created by the government to deceive the people. The non-cooperation tactic is to draw a line between *them* and *us* to awaken the people's spirit so that they can establish their own society. Non-cooperation in the sense of boycotting councils which are *not* people's councils only applies in colonized countries.[51]

Hatta presumed that the issue had been defused, but he was wrong. On December 21, Sukarno again raised it, sparking a heated polemic

---

49 As cited in Hatta, *Memoir*, p. 276.
50 Ibid.
51 Ibid., pp. 278-79.

between Partindo and the New PNI. His hackles up, Hatta pointed out that Sukarno was not himself consistent in his approach since he had "no objections about sending a telegram to Dr. Tjipto in Banda Neira to accept a seat in the Volksraad," as well championing the PPPKI, "who follow a national policy of cooperation, whose right wing can be found in the master's councils."[52] Hatta scoffed: "The 'non-cooperation' promoted by the Partindo leadership as that party's principle is like *gado-gado* [a mixed vegetable dish], with the result that people who study it cannot make a firm decision on 'Partindo non-cooperation.'"[53]

Hatta accused Sukarno of creating disunity by his attacks rather than being a symbol of unity, a charge he would reiterate in the future. Hatta pointed out: "Since Ir. Sukarno entered the party, one sees that streams which were united are now in opposition." Nor did he spare Sartono and the law graduates, indicating that by working for the Dutch legal service, they often worked against their own people's interests, citing the case of Sartono defending a Dutch policeman who had wronged and ill-treated two Indonesian women. Hatta conceded that Sartono probably did not "relish taking an order like this." He pointed out that all advocates had to swear an oath of allegiance to the Dutch Crown. Hatta's tone was sarcastic:

In practice... swearing an oath of loyalty to the Governor-General or Crown is nothing! Becoming an instrument of the imperialists and masters is nothing! Requesting justice in the courts of the *kaum sana* [Dutch] in political cases is nothing! Ordering people to sit in the Volksraad is nothing! And coalescing with the *kaum co* [cooperators] also is nothing! Whatever suits their needs -- it's nothing, go ahead! *Marhaen* who do not have any part in the conspiracy are puzzled by principles like these. What is clear is that Ir. Sukarno is snared by his own words.[54]

Hatta's words had an effect on the Partindo executive, whether because they admired their former PI leader or because they wished to stem the

52 Mohammad Hatta, "Non-Cooperation -- PNI," *Daulat Ra'jat*, December 30, 1932.
53 Mohammad Hatta, "Sedikit Debat Tentang Non-Cooperation," *Daulat Ra'jat*, February 10, 1933.
54 Ibid.

flow of home-truths is unclear. Sartono and Ali Sastroamidjojo opposed Sukarno's suggestion that Partindo revert to its old name to prevent the New PNI from changing its "P" to "Partai." Sartono argued: "If Ir. Sukarno wants to destroy the PNI, then we must play our cards in the open and take a definite stand. That is at least manly."[55] It was almost a PI snub to Sukarno.

The colonial government disliked the New PNI's covert build-up of radical cells, for these methods were difficult to control. Fears that the defense capabilities of the colony were being undermined were aroused when blank New PNI membership cards were discovered in the possession of a union official representing the Indonesian Naval Seamen, following a mutiny of Dutch and Indonesian ratings on February 5, 1933. The attorney-general accused the New PNI of establishing a Communist cell in the Surabaya Naval Establishment. Indicating that he considered the New PNI to be the most dangerous of the nationalist parties, he reported on February 10:

> Its methods of propaganda, its objectives, particularly the way in which it aims at the proletariat (Marhaen), the way in which it gathers into its organizations the scattered elements from both dissolved organisations [*Sarekat Rakyat* and the PKI] and not least the response it finds among the non-intellectual and least level-headed part of the population, are symptoms of a similar nature. I am convinced that it aims at unrest.[56]

At the time that the naval strike was headline news, Hatta was accompanying his Uncle Ayub Rais on a business trip to Japan.[57] According to Iwata Tateo, a Japanese businessman who had met Hatta in Batavia in December 1932, Hatta went to Japan at his invitation, a statement which Hatta later denied.[58] Hatta also denied Iwata's claim that

---

55 See Ingleson, *Road to Exile*, p. 190.
56 See ibid., p. 210.
57 Hatta, *Memoir*, p. 293. Ayub Rais had recovered from his financial setbacks and was prospering as a partner in a large retail business in Pasar Senen. Hatta had agreed to act as an adviser to the firm, although turning down the position of secretary-director.
58 See George S. Kanahele, "Japanese Occupation of Indonesia: Prelude to Independence" (Ph.D. dissertation, Cornell University, 1967), p. 116, n. 18. Iwata published in Tokyo in 1932 a brief

he had introduced him "at Hatta's insistence" to the Indian nationalist, Rash Bahari Bose, then in Japan, or that he had agreed verbally to Bose's suggestion that a Japan-Indonesian Association be formed.[59]

Hatta did admit that he was taken aback when, on docking at Kobe, he was dubbed the "Gandhi of Java" by the bevy of newspapermen who greeted him,[60] probably a reference to his strong stance on non-cooperation. He was asked his opinion of Colijn, recently reelected prime minister in the Netherlands, and replied cautiously, merely commenting that Dr. Colijn's party was adopting a harsh attitude to the Indonesian people, for which they must bear the consequences.[61] Hatta recalled: "I realized that I must be very careful while I was in Japan; the colonial government in Jakarta was certainly following my movements very closely." Hatta could sense the Japanese government stretching out feelers to him during his tour, part of a plan to establish a rapport with Asian nationalist leaders. Similar to the anticolonial League in Europe, Japan seemed to be coordinating Asian revolt against the Western colonial powers. In his memoirs, Hatta remarked: "Linked with the questions of the Japanese newspapermen at the ships, the ones I did not answer, there was certainly a plan by the Japanese government to approach me."[62]

Hatta accepted an invitation to dine with the deputy chairman of the Japanese Parliament, at which his host was determined to explain that Japan's take-over of power in Manchuria had resulted from a need to thwart Soviet Union designs on the region. Hatta remembered his surprise and discomfort when invited to visit Manchuria, an offer he quickly declined.[63] When General Araki, a powerful political figure and

---

study of the Indonesian nationalist movement, drawing attention to statements by Hatta and other Indonesians which had echoed Pan-Asian ideals. In his essay "The Middle of the Asian Revolution" in the *Gedenkboek*, Hatta had waxed enthusiastic about Japan's example in challenging the West, writing: "Was it not from there, from the islands of the Japanese, that there first arose the idea of the freedom of Asian nations after centuries during which their lands had been surrendered to the white man?" See *Portrait of a Patriot*, p. 17.

59 See Kanahele, "Japanese Occupation of Indonesia," p. 246, n. 23.
60 Hatta, *Memoir*, p. 294.
61 Ibid.
62 Ibid., p. 296.
63 Ibid., p. 303. Hatta had been critical of Japan's action in Manchuria, pointing out that Japan had "pounced on Manchuria" to meet its own needs, a strategic move since the West was in a severe crisis and unwilling to "punish Japan." See Mohammad Hatta, "Politik Imperialisme Djepang di Tiongkok," *Daulat Ra'jat*, February 10, 1932.

ardent ultra-nationalist, tried to contact him, Hatta realized that he must return to the Indies. Coming on top of the naval strike, overt meetings with the Japanese military leadership would not be well viewed by the colonial government.

On his return, Hatta described his impressions of Japan and its promotion of the slogan "Asia for the Asians." He clearly did not accept Japan's overtures to Indonesian nationalists unquestioningly, his experiences in Europe having conditioned him to look for underlying motives of self-interest from outsiders. He wrote cautiously:

> The Pan-Asianism which is being promoted by several political writers does not yet have clear guidelines established. We only know that the Pan-Asian community can only be established on two basic principles, lasting peace between China and Japan and the same standards for all its members.[64]

Hatta was making it clear that in any Asian cooperative movement, Indonesians must be equal partners, not subservient to Japan.

Hatta returned home to find that the New PNI was again suffering harassment, the chairman of the Makassar branch having been arrested, and another Makassar branch member detained in Surabaya on May 30.[65] Unknown to Hatta, the party was now the subject of several adverse Politieke Inlichtingen Dienst [Political Intelligence Service -- PID] reports, one of which read:

> The forever extremist and generally agitating tenor of these meetings, during which capitalism and imperialism are continually pointed out as the basic cause of all misery from which the Indonesian people at present are suffering, leaves no doubt about the aim of the movement, i.e., to increase the contrasts in the country in order to get the masses moving against the existing authority. Day by day it becomes clearer that it is the intention of the leaders to unite the small people in one revolutionary mass movement (of

---

64 Mohammad Hatta, "Djepang Maoe Kembali ke Asia," ibid., June 10, 1933.
65 See ibid., July 10, 1933.

farmers, workers and small traders) in the fight for the destruction of capitalism and imperialism to achieve *Indonesia Merdeka*.[66]

In July and August 1933, Hatta concentrated his activities in the Central Java area, always a stronghold of radicalism, where the PKI had mustered great support in the past under the leadership of Semaun and Darsono. He noticed the very considerable increase in police interference, which made it difficult to make public addresses, so that he was forced to meet in private homes, where as many people as possible were squeezed in. In Semarang, he went out of his way to make contacts with the railway workers' union, at that time being pressed by the colonial government to cease all affiliations with Partindo and the New PNI. On June 27, a government order placed a ban on all civil servants associating with these two parties or with the local trade union movement, any infringement of the order leading to dismissal. In the prevailing condition of unemployment and recession, this ban placed workers with dependent families in a very difficult situation, and made open membership of the two parties a genuine sacrifice.

It was while Hatta was in Semarang that the shattering news broke that Sukarno had again been arrested. (Coincidentally the nationalist movement in the Minangkabau also lost top leaders of the Permi and PSII, who were arbitrarily despatched to Boven Digul.) Hatta deliberately kept on publishing as if he must say as much as he could before *Daulat Ra'jat* too was suppressed. He tried to calm the panic sweeping through the nationalist movement, urging Indonesians not to give up, reminding them that they were not the only people to suffer from oppressive regimes. He pointed to the example of Mustapha Kemal Pasha who, although branded a rebel by the government, was later hailed as a national hero. Hatta stressed that leaders were only there to show the way and interpret what was already alive in the people's hearts. He wrote:

The people's movement at this time is like a ship which is being swamped by waves and blown by the wind through an ocean full

---

66 Cited in B. B. Hering, *From Soekamiskin to Endeh*, Occasional Paper No. 1 (Townsville: James Cook University of North Queensland, 1979), p. 48.

of rocks. If the captain becomes confused or loses his head, that is an indication that the ship could founder. For that reason, we must not be afraid, we must not be bemused, but be aware and understand. Let that be our guide in the struggle.[67]

The articles Hatta wrote during the following weeks concentrated on the attributes of good leadership. He emphasized that a leader must expect to suffer in the fight against colonial rule. "This is the period of romanticism in the independence movement," he wrote, explaining that individual sacrifice paved the way for mass action.[68] He stressed: "If the movement is only a leader's movement, ordinary members do not share in carrying the load and the movement then cannot achieve its aims." He advocated that every member of the New PNI, aware of his responsibilities and of his duties as a nationalist, must be a potential leader and an example of "wood which is not cracked by heat or rotted by rain," a well-known Minangkabau aphorism.[69]

Unfortunately Sukarno's second term of imprisonment did crack his spirit, causing him considerable psychological anguish. Dutch records show that he addressed several letters to the attorney-general, pleading for leniency and seeking a reprieve, in return for a promise to withdraw from political life.[70] In October 1933 the colonial government announced that Sukarno had resigned from Partindo, had expressed regret for his previous activities in the nationalist movement, and was now willing to cooperate with the government in the future. The Partindo executive confirmed that Sukarno had submitted his resignation from the party and also from the PPPKI.

Sukarno's capitulation to the Dutch presented Hatta with a golden opportunity to gain the upper hand in the "non-cooperation" debate. On November 30, he published an article in *Daulat Ra'jat* entitled "The

---

67 Mohammad Hatta, "Djalan Sempit," *Daulat Ra'jat*, July 20, 1933.
68 Mohammad Hatta, "Pemimpinan, Madjalah dan Anggauta dalam Pergerakan," ibid., September 10, 1933.
69 Ibid.
70 The letters, dated August 30 and September 7, 21, and 28, 1933, are couched in tones of remorse and supplication. For details of their contents see Ingleson, *Road to Exile*, pp. 218-19, and Hering, *From Soekamiskin to Endeh*, pp. 56-57. The letter of August 30, 1933 was unsigned, which has led some Indonesian scholars to query its authenticity. (See "Benarkah Bung Karno?" *Tempo*, February 21, 1981, pp. 8-10.)

Tragedy of Sukarno" in which he pointed out that Sukarno had become "a victim not only of government action and cruelty but a victim of his own personality, as a consequence of a lowering of his morale and evidently an inherent weakness in his character." Hatta could not restrain a crow of vindication, pointing out to his readers:

> Twice Partindo principles have been changed, the second time in accordance with the wishes and through the influence of Sukarno. The abandoned PPPKI was revived with a new basis, the author being none other than Sukarno himself.

Hatta drew attention to the fact that only ten months earlier Sukarno had been attacking him concerning the acceptance of a seat in the Tweede Kamer, and had declared that "non-cooperation rejected cooperation with the masters in all fields," demanding the "struggle which knows no peace." "Now he himself is the first person to tread the path of peace and submission," Hatta added sarcastically.[71]

Hatta commented that there were rumors that Sukarno had yielded to strong pressures from his wife and parents to withdraw from the nationalist movement, a fact which must have given Hatta some assurance that his own decision to remain celibate until independence was achieved was a wise one. Hatta insisted that a freedom fighter must resist uxorial demands: "A person of character will not be influenced by anything. He is no leader if he is persuaded by the tears of a wife who cannot endure a life of poverty."[72] It was a devastating character assassination of his political opponent.

With Sukarno removed from the nationalist movement, having been sentenced to exile on the island of Flores, Hatta set about reestablishing his own leadership. He had rejected an earlier suggestion that the New PNI disband to confuse the government and operate informally, no doubt a concept too reminiscent of the disbandment of the old PNI which he had criticized so bitterly. Hatta set about strengthening his links with his old PI group, holding discussions in November with Sartono to ensure

---

71 Mohammad Hatta, "Tragedie Soekarno," *Daulat Ra'jat*, November 30, 1933. Hatta did not put his name to the editorial but later claimed to be the author. See Hatta, *Memoir*, p. 335.

72 Ibid.

closer cooperation between Partindo and the New PNI.[73]

Unknown to Hatta, his activities were now the subject of colonial government debate, the attorney-general suggesting to De Jonge that the time had come for further "purification" of the nationalist movement. The adviser for native affairs argued that there was no just case against the New PNI leadership, pointing out that the second-echelon leaders were less level-headed. In a report to the Governor-General in January 1934 he suggested that the New PNI be banned and the leadership warned of arrest if they continued their political activities, stating that "leaders of the mentality of Mohammad Hatta are always dangerous. In comparison, a revolutionary figure such as Dr. Tjipto Mangunkusumo is a child."[74]

The Council of the Indies, the Governor-General's special advisory committee, took the advice of the attorney-general. On February 25, 1934, just a few weeks after Sukarno's despatch to Flores, Hatta was once more confronted in his home by a policeman with a warrant for his arrest. De Jonge reported the action in the following statement:

> The arrest of Hatta and a few other PNI leaders will now be known to you. I hesitated before taking this action because the general political climate is peaceful and I am very much concerned about taking a not wholly motivated measure through which I might cut my own throat. But one cannot let these leaders continue their work; an effective purge cannot always stay on the superficial level.[75]

---

73 See Ingleson, *Road to Exile*, p. 225.
74 Ibid., p. 228.
75 Ibid.

CHAPTER SIX
EXILE

The Indies government permits itself to take, "corrective" action against any resistance by the Indonesian people, with the full force of its might and its judicature, even when the resistance is within the law. But there entirely lacks a power which can protect the people against misuse of power by the authority, whilst the right to moral resistance against arbitrary power is refused to them. Dutch public opinion could throw up a dam against an extreme abuse of power in Indonesia. However, in a number of cases it has been apparent that the conscience of the Dutch people, does not prick them for an injustice committed by their representatives in authority beyond the frontiers of Holland and for which they are ultimately responsible.[1]

Hatta's arrest had not been entirely unexpected. In spite of his efforts to work within the Netherlands Indies legal code, in colonial eyes he was a radical who implemented subversive Marxist methods. The adviser for native affairs had warned that the use of cadres to build up the nationalist movement was more dangerous than mass agitation because more difficult to monitor. Hatta, as one of the masterminds of the movement, was a force which must be neutralized.

The entire New PNI executive was arrested together with several ordinary members. After interrogation, Hatta and Bondan, one of the executive members, were consigned to Glodok jail in Batavia, Sjahrir was detained in Cipinang and four other executive members, Burhanuddin,

---

1   Mohammad Hatta, "Three Years of the Digoel Scandal: The W. P. Hillen Report," in *Portrait of a Patriot*, p. 385. First published in *De Socialist*, 2nd year, No. 102, September 12, 1930.

Maskun, Suka Sumitro, and Murwoto were imprisoned in Bandung. No formal charge was made against them, but Hatta sensed that this time a defense speech was unnecessary. As he had already pointed out in one of his articles, the Indies was a "police state" where sentences were carried out under the Governor-General's "exorbitant rights." The question which burned in the detainees' minds was: would they be sent to Boven Digul, the dreaded, swamp-forest penal settlement in West New Guinea?

Hatta's stoic attitude towards his second term of imprisonment was reflected in a letter written to his associate, Murad, who had taken over the editorship of *Daulat Ra'jat*. He wrote:

> Books are my daily companions and certainly this is a peaceful place to study.... As long as I have books, I can exist anywhere.... No one enjoys prison, yet in spite of its evils, it can also be beneficial. It strengthens one's faith and makes one more resolute. So even here there is light amid the darkness, just as the night sky is illuminated by stars.... My philosophy of life is this: "struggle while one is free; if people have clipped one's wings, then devote oneself to the pursuit of knowledge."[2]

Six months passed without any indication of the colonial government's intention. Hatta was several times interrogated by the police controlleur about the aims and activities of the New PNI, but he sensed that this was a mere formality, that the verdict was a foregone conclusion. Hatta began to prepare himself for the worst -- exile to Boven Digul.

When by October 1934 no decision on the future of the New PNI executive had been announced, Haji Agus Salim took up pen on Hatta's behalf, heading his article: "Will Drs. Mohammad Hatta Be Exiled?" Contained within it was a plea for colonial clemency: "Hopefully, due to the strength of public demands, Drs. Mohammad Hatta and his associates, who are threatened with exile, will be preserved for their work of education and training."[3]

The colonial government evidenced no softening attitude. On the

---

2 Letter from Hatta to T. A. Murad, April 20, 1934, as cited in *Daulat Ra'jat*, May 10, 1934.
3 Haji A. Salim, "Boleh Djadikan Drs. Mohammad Hatta akan Dibuang?" *Pemandangan*, October 2, 1934.

contrary, in September 1934, *Daulat Ra'jat* was closed down and Murad, its acting editor, joined Hatta and Bondan in Glodok jail. Hatta whiled away his time in prison completing a book he had been writing before his arrest, entitled "The Economic Crisis and Capitalism."

The decision to intern seven of the New PNI's executive in the Boven Digul settlement was made official on November 16, 1934. The charge against Hatta read that "when residing in Holland up to 1931 he took a leading role in Perhimpunan Indonesia, which aimed at revolutionary action against the government there," accusing the student association of obtaining support from extremist left-wing groups "such as the Onafhankelijke Socialistische Partij, the Communist Party of Holland, and the League against Imperialism and Colonialism in Berlin."[4] The charge also included accusations of which Hatta had been cleared in a Netherlands court, evidence that the colonial government had resented the verdict exonerating Hatta. The remainder of the charge declared that, after the PKI had been banned, Hatta continued to work with groups whose aims were similar, taking the initiative in establishing the revolutionary groups, the Partai Nasional Indonesia and the Pendidikan Nasional Indonesia.

The colonial decision made headline news in the local press and was loudly condemned. The newspaper *Pemandangan* queried: "When Dr. Tjipto and Mr. Iwa Kusuma Sumantri are exiled to Banda and Ir. Sukarno to Flores, why is Drs. Mohammad Hatta, an international figure, exiled to Boven Digul?"[5] A letter from Dr. Tjipto in *Pemandangan* contended that Hatta's sentence vindicated his own conviction that "non-cooperation" was ineffective. He wrote: "Non-cooperation is only a perfect weapon if the party standing behind it has such a strong position that extra-parliamentary action can achieve something." Otherwise, concluded Dr. Tjipto, "non-cooperation can be destructive in its aims."[6] It was a viewpoint Dr. Tjipto was to change in the next decade.

Despite his arrest, Hatta remained a confirmed non-cooperator as did his increasingly emasculated and clandestine party, the New PNI. Murad remembered his surprise on finding a small piece of paper tucked into his

---

4 As cited in *Pemandangan*, November 20, 1934.
5 See ibid., November 17, 1934.
6 See ibid., November 30, 1934.

prison food. The note was in Hatta's writing and read: "Rad, keep going. Being in and out of jail is better than being exiled to Digul."[7] Murad responded to his leader's challenge, remaining active in the New PNI until his own exile in 1938.

Hatta had no illusions about life in Boven Digul. In 1929, he had written an article based on a report by W. P. Hillen, a member of the Council of the Indies, who had returned from a tour of inspection, suffering from malaria and admitting that there were innocent victims among the internees. Hatta had included in his article a letter written by a Boven Digul inmate, which read: "Death grins at us continuously. Digoel is no longer a place. It has become a heap of consumptives and malaria sufferers, neurotics and semi-lunatics, under the scorching heat of the merciless tropical sun, surrounded by unhealthy marshes in the midst of dense, impenetrable forests,"[8]

Foreign newspaper reports had described the penal settlement as a "hellish pond" where "malaria and blackwater fever will in time wipe out the colony."[9] Yet, Hatta had pointed out, the Dutch government had "tried to lead the public up the garden path by declaring that Upper Digul was malaria-free."[10] Dr. Koningsberger, the former minister of colonies, "without so much as a blush," had declared at a banquet of the Union Coloniale Francais in 1928 that "the interior of New Guinea, where the culprits were sent with their families, is favorable for the creation of an agricultural colony."[11]

The exile order was put into effect in January 1935, the seven New PNI detainees reunited aboard the KPM vessel "Melchior Treub," which would take them as far as Makassar. Perhaps because of their classification as "intellectuals," Hatta and Sjahrir were allocated second-class cabins while the rest of the group traveled as deck passengers, including two wives. In spite of the knowledge that each day the voyage was drawing them

---

7   T. A. Murad, *Perhubungan*, p. 274.
8   Mohammad Hatta, "The Digoel Tragedy of Dutch Colonial Imperialism," in *Portrait of a Patriot*, p. 379.
9   Ibid. According to Hatta, this comment was published by Dr. Van Blankenstein, the "star correspondent" of the *Nieuwe Rotterdamsche Courant*, and reiterated in *Het Haagse Maandlbad* and the *Frank-furter Zeitung*.
10 Hatta, "Three Years of the Digoel Scandal," p. 382.
11 Ibid.

closer to the penal settlement, they could not help reveling in the fresh air and bright seascape, which contrasted so favorably with their prison environment. For a brief few days, their spirits lifted as they laughed and joked together on the deck "like people on a picnic."[12]

At Makassar in South Celebes (Sulawesi), they were again imprisoned while awaiting a ship bound for Ambon. Bondan, who shared a cell with Hatta and Sjahrir, recalled that they tried to counteract the boredom by playing chess, checkers, and word games.[13] For Hatta, the voyage from Makassar to West New Guinea took him for the first time into the eastern boundaries of the Indies, where Asia began to merge into the Pacific Ocean basin. It was an area much less densely populated than Java, although with a long Dutch association.

The last leg of the journey aboard a small police boat brought the seven men to the West New Guinea coast and into the mouth of the Digul River. On January 28, 1935, having navigated the turbid waterway with its overhanging branches, they disembarked at a large raft-like structure serving as a jetty.

Tanah Merah, the pseudo village of which they were now inhabitants, was administered like an ordinary Javanese *desa*, except that its headmen were detainees rather than local residents. A high proportion of the inmates were Minangkabau, Sjahrir remarking that "if that area [Minangkabau] were to be opened to the return of exiles, Tanah Merah would be almost emptied."[14] The "first settlers" were the victims of the round up of PKI members which took place after the 1926-27 revolts.

Internees were further categorized into those who were willing to work, *werkwillig*, the cooperators, and those who would not accept employment, the "naturalists," who were allowed a meager ration of food or "natural nourishment" and must use their own initiative or private means to supplement their rations. Hatta had no hesitation in becoming a "naturalist" in spite of the warning from the Dutch officer in charge of the settlement that cooperators had a better chance of a reprieve. His retort, according to his memoirs, was: "If I wanted to join the *werkwillig* group,

---

12 Burhanuddin, "Bung Hatta Sebagai Kawan dan Guru," in *Bung Hatta: Pribadinya dalam Kenangan*, p. 311, and Sjahrir, *Out of Exile*, p. 43.

13 M. Bondan, "Dari Rotterdam Sampai Brisbane," in *Bung Hatta Mengabdi pada Tjita-Tjita*, p. 92.

14 Sjahrir, *Out of Exile*, p. 192.

I would have been *werkwillig* In Jakarta where several Government jobs were offered to me," adding: "There I could certainly have become a *tuan besar* [great master], there would have been no need to go to Digul to become a coolie on wages of 40 cents per day.[15] In spite of being assured an office job, Hatta refused to change his mind.

Of the six other New PNI internees, only one decided to cooperate. Hatta was more fortunate than his fellows in that he was assigned a small building in which to live, formerly used both as a shop and an office, although its proximity to the police quarters in the village was also of significance. As Hatta commented in exasperation: "I was already living in the middle of dense jungle, yet the watch over my activities continued."[16]

Initially four of the New PNI group moved in with Hatta, Burhanuddin remaining with him for seven months. Hatta was accustomed to being awake at 5 a.m. to observe his morning devotions. Although not always a success as a cook, with the help and advice of experienced settlers, he learned to make good use of the rations and fresh fruits available. The internees also tried to keep fit by joining in games of football. "Hatta usually played back," recalled Bondan, an indication that advancing age had moved him from the forward to the back row.[17]

Living at the level of a peasant in an environment free of modern amenities did at least allow Hatta an opportunity to experience at first hand the hardships faced by the masses he was dedicated to serve. He had frequently written about the toil and suffering of the Indonesian *marhaen*, and, although he was not exactly living off the fruits of hard manual labor, he was experiencing a standard of living well below anything he had known in the past. His exile allowed Hatta an opportunity to impugn Dr. Rival's charge that he was too Western to associate with fellow-*inlander*. Sjahrir too clearly saw that the harsh sentence did have a positive component, that "perhaps just when I have to renounce what I love best in the world, now I feel myself more firmly and indissolubly bound to my people than ever before."[18]

---

15 Hatta, *Memoir*, p. 358.
16 Ibid., p. 353.
17 See M. Bondan, "Mengenal Bung Hatta Dari Dekat," in *Bung Hatta: Pribadinya dalam Kenangan*, p. 282. Bondan recalled that the first time it was Hatta's turn to cook the rice, he burned it.
18 Sjahrir, *Out of Exile*, p. 33.

Hatta had prepared himself for a more rustic lifestyle, requesting his Uncle Ayub Rais to send him a book on chicken farming. He wrote: "I am uncertain whether it will be worthwhile raising chickens at Boven Digul and whether the situation and climate there would permit it. All the same, I'd like to try." He also requested a "variety of vegetables," explaining: "If I obtain a house at Boven Digul with a suitable yard, then I would like to try planting vegetables for my own use. I have been told that rice does not mature at Boven Digul but vegetables are more successful."[19]

Hatta was not cut out to be a full-time farmer. He preferred to use the cool of the early morning for study and writing. He had been offered a contract to write for *Pemandangan*, which he was determined to fulfill as he needed the income to supplement his rations with clothing, oil, and other basic necessities. These items were available in the one local shop run by a Chinese "free settler."

In spite of their circumstances, political divisions and party loyalties persisted within the penal village. The PKI internees were obviously aware that Hatta was now a *persona non grata* in the eyes of the Comintern; nor was he overly popular with many Permi and PSII members. It irritated Hatta that there should be infighting among the internees when, as fellow nationalists, they should be united against the common enemy. He wrote an article drawing attention to the fact that at Boven Digul his two pets, a kitten and a pup, could play together and even share the same dish when eating, although cats and dogs were natural enemies. Yet human beings with similar ideals, such as the inmates of Boven Digul, were antagonistic to one another.[20] When Hatta censured his adversaries, he often evoked a heated response. This time he was confronted by a deputation of PKI members, requesting that he retract his remarks. Hatta refused, defending the truth of what he had written.

Burhanuddin noticed that the debilitating climate and unwholesome environment were taking their toll, making even the New PNI group less tolerant of one another. The usually cool, patient, and well-organized Hatta became irritable and forgetful, showing signs of stress.[21] Despite

---

19 Letter, Hatta to Ayub Rais dated February 11, 1935 cited in *Pemandangan*, February 19, 1935.
20 As cited in Burhanuddin, "Bung Hatta Sebagai Kawan dan Guru," p. 315. According to Burhanuddin, the article appeared in *Pemandangan*.
21 See Ibid., p. 314.

taking health precautions, such as sleeping under nets, every one of the New PNI group succumbed to the endemic malaria, Bondan suffering most seriously and requiring hospitalization. While visiting Bondan in the settlement hospital, Hatta had his first opportunity to make contact with the "incorrigibles," the persistently non-cooperative exiles who were kept in an upstream penal barracks, Tanah Tinggi. Moved by their mental and physical condition, Hatta offered them some of his books to help keep their minds active.[22] As Sjahrir remarked on the penal situation in general: "I am convinced that the real moral undermining comes from the psychic reaction of the individual to this situation of imprisoned exile and the transmutation of this reaction into a profound spiritual misery."[23]

Hatta had inaugurated a teaching program in the settlement to prevent mental stagnation, but it became increasingly difficult to continue it. Recurrent malarial attacks were robbing both him and his students of their vitality. Yet escape from Tanah Merah was not only very difficult and hazardous but also pointless. As a recaptured Menadonese exile, Najoan, made clear to them, there was simply no sympathetic nation in the neighborhood to provide them with a refuge, as most of Southeast Asia was under Western colonization.[24]

In March 1935, Hatta wrote his brother-in-law, Rafi'ah's husband, that he intended to build himself a more comfortable house "which would last about ten years."[25] House building was a communal effort in the village, the colonial authorities providing sheets of galvanized iron while the exiles were expected to cut their own timber from the surrounding forest. Unknown to Hatta, his letter was published both in Indonesian and Dutch newspapers, and it sparked an angry reaction in both the Indies and the Netherlands. When attacked by socialists in the Tweede Kamer, Prime Minister Colijn stressed that Mohammad Hatta's exile in Boven Digul was not intended to destroy him, merely to isolate him from the community.[26]

Possibly to stem the flood of protests, the Dutch government in

---

22 Bondan, "Mengenal Bung Hatta dari Dekat," p. 283.
23 Sjahrir, *Out of Exile*, pp. 62- 63.
24 Burhanuddin, "Sjahrir yang Saya Kenal," in Anwar, *Mengenang Sjahrir*, p. 63. Najoan had managed to get to Tuesday Island but was returned to the Dutch by the Australian authorities there.
25 Hatta, *Memoir*, p, 360.
26 As cited in ibid., p. 361.

November 1935 authorized the transfer of Hatta and Sjahrir to Banda Neira. When informed of the decision, Hatta's immediate sense of relief was mixed with feelings of remorse: the reprieve had not been extended to his other five New PNI colleagues. "I was happy because my lot would be better," he recollected, "But sad because I would be separated from fellow-strugglers, especially PNI comrades."[27] Hatta tried to express his concern for his beleaguered comrades by donating over one hundred of his books to the penal settlement. He also promised to send aid and to continue his lecture program by correspondence.

The colonial government demanded a price for its clemency, insisting that Hatta and Sjahrir sign a declaration that they would have nothing more to do with politics. Sjahrir recalled that "Hafil was astounded."[28] Hatta could not renounce politics; his political cause was akin to a religious vocation. But he was also pragmatic enough to realize that his physical and mental survival might depend on escape from the malarial ravages of Boven Digul.

A compromise solution was finally reached, with the two men agreeing to "refrain from political activity on Banda."[29] Sjahrir anticipated that the authorities would try "to make political capital" out of their removal from Digul to Banda Neira, writing

> For most of the people, politics is not planning and premeditation, but ethical and moral eminence and actions. Political leaders must thus be heroes and prophets and because I realised this, I was sure that there would be difficulties for us connected with our removal to Banda -- and even more difficulties for Hafil than for me. For he is probably the father of the non-cooperation in Indonesia, and in any case he is certainly one of the outstanding champions of this idea.[30]

Sjahrir criticized Hatta for admitting to a ship's officer on the voyage to Banda Neira that they had signed the declaration. He remonstrated:

---

27 Ibid., p. 364.
28 Sjahrir, *Out of Exile*, p. 86.
29 Ibid.
30 Ibid., pp. 86-87.

"Hafil -- before I could prevent him -- naively told him [the ship's officer] everything, so that we even 'cooperated' in this aspect of the case as well."[31] Hatta omitted this uncomfortable incident from his memoirs.

Their declaration was subsequently misrepresented to suggest that the two men had renounced the nationalist movement. Resentful and chagrined, Hatta no doubt recalled the pointed remarks he had made about Sukarno's capitulation to the Dutch in his article "The Tragedy of Sukarno." The last thing Hatta would have wanted in the circumstances was any suggestion that he was following in Sukarno's tracks. Yet, as Sjahrir also commented ruefully: "While it is not true that we are 'converted,' something of the insinuations that have been started will always hang over us."[32]

First impressions of Banda Neira were favorable. Unlike Boven Digul, it was a long-established settlement on a scenic Island with a unique inter-racial society, a blend of European, Chinese, Malay, Arab, and Polynesian with a corresponding *mestizo* culture. Dutch and Christian influences were strong; the Muslim community was predominantly Arab. A totally different society from Java and Sumatra, it was sometimes referred to as a "European town in miniature."[33]

The quality of life of the two exiles was considerably enhanced on Banda Neira. With a monthly allowance of f 75, they could afford to rent a spacious old colonial home. Thrown closely together, the differences in age and temperament between Hatta and Sjahrir began to produce personality clashes. Sol Tas has described them as "a curious pair"; "very unlike in character, they could not avoid irritating each other from time to time." Tas noticed that "Sjahrir would be annoyed by Hatta's bourgeois conventionality," at the same time acknowledging that "Hatta was a much more conscientious and systematic worker."[34] The carefully ordered rhythm of Hatta's life combined with his religious puritanism grated on Sjahrir's nerves. The restless, mercurial, agnostic Sjahrir was not prepared to structure his activities around a timetable geared to Hatta's work

---

31 Ibid., p. 87.
32 Ibid.
33 See Des Alwi, "Oom Kaca Mata yang Mendidik Saya," in *Bung Hatta: Pribadinya dalam Kenangan*, p. 320.
34 Tas, "Souvenirs of Sjahrir," p. 143.

program and devotions. Nor was Hatta prepared to abandon his orderly system to fit in with Sjahrir's whims and impulses.

The local population had been warned to keep away from the two newcomers, referred to by the Dutch controlleur as "those Reds,"[35] although slowly the two men gained acceptance among the indigenous peoples. At first they were dependent on the friendship of their fellow exiles, Dr. Tjipto Mangunkusumo and Iwa Kusuma Sumantri. Hatta already knew Iwa, with whom he had worked closely in the Perhimpunan Indonesia, Yet in many ways, the legendary Dr. Tjipto became a closer friend to both Hatta and Sjahrir, a person they grew to love and admire.

Through Dr. Tjipto's two adopted sons, Sjahrir and Hatta were introduced to three children -- Des Alwi, Lily, and Mimi -- from one of the leading Arab families in the community. On learning that the two girls did not attend school, Sjahrir decided to remedy the situation by opening a small school for them in his half of the house. Sjahrir enjoyed children and had a penchant for teaching them. Although Hatta was relieved to see Sjahrir's severe depression lifting, the presence of the children also created new tensions. Hatta found it difficult to write and study against a background of noise and activity. Sjahrir could sense Hatta's patience wearing thin and decided to move into a vacant "pavilion" adjoining the home of his Arab family. It was a wise move; the normal good relations between them were restored. As Des Alwi observed: "Hatta and Sjahrir were always much closer to one another than to any of the other exiles."[36]

Hatta too was drawn into educational activities. He joined Sjahrir in teaching classes for the older children, including Dr. Tjipto's sons and also two MULO graduates from the Minangkabau sent to study under Hatta. However, any ideas of developing their teaching activities into a nationalist school were curtailed by a colonial government order restricting the number of pupils they might enroll. The government wanted no Pendidikan Nasional Indonesia on Banda Neira.

The Arab children grew very close to Sjahrir, providing a substitute family for him in which Hatta acted as an "uncle." The children liked Hatta

35 Des Alwi, "Oom Kacamata yang Mendidik Saya," p. 321.
36 Interview with Des Alwi, February 6, 1982.

but, because he could not relax with them as uninhibitedly as did Sjahrir, they were more restrained in his presence. They called him "Oom Hatta" to his face, but behind his back he was "Oom *Kaca Mata*," a reference to the large horn-rimmed spectacles which he now wore most of the time.

Lily recalled: "Oom Hatta always had his teaching program well-prepared and was very firm and disciplined."[37] "I trembled if I came late when Oom Hatta was the teacher," admitted Des, "or even more if I obtained a red mark in my report." He added: "The trouble was that Oom Hatta had a tendency to talk above our heads, so we did not understand what he was saying and ended up with bad marks. Then what a fuss he would make about them!"[38]

Yet, Des acknowledged, in spite of his strictness, Hatta was not a punitive person but was basically gentle. He might reprimand with his tongue but never with his fist. "Hatta had a sense of humor," Des recalled. "He was extremely adept at devising whimsical names for local personalities and for his pet cats."[39] Although Hatta could not demonstrate his affection as openly as did Sjahrir, the children were aware that he cared for them. He ordered them story books from Holland at his own expense, books chosen carefully to suit their interests and stimulate their imagination.[40] He was not as strong and adventurous a swimmer as Sjahrir but he enjoyed outings to the beach with the children, although insisting on wearing formal swimwear, including tennis shoes, when in the water.[41]

Both Hatta and Sjahrir were anxious to establish a rapport with the indigenous people by joining in their activities as much as possible, including playing football. Although they were closely monitored by colonial officials, no restrictions were placed on their movements within the island. Hatta also established a friendship with the local Indonesian doctor and school principal, both disliked by Sjahrir. Sjahrir criticized Hatta for sitting up late into the night playing bridge with the two men

---

37 Lily Sutantio, "Perjalanan Kenangan Keluarga Hatta ke Banda: Di Pantai Ini Ia Sering Berenang dan Mau Sepak Bola," in *Bung Hatta Kita* (Jakarta: Yayasan Idayu, 1980), p. 68.
38 Interview with Des Alwi, February 6, 1982.
39 Interview with Des Alwi, February 6, 1982, and Alwi, "Oom Kacamata yang Mendidik Saya," p. 323.
40 Interview with Des Alwi, February 6, 1982.
41 Alwi, "Oom Kacamata yang Mendidik Saya," p. 322.

and listening to their "fatuous" remarks.[42] Yet was it not through local schoolteachers that the New PNI had tried to reach down to the rural masses?

Des noticed that, although Sjahrir was on friendly terms with a bedridden Dutch lady and a young Dutch curate and his wife, "Oom Hatta never associated with Dutch people."[43] Sjahrir too noticed Hatta's reluctance to establish friendships with Dutch residents, which Sjahrir attributed to his Boven Digul experiences. He analyzed Hatta's change of attitude as follows:

> Formerly he was a non-cooperator by political conviction, and yet in many respects he still had faith in the conventional morality and humanity of the colonial government.... In the background of his thoughts he still maintained a high opinion of the respectability and methods of the colonial rulers against whom he made a stand. He now thinks quite differently about these things, thanks to Digul.[44]

Sjahrir was aware of the cultural dichotomy within them, which their long exposure to European education and values had engendered. Their political models reflected the positive values they had observed and admired in Europe, although for Hatta democracy was also a basic principle of the Minangkabau. The cold disregard for human life and dignity, the disdain for justice which had been evident in Boven Digul, had shaken them both, offsetting their fascination for Western culture. As Sjahrir continued: "Boven Digul was really a revelation for Hafil, and he has learned more from it than he did during all his years of 'political life' in Europe."[45]

Sjahrir again alleged that Hatta had acquired a deeper Dutch identity than he had realized:

> While he attacked and criticised colonial conditions in his articles... nevertheless in his heart he was still a Netherlander. He was still

---

42 Sjahrir, *Out of Exile*, p. 110.
43 Alwi, "Oom Kacamata yang Mendidik Saya," p. 322.
44 Sjahrir, *Out of Exile*, p. 203.
45 Ibid., p. 203.

a Netherlander in the sense that he did not really regard that government as a foreign and enemy element, but considered it in the same way that, for example, a left wing socialist opponent considers the Netherlands government in Holland. Hafil thus unconsciously accepted many of the same mutual norms and recognised one very important common basis for cooperation with the Dutch; namely, an internal faith in the humane, democratic and reliable methods of a government that outwardly he called unreliable.[46]

Although forbidden to engage openly in politics, the four exiles used what freedoms they had to undermine the strong Dutch influence on the Island. Iwa and Sjahrir combined their knowledge of law to provide a legal aid service for the people of the kampongs, especially helping in cases of abuse of land rights. Hatta assisted in organizing a cooperative movement among the local produce growers, working through a youth group which the four men helped to establish, the Persatuan Banda Neira [Banda Neira Union], the cooperative's profits being used to rent a house for meetings and to establish a small library filled with simple technical books and other educational material.[47]

As their popularity increased, the four men found themselves drawn into the major local activities and festivals, both Christian and Muslim. Among a predominantly Christian community, it was important that Islam not constitute an obstacle to their nationalist activities. Sjahrir noticed that at first the rather conservative Muslim community frowned upon their bare heads and Western dress, also disapproving of Sjahrir's friendship with the Dutch curate. The unrepentant Sjahrir's comment was that he would probably be placed in the same category as Dr. Tjipto, that is, "not regarded as a real Mohammadan." He added: "I do hope they will not make the same accusations about Hafil. I think that the poor fellow would be deeply troubled by it for he is unquestionably a modern edition of the upright Islamite."[48]

The rise of fascism in Europe absorbed Hatta's attention from 1936

---

46 Ibid., p. 204.
47 Lily Gamar Sutantio et al., "Kenangan-kenangan akan Jasa-Jasa Baik Oom Sjahrir," in Anwar, *Mengenang Sjahrir*, p. 43.
48 Sjahrir, *Out of Exile*, p. 121.

onwards. In spite of a tendency for Indonesians to look to Japan for support, Hatta was determined to dispel any rumors that he was pro-Japanese. Communist insinuations to this effect did not abate while he was in exile, the Dutch Communist Party paper, *Het Volksdagblad* [The People's Daily] publishing on April 23, 1938 an article under the title "Trotskyism in Indonesia," which was a blatant attack on Hatta, Sjahrir, and the New PNI.

Hatta was incensed. Although, as he explained in his defense, an article which he entitled "Stalin's Slave Seeks Trotsky in Indonesia," his intention was not to "indulge in polemics with the C.P.H.," he did feel obliged to respond to "the shrieks and insults of branches of Moscow in Holland," to "illuminate how Moscow teaches a slave-mentality which its servants are ordered to implant in the breasts of the Indonesian people."[49] He contended that, just as the colonial government branded all nationalists as "Communist," so the Stalin regime referred to any independent thinker who deviated from his "general line" as a Trotskyist. Hatta drew attention to Stalin's purges, alleging that Stalin "only wants to run his people like machines who merely wait around for orders from above." Hatta suspected that the author of the article attacking them was Rustam Effendi, and he accused his old PI antagonist of searching for a "Trotsky in Indonesia" because "Moscow no longer supports independence movements in colonies."[50]

Hatta did not conceal his contempt for Moscow's *volte face* in wooing the Western democracies, which led to Rustam Effendi supporting the minister of colonies in the Tweede Kamer and advising Indonesian nationalists to cooperate and abandon their demands for "Indonesia free of the Netherlands." Hatta charged: "It is not just Japanese imperialism which should be feared but also the existing Dutch colonialism and also -- (note well, Rustam Effendi) -- Russian imperialism." Hatta accused Stalin of being no "true communist," concluding with a challenging query: "Think about it, who in truth should be dubbed with the name 'fascist agent'?"[51]

---

49 Mohammad Hatta, "Budak Stalin Mentjari Trotzky ke Indonesia," in *Kumpulan Karangan*, 1: 138. First published in *Matahari*, May 28, 1938.
50 Ibid.
51 Ibid., p. 139.

Not surprisingly, Hatta's riposte evoked a hostile reaction. An article provocatively entitled "Is Hatta a Marxist?" appeared in the Indonesian journal *Sin Tit Po* of April and May 1939. The author, who wrote under the pseudonym Mevrouw Vodegel-Soemarmah, was later discovered by Hatta to be the Indonesian-Chinese communist, Tan Ling Djie. The article attacked Hatta not only for his challenging remarks to Rustam Effendi but also for economic statements he had written in a further article entitled "Some Main Features of the World Economy." In this second article Hatta was strongly critical of the present international economic crisis, contending that capitalism had "become imprisoned in its own world which is 'densely populated' with heavy industry and 'overpopulated' with unemployed."[52] Hatta categorized the Soviet Union's economic system as being in a "separate world of its own" where "socialist development is still in a stage of state capitalism," with economic development controlled by the state.[53]

In a further article, entitled "Marxism or the Wisdom of Epigones?" and headed with Marx's own statement: "I am not a Marxist,"[54] Hatta set out laboriously to make clear once and for all his political ideology and economic position. He acknowledged his admiration for Marx but drew attention to the fact that there were other economic theorists, such as Sombart, more relevant to the present international situation. He also reserved the right to develop theories of his own.

Hatta accused the Dutch Communists of being unable to "rise above narrow-minded, pedestrian polemics," and protested that the damaging article was just another opportunity "to aim communist arrows at me," that "in theoretical fields also must I be annihilated!" He contended:

No one has ever asserted... who knows my great admiration for Marx that I am Marxist. I never set out to wear a label which does not fit me, that is in opposition with many of my compatriots.... At the moment, people can conclude from one or two passages cited that I, while holding to my own logical method, also appreciate Marx's way of thinking. My article is not about the relationship

52 Mohammad Hatta, "Some Main Features of the World Economy," in *Portrait of a Patriot*, p. 94.
53 Ibid., pp. 96-97.
54 Mohammad Hatta, "Marxisme of Epigonenwijsheid?" in *Verspreide Geschriften*, pp. 117-41

of economic basis and ideology, for which Marx's theory is very appropriate.[55]

In the concluding paragraphs of his article, Hatta drew attention to the fact that social concern developed not just from Marx but also from a sense of religious duty, evident both within Christianity and Islam:

> From a deep study of the tenets of Marx one is led irrevocably to socialism. Indeed, as a result of the perception that men themselves are subject to the will of a wholly loving and righteous God, a follower of Islam lives a life of service, brotherhood and justice under men.... He feels the struggle for socialism to be a command of God, from which there is no escape.[56]

Here Hatta was making a clear statement that, while he admired Marx, for him personally the motivation to achieve political, social, and economic justice for his people stemmed from other sources, in particular from his sense of religious vocation.

Hatta and Sjahrir observed with frustration from Banda Neira the slow capitulation of the non-cooperating nationalists under the tough colonial regimes of the thirties. Sartono had given up the struggle to keep Partindo alive as a non-cooperating party, dissolving it in November 1936. By then too Haji Agus Salim had come to the conclusion that cooperation was the only political expedient for nationalists. For this he was expelled from the PSII. The Perhimpunan Indonesia, once so ardent a promoter of non-cooperation, was now obeying Dutch Communist directives to cooperate with the Dutch government against fascism. The name of the PI's journal had been altered from *Indonesia Merdeka* to *Perhimpoenan Indonesia* as freedom for the Indies was no longer being promoted. Three younger Partindo leaders, Muhammad Yamin, Amir Sjarifuddin, and A. K. Gani, all Sumatrans, developed a small, cooperating urbanized party, the Gerakan Rakyat Indonesia [Indonesian People's Movement] or Gerindo which became one of the more spirited and vocal of the

---

55 Ibid., pp. 121-25.
56 Ibid., p. 140.

nationalist groups.

For Hatta and Sjahrir, perhaps the brightest spot in the depressing nationalist scene was that the Pendidikan Nasional Indonesia still survived as an ardent non-cooperating party under the leadership of men such as Hamdani, Subagio, Sastra, and Djohan Sjahruzah. Forced to work secretly, meeting in private homes or organizing itself into cooperative societies instead of local branches to avoid colonial retribution, the party survived.

The more Japan posed a threat to the colonial government, the more the Indonesians rejoiced. As Sjahrir analyzed the situation: "Sympathy for Japan has subconscious causes and these lie in the Asiatic inferiority feelings, which seek compensation in a glorification of the Japanese since the other alternative -- open hatred of the whites -- may involve personal danger."[57] Japanese propaganda, filtering through to the colony, was playing on the cultural sensibilities of the Javanese people by resurrecting the Joyoboyo legend, which predicted that Java would be released from bondage by yellow people from the north who would break white rule and disappear after one hundred days, when the corn harvest was ripe. Hatta was scathing of those who believed such a myth, stressing: "It is our duty, as rational people, to kill such disastrous ideas."[58]

In 1939, the political situation was so critical in Europe that there was an instinctive drawing together of the nationalists in the Indies, as if they sensed the approach of a major international upheaval. In May 1939, a new nationalist front was formed, the Gabungan Politik Indonesia [Indonesian Political Federation] or Gapi, which adopted the slogan "*Indonesia Berparlemen*" [Indonesia with a Parliament] as had been envisaged under the November Promise of 1918. In December 1939, Gapi organized an Indonesian People's Congress at which the need for unity was expressed. A slight alteration was made to the flag, the buffalo's head being removed, so that only two horizontal stripes remained, one white, one red.[59]

The outbreak of war in Europe in September 1939 spurred Hatta to

---

57 Sjahrir, *Out of Exile*, p. 195.
58 Mohammad Hatta, "Rakjat Indonesia dengan Perang Pasifik," in *Kumpulan Karangan*, 1: 145. First published in *Pemandangan*, December 22/23, 1941.
59 See Kahin, *Nationalism and Revolution in Indonesia*, p. 98, n. 101.

take up his pen, producing an article which he entitled "Mendjadi Perang ideologi." He contended that this time the conflict in Europe was "not a war concerned with national pride but an ideological war," "a war between democracy and Nazism." Hatta declared that his sympathies lay with the "democracies" because he feared that "if the spirit of democracy is weakened by the forces of fascism, we get further and further away from what is really true democracy."[60]

Hatta saw the defeat of fascism as being automatically beneficial internationally, causing also a softening of colonial attitudes. "Once the spirit of democracy has regained its strength in Europe, we can only live in hope that this spirit will spread to every place in the world and will even go as far as influencing the attitudes of colonizing governments."[61] The First World War had begun to weaken the colonial structure: another major conflict which engendered a spirit of democracy could benefit Indonesia's cause.

Hatta and Sjahrir were now separated from their fellow exiles, Iwa Kusuma Sumantri and Dr. Tjipto Mangunkusumo, both of whom had been transferred to Makassar. Dr. Tjipto had become ardently pro-Allied, and also sympathetic to the Dutch government in its predicament in Europe, and he organized a demonstration of loyalty in Makassar on May 15, 1940. Although the colonial government's overall response to Indonesian expressions of sympathy was cold and suspicious, the authorities did decide to repatriate the aging Dr. Tjipto to Java, as his health was deteriorating and he required more expert medical attention than was available in the Outer Islands.

The incumbent Governor-General, Van Starkenborgh Stachouwer, dismissed rumors of a Japanese invasion of the Indies, commenting that he believed American military and industrial capacity to be so great "that he could only imagine Japan being an aggressor if it were sure of America's holding aloof."[62] The home government, now in exile in London, had issued instructions to the colonial authorities to retain the

60 Mohammad Hatta, "Mendjadi Perang Ideologi," in *Kumpulan Karangan*, 2: 154.
61 Ibid., p. 156.
62 See Susan Abeyasekere, *One Hand Clapping: Indonesian Nationalists and the Dutch, 1939-42*, Monash Papers on Southeast Asia No. 5 (Clayton, Vic: Monash University Centre of Southeast Asian Studies, 1976), p. 33.

Indies at all costs, as this would ensure Holland's prestige in the postwar negotiations.[63] Only very minor concessions were to be made in order to guarantee the support of the Indonesians in the event of a Japanese invasion.

In December 1941, the news of the devastating Japanese attack on Pearl Harbor shattered colonial government complacency, the Governor-General making the solemn announcement that the Indies was at war. Banda Neira was immediately mobilized into civil defense activities, in which Hatta and Sjahrir spontaneously took part. Hatta was assigned to the task of organizing food distribution, while Sjahrir worked with a former Royal Netherlands Indies Army sergeant on radio monitoring.[64]

Hatta believed that it was his duty, as a nationalist leader, to make a statement on the issues involved in the Pacific War, at the same time explaining his own position. Ideologically it was not a difficult decision. He had made it clear over the last decade that he was not a Japanese agent and that fascism was contrary to his ideal of a democratic state. His admiration for Japan's challenge to the West and economic prowess had dissipated as he observed the rise to power of Japan's militarists and the cruelty of Japanese actions against fellow Asians in China. Yet to air his view publicly in the face of the imminent arrival of the Japanese Army was to invite considerable personal risk.

Nevertheless, Hatta transmitted his thoughts to paper. He entitled his article "The Indonesian People in the Pacific War," and posted it off quickly to the editor of *Pemandangan* before second thoughts could weaken his resolve. He reminded his readers that in 1932 he had predicted the inevitability of a Pacific War, which had become even more likely when Japan joined the Axis. Hatta accused the Japanese of dishonoring their famed *samurai* code by attacking Honolulu, Malaya, and Singapore without first making a formal declaration of war. "A *samurai* does not stab his enemy from behind," accused Hatta, "he meets him face to face."[65]

Hatta advised Indonesians to look at the example of Jawaharlal Nehru who, although opposing British imperialism, did not request or accept aid from Nazis or fascists and who supported the Chinese in their opposition

---

63 Ibid., p. 57.
64 Sjahrir, *Out of Exile*, p. 224.
65 Mohammad Hatta, "Rakjat Indonesia dengan Perang Pasifik," p. 141.

to Japanese imperialism through his writings and actions. Indonesians aimed at self-determination, Hatta pointed out, and "these rights can only be achieved in a world ordered on a democratic basis."[66] Hatta conceded that Western democracy alone would not achieve Indonesia's aims, but under fascism people would only be further enslaved. Therefore fascism must be destroyed. He explained that the "autocratic spirit of the colonizer" at the present time was a result of fascism among the white community in the Indies. "Democracy becomes very conservative because of the existence of fascism," Hatta explained. He added:

> For us, the Indonesian people, the crushing of fascism and of Japanese imperialism will be of great benefit.... Imperialist Japan is the most serious threat to Indonesia and its aims. Therefore every Indonesian who loves his native land and holds to the national goals can have no other viewpoint but to oppose Japanese imperialism.

Hatta concluded with a phrase similar to that he had used in his memoirs in connection with the Kamang incident of 1908, the slogan of the defiant Minangkabau protesting against Dutch injustice: "It is better to drown with one's ideals than live like a corpse. That is the meaning of struggle."[67]

Sjahrir, although also strongly anti-Japanese, was concerned about the possible consequences to Hatta resulting from publication of the article, and the loss to the nationalist movement if he were executed or imprisoned. "I immediately went to see him to advise against publishing it," he wrote in his reminiscences, adding: "Hafil's anti-fascist and pro-Allied leanings were genuine, he had always been a profoundly democratic individual and he was particularly disturbed over the pro-Japanese attitude of the people."[68]

The ironic factor was that the Dutch made use of Hatta's article, translating it into various regional languages, at the same time continuing to treat Hatta as an enemy of the state. Hatta followed up with another article, as if to refute any impression that he had written his previous

---

66 Ibid., p. 143.
67 Ibid., pp. 144-45.
68 Sjahrir, *Out of Exile*, p. 232.

paper at the behest of the Dutch.

> We do not oppose Japanese imperialism because we wish to ingratiate ourselves with the Government.... Howsoever the Government wishes to judge our attitude, that is up to it to decide. But our attitude is based on our own thinking and our own national ideals. This is the only basis upon which we will fight along side the democratic West against Fascism which is now at our very doorstep.[69]

On February 1, 1942, Hatta and Sjahrir were transferred from Banda Neira to Java aboard an American Catalina flying boat at the insistence of the colonial authorities. Hatta had tried to set a condition that their comrades in Boven Digul also be repatriated, the message coming back from Ambon that the West New Guinea exiles were being cared for. In fact, they were being transported to Australia. Sjahrir took three of his Arab protégés with him -- Lily, Mimi, and three-year-old Ali. For Hatta, the order that he must leave without his books caused some personal anguish, relieved to some extent by the promise from young Des Alwi that he would try to get to Java by ship with Hatta's books and join him and Sjahrir there.

Hatta and Sjahrir landed in Surabaya, from where they were taken to Sukabumi in West Java and housed in the Police School, being allocated adjoining residential units. They were allowed to move within Sukabumi but could travel no further afield. One pleasing aspect of the transfer was that they were close to the Mangunkusumo family, who had established a home in the town. Dr. Tjipto was now in very poor health, suffering severe and frequent attacks of asthma.

Through Dr. Tjipto's younger brother, Sujitno, a member of the Governor-General's staff, Hatta and Sjahrir learned that the colonial government, in its desperation, was seeking the support of the nationalist leaders to organize a resistance to the Japanese, especially through broadcasts. The relay of this piece of information was followed up by a

---

69 *Berita Oemoem*, February 12, 1942, as cited in Kanahele, "Japanese Occupation of Indonesia," p. 18, n. 72.

visit from Amir Sjarifuddin, one of the Gerindo leaders and a much more left-wing nationalist than Sartono. Claiming that he was speaking on behalf of Gapi, the new federation of nationalist parties, Amir suggested that, in the event of a Dutch surrender to the Japanese, it might be best if Hatta and Sjahrir agreed to be evacuated to Australia.[70]

According to Hatta's memoirs, he answered that he would only leave the Indies if he received a direct request to do so from other nationalists and in the knowledge that they were paying his expenses and not the Dutch.[71] Hatta clearly suspected that Amir Sjarifuddin was transmitting the wishes of the colonial government. Sjahrir's account of this incident indicated that he was still concerned for Hatta's survival in view of his openly expressed anti-Japanese viewpoint. "I told him I thought Siregar [Sjarifuddin] exaggerated somewhat but was probably sent by the colonial government to sound us out on these matters." He added: "I felt it was obviously too late, and hence absurd, to speak of political cooperation but I approved of the plan to evacuate Hafil."[72] As Hatta commented drily in his memoirs, it was obvious that "Governor-General Tjarda van Starkenborgh Stachouwer had not the moral strength to put forward his request personally as we were still in the status of internees."[73]

Sjahrir continued to press Hatta to reconsider whether he should not seek a safe refuge overseas, promising "to go with him initially and return later to lead our underground work in Indonesia."[74] Hatta was unconvinced: "If leaving the country depends on the Dutch Indies government," he affirmed, "I am not prepared to go."[75] He did however agree to Amir Sjarifuddin's suggestion that he make a public statement, advising the people to remain calm. "The contents were not as Amir Sjarifuddin suggested," recalled Hatta, "I encouraged the people to set up local National Committees with firm leadership which were prepared to meet the Japanese Army when it occupied each locality, informing them that the aims of the national movement are to attain a Free Indonesia."[76]

---

70 Hatta, *Memoir*, p. 388.
71 Ibid.
72 Sjahrir, *Out of Exile*, p. 236.
73 Hatta, *Memoir*, p. 388.
74 Sjahrir, *Out of Exile*, p. 236.
75 Hatta, *Memoir*, p. 388.
76 Ibid., p. 389.

Hatta advised the people to remain neutral as the Great East Asian War was a conflict between the Japanese Army and the Dutch forces.

Hatta had made his decision. He was not going to cooperate with the colonial government or encourage his people to die defending the Dutch. The Dutch had up to the last rejected the pleas of the Indonesians for a share in government and snubbed their expressions of sympathy. In his eyes, and those of Sjahrir, the colonial forces were as fascist as the Japanese. They were both imperialists.

On March 9, 1942, the Dutch Indies government surrendered to the Japanese Army, only two weeks after the landings on Java. The Dutch collapse was so swift and its resistance so weak that the Indonesian people scarcely realized that three hundred years of Dutch penetration of their archipelago was ending. There was no long, drawn-out battle to mark the event. Technically Hatta and Sjahrir were free men, their exile over. The Governor-General was a captive of the Japanese and so unable to hold them any longer under exorbitant rights.

CHAPTER SEVEN
THE JAPANESE INTERREGNUM

We are at war. In a time of war, every nation considers the defense of its native land. The defense of one's country becomes the prior issue underlying every endeavor. The entire physical force of the people and the community is directed towards one aim: to achieve victory.... Young Indonesians, never forget that there is no honorable nation in this world which surrenders completely its self-defense to another nation.... Comrades, don't imagine, we are forming defense forces to serve Nippon's interests. Such a suggestion is quite incorrect.... Dai Nippon knows how to defend itself and, as we have seen since the outbreak of the Greater East Asian War, it is sufficiently strong and daring to subjugate its enemies with its own force and strength.[1]

In 1928, the Dutch socialists had accused Hatta of exaggerating the extent of Indonesian disaffection with colonial rule. In February 1942, the Dutch government realized to its cost how accurate had been the portrayal by Hatta and other nationalists of the Indonesian people's attitudes generally toward the Dutch. This was a rude awakening for a nation which regarded its colony as an integral part of its heritage. In 1941, Minister of Colonies Welter, following a visit to the Indies, had either failed to recognize or deliberately ignored the widespread disillusionment there with colonial rule, commenting confidently on the close relationship between the people of the Netherlands and the Indies, stating that "together we form a unity so mighty, so strong that nothing

---

1   Mohammad Hatta, "Sukarela Membela Tanah Air" [Voluntarily Defending One's Native Land], Speech delivered in Ikada Square, November 3, 1943, in *Kumpulan Karangan*, I: 200-202.

and nobody in the world will be able to break it."[2] Yet the reluctance of the Dutch colonial government to arm Indonesians for local defense activities might appear to throw doubt on the sincerity of Welter's statement.

For Hatta, there was no exultation in the Japanese victory, rather resigned acceptance that Indonesia was again under foreign rule, the main difference being that the new invader was from the East rather than from the West. In view of his recent outspoken anti-Japanese article, which had received wide publicity, Hatta apprehensively awaited his fate. He also had to reach a decision on how far he would cooperate with the Japanese if no punitive action were taken against him. The political relationship with Japan was different from that with the Dutch. Japan had not yet made it clear whether its military occupation of Indonesia was temporary or permanent. Anyhow, how permanent could any occupation be in a wartime situation? "The nature of our present struggle is different from the past," Hatta was to explain in a radio broadcast. "First of all, we are struggling in an atmosphere of war. The education of the people's spirit is aimed at securing final victory."[3]

Hatta seemed to realize the opportunities the Japanese interregnum could provide for developing a "state within a state," no longer as a parallel movement but more in the revolutionary sense of a "bloc within a bloc." The break in Dutch power had taken the independence issue out of the evolutionary category into the area of *realpolitik*. No longer did Hatta use the term "state within a state," his speeches from now on underlined the phrase "*masyarakat baru*," the new society.

Hatta had made clear that he rejected the Japanese, as he did the colonial government, on ideological and nationalist grounds. However, after eight years of political isolation, he was no longer prepared to stand aloof. In 1926 he had forecast that a Pacific War would inevitably involve Indonesians and could be the decisive factor in breaking Western colonial power. As Wilopo, a future Indonesian prime minister, was later to comment, Hatta belonged to a group of Indonesians who were "prepared to cooperate with the Japanese regime because they considered

---

2 See Abeyasekere, *One Hand Clapping*, p. 67.
3 Mohammad Hatta, "Harapan dan Kewajiban Rakyat di Masa Datang," Radio Speech, March 5, 1943, in *Kumpulan Pidato: Dari Tahun 1942 s.d. i949*, arranged by I. Wangsa Widjaja and M. F. Swasono (Jakarta: Yayasan Idayu, 1981), p. 20.

it would not be rational to oppose it."[4] He advised nationalists to demand independence right from the start of the occupation, probably realizing that this would test Japan's sincerity. When the PSII leader, Abikusno Tjokrosujoso, claiming to represent the nationalist movement, called for a parliament and cabinet, the initial benevolent attitude of the Japanese hardened. On March 20, they issued a decree dissolving all political parties and trade unions and denying the use of the Indonesian flag.

Hatta's first encounter with Japanese officials took place on the evening of March 19, 1942, just prior to the announcement of the ban on nationalist activities. Hatta and Sjahrir were still at the Sukabumi Police School, waiting for the Japanese to make the first approach to them, at the same time trying to reestablish contacts with former colleagues.

Unlike Sjahrir, who was merely interrogated, Hatta was ordered to report to Japanese Central Headquarters in Bandung to declare his intention to cooperate with the Japanese Army in "safeguarding the people's safety and fending off Allied attacks."[5] Hatta, according to his memoirs, did not automatically accede to the request, quibbling that "I had to go first to Jakarta to accompany my mother there, after which I would go to Army Headquarters in Bandung."[6] He was allowed three days to settle his affairs.

According to Sjahrir, "Hafil, even more than I, had expected arrest because so much publicity had been given his declaration of support for the Allies," and that therefore "the solicitous attitude of the Japanese was a surprise for Hafil." Sjahrir believed that this conciliatory approach to Hatta was consistent with Japanese designs. "When I had urged him to leave the country, I told him one of my main motives was that I feared he would otherwise be misused by the Japanese for their propaganda. I thought it impossible for him to be active in the underground movement. He was too well known and the people were still too pro-Japanese."[7]

The new regime made a further approach to Hatta, when the next day he received orders from the deputy chief of staff of the Sixteenth Army, General Harada, to leave for Jakarta. Hatta explained to the army

---

4 Wilopo, "Akal, Moral dan Ekonomi," in *Bung Hatta Mengabdi pada Tjita-Tjita*, p. 512.
5 As cited in Hatta, *Memoir*, p. 391.
6 Ibid. Hatta's mother had joined him at the Sukabumi Police School.
7 Sjahrir, *Out of Exile.*, p. 239.

officer sent to accompany him that he was already under orders from the *Kempeitai* to present himself in Bandung. He pointed out that he had observed the body of a Dutch controlleur lying by the roadside with a sign attached, which read: "This is what happens to those who disobey Japanese orders," and he had no desire to suffer a similar fate.[8] Hatta was assured that he could proceed with safety to Jakarta.

There was no summons for Sjahrir, who remained temporarily in Sukabumi. This moment of parting was a turning point in the political association of the two men. Although they remained close colleagues, basically united in ideals and outlook, from now on they would be drawn apart by the different roles they were to play during the Japanese Occupation and subsequently. Hatta, on the verge of forty years of age, would take his place in the ranks of the older nationalists, known as the *Angkatan 28*, the Generation of 1928, many of whom were his former Perhimpunan Indonesia peer group. Sjahrir, in his early thirties, would attract around him the new generation of radical youth, known as the *Angkatan Muda*, the Youth Generation, or the *Angkatan 45*, where his boyish appearance, his socialist ideals and his daring, anti-Japanese stance would make him a cult figure among the young elite. Yet the special bond between Hatta and Sjahrir, combined with Sukarno's mystique, would also serve as a bridge between the old and the young leadership, especially in times of crisis.

Hatta was graciously received in Jakarta, where he was housed in the prestigious Hotel des Indes, usually the preserve of the white community. A spacious De Soto car was provided for his use. In his memoirs, Hatta is anxious to establish that he was not forsaking his non-cooperation stance for the sake of his personal safety and the material benefits offered by the Japanese, and that he was determined not to be enticed into more than the minimum of cooperation. He stressed that he made this clear in his initial interview with General Harada. When asked: "Are you prepared to cooperate with the Japanese military government?" Hatta claimed to have posed a question in response: "Does Japan intend to colonize Indonesia?" This General Harada denied emphatically, Hatta recalled, "on the word

---

8 Hatta, *Memoir*, p. 393.

of a soldier."[9] General Harada assured him that it was Japan's intention to free from colonialism all subjugated Asian nations.

Hatta had little choice but to accept Japan's rationalization of its occupation. The Dutch had defended colonialism as a process of bringing Western enlightenment to the East. The Japanese contended that they were leading fellow Asians out of the grip of the West. Hatta, knowing at least that he had some bargaining power, that the Japanese needed him badly enough to overlook his article, did not offer his services unconditionally.

> I said that I was prepared to cooperate with the Japanese military government, but not as a government official. I would be prepared to be an Adviser who was free to give advice to the military government.... I would not work under a Japanese superior, preferring my advice to be given on my own responsibility.[10]

He also requested his own office and the freedom to appoint his own staff.

Japanese acceptance of Hatta's terms indicated how keen they were to obtain the support of foremost nationalist leaders on Java, having received instructions from Tokyo to obtain popular backing for Japan's war effort.[11] For Hatta, the Kantor Penasihat Umum [Office of the General Adviser], wuth which he was provided until he fell from grace in 1943, became a focal point for trying to build up his "new society." He drew onto his staff both former PI and New PNI colleagues, people he could trust. This was important as he would be liaising with Sjahrir's underground movement. Many nationalists stayed but a short time in Hatta's office before moving on to work in various departments previously staffed by the Dutch. These new vacancies provided the nationalists with an opportunity to build up a government administration which was not subservient to Dutch interests, as in the past. Djohan Sjahruzah and Dr. Tjipto's younger brother, Sujitno, also worked in Hatta's office, with the special task of assisting Sjahrir in organizing an underground network,

---

9 Ibid., p. 400.
10 Ibid.
11 See Kanahele, "Japanese Occupation of Indonesia," p. 27.

financing its operations with whatever funds were available.[12] Hatta had to be very cautious, disciplining his tongue and his pen, although as his confidence grew he became more outspoken. He was always aware that Japanese reaction to subversion would be much more deadly than that of the Dutch and that, although he was free to appoint his staff, a Japanese soldier was always on guard outside his office.

Materially, Hatta's lifestyle was considerably improved. The Japanese were generous in their rewards, providing him with a vacated Dutch colonial house in the prestigious suburb of Menteng, which remained his family home for the rest of his life.[13] Following the pattern set by Dutch officials, Hatta also acquired a small villa in the West Java hills at Megamendung, which was to provide a useful haven for clandestine politics. In the same way Sjahrir made use of his sister's villa in the hills, behind its thick orange groves organizing his nationalist underground and installing a secret radio transmitter.[14]

Amir Sjarifuddin's underground group, which had been amply funded by the colonial government before it surrendered to the Japanese, operated in the sensitive naval port of Surabaya and included illicit PKI members. It soon attracted considerable Kempeitai attention. Sensing that the Kempeitai was closing in on him, Amir sought Hatta's assistance. Hatta responded by requesting that Amir join his staff, offering to be responsible for him -- a risky proposition as Sjahrir had already criticized Amir for lacking discretion in his *modus operandi*.[15] Hatta was no doubt trying to coordinate the operations of the two underground movements in order to transmit the nationalist message more effectively. Perhaps suspecting Hatta's motives, the Japanese did not accede to his request. Amir was instead assigned to the Propaganda Department whose object was to imbue the Indonesian people with the "Japanese spirit," obviously a test of Amir's willingness to cooperate. He was known as an able orator.

---

12 According to Sjahrir, Sujitno (referred to as Boeditjitro) "could not survive" as an underground agent and joined Hatta's staff. See *Out of Exile*, p. 241. See also A. R. Baswedan ("Hatta: Antara Catatan dan Kenangan," in *Bung Hatta: Pribadinya dalam Kenangan*, p. 473), who relates how Djohan Sjahruzah warned Hatta not to record details of the funds he allocated to Sjahrir, remarking: "Bung, isn't it dangerous to make notes like that? If the Japanese find out, you will suffer."

13 Hatta, *Memoir*, p. 413.

14 Sjahrir, *Out of Exile*, p. 241.

15 Hatta, *Memoir*, pp. 409-10, and Sjahrir, *Out of Exile*, p. 236.

The Propaganda Department had begun to sponsor a new movement, the Tiga A or Three A's, to fill the vacuum left following the total ban on nationalist parties and trade unions. Aware that Japan intended to use the Tiga A to mobilize the Indonesian people to serve their war effort, Hatta refused to support the new movement, describing it as "an undisguised attempt to achieve a Greater Japan."[16] He knew from his personal experience with the Dutch that when an Indonesian formed cultural bonds with the foreign power, his assessment of that power's motives could become clouded and his will to resist weakened.

An important consequence of the failure of T1ga A to gain wide Indonesian support was the decision of the Japanese Sixteenth Army to request that Sukarno be released from the service of the Twenty-Fifth Army in Sumatra and returned to Java. Sukarno was the propagandist *par excellence* with a special talent for stirring up the Javanese masses. Hatta did not raise any objections to the return of his prewar rival. On the contrary, according to Sjahrir, Sukarno was brought back to Java "at the request of the nationalists in Java, supported particularly by Hafil."[17]

Hatta and also the nationalists needed to make use of Sukarno's outstanding talent for communicating with the Indonesian people, a skill which Hatta lacked. If Hatta and Sukarno worked together under Japanese sponsorship -- and Sukarno had been prepared to work with Hatta in the past -- they could plan jointly how to use the interregnum to full advantage. No other nationalist was as skillful as Sukarno at translating ideas and instructions into language which the Javanese people could comprehend but which might be less understood by the foreign enemy.

The nationalist movement welcomed the accord between Sukarno and Hatta. Hatta's own response to Sukarno's arrival by motor boat at Tanjung Priok on July 9, 1942 was warm and hospitable. He invited him and his family to be overnight guests in his house, clearly indicating that the issues which had divided them in the past were temporarily set aside. With Indonesia's independence looming as a distinct possibility, the time had come to pool their resources and play down differences in outlook and ideology.

---

16 See Kanahele, "Japanese Occupation of Indonesia," p. 47, n. 38.
17 Sjahrir, *Out of Exile*, p. 245.

Sjahrir joined the two men in their initial discussions. According to Hatta, Sukarno "was convinced that Japan would win in the Second World War because it had been able to paralyze the armadas of America, Britain, and Holland."[18] Hatta, as an economist, did not agree, contending that Japan's industrial capacity was unequal to that of America, that America had the power to recover its strength and possessed the advanced technology to improve its weapons of war. Hatta warned Sukarno of Japan's increasing suppression of radical nationalism, suggesting he avoid the Tiga A. "I explained to him," recalled Hatta, "that the Tiga A movement was generally hated by the people, more rejecting it than supporting it."[19]

In his autobiography, Sukarno showed enthusiasm for this reunion with Hatta. Clearly the fact that both Hatta and Sjahrir were willing to recognize his talents and submit to his leadership was a tremendous boost to his self-confidence. Sukarno indicated that this meeting with Hatta was the beginning of the period of their political partnership, which was to earn them the title of the *Dwi Tunggal*, the two-in-one. He described the scene, when he shook hands with Hatta, declaring: "This is our symbol of *Dwi Tunggal* -- two-in-one. Our solemn oath to work side by side, never to be separated until our country is wholly free."[20]

The note of warmth and delight, so obvious in Sukarno's account, is absent from Hatta's memoirs. By the time he had reached old age, the relationship between the two men had lost its savor and become sour, leaving Hatta with memories which were tinged with bitterness. There was almost a note of resignation in his account, a suggestion that his partnership with Sukarno had been a national duty which he could not avoid at this critical time. "For me," he wrote, "it is clear that Sukarno intended to cooperate with the Japanese government to achieve his aim of establishing a new party which would satisfy his desire for agitation."[21]

Hatta's first public appearance alongside Sukarno took place two weeks later in a fine old colonial building known as the German House in the center of Jakarta. The meeting was attended by thousands of enthusiastic

18 Hatta, *Memoir*, p. 415.
19 Ibid., p. 416.
20 Adams, *Sukarno*, p. 173.
21 Hatta, *Memoir*, p. 416.

Indonesians, excited by the news that the two prewar nationalist rivals had settled their differences. In their speeches, both Sukarno and Hatta stressed that the time had come for the Indonesian people to unite, promising not to allow themselves to be divided again as in the past. The difference in their oratory was immediately noticeable, Hatta's address couched in "bookish" language and Sukarno's in a more popular style. "But those who listened could detect in Bung Hatta's speeches the *Binuang* [buffalo] attacking," a spectator reportedly commented; "Listening to Bung Karno, a person felt he was joining in the leaps and bounds of a *Banteng Ketaton* [a wounded wild buffalo]."[22] But there was an evident sense of relief that the two men were working together and that the nationalist movement was not going to be swamped by the Japanese invasion.

Dr. Tjipto, forced by the continuing deterioration of his health to move to Jakarta, persisted in opposing any collaboration with the Japanese. Hatta frequently visited his dying friend, using his influence to ensure that he was not harassed and was adequately supplied with the medicines he needed. When Dr. Tjipto died on March 8, 1943, one year after the Dutch capitulation on Java, it was Hatta who arranged the details of his funeral, and had his coffin taken under Sjahrir's escort by train to Ambarawa for burial. In a speech in Ikada Square the next day, Hatta paid tribute to his friend, speaking in general of the sacrifices made by nationalists in the colonial period. "Here, full of sadness, I mention a name which deserves to be remembered for the rest of our lives, Tjipto Mangunkusumo, who died yesterday at the age of fifty-eight. The story of his life can be explained in a few words: honest, loyal, chivalrous, struggle, sacrifice, exile, illness."[23]

Sjahrir saw Hatta's relationship with Dr. Tjipto as "unique." "Dr. Soeribno [Tjipto] had only contempt for the nationalists who cooperated with the Japanese, but, from the very beginning, although he was disappointed that Hafil became a leading figure under the Japanese authority rather than a democratic martyr, he always defended Hafil, if not politically then morally. He never spoke harshly of him, not even

---

22 Cited in B. M. Diah, "Manusia Hatta," in *Bung Hatta: Pribadinya dalam Kenangan*, p. 56.
23 Mohammad Hatta, "Organisasi Kita," Speech in Ikada Square, March 9, 1943, in *Kumpulan Pidato*, p. 28.

162 INDONESIA FREE: A POLITICAL BIOGRAPHY OF MOHAMMAD HATTA

when I occasionally expressed my dissatisfaction with him."[24]

Sjahrir did not mention specifically what caused his displeasure. Perhaps Hatta's increasing involvement, along with Sukarno, in Japanese propaganda exercises offended him. Sjahrir may have sensed also that Hatta was once more drawing close to his original PI peer group, especially to Subardjo, a group of men whom Sjahrir regarded as too steeped in Javanese feudal culture, men who had rejected the concept of "people's sovereignty."

At the same time Sjahrir made it clear that Hatta was fulfilling his responsibilities to the underground movement.[25] From a personal point of view, Hatta was also assisting Sjahrir by paying the children's school fees for Sjahrir's adopted family. Des Alwi had finally arrived on New Year's Eve 1942, bringing with him two of Hatta's crates.[26] As on Banda Neira, Hatta insisted that the children pay close attention to their studies, checking their progress and examining their school reports.

Sjahrir had established a home in Jakarta, where he concealed a second radio transmitter to monitor news broadcasts from overseas networks, and the children acted as his messengers, taking it in turns to relay these radio messages to Hatta.[27] At first, Sjahrir included Sukarno in his discussions but, as Sukarno became more deeply involved in Japanese projects, Sjahrir began to draw away from him, confining himself to maintaining links with Hatta and consulting with him alone.

In order to work within the Japanese system Hatta had to show at least a modicum of support for Japanese policies. He selected his words very carefully so that his public statements kept in focus the Indonesian independence issue as much as possible. To such slogans as "Asia for the Asians" and "Asia living in mutual cooperation," he added: "Greater

---

24 Sjahrir, *Out of Exile.*, p. 242.

25 Ibid. There is a strong pro-Hatta element in this section of Sjahrir's account which must be taken into consideration, as it is an addendum to the original collection of letters and extracts from his diary, compiled by Maria and published in the Netherlands in 1945 without Sjahrir's prior knowledge or consent. It is possible that Sjahrir's addendum may be presenting Hatta in more favorable terms to compensate for the publication of the disparaging remarks he made about Hatta on Banda Neira.

26 Des, fifteen years old at the time of his journey, was delayed at Ambon, taking a job until he was able to obtain a passage on a merchant ship as far as Surabaya, where Hatta collected him and his luggage. Interview Des Alwi, February 1982.

27 Lily G. Sutantio et al., "Kenang-kenangan akan Jasa-jasa Baik Oom Sjahrir, Pencinta dan Sahabat Anak-anak," in Anwar, *Mengenang Sjahrir*, p. 45.

Indonesia in the context of Greater Asia." When he stated that "if Japan is defeated now in this violent war, Indonesia too will be conquered," Hatta was not condoning Japan's invasion but explaining that during the period Japan and the Allies remained locked in combat, Indonesia had an opportunity to organize for the final resistance against the Dutch. An immediate Allied victory would merely restore the Dutch colonial government before Indonesians were prepared to resist it. Hatta had no compunction about stressing the positive aspects of the Japanese invasion, declaring that Indonesia "now feels free of the spiritual stress of being ordered to believe in the low status of its nation."[28] In other words, the "colonial hypnosis" was disappearing.

Hatta would frequently end his speeches on a particularly patriotic note as if to fix firmly in the minds of his audience that Indonesia must remain first and foremost in their thoughts and actions. On one such occasion, he quoted the lines of the French poet, Rene de Clercq, with which he himself had ended his defense speech in Holland:

There is but one country that can be mine,
It grows to the deed, and that deed is mine.[29]

The Japanese authorities decided to promote a new organization to replace the unsuccessful Tiga A, acknowledging that it might be more successful if it appeared to be established and led by Indonesians. Sukarno, Hatta, the veteran nationalist, Ki Hajar Dewantoro, and the Islamic leader, Kiyai Mansur, were given the task of organizing the movement. Sukarno was "Great Leader" and Hatta "General Director," roles they were to play during much of their political partnership.

Hatta saw the opportunities this offered for organizing openly a Java-wide nationalist front with a coordinating central administration. The title "Jawa minshu-soryoku kesshu undo," or Movement for the Total Mobilization of the People of Java, was replaced by the Indonesian name Pusat Tenaga Rakyat [Center of People's Power], abbreviated to the acronym Putera meaning son.[30] As its name suggested, Putera was

28 Mohammad Hatta, "Pidato di Muka Rapat Besar, 8 Desember 1942," in *Kumpulan Pidato*, p. 15.
29 Hatta, "Harapan dan Kewajiban Rakyat di Masa Datang," in ibid., p. 25.
30 Mohammad Hatta, *The Putera Reports: Problems in Indonesian-Japanese Wartime Cooperation,*

intended to be the nerve center of the nationalist movement, the governing body of the long-desired "state within a state."

When describing the aims and purpose of Putera at its official launching on March 9, 1943 in Ikada Square, Hatta again referred to the "development of a new society," reassuring his audience that, unlike Tiga A, Putera was a wholly Indonesian movement: "Today cooperation between the government and the people is strengthened by the establishment of the movement 'Pusat Tenaga Rakyat,'" which, Hatta claimed, would "help the government achieve the final victory in the Greater East Asian War."[31] Significantly Hatta used the word "government" not the "Japanese Army" as if to indicate that Putera's central administration was the nucleus of an Indonesian government acting in conjunction with the people. He explained that Putera was open to all Indonesians, it was not an ordinary organization with restricted membership and set fees. "Everyone is eligible to contribute to it with a new spirit and soul," he declared.[32]

Hatta appealed to his audience to support Putera as wholeheartedly as possible. He tried to convey the message that the present occupation was a temporary arrangement:

> Time passes. We live but a small part of our lives now, the greater part will be in the future. Because of this, struggle on to achieve a radiant and happy future. Let us make the sacrifice for our descendants, our grandchildren, our homeland, our Native Land, and to achieve what we long for: Asia for the Asians. Long live Putera, in its efforts and struggle.[33]

Unfortunately Putera did not live up to Hatta's expectations, surviving for less than a year. The Kempeitai disliked the movement from the start. It criticized the Japanese administration for assigning Japan's mobilization efforts to radical nationalists, whose motives were always suspect. The authorities heeded the warning, and, determined to prevent Putera from developing any political "teeth," they used the old Dutch ploy of

---

translated by W. H. Frederick (Ithaca: Cornell Modern Indonesia Project, 1971), p. 29.

31 Hatta, "Organisasi Kita," in *Kumpulan Pidato*, p. 29.

32 Ibid., p. 30.

33 Ibid., p. 32.

mobilizing through the indigenous rulers and cooperative civil service, the *pangreh praja.*

In his two reports written as general director and head of planning of Putera, Hatta could barely contain his anger and frustration, not just with the Japanese but even more with the *pangreh praja*, especially the Javanese ruling elite, who had followed past practices of sheltering the rural masses from nationalist penetration of their regions. Hatta defended the branch leaders appointed by Putera as leaders whom the people trusted, although not necessarily of high social status, and he denied the *pangreh praja's* claims that they were inexperienced and inept. Urging the traditional rulers to discontinue the practices of the past, Hatta pleaded: "the people's cry must be heeded. Otherwise the people will become disillusioned." Again Hatta was returning to the theme of *kedaulatan rakyat*, stressing that the "involvement of the people is imperative in order to inculcate a determined spirit on the home front."[34]

Hatta did not confine his remarks to Indonesians. In his report, he also criticized the Kempeitai, accusing it of listening to the advice of former PID officers and arresting leftists "who had earned the gratitude of the Japanese Army when it entered Java."[35] He censured the Japanese authorities for forbidding high school teachers to join Putera. Both Hatta and the Japanese realized the power of the schoolroom in inculcating nationalist ideals. "Is Putera a group of bandits capable of corrupting teachers who come too close?" he challenged, storming: "If the Japanese persist in this narrowminded attitude towards an organization which was expressly established by the government to support the Army behind the front lines, it will be difficult for Indonesians to respect them."[36]

In May 1943, the Minister of Greater East Asia, Aoki, paid a visit to Java. As Sukarno was absent from Jakarta, Hatta acted as spokesman for Putera and demanded to know why Prime Minister Tojo had promised independence to Burma and the Philippines but had ignored Indonesia. Hatta warned that it would be difficult to guarantee continuing support for Japan unless an assurance was given that Indonesia would be self-governing. He requested that the use of the national flag and anthem

---

34 Hatta, *Putera Reports*, p. 33.
35 Ibid., pp. 38-39.
36 Ibid., p. 45.

be permitted and that the Japanese system of dividing Indonesia into three completely separate war zones be discontinued.[37] Minister Aokl assured Hatta that his government appreciated Indonesian support and understood the "desires of the people," but he was unprepared to make any statement until he had discussed the matter with Premier Tojo.[38]

Determined to press the independence issue, Hatta broke the regulations by sending a letter direct to Aoki in Tokyo to confirm their conversation, using a naval courier rather than the normal channels. In the Naval Liaison Office in Jakarta, Subardjo was working closely with Rear-Admiral Maeda an officer consistently supportive of the nationalists and with clear socialist sympathies. Maeda also seemed to have an inkling that the victory would not be Japan's and that it was important to prevent recolonization of Asia by the West. As might be expected, Hatta's breach of regulations embarrassed the Japanese Army administration when they learned of it, exacerbating also its relations with the Naval Liaison Office. This, combined with Hatta's gibe at the Kempeitai and his outspoken criticisms of the Japanese administration to convince the Kempeitai that Hatta should be eliminated.

Hatta realized that he had overstepped the security mark when Kempeitai officials came to his office to demand an explanation of his breach of the rules, reminding him that "no letter may leave Indonesia without the permission of the Gunseikan [Head of Army Administration]."[39] Hatta explained that "The subject matter of the letter was already known here, that is, the question of Japanese policy decisions concerning Indonesia," and pointed out: "If we had raised the matter here, undoubtedly the answer would have been 'That is Tokyo's affair,' so we raised the matter directly with Tokyo."[40]

Hatta's communication with Aoki bore fruit. On June 16, 1943, Prime Minister Tojo, speaking in the Japanese Diet, promised "political participation within this year to Malaya, Sumatra, Java, Borneo, and the Celebes." "Political participation" was to be granted to each area

---

37 Kanahele, "Japanese Occupation of Indonesia," p. 92, citing an interview with Hatta, August 26, 1964 and Miyoshi Shunchiro's Memoirs (no pagination).
38 Ibid.
39 Hadji Soebagijo, "Bung Hatta Kita," in *Bung Hatta Mengabdi pada Tjita-Tjita*, p. 32.
40 Ibid.

"according to their abilities."[41] However, the announcement did not include the eastern archipelago, areas such as the Moluccas and Bali, nor was there a clear definition of the nature of the "political participation" to be conceded, disappointing in view of the fact that Burma and the Philippines already had committees actively planning for independence.

In a speech broadcast on June 19, 1943, however, Hatta urged the Indonesian people, especially those in the Outer Islands, to accept Prime Minister Tojo's statement as a step in the right direction, in spite of its shortcomings. The Japanese Navy, which controlled the eastern islands, was clearly unprepared to offer "political participation" to the local people. "Don't be worried that the Outer Islands are being kept back," Hatta reassured his compatriots, "If we analyze properly the explanation offered by the Tokyo Government, it is obvious that, in view of the critical war situation, the Japanese are implementing rational policies."[42] Hatta knew that the Americans had landed on Guadalcanal and that Allied bombers were attacking Ambon and Makassar. He advised the Outer Islanders to build up the nationalist movement, reminding them that, as a result of colonial policies, their foremost leaders had either been concentrated on Java or sent to Boven Digul. He urged his listeners to "organize your manpower as actively as possible, building a new force with a sense of responsibility."[43] The Moluccas in particular needed to strengthen their nationalist sentiment because of long established ties of fealty to the Dutch. Radio was the nationalists' most effective weapon at this time for penetrating the zoning barriers created by the Japanese forces, which were fragmenting their movement.

On July 7, 1943, Tojo made a brief visit to Java. Although no further explanation of Indonesia's political participation was offered, Hatta conceded that he was impressed by Tojo's willingness to meet and talk to the nationalists on Java.[44] The matter became clear when in August 1943 General Harada announced the establishment of a Central Advisory Council and regional councils. As in the case of the "November Promise,"

---

41 See Kanahele, "The Japanese Occupation of Indonesia," p. 93.
42 Mohammad Hatta, "Sambutan Atas Pidato Perdana Menteri Tojo," in *Kumpulan Pidato*, pp. 34-35.
43 Ibid., p. 35.
44 See Kanahele, "Japanese Occupation of Indonesia," p. 94.

the reality was a shadow of the expectation. The councils, apart from having no legislative power, were more restricted than the Dutch Volksraad in that they could not be used as forums for criticizing Japanese policies. Election for leadership positions was allowed, which resulted in Sukarno being elected chairman and Hatta and Ki Hadjar Dewantoro as vice-chairmen. To the nationalists' surprise, General Harada canceled Hatta's and Ki Hadjar's names, although, after protest, Hatta was appointed an ordinary member of the Central Advisory Council.

It was evident that Hatta was out of favor and that the Japanese were determined to break up the nationalist oligarchy of four, known whimsically as the *Empat Serangkai* or Four-Leaved Clover, the Putera leadership. At the reception for members of the Central Advisory Council held in the former Governor-General's residence in Bogor, Hatta was noticeably low down in the protocol ranking.[45] The Japanese appeared to be trying to undermine his leadership position.

It was almost immediately following the Japanese prime minister's visit that Hatta's Japanese interpreter and liaison officer, Miyoshi, discovered a Kempeitai plot to assassinate Hatta. Convinced that Hatta's criticisms and independent behavior were related to his prewar "Communist" background, the security police devised a simple plan. While Hatta was being driven to Bandung from Jakarta, his car would be forced off the road over a steep mountain pass at Puncak, resulting in his "accidental" death. Miyoshi, whose duty was to accompany Hatta, would also have been killed. Naturally he was concerned, not just for Hatta, whom he liked, but also for his own life.[46]

Miyoshi tried to persuade the deputy head of the Kempeitai, Murase, to revise his plans, and Murase agreed to interrogate Hatta personally, inviting him to morning coffee in his house.[47] Hatta recalled that it was the month of Ramadan, the yearly Islamic fast, so he could partake of neither food nor drink, and that Murase courteously ordered that the refreshments be removed without partaking of any himself.[48]

---

45 Hadji Soebagijo, "Bung Hatta Kita," p. 33.
46 Kanahele, "Japanese Occupation of Indonesia," p. 95, where he cites Miyoshi's Memoirs.
47 This could have been interpreted as a threat as the Kempeitai was noted for hosting its victims before their demise. See John Coast, *Recruit to Revolution* (London: Christophers, 1952), p. 9.
48 Hatta, *Memoir*, p. 425.

According to Hatta's account, he was questioned about capitalism and imperialism. "I put forward my opinions based on the theories of Sombart and Max Weber," recalled Hatta, obviously deliberately avoiding Marx. Stating firmly that he "very much regretted that Japan was attracted to imperialism," he was careful to cite China as an example rather than Indonesia.[49] He informed Murase that he had discussed the question of Japanese imperialism with the civilian adviser to the Japanese Administration, Mr. Hayashi Kyujiro, who had agreed that, in a sense, Japan's war was imperialistic.[50] If Hatta's account is accurate, he was clearly playing on rivalries and ill-feeling which often existed between the Japanese civilian and military personnel, practicing a policy of "divide and survive." Murase was doubtless irked by Hayashi's statement but could not refute it in front of an Indonesian.

No immediate action was taken against Hatta, although the Kempeitai interview alerted him that he would have to be more reticent if he wanted to remain effective. As the war turned increasingly against the Japanese, the possibility of Indonesia becoming a battleground mounted. In October 1943, the Japanese established several defense corps on Java, the most significant being the Sukarela Tentara Pembela Tanah Air [Volunteer Army for the Defense of the Native Land], abbreviated to Peta. Its creation was received enthusiastically by the nationalists, for it meant that at last the Indonesian people were to be trained to fight and use weapons, one of the major factors limiting their earlier efforts to oppose the Dutch.

Hatta reminded his youthful audience at a public meeting in Ikada Square on November 3, 1943 that they were there to defend their own country, not Japan, although he acknowledged diplomatically that "Nippon has freed us from Dutch imperialism: we thank heaven for this and also thank the Japanese Army." He appealed: "Young Indonesians, never forget that no respected nation in this world surrenders its entire defense to another nation."[51]

B. M. Diah, a young journalist and active nationalist, who was in Ikada Square, recalled that Hatta displayed unusual fire, "shrieking out" his

---

49 Ibid.
50 Kanahele, "Japanese Occupation of Indonesia," p. 96, n. 27.
51 Mohammad Hatta, "Sukarela Membela Tanah Air," in *Kumpulan Pidato*, p. 297.

message, which received a warm reception from his youthful audience.[52] By stressing the words *"Tanah Air"* or "Native Land" in the acronym Peta, Hatta and Sukarno pressed home that the Japanese instructors' encouragement to fight to the death meant self-sacrifice for Indonesia not for Japan.

Hatta's first intimation that he might be about to undergo another period of exile was when he noticed an announcement in the local newspaper that Sukarno and a religious leader would be visiting Tokyo, accompanied by a third person, an intellectual, who would remain there to study *Nippon Sheishin* in Japan. "I already guessed that the third person was me," commented Hatta ruefully.[53] His associates suggested that he go into hiding rather than allow himself to be exiled to Japan, but Hatta knew that this was impossibly dangerous because of the ubiquity of Japanese informers.[54] When people were starving, the temptation to betray their brothers for a ration of rice was very strong. One of the unpleasant factors of the Japanese occupation was the extent to which the traditional communal spirit was broken down.

Before leaving for Tokyo, Hatta was interviewed by Harada, who explained to him that Sukarno and Ki Bagus Hadikusumo, an Islamic leader, were being sent to Japan at Tokyo's request but that he, on the contrary, was going there to study *Nippon Sheishin*, so that on his return to Indonesia he could write a book on the subject.[55] Harada advised Hatta not to discuss any matters concerning Putera while in Japan; in other words, not to stir up any unnecessary trouble.

On November 10, Sukarno, Hatta, and Ki Bagus Hadikusumo boarded an airplane for Tokyo, traveling via Manila and Taipeh. In Manila, they noticed that the city streets were still sporting the decorations erected for the celebration of Philippine independence, which had been declared a month previously. Sukarno was so moved that he burst into tears, Miyoshi recalled.[56] A further insult was that Indonesia had been omitted from the Greater East Asia Conference, held the week before their arrival

---

52 B. M. Diah, "Manusia Hatta," in *Bung Hatta: Pribadinya dalam Kenangan*, p. 569.
53 Hatta, *Memoir*, p. 426.
54 Ibid.
55 Ibid., p. 427.
56 Myoshi's Memoirs, as cited in Kanahele, "Japanese Occupation of Indonesia," p. 294, n. 62.

in Tokyo, at which Burma, the Philippines, Thailand, Manchukuo, China, and "Free India" were represented. The meeting had been convened to solidify mutual cooperation between Japan and her Asian partners,[57] which seemed to cast doubt on Indonesia's status as a partner.

Perhaps to mollify the visiting Indonesians, they were given a particularly warm reception in Tokyo. Miyoshi was puzzled as to what to do about Hatta, and he approached Army Headquarters to find out exactly where he was to be taken. To his surprise, he discovered that the Headquarters staff knew nothing about the plan to exile Hatta, nor did they approve of it, declaring it to be impossible to provide proper supervision for him in Tokyo.[58] Meanwhile Sukarno had also pleaded with Tojo on Hatta's behalf, declaring that he personally needed Hatta's assistance. Tojo agreed to Sukarno's request, and also ordered that, along with his two associates, Hatta too should be honored with an award from the Emperor, the Holy Gem Star, Class III.

For Hatta the award had special significance; it meant that he was now inviolable; the Kempeitai was not allowed to harm anyone who had been honored by the Emperor: "From that moment, I felt free of the Kempeitai threat," Hatta recorded. "Truly at that time I felt protected by God the Almighty, to whom be praise!"[59] (As a matter of interest, this was not Hatta's first meeting with Emperor Hirohito. They had been fellow students in a vacation course in Europe in the 1920s.[60])

Hatta returned home with a new sense of security and an even greater assurance that he was divinely protected. He noticed at once that an explosive situation was building up in Indonesia, as the people experienced hunger and oppression on a scale far exceeding the vicissitudes under the Dutch regime. Anwar Tjokroaminoto, a son of the former Sarikat Islam leader, who worked closely with Sukarno and Hatta, remarked on Hatta's anguish at the widespread starvation. "He could not stand seeing the fate of his people who every day seemed to be sprawled around, dead from hunger."[61]

---

57 Kanahele, "Japanese Occupation of Indonesia," p. 108.
58 Ibid., p. 107.
59 Hatta, Memoir, p. 432.
60 See Julinar Idris Koestono, "Bung Hatta: Pembimbing Rakyat dan Keluarga Kami," in Bung Hatta: Pribadinya dalam Kenangan, p. 15.
61 H. Anwar Tjokroaminoto, "Jang Utama Bung Hatta," in Bung Hatta Mengabdi pada Tjita-Tjita, p.

Hatta's second Putera report, although less aggressive than the first, drew attention to inadequacies in the Japanese administration of the country. In particular it highlighted the rice shortages on Java and the hunger of the masses. Hatta pointed out that "if the distribution of rice in the villages were regulated to ensure that each person would be able to buy his daily rice on the spot in the established amount," people might increase production. He also pointed to the acute clothing shortage, claiming "indeed there are many who are almost naked."[62] Although Hatta did not directly attack the widespread recruitment of young Indonesians as *romusha*, now a bitter issue among the people, he did underline a sentence in his Public Welfare section, which could be construed as an indirect reference to the *romusha* and the shortage of rural labor. It read: "It is not the people who need jobs, but the jobs that need people."[63]

Hatta's report heralded the demise of Putera and its replacement by a new organization firmly under Japanese supervision, the Jawa Hokokai [Java Service Association]. Although appointed a vice-chairman, an appointment he tried to refuse at first, Hatta could not disguise his dislike for the new movement. "Under Putera, the nationalists actively guided the people," he remarked, "now under Jawa Hokokai they sit idly by in their Jakarta Offices."[64]

It was clear that young Indonesians were becoming restive and rebellious, impatient at the inability of their traditional and nationalist leaders to stop the widespread exploitation and deprivation of the masses, while the leaders themselves lived in relative affluence in their comfortable offices and well-appointed ex-colonial houses. Indonesian youth were caught in a love/hate relationship with their Japanese rulers, admiring the spirit of sacrifice and discipline of the officers who organized their militia training, and yet hating Japanese cruelty and inhuman indifference to the plight of the people around them.

In the initial period of the Occupation, the Japanese Propaganda Department had encouraged the establishment of youth hostels or *asrama* for indoctrination purposes, aiming especially at the educated

491.
62 Hatta, *Putera Reports*, p. 67.
63 Ibid., p. 111.
64 As cited in Kanahele, "Japanese Occupation of Indonesia," p. 143.

youth for whom no tertiary institutions existed. Even before Sukarno returned to Java, Hatta had established links with the *Asrama Angkatan Baru Indonesia* [Indonesian New Generation Hostel] situated at Jalan Menteng 31 in the heart of Jakarta, encouraging the young men to form cadres.[65] Sjahrir's main contacts were with the medical school hostel, the only tertiary institution allowed to continue to operate in Jakarta. Both Sukarno and Hatta remained close to the radical *asrama* youth leaders, and they were permitted to lecture to the students on political themes.

In October 1944, Rear-Admiral Maeda established a new *asrama* in Jakarta under Subardjo's supervision,[66] following the announcement in the Diet by the new prime minister, Koiso, that in view of the endeavors of the East Indies to "carry out the Great East Asia War... we declare here that we intend to recognize their independence in the future."[67] From the time of the Koiso declaration, a statement which sounded like music in Hatta's ears, the Japanese were noticeably more accommodating to the nationalists.

In retrospect, Maeda alleged that he "felt very strongly that Indonesia would need capable leaders of the younger generation," so he invited leading nationalists, including Sjahrir, to lecture at his *asrama*.[68] Sjahrir was convinced that Maeda's primary purpose in establishing the *asrama* was to penetrate and control the PKI underground, while Hatta believed Maeda's motives to be less Machiavellian, commenting that "Maeda and many of the naval officers under him were genuinely sincere in their desire for Indonesian independence."[69]

Amir Sjarifuddin's underground network, which had strong support from PKI sympathizers, had suffered considerable harassment from the Kempeitai. In 1943 Amir himself was arrested by the Kempeitai and later sentenced to death. Sukarno and Hatta pleaded with General Harada for clemency, pointing out that Amir's death would engender anger and resentment. In a climate when Indonesians were increasingly reluctant

---

65 Boerhanoedin Harahap, "Bung Hatta Dalam Dwitunggal," in *Bung Hatta: Pribadinya dalam Kenangan*, p. 431.

66 Kanahele, "Japanese Occupation of Indonesia," p. 172.

67 Ibid., p. 163, n. 5, citing *Teikoku Gikae Shugiin Gijinoku Dai Hachi-ju-go-kai* [Imperial Diet Lower House Proceedings, 85th Session].

68 Anderson, *Java in a Time of Revolution*, p. 44.

69 Kahin, *Nationalism and Revolution*, pp. 117-18.

to aid the Japanese war effort, Harada heeded the warning, commuting Amir's sentence to life imprisonment.

At a public rally in Ikada Square, Hatta expressed his joy at Japan's promise of independence and the immediate restoration of the right to sing the national anthem and fly the Indonesian flag. He reached out to the youth around him, trying to convey to them within the limits of the Occupation's censorship the struggle which would lie ahead in defending any grant of independence. He pleaded:

> You who have been trained by the Japanese Army, be willing to fight, be willing to defend your own country. The past decade of our movement shows that young people are prepared to struggle in the front lines, are prepared to pioneer our national struggle. I believe in the sincerity of Indonesian youth, I believe in their willingness to struggle and suffer. *Young Indonesians, you are heroes in my heart.*[70]

Hatta was to use this last sentence many times in the future, and it was to become especially associated with him as time and time again he looked to the oncoming youthful generations to fulfill his concept and ideal of independent Indonesia.

---

70 Mohammad Hatta, "Pidato Pembukaan Rapat Besar di Lapangan Ikada," September 11, 1944, in *Kumpulan Pidato*, p. 51.

CHAPTER EIGHT
INDEPENDENCE PROCLAIMED

We appeal to the world powers, who are now determining the future world structure, to approve of Indonesia's independence. We are ready to receive help and guidance from the International Body entrusted with the safeguarding of would peace; and we are anxious to give of our manpower and of our country's material wealth towards the building up of would prosperity. But do grant us the right to self-determination, do give us the opportunity to live under a government of our own choice and of a form suited to our national needs.[1]

The year 1945 opened in an atmosphere of gathering storm and impending crisis. The Allied forces were pushing strongly to regain occupied territories; it was assumed that they must soon land on Java. Japan's inevitable defeat, although not unwelcome, would not bring relief; it would herald the return of the Dutch. For Sukarno and Hatta personally there was an added element of danger. Monitored Allied broadcasts contained statements which placed them both in the category of war criminal. There was a clear threat in the Dutch assertions that "when we get back to Java we shall never forget those who cried: 'Let's iron out America and use a crowbar on England.'"[2] Hatta's name was now so closely linked with that of Sukarno that he would share the blame for Sukarno's more defiant propaganda outbursts. There was another consideration. By eliminating both Sukarno and Hatta, the Dutch would again deprive the nationalist movement of its most effective leadership, as they had done

---

1 Mohammad Hatta, "Indonesian Aims and Ideals," in *Portrait of a Patriot*, p. 503. Speech, August 23, 1945.
2 See Anderson, *Java in a Time of Revolution*, p. 66.

from 1934 to 1942.

Hatta and Sukarno continued to press the Japanese Army authorities to widen defense training so that Indonesians could more effectively resist a resumption of Dutch power. Yet the Japanese were themselves in a dilemma. They needed to use the Indonesian militia to defend the archipelago against Allied forces but they were uncertain of how far the Indonesians would support them. A mutiny by Peta units at Blitar in East Java on February 14, 1945 warned the Japanese that Indonesian resentment against them was reaching boiling point.

Hatta and Sukarno also sensed that the patience of the young people was wearing thin, that the spirit of the *samurai* instilled in the *pemuda* by their Japanese mentors was seeking an immediate target. The acute shortage of basic necessities and the widespread malnutrition and suffering had by early 1945 created a wave of hatred of everything associated with the Japanese. Having acquired a fighting spirit, the *pemuda* were ready to vent their wrath on their present enemy.

But news broadcasts indicated that Japan was now a spent force. It would be wasteful for the *pemuda* to dissipate their resources and manpower on avenging the indignities of the last three years. Their fighting skills and spirit had to be held in check for the ultimate trial, the return of the Dutch under the protection of the Allied forces.

Disaffection with the current situation and a sense of approaching danger inevitably created a volatile atmosphere. There was mounting criticism of the leaders most closely associated with the Japanese, in particular Sukarno and Hatta. The *pemuda* leaders accused the two of having failed to alleviate the distress of the forced laborers, the romusha. According to one *pemuda* in Sjahrir's group, "it was felt that the Japanese were benefitting from Sukarno's power and leadership, that the community was not being protected."[3] Indonesian officials connected with *romusha* recruitment were earning the title "*Anjing Jepang*" ["Japanese Dog"], including Sukarno, who had participated overenthusiastically in a well-publicized Propaganda Department campaign to incite young men to "join the army of laborers." In his autobiography, Sukarno admitted with a sense of genuine remorse that he had "shipped to their death" thousands

---

3 Subadio Sastrosatomo, "Bung Karno dengan Keyakinan dan Takdirnya," p. 87.

of *romusha*, but defended this as the only way to "save millions."[4]

Hatta had begun to carry out an investigation into the situation of the *romusha*, establishing and leading a group, the Badan Pembantu Prajurit Pekerja [Body to Help the Worker Soldier], aimed at providing relief aid for them.[5] At a meeting of the Central Advisory Council on February 21, 1945, Hatta launched an attack on the Japanese authorities for their treatment of these young laborers, putting forward evidence which he had collected over the previous six months to show the extent of their maltreatment.[6] It was a much more weighted critique than the veiled protests contained in his Second Putera Report, an indication that he had regained confidence following his near escape from liquidation at the hands of the Kempeitai.

The nationalists generally displayed a bolder spirit at this meeting, with demands that Indonesia's independence preparations be set in motion in the spirit of the prevailing catch-cry: "*Merdeka atau Mati*" ["Freedom or Death"]. On March 1, the Japanese administration announced that Tokyo had given permission for the establishment of a body to plan the details of Indonesian independence in fulfillment of Koiso's promises. On April 29, 1945, the membership of this body, the Badan Penyelidik Kemerdekaan Indonesia [Body to Investigate Indonesian Independence] or BPKI was announced.[7]

Surprisingly, the pattern of leadership was altered, and neither Sukarno nor Hatta was appointed to a top position. Instead an elderly, conservative ex-Budi Utomo member, Dr. Rajiman Wediodiningrat, took the chair. It might appear that the Japanese were trying to reduce the influence of the radical nationalists in favor of the conservative Javanese elite to balance the granting of greater political freedom. The sixty-two Indonesian members appointed to the BPKI were a mixture of prominent nationalists and senior *pangreh praja*, with a noticeable minority of Muslim representation. There were eight Japanese delegates.

Despite criticism from the general public as well as the various youth

---

4   See Adams, *Sukarno*, pp. 192-93.
5   Kanahele, "Japanese Occupation of Indonesia," p. 189, n. 9.
6   Ibid.
7   See B. R. O'G. Anderson, *Some Aspects of Indonesian Politics under the Japanese Occupation*, 1944-45 (Ithaca: Cornell Modern Indonesia Project, 1961).

groups, Sukarno and Hatta were still regarded by most Indonesians on Java as the foremost leaders of the drive towards independence. But in the mood of disillusionment with everything Japanese which was gathering strength by early 1945, Sjahrir's prestige too was very high. Because of his non-collaboration, he had acquired considerable heroic kudos among urban youth. "To be free of the stain of cooperation with the Japanese was very unusual in the circles of the national leadership at that time," commented the Indonesian writer, Y. B. Mangunwijaya.[8] According to Subadio, then a youth in the Sjahrir group, "The *Tritunggal* of Sukarno, Hatta and Sjahrir constituted the most effective leadership in Indonesia. Sjahrir respected Hatta's integrity and leadership qualities, Hatta admired Sjahrir's political acumen."[9] Both relied on Sukarno's mass appeal for Javanese support. Sjahrir's activities, however, had obscured him from the public eye and his identification with youth and his brand of socialism alienated him to some extent from the older generation. Sukarno and Hatta, then, in the eyes of the general public, stood above Sjahrir as well as all the other national leaders. And now that these two men were working in harmony, they provided a satisfying type of leadership because they "*Saling isi-mengisi*," they complemented one another.[10]

Sukarno on his own was not sufficiently stable. His eloquence and fiery emotionalism, although highly effective in drawing Indonesians to his cause, were not the only leadership qualities required. Charisma had to be backed by firmness and concentrated effort. While people delighted in Sukarno's warmth and color, drawing reassurance from his exuberance, they also appreciated the presence of the rock-like, level-headed Hatta by his side. In the spheres of planning and organization, Hatta came to the fore, his industriousness, careful attention to detail, and ability to judge the long-range consequences of an action blending well with Sukarno's romanticism and sensibility towards Javanese cultural traits.

The two men had one strong characteristic in common to bind them together: their total and unequivocal dedication to the achievement of Indonesian independence. In 1945, they were also drawing together to counter charges of being leading collaborators and to ward off verbal

---

8 Y. B. Mangunwijaya, "'Archetype' Sutan Sjahrir," in *Mengenang Sjahrir*, p. 220.
9 Interview with Subadio Sastrosatomo, February 22, 1982.
10 As reported in *Kompas*, March 15, 1980.

attacks from militant youth, defending one another rather than putting forward their individual viewpoint as in the 1930s. Yet, inevitably there were strains when two men of such totally different personality worked together. Hatta, as was his nature, did not refrain from speaking out bluntly if Sukarno's ideas were, in his opinion, far-fetched, bridling him. Hatta's stern rejection of Sukarno's over-fanciful suggestions acted as a control mechanism, as acknowledged by fellow nationalists.

Sukarno himself graphically admitted: "Hatta always gave the impression of rain. If I was in a real good mood and full of ideas and then happened to encounter Hatta, I felt I was suddenly surprised by a shower of rain and got wet all over the body. My good mood was gone, and also my ideas."[11] "That was why Sukarno always rather resented Hatta," commented Abu Hanifah, one of the youth leaders, when later recording Sukarno's statement, adding: "but it was a fact that many times Hatta prevented Sukarno from doing things he would have been sorry for afterwards."[12]

It is possible to detect a certain similarity between the Sukarno-Hatta relationship and that of their former mentors, the Javanese Tjokroaminoto and the Minangkabau Haji Agus Salim, if one examines Alfian's description of the two Sarikat Islam leaders:

He [Haji Agus Salim] was, in a significant way, the real power-house behind Tjokroaminoto in running Sarikat Islam and facing all its problems. As Tjokroaminoto was the orator *par excellence* of Sarikat Islam and a remarkable politician in his own right, Salim was to provide it with his intelligence and knowledge, things which might seem more important since they represented the very soul of the movement.[13]

Alfian here indicates that the outstanding Minangkabau nationalists were forced to work in the shadow of Javanese leaders. The Javanese people responded to a father-figure who was unmistakably imbued with Javanese

---

11 Cited in Abu Hanifah, *Tales of a Revolution*, p. 163.
12 Ibid.
13 Alfian, "Islamic Modernism in Indonesian Politics, the Muhammadijah Movement during the Dutch Colonial Period (1912-1942)" (Ph.D. dissertation, University of Wisconsin, 1969), p. 177.

culture. Nor was eloquence in itself sufficient. Mohammad Roem, a young colleague of Haji Agus Salim, described him as "a good talker!" In this he was different from Hatta, who "was a listener."[14] Eloquence, too, required a framework of Javanese culture.

For both Sukarno and Hatta, the forthcoming deliberations of the independence planning committee, the BPKI, were taking precedence over other matters. Sjahrir had strong doubts about the capacity of a predominantly Javanese cooperating elite working under the auspices of an authoritarian Japanese regime to shape a democratic nation. He feared that the masses would be locked into a political system as "feudalistic" as past regimes. His forebodings and his criticisms of the Committee's resolutions he formulated into a small booklet, *Our Struggle*.[15] Six months later this work would have a profound impact on political thought and action, making Hatta the mediator trying to keep the balance between Sjahrir and his *pemuda* group on the one side and Sukarno and many of the leading figures in Hatta's PI peer group on the other.

Sukarno clearly sensed the incompatibility between himself and Sjahrir, and may have resented Sjahrir's prestige among the youth. In his autobiography, Sukarno suggests that Sjahrir deliberately undermined his position among the *pemuda* in the final days of the Japanese Occupation:

> Never to my face but secretly, always he [Sjahrir] sneered, "Sukarno is crazy... Sukarno is Japanese-minded... Sukarno is a coward." He was vicious. And what exactly did Sjahrir do for the Republic?... His entire underground effort can be summed up by saying that he sat quietly and safely away somewhere listening to a clandestine radio.[16]

---

14 Interview Mohamad Roem, February 1982. See also Ny. Maria Ullfah Soebadio, "Bung Hatta dan Saya," in *Bung Hatta: Pribadinya dalam Kenangan*, p. 262. Ny. Soebadio recalls her first meeting with Hatta in the Netherlands when he came with Haji Agus Salim to visit her father. She comments: "Bung Hatta hardly spoke at all, quite different from Oom Salim who told many stories. In this my first meeting with Bung Hatta, I judged him to be a shy and unassuming person."

15 Sutan Sjahrir, *Our Struggle*, translated with an introduction by B. O'G. Anderson (Ithaca: Cornell Modern Indonesia Project, 1968).

16 Adams, *Sukarno*, p. 210.

The first session of the BPKI opened on May 29, 1945, in the former Volksraad building, proceeding until June 1. During the session the issue of whether Indonesia should be an Islamic state was debated. Hatta proposed the establishment of a state which separated the affairs of government from religious affairs. When commenting on this opening session of the BPKI in the latter years of his life, Hatta recalled:

> At that time, I said that if we established a free state, don't let us just have the same basis as European states; there is no need to repeat the history of Western countries which experienced opposition between religion and state.[17]

Islam seeks to be a system which penetrates every corner of a person's life, including politics. In traditional Minangkabau society, apart from the extremist *Padri* period, Islam and *adat* had constituted separate yet interlocking systems, Islam providing the spiritual buttress required to enhance *adat*. In the opening chapters of his memoirs, Hatta commented that "the Prophet Mohammad permitted the use of customary law in Arabia which ensured public well-being,"[18] signifying that it was quite in order to have separate state and religious legal and governing systems.

Hatta, in his memoirs, described the idealistic influences which were inspiring the committee members during their deliberations, as if to refute charges that they were not socialist in outlook:

> In their spirit was brought to life a divine message to shape an Indonesian State which protected every Indonesian person and the whole land of Indonesia, to advance public welfare, to improve people's lives, implementing a world order which is based on freedom, lasting peace, and social justice.

Hatta recalled that the majority of members were reluctant to answer directly the question raised in the chairman's opening address: "What will be the foundation of the state which we are about to shape?"[19] If Islam was

---

17 Hatta, *Bung Hatta Menjawab*, p. 89.
18 Hatta, *Memoir*, p. 2.
19 Ibid., p. 435.

not directly designated as the basis, what was the alternative?

Hatta was not present at the fourth and final day of the session when Sukarno delivered his famous speech proposing that the new nation should be founded on five principles, the *Panca Sila*, which in themselves were a "*philosophische grondslag*" [philosophical basis].[20] The five principles proposed were: *Kebangsaan* [Nationalism], *Internationalisme* or *Peri-Kemanusiaan* [Humanitarianism], *Mufakat* or *Demokrasi, Kesejahteraan Sosial* [social Welfare], and *Ketuhanan* [Belief in God], all of which Sukarno believed could be reduced to the one term *gotong-royong*. Sukarno admitted that his *Panca Sila* were based on the general ideals of the international socialist movement, Nationalism, Democracy, and Socialism being akin to Sun Yat-sen's "Three Principles of the People," symbolic of a socialist state, although in Indonesia's case, in view of the fifth *sila*, also a theist one.[21]

When reviewing the committee's deliberations many years later, Hatta acknowledged that he had always approved of the *Panca Sila*. He pointed out that as long as "Belief in God" was written into the basic principles of the state, the Islamic tenet that God must be at the center of every Muslim's activities was ensured:

> Belief in God is not just a way of respecting each person's creed, as was first suggested by Bung Karno, but is a basic principle which leads towards truth, justice, goodness, honesty, and brotherhood.[22]

The broad concept of "Belief in God" also allowed an escape route for Hatta from any obligations, as an orthodox Muslim and the son of an *ulama*, to support the Islamic state.

---

20 Saifuddin Anshari, *The Jakarta Charter of June 1945; The Struggle for an Islamic Constitution in Indonesia* (Kuala Lumpur: Muslim Youth Movement of Malaysia, 1979), p. 17, n. 1.

21 Ibid., p. 14. Sukarno admitted that the Dutch Marxist, Baars, had influenced his thinking. Hatta has defended Sukarno as the originator of the *Panca Sila* and, according to his secretary I. Wangsa Widjaja, was critical of Yamin's documentation of the preparatory committee. (Interview, I. Wangsa Widjaja, February 1982.) Frans Seda claims that Sukarno was already working on the *Panca Sila* concept while in exile on Flores. See Frans Seda, "Bung Karno, Mikul Duwur, Mendem Jero," in *Bung Karno dalam Kenangan*, ed. Solichin Salam, p. 74.

22 Mohammad Hatta, *Menuju Negara Hukum.* An address delivered on receiving the degree of Doctor *Honoris Causa* from the University of Indonesia on 30 August 1975 on the Thirtieth Anniversary of Indonesian Independence (Jakarta: Yayasan Idayu, 1975), pp. 9-10.

In deference to Islamic dissatisfaction with the *Panca Sila*, Sukarno and Hatta led a Committee of Nine whose task was to examine the five "*sila*" further. A compromise solution was reached. "Belief in God" was placed before the other four principles with the addition of a short clause: "with an obligation to carry out the *shari'ah Islam* [Islamic law] for its adherents."[23] This decision was incorporated into a special document, entitled the Jakarta Charter, which was to serve as a Preamble to the Draft Constitution.

Hatta later described the dilemma facing the committee drafting the constitution:

> When first we discussed the governmental design of our democracy in the Committee for the Preparation of Indonesian Independence, we had before us two systems of democracy proposed by the members, that is the system of democracy with a parliamentary cabinet, such as was customary in Western Europe prior to the Second World War, and a system of democracy with a presidential cabinet as used in the United States of America.[24]

Hatta explained that, although parliamentary government was believed to be more progressive, on weighing up the two systems, the committee "almost unanimously chose the Presidential Cabinet system," He added: "The deciding factor was that, although in theory the parliamentary cabinet system was more advanced democracy, yet in the transitional period and time of development for Indonesia, action and decision must be taken more quickly."[25] Hatta's basic common sense combined with experience gained over the last three years no doubt persuaded him to accept the majority decision. It was not one which met with Sjahrir's approval.

Undoubtedly a strong presidency suited Sukarno, who knew he was the most likely candidate for the position. In some ways, the Draft Constitution compromised between the Javanese conception of strong

---

23 See Anshari, *Jakarta Charter*, p. 19.
24 Mohammad Hatta, *Sesudah 25 Tahun*, a Speech delivered on the Ninth Anniversary of Sjiah Kuala Darussalam University in Banda Atjeh on 2 September 1970 (Jakarta: Djambatan, 1970), p. 15.
25 Ibid.

184 INDONESIA FREE: A POLITICAL BIOGRAPHY OF MOHAMMAD HATTA

centralized rule and the democracy of the Minangkabau, as the President's authority was balanced by two representative bodies. Yet the framers of the Constitution were aware that Sukarno was not the only leader of the nationalist movement, that the accepted formula was "Sukarno-Hatta." It was decided to institute a vice-presidency to cover the problem of where to place Hatta.

Although the Vice-President's duties were to assist the President, in practice the two leaders continued to play the type of leadership role at which they were most talented. According to Karim Pringgodigdo, who was to become chief of the Presidential Secretariat, "the establishment of the office of Vice-President is, of course, essentially related to the emergence of the dual unity of Sukarno and Hatta (*Dwi Tunggal*) in 1945," adding: "Thus the Vice-President was not allotted functions apart from the functions of the President, for the status of the Vice-President was no different from that of the President."[26] In theory, this statement was not quite accurate but in practice Hatta did have very strong powers to act independently of the President.

Hatta later commented that he considered the *Dwi Tunggal* to be a unique relationship between a President and Vice-President.[27] It freed Sukarno to tour the countryside, speaking to the people and arousing their spirit, while Hatta tackled the intricate details of administering a nation, the job at which he was most skilled.

The decision of the drafting committee which did concern Sjahrir and the *Kedaulatan rakyat* group was the granting, under Article IV, of Transitional Provisions which stated that, until the formation of the representative assemblies, the Majelis Permusyawaratan Rakyat [People's Deliberative Council -- MPR] and the Dewan Perwakilan Rakyat [People's Representative Council -- DPR], "all state powers would be exercised by the President assisted by a National Committee."[28] As Pringgodigdo admitted, these provisions gave the President legal power "to act with dictatorial authority since there was absolutely no basis for interpreting

---

26 A. K. Pringgodigdo, *The Office of President in Indonesia as Defined in the Three Constitutions in Theory and Practice*, trans. A. Brotherton (Ithaca: Cornell Modern Indonesia Project, 1957), p. 30.

27 Hatta, *Memoir*, p. 461.

28 Pringgodigdo, *Office of President*, p. 6.

what was described as the assistance of a National Committee as a factor of restraint." The Draft Constitution, however, also made clear that this was only a temporary arrangement as "within six months from the date of the termination of the war in Asia, the President of Indonesia will give effect to all requirements specified in this Constitution."[29] In other words, the Transitional Clauses were an attempt to legitimize the new government until general elections for the various legislative bodies could be arranged.

Hatta later defended the democracy of the presidential system in the Draft Constitution:

> In a system of democracy with a Presidential Cabinet, the two governing bodies, President and Parliament, are equally strong. The President cannot dissolve the Parliament and the Parliament cannot dismiss the President. In order to prevent continual discord between the President and the People's Representative Council, which could paralyze government, the two must cooperate in a business-like way.[30]

To Hatta, the important factor in achieving *kedaulatan rakyat* was to institute a system of local autonomy. The power of the ruler in the Minangkabau had been kept in check because of the strong *demokrasi asli* in the village or *nagari*. Hatta, as his Perhimpunan Indonesia colleagues knew from past discussions, was a federalist, believing that Indonesia must have a constitutional system which allowed regions the opportunity to govern their own affairs. There was obviously a general sense of disquiet in the nationalist movement that Hatta might not be prepared to yield on this important issue, that this could be the breaking point of the *Dwi Tunggal*. So great was the anxiety that Hatta would stick by his individual viewpoint, that on the evening before the issue was scheduled to be aired in the BPKI, Hatta was awakened from his sleep to find a group of *pemuda* urgently requesting an interview. B. M. Diah, the journalist, recalled the intrusion into Hatta's home. "Their aim was that Bung Hatta should not

---

29 Ibid.
30 Hatta, *Sesudah 25 Tahun*, pp. 15-16.

impede the independent state of Indonesia being organized as one unity rather than as a proliferation of small states." He added: "They were aware that if Bung Karno upheld to the death the unitary state, a great conflict might arise between the two leaders." Hatta promised that "a dangerous controversy" between him and Sukarno would not develop.[31] Hatta believed that as long as the Constitution guaranteed regional autonomy, the question of whether the state was unitary or federalist was largely irrelevant. From now on, Hatta concentrated on pressing for regional autonomy.[32]

There were other sections of the Constitution where Hatta also had to battle for his point of view, such as to obtain a Bill of Rights. A hotly debated issue was whether to permit the formation of political parties. This time Sukarno won, pointing out that such organizations might threaten unity. Hatta had always seen political parties as a means of allowing factions in society to express their individual viewpoint. A parliament was in itself a "unity in diversity," a concept which was to become the motto of the new state: *Bhinneka Tunggal Ika*.

In the economic section, Chapter 33 of the Draft Constitution, Hatta was allowed his head, putting forward his views on the importance of cooperatives both as an economic concept and to build up the strength of weak economic groups. He proposed that the following clauses be inserted: "The economy of the country is built upon terms of a cooperative effort based on the principle of human relations." He stressed that "the main branches of production... must be owned by the State," "the land and water and the natural products in them must be owned by the State and must be used for the maximum prosperity of the people."[33]

In an address to an Economic Conference which he chaired in Yogyakarta six months later, Hatta explained that "the economy of a country is generally determined by three things. Firstly, the wealth of the

---

31 B. M. Diah, "Manusia Hatta," in *Bung Hatta: Pribadinya dalam Kenangan*, p. 570.

32 According to Hatta in his booklet *Pendidikan Nasional Indonesia*, p. 29, "the aims of decentralisation and autonomy which were supported by the *Pendidikan Nasional Indonesia* lived on in Article 18 of the Constitution concerning regional government." According to Professor Kuntjoro Purbopranoto, "Bung Hatta dan Demokrasi Kita," in *Bung Hatta Mengabdi pada Tjita-Tjita*, p. 349, Hatta rejected the creation of a *Machtstaat*, where the state had excessive powers.

33 Cited in M. Hatta, "Message to the Chinese Group Conference," in *Portrait of a Patriot*, p. 496. Yogyakarta, September 17, 1946.

land, secondly, its position towards other countries in the international sphere; thirdly, the nature, capability and aims of its people." He added:

> In Indonesia's case, another section must be added, that is its history as a colony. Because Indonesia was constrained under Dutch colonialism for three centuries, its economic situation as a whole is not as mentioned above. Indonesia's land is rich, producing hundreds of thousands of products every year for the outside world but the Indonesian people themselves are poverty-stricken and miserable in the midst of abundant riches.... The economic basis in the future will avoid individualism as much as possible and come as close as possible to collectivism, that is of maintaining an equal level of prosperity.[34]

Hatta knew that the Indonesian trader and farmer was vulnerable to international consortiums and world marketing systems. Although opposing individualism, he never suggested that an individual should not have rights to trade or hold private property, which would anyway be against Islamic teaching. The emphasis in economic policies formulated by Hatta was the protection of the weaker members of society involved in the economic process.

On July 16, 1945, the BPKI completed its deliberations accepting the Draft Constitution. On the same day, news was received from Tokyo that Japan would recognize the independence of the East Indies as soon as possible, with an acknowledgement that the three war zones must now liaise more closely on the independence issue. It was decided to establish an archipelago-wide Panitia Persiapan Kemerdekaan Indonesia [Committee for the Preparation of Indonesian Independence -- PPKI] which would allow regional representatives to pool their viewpoints on independence issues, such as the Draft Constitution formulated in Java.

This decision was warmly received by Hatta, who had been conscious of an underrepresentation of the Outer Island viewpoint in the sessions of the BPKI. Hatta had been permitted to fly to Banjarmasin in Kalimantan

---

34 Mohammad Hatta, "Ekonomi Indonesia di Masa Datang," in *Bung Hatta Berpidato, Bung Hatta Menulis* (Jakarta: Mutiara, 1979), pp. 7-10.

[Borneo] the previous month, where at a meeting of local dignitaries in the Town Hall he had faced a barrage of questions on how independent Indonesia would be governed and what would be its territorial limits. Hatta assured his listeners that the boundaries of the new nation would correspond to the former Netherlands East Indies.

Hatta's speeches seemed to have an impact in the Outer Islands, winning considerable support from the local elite. The journey was not uneventful. Noor, an engineer from Kalimantan who accompanied Hatta, recalling that their airplane had to skirt a force of Allied bombers, remarked on Hatta's cool indifference to the dangers around him. He reportedly showed more interest in the areas of tall *alang-alang* grass through which their vehicle passed on the journey from the airport to the town, querying whether the area could be drained and developed for rice production.[35] Hatta's first meeting with the local people had to be carried out in blackout conditions in the courtyard of the house where he was lodging because of air-raid warnings. His address was significant in that, for the first time, he spoke out openly about Japan's impossible military situation and the likelihood of its imminent defeat, comments usually expressed privately but never aired in public.[36]

The extent of devastation on Hiroshima resulting from the drop of an atomic bomb on August 6 highlighted the proximity and strength of the Allied forces. On August 9, Sukarno, Hatta, and Dr. Rajiman Wedioningrat were unexpectedly summoned to Saigon to hold discussions with Marshal Terauchi, the Japanese commander-in-chief for the Southern Territories. Japan wanted an assurance of Indonesian support in return for independence. Their airplane never reached Saigon, crash-landing in a field several miles from the city.[37] Following an overnight stop in Saigon, the party was driven to a villa at Dalat where Marshal Terauchi was convalescing following an illness.

Hatta recalled that the Marshal confirmed the granting of independence to Indonesia, allowing the new PPKI to set the date for a proclamation to be made. "I was unusually happy because, being August 12, it was

35 P. M. Noor, "Inspirasi-Inspirasi jang Timbul Selama Pergaulan Saja dengan Bung Hatta," in *Bung Hatta Mengabdi pada Tjita-Tjita*, p. 304.
36 Kanahele, "Japanese Occupation of Indonesia," p. 222.
37 Ibid., p. 218.

my birthday," commented Hatta, continuing: "In my innermost heart I considered Indonesian independence to be my special gift for those long years of struggle for the freedom of Indonesia."[38]

On the return journey, Sukarno and Hatta learned the strategic news that Russia had entered the war and was advancing on Manchuria. They now realized that the battlefront might never reach Java, that Japan would be forced to surrender, handing Indonesia back to the Allied forces, including the Dutch, before independence was declared. This meant that members of the new preparatory committee must act fast to proclaim independence. Fortunately the Japanese had announced the committee's membership and arrangements were under way to bring the Outer Island delegates to Jakarta for an inaugural meeting on August 18.

On the section of the return flight between Singapore and Jakarta, Hatta and Sukarno had an opportunity to confer with the three Sumatran delegates to the PPKI who were sharing their plane. Hatta urged the three Sumatrans to accept the Draft Constitution in its present form to prevent any hold-up.[39] He believed the most contentious issue for Sumatrans might be the decision to designate the whole of Sumatra as one Indonesian province rather than three. There was no suggestion in Hatta's account, at this stage, that the Sumatrans might be dissatisfied with the *Panca Sila*.

A crowd of people was awaiting the return of Sukarno and Hatta, pressing for information as the two leaders disembarked at Jakarta. As the Japanese officers were anxious to whisk them away for briefing, Sukarno made an unusually short speech. His words had special meaning for the Javanese, referring back to the Joyoboyo legend. "If I used to say that Indonesia would be free when the corn ripens," he stated, "I can now say that Indonesia will be free before it blossoms."[40] The crowd understood. Hatta recalled that Sukarno's words were greeted with enthusiastic applause and cries of "*Indonesia Merdeka!*"[41]

During their briefing session, Hatta noticed that no mention was made of Japan's impending defeat, but that discussion centered on preparations for independence. On returning home in the early afternoon, Hatta was

---

38 Hatta, *Memoir*, p. 437.
39 Ibid., p. 439.
40 Cited in ibid., p. 440, and *Asia Raja*, August 14, 1945.
41 Hatta, *Memoir*, p. 440.

greeted by an impatient Sjahrir, who had just picked up the news on his radio that Japan had requested peace terms of the Allies. Sjahrir urged Hatta to contact Sukarno immediately to try to persuade him to proclaim independence over the air in the name of the Indonesian people. He was convinced that such a spontaneous declaration would carry more weight with the Allied forces than a declaration made under Japanese auspices.[42] Hatta, according to his memoirs, agreed that independence must be proclaimed quickly but "doubted whether it could be done by Sukarno alone as the people's leader in the name of the people" rather than as chairman of the PPKI. As far as the Allies were concerned, Sukarno would still be viewed as a collaborator whatever way he proclaimed independence.[43] The situation was reminiscent of 1942 when Hatta contemplated his chances of survival under the advancing forces because of his anti-Japanese sentiments. Now he was a *persona non grata* in the eyes of the Allied forces for having collaborated.

Hatta realized that a spontaneous declaration of independence would not only violate Indonesia's agreement with Tokyo but would rob the Outer Islanders of a voice in the independence preparations at a time when they were already suspicious of Java domination. Hatta pointed out to Sjahrir that if Sukarno acted on his initiative, "he would be considered to be expropriating and usurping the rights of the Panitia Persiapan Kemerdekaan Indonesia,"[44] in other words, acting undemocratically, an issue about which Sjahrir was usually very sensitive.

The events surrounding the proclamation of independence and Hatta's writings on the period reveal his exasperation with Sjahrir and the *pemuda* for their lack of sensitivity to the dangers inherent in rash action and the need to rein in revolutionary ardor until the Dutch return. His tone is that of someone who is convinced that he has moved a rung higher on the ladder towards mature statesmanship, that he considered the stance taken by Sjahrir and the *pemuda* leaders to be unrealistic. As Hatta summed up the situation in his later writings:

---

42 Sjahrir, *Out of Exile*, p. 253, and Hatta, *Memoir*, pp. 441-42. Sjahrir suggests strongly that Hatta was in sympathy with his viewpoint but stressed that it would need Sukarno's cooperation.
43 Hatta, *Memoir*, p. 442, and Anderson, *Some Aspects of Indonesian Politics*, p. 66.
44 Hatta, *Memoir*, p. 442.

In our opinion, the Proclamation of Independence had to be confirmed by the PPKI because its membership consisted of several Indonesian experts and it was considered to represent the whole of Indonesia. Although the delegates from Java, Sumatra, Kalimantan, Sulawesi, the Lesser Sundas and the Moluccas were appointed by the Japanese, the opinions which they expressed... were the opinions and aims of the people....

Thus the principal difference of opinion was between the Sukarno/Hatta group, which followed a legal course, and the API [Angkatan Pemuda Indonesia]-Students-Sjahrir group which considers its course to be the revolutionary way. It is difficult to reconcile a standpoint which is based on the logic emanating from a warm heart and a cool head with a point of view which is rebellious and hot-headed.[45]

After three years of collaboration, Hatta was much more finely tuned than Sjahrir to the ebb and flow of compromise between the Japanese and Indonesian leaders. In this delicate period, while hovering on the brink of nationhood, a false step could spell disaster.

According to Sastra, an active member of the New PNI during Hatta's and Sjahrir's exile, Sjahrir was prepared to consider Tan Malaka as a possible alternative proclaimant.[46] Sastra further commented: "Remembering that Sukarno and Hatta, although certainly well known to the people, were tainted in the people's eyes and in the international world because of their collaboration with the Japanese, we decided to contact Tan Malaka, the PKI leader who *opposed the 1926 Communist Insurrections* and later established and led a clandestine organization, PARI... who had slipped back into Indonesia and was hiding in Bayah Banten under the alias Ibrahim." When contacted, Tan Malaka bluntly declared that he was not prepared to proclaim independence so, concluded Sastra, "for us there were no other alternatives but Bung Karno and Bung Hatta."[47]

---

45 Mohammad Hatta, *Sekitar Proklamasi 17 Agustus 1945* (Jakarta: Tintamas, 1969), pp. 10-11.
46 Sastra, "Makna Sjahrir untuk Sastra dan Sastra untuk Sjahrir," in *Mengenang Sjahrir*, p. 90.
47 Ibid., p. 90. Sastra's italics. Hatta was aware of Tan Malaka's return to Indonesia and had, he claimed, actually seen him at Bayah Banten where Tan Malaka had deliberately tried to avoid him. See Hatta, *Bung Hatta Menjawab*, p. 16. Tan Malaka was said to consider "Sukarno and Hatta to be symbols of the old group who collaborated with the Japanese authorities," deeming them,

Sjahrir believed that the period between the Japanese request for peace terms and their acceptance by the Allied forces was the "psychological moment" for independence to be proclaimed, because Japan was then powerless. The proclamation would therefore signify seizing independence from Japan, not from the Allies.[48] It was a convincing argument which, according to Sjahrir's account, both Sukarno and Hatta were willing to explore, although both preferred to act under the auspices of the PPKI. They learned from Rear-Admiral Maeda the following day, August 15, that the Japanese Emperor had broadcast his country's intention to surrender. Maeda also made it clear that no instructions had been received from Tokyo as to what action the authorities on Java should take. According to Hatta's account, he suggested that the PPKI meeting be held the next morning instead of on August 18, since all the delegates were assembled in Jakarta.[49]

The rumors of Japan's surrender increased tension among the *pemuda*. That evening, while frantically preparing papers for the PPKI meeting, Hatta was interrupted by the arrival of two *pemuda*, who pleaded with him to ensure that the proclamation of independence was not made under the auspices of the PPKI, thus branding it forever as "Japanese made." Hatta, according to his memoirs, tried to convince the young men that he and Sukarno were adopting a sensible, rational stance. He recalled that he was accused of being "no longer a revolutionary."[50] Hatta retorted that he wanted to stage a revolution but wanted first of all to organize it properly. He pointed out that the action proposed by the *pemuda* was not a revolution but more like Hitler's "putsch" in Munich in 1923 which had failed.

Pemuda pressure switched to Sukarno, perhaps viewing him as more malleable than the steely Hatta. Wikana, a young protégé of Sukarno who worked with Subardjo in Maeda's office, was the spokesman for the *pemuda* delegation, many of whom were from Sjahrir's group and also from the Menteng 31 *asrama*.[51] Wikana brought the confrontation to

---

and especially Sukarno, to be "opportunists." See Alfian, "Tan Malaka: Pejuang Revolusioner yang Kesepian," in *Prisma*, August 8, 1977, p. 90.

48 Sastra, "Makna Sjahrir untuk Sastra dan Sastra untuk Sjahrir," p. 91.

49 Hatta, *Memoir*, p. 443.

50 Ibid., pp. 443-44.

51 A. Subardjo Djoyoadisuryo, *Lahirnya Republik Indonesia* (Jakarta: Kinta, 1977), p. 85.

crisis point by accusing Sukarno of failing as a leader, threatening that if he did not make the proclamation, "tomorrow there will be murder and bloodshed." Sukarno's patience snapped under the pressure and heatedly he shouted at the startled young men: "Here is my throat! Don't wait until tomorrow."[52]

Hatta, summoned by Subardjo to come to Sukarno's aid, arrived shortly after this emotional outburst. He took it upon himself to inform the *pemuda* that neither he nor Sukarno would be forced into taking actions which were unwise. "If you are prepared to proclaim independence yourself, go ahead," he challenged.[53] Hatta, when angry, could be awesome and cold. The severity of his tone cut short any further argument but his riposte, provoked in anger, bit deeper than he had intended. Hatta admitted that the *pemuda* delegation "had been shamed" and they took the humiliation as a challenge.[54] Their rejoinder to him as they left Sukarno's house was: "We the *pemuda* cannot allow the postponement of the proclamation for another day. We will take action and prove our ability as Bung suggested."[55]

Yet the *pemuda* realized that they did not have the prestige to make a declaration of independence. They devised a plan to kidnap Sukarno and Hatta, taking them to a Peta barracks at Rengasdenglok, a small town northeast of Jakarta. It was planned that the *pemuda* would either stage a rally in Ikada Square, in an effort to seize control from the Japanese, or would at least threaten to do so, in the hope that Sukarno and Hatta would accede to their request.[56] According to Des Alwi, there was also a plan to broadcast a text prepared by Sjahrir on the evening of August 15, if Sukarno and Hatta were prepared to sign it, which they refused to do.[57]

The blame for the kidnapping of Sukarno and Hatta early on the

---

52 As cited in Anderson, *Some Aspects of Indonesian Politics*, p. 69.
53 Subardjo Djoyoadisuryo, *Lahirnya Republik Indonesia*, p. 85. According to Adam Malik, *Riwajat dan Perdjuangan Sekitar Proklamasi Kemerdekaan Indonesia 17 Agustus 1945* (Jakarta: Widjaja, 1950), p. 35, Sukarno and Hatta would not have proclaimed independence without Japanese permission whatever the circumstances.
54 Anderson, *Java in a Time of Revolution*, pp. 73-74.
55 As cited in Subardjo Djoyoadisuryo, *Lahirnya Republic Indonesia*, p. 85.
56 Anderson, *Java in a Time of Revolution*, p. 75.
57 Des Alwi, "Oom Kacamata yang Mendidik Saya," in *Bung Hatta Pribadinya dalam Kenangan*, p. 326.

morning of August 16 may be attributed in some degree to Hatta's angry challenge to the *pemuda*. It should be remembered, however, how physically exhausted he was at the time, after traveling to Saigon under hazardous conditions the previous week and surviving a near-fatal air crash. It was also Ramadan, the month of fasting, always a tiring time.

The kidnappers used no force apart from a pointed gun when they bundled Hatta, Sukarno, and his wife, Fatmawati, and baby son, Guntur, into a car to take them to Rengasdenglok barracks. Hatta's heart sank as he visualized the PPKI members arriving for the fateful meeting at which independence was to have been proclaimed, only to find that both he and Sukarno were absent. He recalled: "In my eyes I pictured the destruction of our aims to implement Free Indonesia."[58] "Oom Hatta was furious about the kidnapping," Des Alwi admitted.[59] Hatta's anger and frustration were understandable; he had been within hours of achieving his life's goal only to see it snatched away by action for which he himself must accept a degree of responsibility.

The kidnapping did not weaken the two leaders' resolve, nor change their viewpoint. The two men merely spent an anxious day speculating on the events taking place in Jakarta. Hatta's main concern was whether the PPKI meeting would go ahead and what would be the outcome of the *pemuda* putsch. If this were not sufficient trial, Hatta suffered the further physical discomfort of having his only available pair of trousers wet through while taking a turn at nursing baby Guntur![60]

Sjahrir did not support the kidnapping, although he backed the *pemuda* plans to proclaim independence in Ikada Square. Subardjo and Rear-Admiral Maeda at first suspected that the Japanese Army had arrested Sukarno and Hatta, but the Gunseikan denied responsibility. The Kempeitai was ordered to search for them. Through Wikana, Subardjo managed to ferret out details of what had happened, finally persuading the young man to take him to Rengasdenglok. Hatta was relieved to hear that no youthful uprising had in fact taken place. The PPKI members had decided to postpone their meeting.

Hatta resolved to make up for lost time, and on his return to Jakarta

---

58 Hatta, *Memoir*, p. 448.
59 Interview with Des Alwi, February 6, 1982.
60 Hatta, *Memoir*, p. 448.

that evening tried to arrange an immediate meeting of the PPKI. He gladly accepted Maeda's offer of his house as a venue, knowing it was free of Kempeitai and Japanese Army interference. But a new obstacle had arisen. Sukarno and Hatta were informed that, under the surrender terms, Japan was ordered to maintain the status quo in all occupied territories from the date of acceptance of the Allied ultimatum. They were also warned not to try to convene the PPKI meeting in Admiral Maeda's house. Maeda did, however, manage to extract from the Army a reluctant assurance that, as long as independence was proclaimed quietly and the *pemuda* remained calm and under control, the military authorities would remain passive.[61]

Word was quickly passed to the *pemuda* to send representatives to Maeda's house so that not only the PPKI members but the *pemuda* as well could join in drawing up the proclamation of independence. Sjahrir, anti-Japanese to the end, refused to enter Maeda's house, but his *pemuda* group took along the text which he had helped them to prepare.

Sukarno and Hatta rejected Sjahrir's text, sensing that its tone was too provocative. They decided instead to use a sentence from the Preamble to the Draft Constitution: "We the Indonesian people declare herewith Indonesia's independence," merely adding a short sentence: "Matters concerning the transfer of power and other matters will be executed in an orderly manner and in the shortest possible time."[62] The *pemuda* leaders protested that the proclamation was too "tame" but the PPKI delegates supported it wholeheartedly. It was suggested that all present sign the proclamation. The *pemuda* refused to sign in conjunction with the PPKI members but agreed that six of their members would sign under Sukarno and Hatta's signature. This was unacceptable to the PPKI delegates. Finally, it was agreed that only Sukarno's and Hatta's names should appear on the proclamation. Hatta expressed exasperation and disappointment: "I hoped that they would join in signing such an historical document which would carry their names to the pride of their future descendants."[63]

Sukarno and Hatta rejected any suggestion that the proclamation be made in Ikada Square, knowing that a mass gathering would alarm the

---

61 Anderson, *Java in a Time of Revolution*, p. 79.
62 Ibid., p. 82, and Hatta, *Memoir*, p. 454.
63 Hatta, *Memoir*, p. 455.

Japanese Army. Instead it was decided that independence be proclaimed in the courtyard of Sukarno's house at ten o'clock that morning, five hours hence. Dawn was already beginning to break.

The proclamation of Indonesian independence was not made amid great fanfare. Sukarno, with Hatta at his side, read the brief proclamation while a home-made red and white flag was raised and the anthem *Indonesia Raya* sung. Hatta obviously felt a great sense of release and happiness, relating how he embraced his family and friends amid tears of joy.[64] He knew it was not the final seal of independence, only the beginning of the bitterest conflict of all. But at least now they had a foundation of nationhood on which to build, much more than a seemingly impossible dream.

In later years, when the *Dwi Tunggal* no longer existed as a political unity, Sukarno in his autobiography made a particularly spiteful attack regarding Hatta's presence at the proclamation ceremony:

No one shrieked "We want Bung Hatta." I did not need him. Just as also I did not need Sjahrir who refused to show himself at the time of the reading of the Proclamation. Indeed, I could do it myself and indeed I did it alone. In those nerve-wracking days, the role of Hatta in history did not exist. He had no individual role in the time of our struggle. It was just Sukarno who continually pushed him to the fore. I needed this person who was called "a leader" because of one consideration. I needed him because I am a Javanese and he is a Sumatran and in those days I needed a person from Sumatra.... At this grave historical moment, Sukarno and the native land of Indonesia awaited the coming of Hatta.[65]

Not surprisingly, Hatta was forced into print to list his movements on the morning of August 17. His response was quiet and restrained: "People knew that I am always punctual. Sukarno need not have worried because he knew my habits."[66] Nevertheless, it was an occasion when Hatta might have relieved tension if he had arrived before schedule. Those organizing

---

64 Ibid., p. 458.
65 Adams, *Sukarno*, p. 219.
66 Hatta, *Sekitar Proklamasi*, p. 54.

the ceremony were growing nervous about Japanese reprisals as the morning progressed. As Sudiro later remarked: "Up to 0950 Bung Hatta had not put in an appearance but Bung Karno was not prepared to read the Proclamation unless Bung Hatta was present."[67] Sudiro's reminiscences seem to refute Sukarno's willingness to act alone. Indeed the historical record would seem to indicate that at the moment of the declaration of Indonesia's independence, Sukarno and Hatta were working together as a very close-knit team.

With Maeda's cooperation, the Naval Office press was used to issue copies of the proclamation for distribution in the capital and the news was telephoned and telegraphed across Java. At 7 p.m. that evening, broadcasts of the independence proclamation were made, Des Alwi relating how he had helped to smuggle the text past the Kempeitai guards into the radio building.[68] Hatta had also prepared a personal message for transmission to his nationalist friends.

Sjahrir, although remaining aloof from the declaration because of its association with the Japanese, nevertheless acknowledged that it had the desired impact on the Indonesian people:

> The effect of the proclamation was tremendous. It was as though our people had been electrified. A majority of the Indonesian civil servants, administrators, police and military groups immediately declared their support for the Republic. National strength and unity reached greater heights than anything we had known before.[69]

67 Pak Diro, "Bung Hatta yang Saya Kenal," in *Bung Hatta: Pribadinya dalam Kenangan*, p. 410.
68 D. Alwi, "Oom Kacamata yang Mendidik Saya," pp. 326-27.
69 Sjahrir, *Out of Exile*, p. 259.

CHAPTER NINE
INDEPENDENCE DEFENDED

Every revolution invariably gives rise to an atmosphere influenced by a mass psychology, which is itself strongly affected by romanticism and heroism. The primary problem in a revolution is how to channel the burning but anarchic energies of thee masses, and to mould them into a body, strong at heart, capable of enduring suffering and undergoing trials in facing reactions that may arise, until the final victory is achieved.[1]

"How to channel the burning and anarchic energies of the masses" and maintain national strength and unity were major problems facing the *Dwi Tunggal* in the newly proclaimed Republic of Indonesia. In the preceding two years Hatta had stressed to the youth that the fate of the nation rested on them, that they were "heroes in his heart." For the next four years, he would find himself tossed about amid a current of youthful tumult, far more aggressive and impetuous than the ferment he had experienced in his own period of youthful nationalism. The *pemuda* basically needed to relate to and work under mature national leaders; they were prepared to accept the *Dwi Tunggal's* direction but, as if to punish them for prospering under the Japanese regime, were reluctant to accord them traditional respect. Both Sukarno and Hatta would be stretched to the limits of their leadership capabilities to maneuver within this youthful whirlpool. Many times they would find themselves fighting both internal

---

1 Mohammad Hatta, "Isi Proklamasi," in *Fakta dan Dokumen-Dokumen untuk menjusan buku 'Indonesia memasuki Gelanggang Internasional', Supplemen I*, Vol. II (Kemlu R.I. Direktorat V, Seksi Penjelidikan Dokumentasi dan Perpustakaan [ed. Emzita], 1958), p. 1, as cited in Anderson, *Some Aspects of Indonesian Politics under the Japanese Occupation*, pp. 99-100.

and external foes for survival.

The *pemuda* groups were invited to send representatives to the final sessions of the PPKI, but their delegates insisted that the PPKI first convert itself into the Komité Nasional Indonesia. Hatta tried to defuse the issue by explaining that the nationalist leaders were still responsible to the Japanese authorities and that the PPKI would in due course reconstitute itself as a national body. "For this reason we tell the Japanese that this is a meeting of the PPKI," Hatta contended, "while we guarantee to the people that this is the first meeting of the Komité Nasional Indonesia [Indonesian National Committee],"[2] a remark which the *pemuda* leader, Adam Malik, dismissed as "Hatta's hermaphroditic statement."[3]

Hatta was also concerned that territories outside Java and Sumatra, especially ethnic groups in the past favored by the Dutch, such as the Menadonese and Ambonese, might opt for a continuing Netherlands association. Only a few hours after the proclamation, a Japanese naval officer warned Hatta that Christian groups in the eastern islands were concerned by the clause in the *Panca Sila* referring to Islamic obligations. Aware from his period of exile in Banda Neira of the strength of Ambonese loyalty to the Dutch, Hatta immediately sought out influential Muslims in the PPKI to obtain their support. Teuku Hasan, the Acehnese delegate and an influential Muslim representative, recalled that Hatta requested his assistance in persuading the Javanese Muhammadiyah leader, Ki Bagus Hadikusumo, to agree to the omission of the phrase "with an obligation to carry out the *shari'ah* for its adherents."[4] Hatta commented in his memoirs that the attitude of the Islamic delegation was "a sign that the leaders at that time really were concerned about the future and unity of the nation,"[5] perhaps a subtle suggestion that national and religious leaders should be more accommodating about constitutional matters in future crises.

Sukarno and Hatta were unanimously elected President and Vice-President, amid thunderous applause, a spontaneous rendering of

---

2 See Anderson, *Java in a Time of Revolution*, p. 86.

3 Malik, *Riwajat dan Perdjuangan*, p. 6.

4 Teuku Mohammad Hasan, "Bung Hatta di Sumatera," in *Bung Hatta Mengabdi pada Tjita-Tjita*, pp. 182-83. Hatta did not obtain Hasan's support for the division of Sumatra into three provinces. Hasan was later appointed governor of Sumatra.

5 Hatta, *Memoir*, p. 460.

the anthem *Indonesia Raya*, and with a firm proposal that the offices constitute a special *Dwi Tunggal*. There was a challenge inherent in the term. It signified that the two leaders must maintain a united front, and be prepared to settle their differences behind the scenes. They were expected to pool their talents in order to produce a rounded, stable leadership, a leadership made up of elements with which the various streams in Indonesian society could identify. With Sukarno as the orator and magnetic force, Hatta would provide planning and attend to administrative detail. Sukarno would reflect the "*abangan*" Muslim, Hatta the more orthodox. Sukarno would project the brilliance and sensuality of the Javanese ruler while Hatta would offset it with his puritanism and incorruptibility. Sukarno would represent autocratic centralist Javanese rule while Hatta would reflect *kedaulatan rakyat* modeled on the *demokrasi asli* of the Agam plateau. Together they would provide a symbol of national unity, in particular a microcosm of the macrocosm of Java and the Outer Islands, so vital a concept at this particular time of crisis.

While the *pemuda* accepted the *Dwi Tunggal*, they reacted angrily to the PPKI's decision to disband Peta and Heiho, the most widespread militia forces on Java. *pemuda* spokesman Wikana urged that a national army be established incorporating all Peta and Heiho units.[6] The compromise offered by the PPKI was to establish a Badan Keamanan Rakyat [People's Security Body] or BKR, which, although posing as a police force to allay Japanese fears, was regarded as the nucleus of an Indonesian army. This response was still too passive for the *pemuda*, who independently regrouped into their former Peta and Heiho units, loyal to local officers rather than to any central administration. On August 29, 1945, Hatta broadcast an appeal for coordination. "The youth must not act alone," he warned, "failing to bind themselves to the people and outside the main movement of the people."[7]

Hatta did not underestimate the need for defense forces, and his memoirs suggest that he played an important role in the establishment of the national army. On October 4 he was introduced to Urip Sumohardjo, a former officer in the Koninklijk Nederlands Indisch Leger [Royal

---

6   See Anderson, *Java in a Time of Revolution*, p. 102.
7   Mohammad Hatta, "Bulat Bersatu Menghadapi Masa yang Genting," Radio Speech, August 29, 1945, in *Kumpulan Pidato: Dari Tahun 1942 s.d. 1949*, pp. 69-70.

Netherlands Indies Army known as KNIL], who expressed his willingness to participate in establishing the Republic's army.[8] Hatta recorded that he appointed Urip chief of staff, "empowering him to appoint his own auxiliary staff, as much as possible consisting of former Peta and KNIL officers."[9] Hatta's wife, when reminiscing on her husband's insistence on attending an anniversary of the founding of the armed forces on October 5, 1974, recalled that Hatta expressed a sense of duty to be present, in spite of ill-health and advanced age. "Wasn't it I who first built up our national army," he maintained, adding: "Who cares if people forget about me, for me that is not important. It is sufficient that I personally know that it was I who established the armed forces of the Republic of Indonesia."[10]

Both Sukarno and Hatta played major roles in the appointment of the first presidential cabinet, which incurred Sjahrir's strong disapproval. In response, Hatta explained that by selecting "those men who were already placed at the top of the departmental hierarchies... the downward channels of command could be controlled and the Japanese easily set aside."[11] Hatta admitted that they could have built up "a national governmental administrative arm alongside" the Japanese administration, a course which in many respects would have resembled his past formula of a "state within a state," "This way might seem to be revolutionary," Hatta conceded, "but it would not be rational. And what is not rational in a revolution is not revolutionary." Hatta believed that, if the administrative structure had not been infiltrated by nationalists, it would simply have been handed on from the Japanese to the Allies, "and from the Allies it would have been transferred to the control of Holland."[12]

The cabinet was made up of many of Hatta's former companions in the

---

8   Hatta, *Memoir*, p. 470. According to Hatta, it was Amir Sjarifuddin who made the introduction.

9   Ibid., p. 471. The name was changed to Tentara Keamanan Rakyat [People's Security Army] from October 5, 1945 and finally designated Tentara Nasional Indonesia [Indonesian National Army]. As Sukarno was out of the capital, Hatta as Acting President commissioned the establishment of the national army.

10 As cited in Ny. Rahmi Hatta, "Prinsip-Prinsip Bung Hatta tak Pernah Luntur," in *Bung Hatta: Pilbadinya dalam Kenangan*, p. 44. According to two future chiefs of staff, Generals Nasution and Simatupang, the armed forces did not view Hatta as their founder. Simatupang believed Amir Sjarifuddin took more initiative than Hatta. Both agreed that Hatta was effective as a minister of defense. Interviews: General A. H. Nasution, February 22, 1982, and General T. B. Simatupang, February 4, 1982.

11 Hatta, "Isi Proklamasi," p. 2, as cited in Anderson, *Java in a Time of Revolution*, p. 112.

12 Ibid., pp. 2, 4.

Perhimpunan Indonesia, including Subardjo as foreign affairs minister and Iwa Kusuma Sumantri as minister of social affairs. To prevent its being labeled a cabinet of collaborators, Amir Sjarifuddin was appointed minister of information, although Ali Sastroamidjojo deputized for him while Amir recovered his health after the ordeal of Kempeitai imprisonment. Both Tan Malaka and Sjahrir refused seats in the cabinet, Sjahrir stating bluntly in his political manifesto, *Our Struggle*, that it was composed of "men without real character," most of them "too accustomed to kowtow or run errands for the Dutch and Japanese." Sjahrir further charged: "Psychologically they are irresolute and have proved quite incapable of acting decisively and assuming responsibility."[13] For practical reasons, Hatta needed the skills of his peer group. He had experienced *realpolitik* for three years and had learned to temper idealism with realism.

Although he still advocated *kedaulatan rakyat*, Hatta had to admit that the present situation of people's sovereignty "differed from its intentions,"[14] as the masses increasingly acted independently of the newly appointed government. Yet, while Hatta deplored the growth of disorder in Indonesian society, fearing it would create an adverse impression internationally, Tan Malaka applauded the radical revolutionary mood of the masses, and began to move more openly among the *pemuda*. He was supported by nationalists who had tried to keep alive his Partai Republik Indonesia in the thirties. According to Abu Hanifah, it was known that the Dutch had plans to capture Sukarno and Hatta as collaborators.[15]

Supported by Subardjo and the *pemuda* group led by Sukarni, Chaerul Saleh, and Adam Malik, Tan Malaka pressed Sukarno to seek refuge in the interior. Depressed and insecure, Sukarno impetuously agreed that, if he and Hatta were taken prisoner by the Allied forces, Tan Malaka could hold the fort as President in his place.[16] According to Hatta in one of the final interviews of his life, Sukarno regretted his agreement with Tan Malaka and sought a compromise. Hatta claimed to have suggested to Sukarno that the presidential mandate be transferred

---

13 Sjahrir, *Our Struggle*, p. 20.
14 Mohammad Hatta, "Kedaulatan Rakyat," a speech given to a meeting of civil servants at Solo, February 7, 1946, in *Bung Hatta Berpidato, Bung Hatta Menulis*, p. 25.
15 Abu Hanifah, *Tales of a Revolution*, p. 191.
16 Interview with Sajuti Melik, September 24, 1962, in Anderson, *Java in a Time of Revolution*, p. 278.

to a quadrumvirate, including Tan Malaka, Sutan Sjahrir, Iwa Kusuma Sumatri, and Wongsonegoro.[17] Hatta's suggestion mirrored the concept of the *Empat Serangkai*, a joint leadership representative of mainstreams in Indonesian society during the Japanese Occupation. According to Adam Malik, Tan Malaka viewed this new arrangement as a breach of promise[18] and certainly the *Dwi Tunggal's* decision failed to scotch rumors that Tan Malaka was Sukarno's sole successor.

With the Labour Party under Clement Attlee in power in Britain and the Dutch Labor Party dominating a coalition government in the Netherlands, Hatta grasped the opportunity to gain support from overseas socialists, especially those with whom he had worked in Europe. On August 30, he launched a radio appeal in the hope of winning an acknowledgment of Indonesia's independence, reminding his listeners:

> In the past, when we were comrades in the common fight for the realization of the principles of humanity and justice, you threw your whole heart and soul into the struggle for Indonesian independence. Today you sit in high positions wielding much power. Now, then, it is the time for you to give us the assistance we seek.[19]

The response from Britain was cautious, but not entirely unsympathetic. Attlee, like Hatta, was a social democrat; but the British prime minister was in a dilemma. Like Hatta, he tended to conform to the rules, and the established principle in Europe was that one did not interfere in the colonial affairs of an ally.

General MacArthur's relegation of Indonesia to Lord Louis Mountbatten's South East Asia Command (SEAC) had been a last-minute decision, throwing both Mountbatten and the Dutch government into confusion. Van Mook, the Acting Governor-General and head of the

---

17 Hatta saw Tan Malaka as representative of the radical group, Sjahrir of the semi-radical, Sukiman of the Muslims, and Wongsonegoro of the conservatives. As Sukiman was in Yogyakarta, it was agreed that Iwa Kusuma Sumantri represent the Islamic body. See Hatta, *Bung Hatta's Answers*, p. 15.

18 Adam Malik, *In the Service of the Republic* (Singapore: Gunung Agung, 1980), p. 204.

19 Mohammad Hatta, "A Personal Message to My Old Comrades Wherever They May Be," in *Portrait of a Patriot*, p. 505.

newly formed Netherlands Indies Civil Affairs Administration (NICA), had been liaising directly with MacArthur in Australia and now had to brief Mountbatten, reiterating that the proclamation of independence was merely a Japanese stratagem. Mountbatten was hesitant, having observed the strength of nationalism in Burma at first hand, and he delayed inaugurating the repossession of Indonesia until he had established a new base in Singapore.

When on September 15, 1945, Mountbatten's representative, Rear-Admiral Patterson, landed at Tanjung Priok, almost a month had elapsed since the proclamation. Patterson accepted General Yamamoto's advice not to treat Sukarno and Hatta as war criminals, assessing that, with its present extended commitments, SEAC would be unable to engage in large-scale combat. He suggested to Mountbatten that the Allied forces concentrate in the key coastal cities, using them to evacuate Japanese forces and internees and acting in cooperation with the Indonesian government. Further penetration would be the responsibility of the Dutch.[20]

Mountbatten accepted Patterson's recommendations and instructed General Christison, the newly appointed Allied commander for the area, to instruct the Republic of Indonesia to continue its administration of all areas in Java and Sumatra except the coastal bases. Christison relayed this information by radio from Singapore, at the same time confirming that the Republic's leaders would not be removed as collaborators; in fact he would "ask the present Party leaders to treat him and his troops as guests."[21] For Sukarno and Hatta, Christison's statement was tantamount to a reprieve, although they recognized that the Dutch might not concur in it.

Patterson's recommendations had not only been based on Japanese advice. During his short stay in Jakarta he himself had witnessed the *Dwi Tunggal's* leadership abilities. The *pemuda* and several of the older nationalists, under the sponsorship of Tan Malaka and against Sukarno's and Hatta's wishes, had held a mass meeting in Ikada Square while

---

20 See Anderson, *Some Aspects of Indonesian Politics*, pp. 120-21.
21 See Anderson, *Java in a Time of Revolutlon*, p. 135. According to Anderson, no official transcript of this broadcast was released and SEAC tried to play it down. Anderson's source is British Intelligence Files, IC-RVO doc. no. 014235-42.

Patterson was conferring with the Japanese administration. The *pemuda* were in a highly volatile mood, but Sukarno again proved that he held the trump card. His speech before the massed audience was short, soothing, an appeal for their confidence. It was an appeal that immediately evoked an enthusiastic avowal of loyalty. Quietly Sukarno ordered: "Let us all go home now, calmly and serenely, but maintain our vigilance."[22]

This incident confirmed for Sjahrir that, although he disliked the present government, Sukarno himself was an essential ingredient in rallying anti-Dutch resistance in Java and must be protected, although preferably detached from his tainted colleagues. When approached by Tan Malaka in early October with a suggestion that he join forces with him to overthrow Sukarno, Sjahrir rejected the proposal, perceiving this to be disastrous for national unity.[23] Likewise, when the *pemuda* leader Sukarni, on October 31, proposed to Hatta that he support a move to dislodge Sukarno from the presidency, replacing him with Tan Malaka, Hatta's response was cold and disapproving.[24] However, these approaches did warn Hatta that a power struggle could be imminent, exacerbated by Dutch threats to Sukarno.

The Dutch embassy in London on September 30 had issued a statement denouncing Mountbatten's concessions to the Indonesian government and reiterating that it was "a Japanese puppet government of a totalitarian character dependent on the Japanese military organisation."[25] Yet Van Mook, now in the Indies, had to admit that dramatic changes had occurred in Indonesian society during the Japanese Occupation. Observing the widespread resistance to the Dutch return, he could now understand Christison's desire to maintain the *Dwi Tunggal's* goodwill. Van Mook compromised, informing the media on October 14 that he was prepared to meet representatives of Indonesian groups, including Sukarno.[26] Unfortunately, his statement was immediately repudiated by The Hague,

---

22 Anderson, *Java in a Time of Revolution*, p. 123.
23 See Kahin, *Nationalism and Revolution in Indonesia*, p. 149.
24 Hatta, *Memoir*, p. 479. According to his memoirs, Hatta admonished Sukarni, reminding him that "the Republic of Indonesia is not a group whose chairman can be replaced just on the whim of some of its leading members. The Republic of Indonesia is a State whose President is elected constitutionally."
25 See Dorothy Woodman, *The Republic of Indonesia* (London: Cresset Press, 1955), p. 209.
26 Ibid.

which forbade any dealings with Sukarno, although conceding that the Dutch government was prepared to grant dominion status to Indonesia.

On October 18 Hatta held a press conference in which he emphatically rejected the Dutch government's proposals for "dominion status" within a Netherlands Union, querying: "And why must Indonesia willy-nilly be made partner of a commonwealth in which the Dutch tail will wag the Indonesian dog," adding: "The Dutch are graciously permitting us entry into the basement while we have climbed all the way to the top floor and up to the attic!"[27] This Hatta back in prewar form, doing what he enjoyed most, needling the Dutch, attacking their colonial *hauteur*. There never had been the same degree of satisfaction in Hatta's cuts at the Japanese, apart from the danger of reprisal.

Van Mook and his deputy, Van der Plas, undoubtedly caught the confident determination of Hatta's statement. In spite of their home government's hard-line attitudes, they agreed to Christison's call for negotiations. Hatta recalled that he, Sukarno, Subardjo, and Haji Agus Salim met with Christison and the two Dutch representatives on October 23. The Republicans stressed that any links formed between the Netherlands and Indonesia must be on the basis of two independent nations, with a preliminary requirement that the Dutch propose Indonesia's admittance to the United Nations. "Van Mook, as Lieutenant-Governor of the Netherlands Indies, could not make a reply," commented Hatta, "so our discussions had to be discontinued."[28]

Van Mook has been described by P. J. Idenburg, a former colonial associate, as "belonging to a group of Dutchmen whose being and existence were so linked to the Indies... that the Netherlands-Indies portion of the Netherlands had in fact become their fatherland."[29] In January 1930, as an ardent associationist, Van Mook had been among a group in the Indies to form the movement "Stuw." This movement aimed at making the Indies an independent commonwealth in which the Indonesian would have a part "in proportion to his political and social significance," a suggestion of a situation similar to South Africa, where the Afrikaner minority is

---

27 As cited in David Wehl, *The Birth of Indonesia* (London: Allen and Unwin, 1948), p. 90.
28 Hatta, *Memoir*, p. 470.
29 See Yong Mun Cheong, *H. J. van Mook and Indonesian Independence: A Study of His Role in Dutch-Indonesian Relations, 1945-48* (The Hague: Nijhoff, 1982), p. 8.

considered to be of greater political and social significance than the African majority.

In a radio broadcast Hatta summed up his views on Van Mook:

> The inability to keep pace with the forward march of the subject peoples is an occupational disease to which all bureaucrats fall victim, but it was in Indonesia that that disease manifested itself in its most virulent form. And the worst sufferer was undoubtedly Doctor van Mook. He fell victim to the delusion that, because he was born in Java, he was possessed of clairvoyantic powers which enabled him to see what was missed by other Dutchmen. The truth of the matter is that Doctor van Mook, like the old China hand, is *in* the country but not *of* it.[30]

Although relations with the British remained relatively cordial, incidences of confrontation increased as Dutch forces entered in greater numbers. Hatta described the uneasy atmosphere in the capital: "Dutch troops, the majority of them Ambonese, cruised around Jakarta in jeeps or trucks, shooting at random, in particular at the cars of Indonesian dignitaries which they identified by the red and white flag flying at the front."[31]

In view of the Dutch government's continued rejection of the Republic of Indonesia on the grounds that it was a totalitarian state, the national leaders felt they had to present a more democratic image. Sjahrir, who had been critical of the extra transitional powers allowed the presidency, suggested that the Central National Committee, KNIP, should assume temporarily the role of the proposed legislative bodies, the MPR and DPR.[32] Sukarno accepted Sjahrir's proposals, sensing how precarious was his own position and the need to present a more liberal image to the Allied powers. Yet he was reluctant to associate himself fully with legislation which not only diminished his power but was thrust upon him by external pressures, especially the need to placate the Dutch.

---

30 See ibid., p. 73.
31 Hatta, *Memoir*, p. 467.
32 To back his proposal, Sjahrir obtained the signatures of fifty members of KNIP, which he presented to Sukarno and Hatta on October 7.

Sukarno therefore assigned to Hatta the duty of issuing a decree to give KNIP legislative powers, and at the same time removed himself from the capital.

Hatta was willing to perform the task; he had always perceived wider power sharing as closest to his ideal of democracy. "Hatta appreciated the logic behind Sjahrir's strategy," confirmed Subadio.[33] Not only would the Republic be less totalitarian but the decree would institute the system envisaged in the Draft Constitution where the presidential cabinet was balanced by a popular assembly. Under the unusual appellation of *Maklumat x* [Decree x], on October 16 Hatta decreed the conversion of the KNIP into a legislative assembly.

The decree was not unchallenged, and there was a sharp division between the supportive *pemuda* and older nationalists such as Sartono. A Badan Pekerja or Working Body led by Sjahrir and Amir Sjarifuddin was instituted to deal with day-to-day affairs of KNIP. Sjahrir took his democratization efforts one step further, calling for the establishment of political parties, in an effort to ensure that any plans to establish a one-party system were blocked. Although in principle supportive of political parties, Hatta omitted from his memoirs any mention of the decree of November 3, 1945, which permitted political parties to operate. This may have been a result of the future implications of his action, or his own subsequent disillusionment with the implementation of the multiparty system.

Two days previously, on November 1, Hatta had also issued a "political manifesto," which criticized Dutch attitudes to the new Republic. Denying that the Dutch had any moral right to "take the virtuous stand that we cooperated with the Japanese," Hatta claimed that the nationalists who collaborated never "forsook the nationalistic ideals which for years had been their guide."[34] He warned that failure to accept Indonesia's independence "will be nothing but a deliberate violation of the Atlantic Charter and the United Nations Charter" and "it will result in endless bloodshed and sacrifice of life, for only by force and force alone can the

---

33 Interview with Subadio Sastrosatomo, February 22, 1982.
34 "Political Manifesto of November 1945" as cited in Feith and Castles, eds., *Indonesian Political Thinking 1945-1965*, p. 52.

Dutch try to pull down the government which we have set up."[35]

Hatta assured the Dutch that Indonesians entertained no personal hatred for them and that Indonesian sovereignty would not "affect Dutch capital or Dutch lives"; in other words, Dutch business interests would be safeguarded. "All property of foreigners will be handed over to them," Hatta promised, with a stipulation that "we reserve the right to acquire at fair prices such property as shall be deemed necessary for the welfare of the country." He concluded: "All debts incurred by the Dutch East Indies government previous to the Japanese surrender and fairly chargeable to us we will unhesitatingly take over,"[36] an issue which was to provide difficulties for him in the years ahead.

Tan Malaka challenged Hatta's concessions to the Dutch and advocated instead seizure by the masses of foreign properties without compensation, no doubt remembering the extent of exploitation he had witnessed in the plantations of East Sumatra.[37] Tan Malaka also challenged Sjahrir to oust the *Dwi Tunggal* since he had been so contemptuous of them and of the presidential cabinet in *Our Struggle*.[38] Sjahrir's response was to recommend to Sukarno and Hatta that the presidential cabinet be disbanded, that Sukarno and Hatta become heads of state, and thus inviolate, while KNIP be permitted to appoint its own cabinet, with the leader of the KNIP becoming prime minister. This strategy would both thwart Tan Malaka's attacks on the *Dwi Tunggal* and provide a national leader acceptable to the Dutch, for Sjahrir's standing was high with the Allies in view of his anti-Japanese activities.

The fact that Sukarno was prepared to transfer his powers to Sjahrir, a man he disliked, indicated how far his confidence had been undermined. But Sukarno was also aware that Sjahrir's position depended on Sukarno and Hatta remaining as heads of state and that he therefore did not pose such a personal threat as Tan Malaka. Sukarno agreed to the implementation of a system he had always disliked as being too individualistic and Western: parliamentary democracy. Again Hatta was

---

35 Ibid., p. 53.
36 Ibid., pp. 54-55.
37 See Rudolph Mrazek, "Tan Malaka: A Political Personality's Structure of Experience," in *Indonesia* 14 (October 1972): 9.
38 According to Mohamad Roem, Hatta had been included in Sjahrir's criticisms of the national leadership. Interview, February 2, 1982.

assigned the task of issuing on November 14 a decree which in effect ended presidential government and converted the Republic of Indonesia into a parliamentary democracy. Sjahrir, at the age of thirty-six became Indonesia's first prime minister.

This final decree was to remain a source of disquiet for Hatta, one of the issues in his political career on which he was most ambivalent. Undoubtedly, he concurred with Sjahrir that parliamentary democracy had always been his goal for Indonesia. But Hatta had also contended that this goal had to be preceded by a period of education in political responsibility, because it was not a system with which the Javanese masses were familiar. There was another more pressing consideration. The difficulty in controlling the *pemuda* groups alone was an indication that the wartime situation demanded strong central control.

The British commander in Surabaya, Brigadier-General Mallaby, voiced concern at the militant spirit of the *pemuda* in his area, appealing to Sukarno and Hatta to intervene personally to try to prevent further bloodshed. On arrival in Surabaya, both men sensed the frenzied atmosphere prevailing in the city. Des Alwi, who was among the *pemuda* fighting there, recalled Hatta's anger when his vehicle was halted by two armed *pemuda* who demanded that their British driver be handed over as a prisoner. "On hearing this, Oom Hatta was furious," Des recalled, "admonishing the two young Indonesians, inquiring: 'Hey, is killing all you want to do? That won't achieve our struggle!'"[39]

Sukarno and Hatta tried to mediate between the Allies and the *pemuda* leaders in Surabaya, but they only achieved a fragile settlement. No sooner had their airplane flown out than Mallaby was caught by a bullet in cross-fire and killed.[40] British sympathy for the Indonesian cause declined, Christison issuing an immediate warning that he would "bring the whole weight of his sea, land and air forces against the Republic forces unless the culprits surrendered."[41] When on November 10, the British

---

39 Des Alwi, "Oom Kacamata yang Mendidik Saya," p. 328. Hatta himself relates the story of Indonesian soldiers who originated from Aceh who drank the blood of Gurkha soldiers before the corpses were thrown in the nearby river. See *Memoir*, p. 477.

40 See J. G. A. Parrott, "Who Killed Brigadier Mallaby?" in *Indonesia* 20 (October 1975): 87-111, in which the writer presents evidence that Mallaby's death was more likely to have been caused by a blunder on the part of his own troops than by an Indonesian bullet.

41 See Wehl, *Birth of Indonesia*, p. 62.

insisted on a surrender of all weapons in Surabaya, the pent-up emotion of the *pemuda* erupted in a fury which astounded not only the British but the nationalists. It has been estimated that thousands of Indonesians died in what was regarded as one of the most heroic battles of the struggle for independence.

In the midst of this frenzied maelstrom of internal and external threat and political intrigue, Hatta at last ended his self-imposed celibacy. His bride was Rahmi Rachim, the elder daughter of Anni Nurdin, the girlfriend he had rejected for the nationalist cause. Sukarno, a man with a discerning eye for feminine charm, approved of Hatta's choice, describing his bride as "the most beautiful girl in Bandung."[42] Whether Hatta saw in Rahmi Rachim the qualities he had previously admired in her mother, he does not mention. In fact, in Hatta's memoirs the wedding is marked only by a photograph of the bridal couple.

Anni Rachim admitted that she was surprised when Sukarno, acting as a marriage broker on Hatta's behalf, asked for her daughter's hand in marriage. She recalled: "I considered that the age difference between Yuke and Bung Hatta was too great, but I merely replied: 'Mas Karno, about this proposal, I must ask my daughter first. She's nineteen years old and adult enough to decide her own future.'" Rahmi's younger sister, Titi, was more candid than her mother: "Don't accept, Yu," she advised, "He's too old!"[43] Titi was later to revise her opinion of Hatta's senescence when she discovered that, when climbing mountains, she could not keep up with him. "He walked so quickly, like a Westerner," she acknowledged.[44] Sukarno assured Rahmi of Hatta's suitability as a prospective husband: "The main thing is that Hatta is a fine person, he is a good leader and he's my own very close friend," adding: "You won't be disappointed. Hatta is a perfect gentleman with the highest principles."[45]

Rahmi married Hatta on November 18, 1945, a union which endured until Hatta's death. "Every opportunity we had of being together felt beautiful and valuable," Hatta's wife recalled, "like a string of precious

42 See Nyonya H. S. S. A. Rachim, "Pribadinya Bung Hatta yang Saya Kenal," in *Bung Hatta: Pribadinya dalam Kenangan*, pp. 25-26.
43 Ibid., p. 26. "Yuke" was Rahmi's pet name.
44 Raharty Subijakto, "Sebuah Kenangan," in *Bung Hatta: Pribadinya dalam Kenangan*, p. 38.
45 Rachim, "Pribadinya Bung Hatta yang Saya Kenal," p. 27.

jewels."[46] Many Indonesians claimed that, as a good Muslim, Hatta had four wives: the first was Indonesia, the second the Indonesian people, the third his work, and fourth -- Nyonya Hatta![47]

In view of the war-time situation, Hatta requested that the wedding ceremony be simple, attended only by close family friends. It was at his small villa in the hills at Megamendung that he ceased to be Indonesia's most eligible bachelor. Hatta's wedding gift to his bride, his recently completed book *Alam Pikiran Yunani* ["The Greek Thought-World"] did not meet with his mother's approval, although Rahmi accepted the gift in the spirit in which it was offered, knowing that books were Hatta's most treasured possessions and that Greek views on democracy accorded in many respects with his own.

The first years of their married life were difficult and dangerous, affording Hatta scant time to devote to his wife. On December 26, Sjahrir narrowly escaped death, when a pistol fired at him by a KNIL soldier miraculously jammed.[48] Two days later an assassination attempt was made on Amir Sjarifuddin. By January 1946, the situation in the capital was so tense that Sjahrir evacuated his government, accepting the offer from the Sultan of Yogyakarta of his royal domain as an alternative capital.

It was a move which restored leadership significance to the *Dwi Tunggal* because, while Sjahrir remained in Jakarta for negotiations, Sukarno and Hatta acted as de facto heads of government in Yogyakarta. Sukarno's confidence recovered in this center of Javanese culture. For Hatta, too, the transfer was satisfying as it allowed him an opportunity to concentrate on consolidation, especially in the economic sector.

One of Hatta's priorities was to commission a printing press to produce Republican currency to replace the Japanese money still in circulation and to prevent Dutch NICA notes being used. Republic of Indonesia money [*Oeang Republik Indonesia* -- ORI] had been printed in Jakarta, but because of the abundance of Japanese notes in circulation, it was decided to delay their issue until February 1, 1946.[49] However, when

---

46 Rahmi Hatta, "Prinsip-Prinsip Bung Hatta Tak Pernah Luntur," p. 41.

47 See Coast, *Recruit to Revolution*, p. 153.

48 Interview, Nyonya Siti Wahjunah Sjahrir, February 5, 1982.

49 According to Sjafruddin Prawiranegara, later to become finance minister, he had pressed Hatta to print Republican money from the time of the proclamation. See Sjafruddin Prawiranegara, "Bung Hatta Demokrat Sedjati dan Pemimpin jang Saja Hormati," p. 322. See also Robert Cribb,

the Allies occupied the state printing works in Jakarta in January 1946, they confiscated the Republican currency, necessitating the production of new notes. Dening, the SEAC adviser, warned that the economy of the country would be ruined if the Republic issued its own currency, although Hatta had already made clear that Republican money would be backed by goods rather than gold.[50]

Hatta managed to find an alternative printer for the new currency at the Kolff printing works at Malang in East Java, although the quality was inferior to that of the state printing works in Jakarta. When the new currency was finally issued on October 31, 1946, Hatta made a radio broadcast to the nation, urging that Indonesians regard it as a symbol of independence and economic development, rejecting the NICA money. Hatta explained that the power of the rupiah would be roughly equivalent to the prewar Netherlands Indies guilder.[51] Hatta had also, on the first anniversary of the proclamation of independence, opened the *Bank Negara Indonesia*, the Indonesian State Bank. From now on the Dutch and Republic of Indonesia were strongly competing for control of the nation's financial affairs.

Hatta was also active in the field of education, supporting the establishment of a new national university in Yogyakarta, named in honor of the famed Majapahit leader, Gajah Mada. An American observer has commented that the man who in those first years was responsible for the day-to-day functioning of the Republic was "neither Sukarno the spellbinder nor Sjahrir the thinker, but Hatta the administrator."[52]

During 1946, the Sjahrir government came under fire for dampening revolutionary ardor by its efforts to restrain the anarchical spirit prevalent in the archipelago. The Tan Malaka group accused Sjahrir's government of pursuing policies which were too conciliatory to the

---

"Political Dimensions of the Currency Question 1945-1947," in *Indonesia* 31 (April 1981): 115.

50 See Cribb, "Political Dimensions of the Currency Question," pp. 121-22. According to Cribb, the British were not consistent. One group of officers advised Hatta to accept the NICA currency while another encouraged him to go ahead with the issue of Republican notes. Mountbatten urged the Dutch to withhold the NICA money to avoid provoking the Indonesians, while on December 10, Christison wrote to Van Mook suggesting that he circulate NICA currency from January 1, 1946.

51 Ibid., p. 128.

52 Charles Wolf, Jr., *Indonesia Story: The Birth, Growth and Structure of the Indonesian Republic* (New York: John Day, 1948), p. 95.

Dutch, thus contrary to its ideological commitment to social revolution. In a pamphlet, *Moeslihat* ["Strategy"], the Tan Malaka group argued that "armed struggle" rather than "diplomacy" should be adopted by the Sjahrir government. The group formed a Persatuan Perjuangan [PP or Struggle Union], stressing the goal of "100% *Merdeka*" to be attained through a struggle which included the confiscation of enemy property.

Tan Malaka's program received wide support. Its fiery, revolutionary ring appealed to the *pemuda* at a time when the Republican government seemed to be losing ground in its negotiations with the Dutch. When on February 10, 1946, Sjahrir announced to the KNIP that Van Mook insisted on the formation of a United States of Indonesia under the Dutch Crown in which the Republic of Indonesia would merely represent Java, the reception he received was so hostile that he submitted his resignation to Sukarno.[53]

When the Persatuan Perjuangan group pressed Sukarno and Hatta for a mandate to form a coalition cabinet, Hatta made clear to its spokesman, the *pemuda* leader, Chaerul Saleh, that "neither Sukarno nor I can accept as cabinet policy the Persatuan Perjuangan program."[54] The PP discovered that, although it had succeeded in ousting Sjahrir from office, it could not gain support for a cabinet which did not have the *Dwi Tunggal's* approval. On March 2, Hatta announced that Sjahrir would form a new coalition cabinet based on a Five-Point program, incorporating the PP's emotive theme "100% *Merdeka*." Hatta stressed that the second cabinet would be more widely representative and less accommodating to the Dutch.

The Tan Malaka group did not accept its rejection passively, arranging a congress to be held on March 17 to coincide with Sjahrir's negotiations with Van Mook. Sjahrir relayed a secret request to Yogyakarta that the *Dwi Tunggal* and Amir Sjarifuddin detain the PP leadership temporarily, as their antigovernment sentiments were making it difficult for him to achieve a satisfactory settlement.[55] On the charge that inflammatory, antigovernment sentiments had been expressed at the PP congress, Tan

---

53 Anderson, *Java in a Time of Revolution*, p. 306.
54 Hatta, *Memoir*, p. 484.
55 See Anderson, *Java in a Time of Revolution*, p. 323. Anderson in footnote 35 states that Subadio, in an interview on June 4, 1967, admitted that he was one of the couriers of the message from Sjahrir, which was delivered orally.

Malaka, Yamin, Sukarni, Chaerul Saleh, and Abikusno Tjokrosujoso, the Muslim leader, were arrested.

Aware of having adopted tactics which were in sharp conflict with democratic principles, Sjahrir's government issued an explanation on April 1, which read: "The purpose and aim of these arrests, based exclusively on the government's full responsibility, was to avoid the possibility of still graver dangers to the security and well being of the state."[56] Press response was critical, comparing Sjahrir's actions with those of the PID and Kempeitai. Sukarno defended Sjahrir, stressing that "the object was to maintain maximum unity while solutions to political difficulties were being sought."[57]

Increasingly, it became the task of the *Dwi Tunggal* to ward off attacks on Sjahrir's government and to present the unpleasant realities of the negotiations to the public. On June 27, Hatta announced on Sjahrir's behalf that the Republic of Indonesia could at most claim sovereignty over the islands of Java and Sumatra, that the Dutch had reestablished colonial rule in the remaining territories. The resentment aroused by Hatta's announcement was sufficiently heated for the PP to attempt a coup, kidnapping Sjahrir and his party while they were traveling in Central Java.[58]

On June 28, Sukarno proclaimed a state of emergency and resumed his presidential powers. Members of the pro-Tan Malaka group who had now been released from jail presented Sukarno and Hatta with four decrees to sign instituting a new "Supreme Political Council" headed by Tan Malaka, with demands that Sukarno's military powers be delegated to the army commander, Sudirman. Sudirman was persuaded to remain loyal to the government and he agreed to arrest Subardjo, Iwa Kusuma Sumantri, Yamin, and Sukarni. Hatta was faced with authorizing the arrest of two former PI colleagues with whom he had enjoyed particularly close associations in the past -- Subardjo and Iwa. He was many times to learn that politics play havoc with personal friendships.

---

56 Ibid., pp. 327-28.
57 *Merdeka*, March 29, 1946.
58 See Kahin, *Nationalism and Revolution in Indonesia*, p. 189, n. 64. Kahin quotes Sjahrir as stating that his kidnapping came as no surprise since the Dutch army radio had already announced it the evening prior to the event.

The removal of the PP leadership did make it easier for negotiations with the Dutch to continue. On October 2, the *Dwi Tunggal* handed back their legislative powers to Sjahrir, allowing him to form a third cabinet, this time a body representative of a wide spectrum of parties and nationalist groups. On November 15, 1946, under the chairmanship of the British mediator, Lord Killearn, Sjahrir initialed a treaty with the Dutch, the Linggajati Agreement, in which the Dutch representatives finally recognized the Republic of Indonesia as the de facto authority on Java and Sumatra, agreeing that the Republic and the Netherlands would cooperate to establish a United States of Indonesia, consisting of three entities, the Republic of Indonesia, Borneo, and the Great Eastern State, all part of a Netherlands-Indonesian Union.[59]

There was widespread hostility to the Linggajati Agreement, which now had to go before KNIP for ratification, in spite of the fact that Sjahrir had obtained recognition of Sumatra as Republican territory. Feelings became polarized into two opposing fronts, the Benteng Republik [The Republican Fortress], which included members of the two most influential parties, Masjumi and the PNI and which opposed the agreement, and the Sayap Kiri [The Left Wing], consisting of Sjahrir's Partai Sosialis, the renascent PKI, the Labor Party, and Pesindo, the Indonesian Socialist Youth [Pemuda Sosialis Indonesia], which supported it. Seeing that the Sayap Kiri would be outnumbered in the vote for the Linggajati Agreement, on December 30, 1946 Sukarno took back power in order to issue a presidential decree increasing the membership of KNIP from 200 to 513, thus allowing the Sayap Kiri a sufficient majority to ensure the agreement's ratification.

Masjumi and the PNI were furious, condemning Sukarno's action as a violation of Hatta's decree of October 16, 1945. Sukarno defended his action by declaring that he was not a President of the French or American type but a "President à la Indonesian revolution," whose responsibility was to guide and lead the people.[60] But resentment ran too deeply for the KNIP to accept Sukarno's explanation and heated debate continued for two days.

59 For details and text of Linggajati Agreement, see C. Smit, *Het Akkoord Van Linggadjati: Uit Dagboek van Prof. Dr. Ir. W. Schermerhorn* (Amsterdam: Elsevier, 1959).
60 See Reid, *Indonesian National Revolution*, p. 97.

On the third day Hatta intervened, making an *ex tempore* speech before the KNIP assembly. It was, as a member of his audience recalled, "very strong and fiery, quickening the heart beats of those who heard him."[61] Gone was the phlegmatic Hatta, to be replaced by an emotionally charged revolutionary, whose "voice trembled" and whose face "grew red."[62] Hatta drew the KNIP's attention to the seriousness of the crisis facing the new nation, and declared that if KNIP were "not satisfied with the leadership of the President and Vice-President, let us look for another President and Vice-President."[63] Hatta's outburst had the desired effect. No further objections were raised. The audience broke into wild clapping, Hatta recalled in his memoirs, people "coming over to where I was sitting, congratulating me and expressing thanks."[64] According to Abu Hanifah, "Hatta's speech was a psychological masterpiece because the big majority did not fancy the idea of a Republic without Sukarno and Hatta."[65]

In the brief lull which followed the initialing of the Linggajati Agreement, as both governments mulled over its implications, Hatta's first daughter, Meutia, was born. The birth took place in the large house in Yogyakarta, which had been allocated as the vice-presidential residence. But Hatta found that he had little time to spend with his wife and baby.

It was clear that the implementation of the Linggajati Agreement presented problems. On May 27, 1947, the Dutch issued a further challenge to Sjahrir, demanding Indonesian recognition of Netherlands *de jure* sovereignty and the immediate establishment of an interim government to administer the whole archipelago until the United States of Indonesia was formally inaugurated on January 1, 1949. In this interim government, the representative of the Dutch Crown would have ultimate power, in Republican ears an echo of past colonial governors' "exorbitant rights."[66] At the same time, Dutch troops continued to press into the Javanese interior, raising speculation in Republican circles that the struggle might eventually have to be fought out in the mountains and

---

61 See Rahendra Koesnan, "Membantu Perdana Menteri Bung Hatta," in *Bung Hatta Mengabdi pada Tjita-Tjita*, p. 222.

62 Ibid.

63 See Reid, *Indonesian National Revolution*, p. 98.

64 Hatta, *Memoir*, p. 494.

65 Hanifah, *Tales of a Revolution*, p. 207.

66 See Wehl, *Birth of Indonesia*, p. 156.

forests of Sumatra.

Hatta had been concerned for some time about the situation in Sumatra. Two social revolutions had already taken place, one in Aceh and the other in East Sumatra, both directed against the local rulers. The Acehnese revolt, which was Islamic rather than Marxist, was less worrying for Hatta than the uprising in East Sumatra, which had direct links with Tan Malaka's Persatuan Perjuangan. Tan Malaka's standing was high in Sumatra, including in the Minangkabau region, and his strategy of "armed struggle" accorded more with the spirit of militancy among the Sumatran nationalists than Sjahrir's and Amir Sjarifuddin's advocacy of "negotiation."

A minor uprising in West Sumatra directed against the Republic administrators, several of whom were former members of the New PNI,[67] alerted Hatta to a potentially dangerous mood of dissatisfaction prevailing in his home region. On May 20, he accepted an invitation to tour Sumatra in an attempt to strengthen local support for the central government. Teuku Hasan, whose influence outside Aceh was limited, was facing immense difficulties in carrying out his task as governor of Sumatra. Hatta could see that his plea to the PPKI to divide the island into three provinces had been justified. In a subsequent report he pointed out that "the Governor of Sumatra was only the Governor of Pematang Siantar because of the lack of communication with the Residents."[68] Teuku Hasan had moved his capital to Pematang Siantar because of the build-up of Dutch forces in Medan.

Hatta commenced his tour in South Sumatra, traveling up through Jambi and across to Bukit Tinggi. His itinerary was interrupted when he received a request from Sukarno to fly to India to negotiate for arms with his old friend Nehru. At the time the Republicans were in desperate need of defense equipment. On May 7, 1947, Dutch ministers Beel and Jonkman had held talks in Jakarta which foreshadowed a military offensive as a means of solving the Republican deadlock. Economic factors were involved, as the Dutch were anxious to resume plantation operations in a

67 Among them were Chatib Suleiman, Leon Salim, and Darwis Thaib as was also Mohammad Sjafei, a personal friend of Hatta's.
68 "Outline of Vice-President's Statement on the Situation in Sumatra," January 17, 1948, as cited in A. Kahin, "Struggle for Independence," pp. 246-47, n. 7.

more secure atmosphere. Sukarno's message was relayed to Hatta by Biju Patnaik, an Indian nationalist, the pilot of an Indian plane which had landed at Bukit Tinggi on its return flight, having delivered aid supplies to the Republican government on Java. Sukarno suggested that Hatta accompany Patnaik disguised as his co-pilot.

The two "Indias," the British and the Dutch, had already established a supportive relationship. The former was now self-governing and on the brink of full independence, so more free than Indonesia of colonial interference. In June 1946, Sjahrir's government had consigned 7,000 tons of rice to relieve famine in India. Hatta admitted that, although the amount was not large, "as a contribution from the Indonesian people to the people of India, it has great significance, clearly influencing international politics, because by offering rice to India, the eyes of the world are redirected to Indonesia."[69] The gesture established Indonesia as a nation engaging in foreign relations independently of the Dutch. Haji Agus Salim, as deputy foreign minister, also signed treaties of friendship with Egypt and Syria.

India's prime minister had given what support he could, organizing an Inter-Asiatic Conference in New Delhi in March 1947 to coincide with the signing of the Linggajati Agreement. He established a rapport with Sjahrir, who arrived at the conference just in time to address the closing session.[70] Now it was Hatta's turn to use his influence with an old friend to gain arms for Indonesia.

As he knew the Dutch would be watching his movements carefully, Hatta had to maintain his disguise even when in India. In New Delhi, he had to decine Nehru's offer of hospitality for the sake of secrecy. Patnaik recalled that even when Nehru introduced Hatta to Gandhi his real identity was not revealed, "for which Pandit Nehru was later reprimanded by Mahatma Gandhi."[71] Hatta remembered that Gandhi was confident that Indonesia would attain its independence, commenting that "however aggressive the Dutch, Indonesia will be victorious."[72]

---

69 Hatta, "Beras Kita ke India," in *Kumpulan Pidato*, p. 81.
70 Biju Patnaik, "Mengenang Dr. Mohammad Hatta, Bekas Wakil Presiden Republik Indonesia," in *Bung Hatta: Pribadinya dalam Kenangan*, p. 358.
71 Ibid., p. 361.
72 Hatta, *Memoir*, p. 504.

The British army was still in control of military supplies, its presence required to prevent Hindu/Muslim rioting on the eve of India's independence and partition. Because of this Hatta did not succeed in obtaining arms, although the Indian leaders did offer moral support.

Hatta returned to East Sumatra to find Governor Hasan's capital at Pematang Siantar was about to fall to Dutch military forces. Hatta and Hasan had little alternative but to find a new capital, their choice being Bukit Tinggi.

The whole Republic was in a state of crisis. While Hatta was overseas, Sjahrir had again handed back his mandate to govern, disillusioned by the Dutch failure to honor their agreements and worried by the extreme left wing group within the Partai Sosialis. The tense situation was heightened by the receipt on June 28 of an *aide-memoire* from the United States of America advising the Republican government to "cooperate without delay" with the Dutch.[73] On July 3, Amir Sjarifuddin managed to form a coalition cabinet, following Sjahrir's example of "diplomacy" rather than "armed struggle," agreeing to meet Dutch demands for an interim government.

Hatta made use of the spacious quarters of the former Dutch Assistant-Resident of Agam as his vice-presidential palace in Bukit Tinggi. His first concern was to coordinate the activities of the various national groups in West Sumatra and to try to regulate the economy. He quickly caught the prevailing air of resentment against the Republican government for its neglect of Sumatra and a general distaste for the Linggajati Agreement.

A difficulty experienced by Sumatran administrators was an inadequate supply of Republican currency, forcing them to print their own. Although special Republic of Indonesia, Sumatra Province, currency was printed in Pematang Siantar and issued in April 1947, the supply was still insufficient.[74] Hatta's nationalist colleague, Hazairin, who held the position of Resident in Bengkulu, recalled that he challenged Hatta to provide him with legal currency when reprimanded for printing his own

73 According to R. E. Elson, "American Policy and the Indonesian Dispute, 1945-1949" (B.A. Honours Thesis, Monash University), p. 28, the US State Department failed to comprehend the nature of the gulf separating the Dutch and Indonesians.
74 See Cribb, "Political Dimensions of the Currency Question," p. 132, n. 103.

notes. "Pak Hatta was silent," he recorded.[75]

Hatta tried to regularize Sumatra's important external trade with Singapore and the Malay peninsula, establishing in July 1947 the Central Trading Corporation. He also tried to coordinate the activities of the various nationalist groups in West Sumatra. Hamka, a local Masjumi leader, recalled how on June 30 Hatta invited all "those holding responsible positions in parties, local groups, the military, religious teachers and civil servants" to meet with him for a "briefing" in which Hatta reiterated the importance of unity of command, "because, even if the spirit were bubbling over, if mature decisions were not made under a unified command, it would be very difficult to achieve their goals."[76] But the concept of a paramount chief was not one which was easy to accept in this part of the Minangkabau.

Audrey Kahin, in her study of West Sumatra during this period, has observed that "Hatta was the principal agent ensuring the subordination of local to national issues. As a Minangkabau and one of the two highest leaders of the Republic, he exerted great influence over the situation in West Sumatra,"[77] sentiments echoed by Hamka, who declared: "He could hold the hearts of the Minangkabau people in his hands."[78] Yet, despite the psychological strength which the people derived from Hatta's presence in their midst, Audrey Kahin felt that some of the policies which he pursued were incompatible with the most effective marshalling of the Republic on Sumatra to confront the Dutch.[79] In trying to impose centralized control on his people, Hatta was running contrary to traditional patterns of working in independent local groups. One of Hatta's first initiatives had been to merge the numerous Sumatran parties and organizations into a National Defense Front and to incorporate the disparate combat units into the regular army, a move which was to prove unworkable. Yet, in other ways, Hatta tried to correct Javanese centralist influences, aiming to restore local autonomy by abolishing the residencies. The problem was that the Residents had become effective regional administrators.

75 Hazairin, "Kenang-Kenangan tentang Pak Hatta," p. 191.
76 Hamka, "Memimpin Perdjuangan Revolusi dari Bukit Tinggi," p. 165.
77 Kahin, "Struggle for Independence," p. 241.
78 Hamka, "Memimpin Perdjuangan Revolusi dari Bukit Tinggi," p. 165.
79 Kahin, "Struggle for Independence," p. 241.

It was while Hatta was in Sumatra that the Indonesian struggle assumed a much more international character. On August 14, 1947 at Lake Success in New York, Sjahrir became the first Indonesian to address a United Nations assembly, appealing to the Security Council to back Indonesia's bid for independence. In response, the Security Council appointed a Good Offices Committee from among its members, allowing the Dutch and Indonesians to choose one delegate each. The Dutch chose a Belgian representative and the Indonesians an Australian, sensing that Labor Prime Minister Chiffley was sympathetic to their cause. The third member was a representative of the United States of America.[80]

Hamka recalled the determination of the Minangkabau people to impress the Good Offices Committee members when they made a tour of inspection of Sumatra, rallying the people by "using old-fashioned but tried methods of beating the mosque drums." He remembered Hatta's look of surprise when seeing mass formations streaming up to his Vice-President's mansion, the majority carrying bamboo spears and shouting "Long live Bung Hatta!"[81]

Hamka delivered the speech of welcome to the Good Offices Committee. He appealed:

> Sirs, have you ever seen a place as beautiful as this? Its mountains, its ricefields, its green forests and villages? For three hundred and fifty years this land which we love has been taken from our hands, although it is we who own it. We lived in it but we did not control it. We were considered to be slaves in our own country.... Sirs, you see our bamboo spears! Even if these are the only weapons we have to defend ourselves, we will never allow our native land to be plundered again.[82]

Glancing at Hatta, Hamka noticed to his astonishment that the Vice-President's eyes were moist and red, that the self-contained Hatta was actually weeping.[83] It was one of the few occasions when Hatta allowed

---

80 The United States member was chosen by the Australian and Belgian appointees.
81 Hamka, "Memimpin Perdjuangan Revolusi dari Bukit Tinggi," pp. 168-69.
82 Ibid., pp. 170-71.
83 Ibid., p. 171.

his emotions public display.

For Hatta, his own close personal relationships with members of the Good Offices Committee, especially the Australian and American representatives, would play an important part in the final attainment of Indonesian independence. Hatta had always supported the concept of an international forum and judiciary to protect the interests of the weaker nations. As 1947 drew uneasily to a close, Hatta appealed to his people to maintain the fight:

> Struggle demands sacrifice, suffering, patience and a conviction that our goals will be achieved. We must be prepared to fight on for a very long time and we must safeguard that the base of our effort is pure because it is the purity of our goals which is our strength. This last year has shown us that our freedom depends on two things: firstly, our own personal strength, and secondly, the sympathy of the international world towards us.[84]

---

84 Hatta, "Pidato Pada Perpisahan Tahun 1947-1948," in *Kumpulan Pidato*, p. 135.

Proclamation of Independence

Linggajati Discussions
(L to R: Sukarno, Prof. Dr. Schermerhorn,
Lord Killearn, Hatta, H. J. Van Mook)

Sjahrir, Sukarno, Hatta being taken prisoner by Capt. Vosveld of Dutch Military Intelligence, Yogyakarta, December 19, 1948

Family members and staff at Presidential Palace as Sukarno, Hatta, and Sjahrir are driven away, December 19, 1948. Mrs. Hatta is second woman from R.

Hatta on Bangka, April 1949
(L to R: Abdul Gafar Pringgodigdo, Sudarpo, Hatta, Assaat)

Transfer of Sovereignty
(Hatta is on Queen Juliana's right)

Hatta with his wife and daughters

At Sjahrir's graveside, 1966

With his family, following conferral of honorary doctorate at University of Indonesia, 1975

At Panca Sila commemoration conference, June 1977.
At R is his daughter Halida, who completed his speech for him.

Hatta as Prime Minister

CHAPTER TEN
PRIME MINISTER

However emphatically the Dutch government produces legal arguments that the sovereignty over Indonesia lies in the hands of the kingdom of the Netherlands, the Indonesian people of the republic is of the opinion and feels that its state is sovereign. It has its own government which is not subject to any other government. It has its own army and its own police force to maintain law and order, it has its own monetary system and last but not least it has its own foreign policy and representation abroad.[1]

1948 was one of the most critical and challenging years of Hatta's life. In January he returned to Java where a political crisis had developed following Prime Minister Amir Sjarifuddin's acceptance of the Renville Agreement.[2] Under the new treaty with the Dutch, the Republic was reduced to a "sub-state"[3] among many, its territory comprising merely Central Java and less resource-rich areas of Sumatra, although including the indomitable Aceh. The "Van Mook line," an arbitrary boundary joining up Dutch military spearheads, ceded to the Dutch Republican territory in which some of its most efficient fighting units were well established.

In the face of bitter resentment and accusations of being pro-Dutch, Amir Sjarifuddin tendered his resignation. For six days the government hung in the balance, no party prepared to face the repugnant task of

---

1 Mohammad Hatta, "On the Road to Transfer of Sovereignty," in *Portrait of a Patriot*, p. 508. Speech delivered at the Opening Session of the Round Table Conference on August 23, 1949.
2 The agreement was signed aboard the American battleship, the USS *Renville* anchored off Jakarta, a venue suggested by Sukarno.
3 This is how Subadio Sastrosatomo described the Republic's reduced status. Interview, February 22, 1982.

implementing the Renville Agreement, especially persuading Indonesian military units to withdraw to the Republic's reduced territory. "Renville was a low point in the struggle," Mohamad Roem recalled, "Everyone felt the need for a strong cabinet and Hatta seemed to be the strongest leader."[4]

Hatta was initially reluctant to accept the prime ministership, not surprising since assuming the office was tantamount to committing political suicide. There was an anomaly in the person who had decreed parliamentary government heading a presidential cabinet, although Hatta did consult the Working Body of KNIP on most major decisions.[5]

Hatta returned briefly to Bukit Tinggi to seek support for his government, pleading that the unfavorable terms of the Renville Agreement be regarded as "just a link in our long struggle."[6] He pointed out to his mass audience:

> People say that we are defeated, but let me remind you that a defeated nation is one which admits it has lost. Our struggle still continues, despite the risks. The United Nations has accepted that we are entitled to defend our freedom. Indonesia will never again be wiped off the map of the world.[7]

The Renville Agreement marked a turning point in the close relationship of both Hatta and Sjahrir with Amir Sjarifuddin. Sjahrir in February 1948 led his own socialist faction out of the Partai Sosialis, forming a new party, the Partai Sosialis Indonesia or PSI, a party considered to be a continuation of the policies of the New PNI of the early 1930s. The Sayap Kiri now consisted of Amir Sjarifuddin's Partai Sosialis group, the PKI, the Labor Party, and Pesindo. Formerly dependent on strong support

---

4 Interview with Mohamad Roem, February 5, 1982.
5 John Coast, a young English socialist who was working for the Republican cause, recorded widespread approval of Hatta's apointment as prime minister, and Critchley, the Australian representative on the Good Offices Committee, has remarked: "Hatta was a man who commanded respect, a man of unusual quality. He may not have sought to arouse the emotions of the people, but he always remained a man of the people." Personal communication from T. K. Critchley, May 1, 1983.
6 Hatta, *Memoir*, p. 522.
7 Ibid., and T. Mohammad Hasan, "Bung Hatta di Sumatera," in *Bung Hatta: Mengabdi pada Tjita-Tjita*, p. 186.

from the *Dwi Tunggal*, the Sayap Kiri was now bitterly critical of Hatta heading a presidential rather than a parliamentary cabinet.

Several of Hatta's former antagonists now had strong leadership positions in the Sayap Kiri, such as Abdul Madjid, Tan Ling Djie, and Setiadjit, men who had supported Rustam Effendi and the Communist Party of Holland in their attacks on Hatta. Rustam Effendi was back in Indonesia but had switched his allegiance from the Stalinists to Tan Malaka, thus as a national Communist perhaps qualifying for the label "Trotskyist." Hatta's gibes that he was "Stalin's slave" may have borne fruit. A disquieting factor for Hatta was that, during his absence in Sumatra, the Communist group had been wooing Sukarno. As Abu Hanifah commented: "At that time it was very difficult to approach Sukarno. If one wanted to talk to him, one had to ask for an appointment through Setiadjit,"[8] possibly an exaggeration.

Hatta offered the foreign affairs portfolio to Sjahrir, highly regarded internationally since his defense of the Republic of Indonesia before the United Nations Security Council. Sjahrir refused, preferring to remain a special adviser, disliking the return to a presidential rather than a parliamentary cabinet and, since the Renville Agreement, opposing the policy of continuing negotiation.[9] As Haji Agus Salim had been liaising closely with Sjahrir in building up a diplomatic corps overseas, Hatta offered him the foreign affairs portfolio instead. His former PI colleagues, Sukiman, Maramis, and Ali Sastroamidjojo, now representing Masjumi and PNI, he appointed ministers of the interior, finance, and education respectively.

Hatta's cabinet program had four main goals: implementation of the Renville Agreement with continued negotiation through the Good Offices Committee, acceleration of the formation of a sovereign, democratic United States of Indonesia, rationalization of the Republic's army and civil service in view of the nation's limited resources, and an attempt at national reconstruction. In defending his government's policies, Hatta pointed out that "like it or not, the Republic of Indonesia is bound to implement the Renville Agreement."[10] He recalled in his memoirs: "What was amusing

8   Hanifah, *Tales of a Revolution*, p. 272.
9   Interview with Subadio Sastrosatomo, February 22, 1982.
10 Hatta, *Memoir*, p. 525.

was that, in the following debates, it was the Amir Sjarifuddin group in the Working Body which opposed my Government's policies. They, who had produced the Agreement, wanted it to be rejected."[11]

The Sayap Kiri, following the pattern set by Tan Malaka's Persatuan Perjuangan, on February 26 transformed itself into an antigovernment group calling itself the Front Demokrasi Rakyat [People's Democratic Front], abbreviated to FDR. Its program mirrored that of Tan Malaka, advocating mass struggle, nationalization of foreign properties and a cessation of negotiations with the Dutch while they remained on Indonesian soil.[12] "Diplomacy" was now a very unpopular concept to the humiliated Indonesians.

When on May 26, the Soviet Union announced that it had ratified an agreement for the exchange of consuls between their nation and the Republic of Indonesia, Hatta was considerably embarrassed. He took shelter behind the Renville Agreement, claiming that the Dutch and Americans might misinterpret an agreement between Indonesia and the Soviet Union as the treaty did stipulate Dutch control of Indonesia's foreign relations, a concession made by Amir Sjarifuddin.[13] Yet Hatta had ignored this clause in appointing Haji Agus Salim to the foreign affairs ministry and in continuing Indonesia's diplomatic offensive overseas. His government assured the American representative on the Good Offices Committee, Du Bois, that, as long as Hatta was prime minister, there would be no exchange of consuls with the Soviet Union.[14]

Undoubtedly the most contentious issue in Hatta's program, both in Java and Sumatra, was "rationalization" of the civil service and armed forces. In defending the program before the KNIP's Working Body on February 16, 1948, Hatta stated:

That the revenues of the state do not cover expenditures should be no reason for wonder. But the difference can be narrowed by judicious rationalization, by transferring labor from unproductive

---

11 Ibid.
12 Kahin, *Nationalism and Revolution in Indonesia*, p. 260.
13 See Reid, *Indonesian National Revolution*, p. 131.
14 Oey Hong Lee, *War and Diplomacy in Indonesia 1945-1950* (Townsville, Qd.: James Cook University, 1981), p. 177.

work to productive fields of activity. This transfer of labor will not at once show a decrease in the state's expenditures; the contrary may even be the case in the beginning, because the creation of productive enterprises requires previous preparation and investment to work on. But once the preparations are completed, the productive labor will begin to yield its profits and the income of the State will increase.[15]

This was Hatta the economist speaking, applying business management principles to his government. The problem was that a chaotic revolutionary situation was not an ideal basis for sound planning.

Due to the large numbers of refugees flooding into the now pocket-sized Republic, Hatta's government had a massive unemployment problem on its hands. The refugees had to be fed and offered sustenance, but the main government employment opportunities, apart from the already cumbersome defense forces and civil service, were in the oilfields at Cepu and the railway workshops at Madiun, both overstaffed. Hatta instituted a Ministry of Youth and Reconstruction to try to retrain and rehabilitate excess labor. The problem was that, in the atmosphere of war, the prestigious course open for young men was to take up arms. Hatta's attempts to establish agricultural cooperatives also received a weak response. The Japanese had discredited such enterprises by using them as a means for extorting produce from the Indonesian people.

Hatta was uneasy about the nationalization of the armed forces already begun under Amir Sjarifuddin's government, which included the demotion of General Sudirman and the sacking of Urip, both of whom Hatta reinstated. In his memoirs Hatta cited the existence of a marine corps, part of the left-wing Fourth Division, which was "led by nine admirals, all friends of Amir Sjarifuddin."[16] The admirals Hatta dismissed, informing them that, as the Republic's armada was insignificant, it "had no need of nine admirals." Hatta also recorded the case of a militia unit "which was considered to be the FDR's army," explaining that "I began by removing this People's Army, which was financed by the ministry

15 As cited in Kahin, *Nationalism and Revolution*, p. 262.
16 Hatta, *Memoir*, p. 527.

of defense."[17] The detailed reports from Colonel A. H. Nasution do not confirm Hatta's figures, but do state that "the top leadership of the ALRI was eliminated."[18] Nasution also pointed to persistent conflict between his own Siliwangi Division and the Marine Corps, the Tentara Laut Republik Indonesia,[19] and stated that the Sayap Kiri controlled more than 80 percent of the People's Army and almost all of the Marine Corps.[20]

In his rationalization efforts Hatta was strongly supported by Nasution, the young but highly regarded Sumatran officer who was chief of the Siliwangi Division, and with whom Hatta was to work very closely both as minister of defense and prime minister. T. B. Simatupang, another senior Siliwangi officer close to Sjahrir, agreed that the forces needed tidying up.[21] Generals Sudirman and Urip, however, aware of a crisis situation within the armed forces, were of the opinion that such drastic pruning should be postponed in spite of the high cost of maintaining irregular units.

Dissatisfaction among the military was particularly evident in the Surakarta region where a number of officers refused to relinquish their commands, and many were resentful of the Siliwangi Division's favored status. For the rest of his life, Hatta was to be the target of recriminations that he was the direct cause of the internal revolt which broke out in the latter half of 1948. Both Nasution and Simatupang defended Hatta, claiming that, apart from defusing antigovernment elements in the forces, Hatta's motives were defensible on economic grounds.[22]

Undoubtedly the Dutch blockade was impoverishing the Republic, cutting it off from sources of income, from arms purchases and medical supplies. The Republic was forced to exploit a stockpile of opium left over from the Dutch and Japanese regimes. Morally it was not a situation which Hatta enjoyed, but he felt that the opium's exchange value and its neatness as a smuggling commodity were too advantageous to be ignored. John Coast, an English socialist working for the Republic, recalled that one of

---

17 Ibid.
18 A. H. Nasution, *Sekitar Perang Kemerdekaan Indonesia*, vol. 7: Renville Period (Bandung: Angkasa, 1978), p. 135.
19 Ibid., pp. 213-14.
20 Nasution, *Sekitar Perang Kemerdekaan Indonesia*, vol. 8, p. 75.
21 Interview with T. B. Simatupang, February 4, 1982.
22 Both Nasution and Simatupang confirmed this point in interviews in February 1982.

his assignments was to report to Hatta on the Republic's opium-running operations centered on Singapore, which had become the subject of Dutch criticism. Hatta's delicate way of delegating this task amused Coast. "As an afterthought and smiling like a benign sphinx, he commented: 'And at the same time, John, please see if you can clear up this opium business for me!'"[23] Coast sensed Hatta's discomfiture. "To Hatta, I knew the Republic's reputation in this vital commercial centre was all that mattered. To settle 'this opium business' which was boomeranging round the world with the full power of the Netherlands foreign minister's information service behind it, was hardly likely to be a sinecure."[24]

Like many of Hatta's fellow Indonesians, Coast saw that the *Dwi Tunggal* was an effective leadership combination, commenting:

> Hatta is too good and too quiet to be popular in the Sukarno sense, but between the two of them, with the parallel characteristics of showmanship and solid administrative ability, of artistry and applied economics, of brilliant demagogic appeal and a reputation for utter integrity, they were as President and Vice-President a most happy combination for Indonesia.[25]

Coast also noted the physical contrast between the two men. "Sukarno is tall and unusually handsome, with brooding, thoughtful eyes. There is about him a mixture of missionary, orator and actor." Hatta he described as "small, slightly chubby, bespectacled," sitting on his chair like an Indonesian Buddha, "calm, imperturbable and steady-eyed. In his looks there was nothing of the fanatic and no indication of his revolutionary past. A solid sincerity sat about him."[26]

Critchley, the Australian representative on the Good Offices Committee, also considered that "Sukarno and Hatta had a unique and complementary partnership during the independence struggle," at the same time remarking:

---

23 Coast, *Recruit to Revolution*, p. 163.
24 Ibid., p. 164.
25 Ibid., pp. 153-54.
26 Ibid., p. 100.

But it was Sukarno with his charismatic oratory who captured the imagination and allegiance of the Indonesian people. I remember travelling from Yogyakarta to Wonosobo with Sukarno in 1948. Hatta followed in a car behind. Villagers along the way flocked to Sukarno's car to cheer him and they filled our car with fruit and vegetables. Sukarno went out of his way to tell them that Bung Hatta was following and that they should give some of their attention to him, but their interest was primarily in Sukarno.[27]

Sukarno's strong support for Hatta at this time undoubtedly made his task easier as the Dutch relentlessly pressed the Republic to the limits. Hatta sounded out Van Mook's sincerity regarding the Republic's eventual inclusion in the United States of Indonesia by offering to participate in planning of the interim federal government. As he had suspected, this was the last thing Van Mook wanted, and Van Mook's reply made it clear that the Republic would not be welcome in any planning until a final political settlement had been achieved, which would depend on the Republic's full acknowledgement of Dutch authority.[28] On March 9 Van Mook had already announced that he was to be President of the interim government, with key secretariats headed by Dutch colonial officers. Hatta made clear that in any transfer of sovereignty, Sukarno would replace Van Mook as President.[29]

The American and Australian delegates to the Good Offices Committee, Du Bois and Critchley, offered compromise proposals, suggesting that elections be held for the federal government's Constituent Assembly, and that this body be allowed to delineate the constituent states and elect the President, with a proviso that the Netherlands high commissioner retain certain rights of veto.[30] Hatta supported the Du Bois-Critchley proposals, which were rejected by the Dutch government. The 1948 elections in the

---

27 Personal communication from T. K. Critchley.

28 United Press Dispatch, February 14, 1948, as cited in Kahin, *Nationalism and Revolution in Indonesia*, p. 245.

29 Oey Hong Lee, *War and Diplomacy in Indonesia*, p. 171. According to Harmani, Hatta's envoy to discussions on the provisional federal government, Hatta requested the position of second man for himself. De Villeneuve, one of Van Mook's assistants, interpreted this as meaning Hatta "wants to be the boss."

30 For the Du Bois-Critchley Plan, see Kahin, *Nationalism and Revolution in Indonesia*, p. 248.

Netherlands had consolidated the power of the conservative Catholic Party, which considered Van Mook too conciliatory, replacing him in October 1948 with the more hardline former prime minister, Beel. Beel was given the new title "High Representative of the Crown," an indication of how important it was to the Dutch not to let the Indies slip from their grip.

As had been the experience of Sjahrir and Amir, Hatta was not only faced with Dutch intransigence and intensification of Dutch forces around the Republican perimeter, but he was also under increasing attack on the home front. In May 1948, the Front Demokrasi Rakyat launched a strong offensive against Hatta's government, demanding key ministries, and proposing a new "National Program" with a new "National Government" in which they would be represented. Labor unrest accompanied their demands, the most serious incident being a strike at Delanggu, a cotton-growing area providing raw materials for much needed textiles. Yet Hatta refused to use force to bring about a return to work. On July 27, as a gesture of reconciliation, he announced that he would accept the FDR's National Program, as it differed little from his own. However, he was not prepared to offer the ministries which the FDR demanded, in particular his own defense ministry.[31]

Hatta was on the alert for more serious confrontation when the veteran PKI leader, Musso, returned from Russia on August 3. Musso immediately advocated a *Jalan Baru*, a New Way, insisting that the PKI become a single party of the working class, taking over from the FDR the task of wresting control of the government from the "national bourgeoisie."[32] When reminiscing on Musso's return, Hatta expressed the opinion that "Musso's original plan was to proclaim an Indonesian Soviet State,"[33] Hatta had grounds for making this assumption in that Musso openly declared that his strategy was based on the "Gottwald Plan," by which power in Czechoslovakia had passed relatively bloodlessly to the Communist party.

The FDR responded to Musso's call, its member parties, including Amir Sjarifuddin's Partai Sosialis, agreeing to merge into the PKI. For

---

31 Ibid., p. 267.
32 Reid, *Indonesian National Revolution*, p. 137.
33 Hatta, *Bung Hatta's Answers*, p. 16.

Indonesians in general, a surprising aspect of the merger was Amir's public announcement that he had been a member of the Communist party for many years. Most people, including Hatta, found it difficult to accept this statement.[34]

Hatta was aware that Amir commanded considerable popular support and that therefore the PKI threat must be taken seriously. On the third anniversary of the proclamation of independence, August 17, 1948, Sukarno announced an amnesty for the jailed leaders of the Persatuan Perjuangan, releasing Tan Malaka, Subardjo, Iwa Kusuma Sumantri, Sukarni, and Abikusno. The Tan Malaka group, now calling itself the Gerakan Revolusi Rakyat [People's Revolutionary Movement] or GRR, was strongly hostile to Musso, who had consistently accused Tan Malaka of thwarting the PKI revolts of 1926-27. What better strategy than to set two of the government's most ardent opponents at each other's throats?

In his major address to the Working Body of KNIP on September 2, 1948, Hatta was determined both to defend his government's policies and at the same time to alert the Republic to the Communist threat:

> If our struggle were to be regarded merely from the Communist point of view, then indeed there would be much to say for identifying ourselves with Soviet Russian policy. To the Communist, Russia represents the foundation on which to work for the realization of his ideals; for the Communist, struggle rises or falls with the Soviet Union... and therefore the interests of the Soviet Union take precedence over all other matters in international political controversies.[35]

Hatta pointed out that a nationalist, "even though he may have a socialist outlook," must give precedence to his country's independence and therefore "the methods he follows in his struggle differ widely from the methods to which the Communist resorts." Hatta directed attention to the bipolar power structure which had emerged internationally in the wake of the Second World War, contending:

---

34 Hanifah, *Tales of a Revolution*, p. 278.
35 As cited in Kahin, *Nationalism and Revolution in Indonesia*, p. 281.

No matter how weak we appear to be as a nation that has only recently won its independence when compared to the two giants in the conflict -- the United States and the Soviet Union -- it is the view of the government that we must continue to base our struggle on the principle that we must have confidence in ourselves and that we must struggle on our own strength and abilities.[36]

Here Hatta was reiterating Sjahrir's call for an independent policy free of great power domination.

Hatta also pointed out that it was premature to stage a social revolution, using Marxist theory to back his statement. "Even those, who formerly quoted Marx's and Mao Tse-tung's maxims to remind us of the fact that we have not yet passed the stage of national revolution and that therefore the time has not yet arrived for a social revolution, have forgotten their own theories and are ardently advocating a social revolution." Hatta defended his government's record, claiming it had achieved results in spite of the emergency situation, including the cultivation of an extra 75,000 hectares of land, the organization of agricultural cooperatives, price control, and attacks on hoarding.[37]

As a response, Musso wrote directly to the leaders of the two major parties, the PNI and Masjumi, seeking support for a united front against the Dutch and American imperialists. Musso realized that the Republic's tense situation was making the policy of continuing negotiation increasingly unattractive. Both parties remained loyal to Hatta, Masjumi further accusing the Communists of "insulting the Hatta government and organizing anti-tax campaigns."[38] Musso now turned to the Javanese peasantry for support. On September 4 he addressed a congress of the radical Barisan Tani Indonesia [Indonesian Farmers' Brigade] or BTI, groups reminiscent of the former Sarekat Rakyat, insisting that "agrarian revolution, the division of land to the peasants, must be carried out in this time of revolution."[39] Musso was playing on a very emotive issue, as the

36 Ibid., p. 282.
37 Ibid., p. 282, n. 46.
38 Ibid., p. 285.
39 *Buruh*, Yogyakarta, September 4, 1948, as cited in Reid, *Indonesian National Revolution*, p. 138, n. 19.

influx of refugees had increased demand for available land, exacerbating the latent religious animosity between the more affluent landed *santri* and the poorer *abangan* Muslims in the villages. Musso also had strong support from discontented combatants who had been demobilized under Hatta's drastic pruning operation, who were now eager to rally behind a leader out to attack the man they considered was most to blame for their unhappy circumstances.

The Americans were watching closely the confrontation between Hatta and the PKI. Hatta had also clearly put out feelers to see how the Americans, in their present sensitivity to the Communist threat in China and Asia generally, were reacting. Consul General Livengood in Jakarta informed Secretary of State Marshall that Hatta was "prepared to take strong action against intransigent elements" and wished to know "the official US stand, particularly regarding assistance to the Republic against Communists."[40] Replying on September 9, Marshall instructed Livengood to inform Hatta that "US Govt will in every practical way assist democratic non-Communist govt of Indonesia," but he also made clear that extension of financial help would only be forthcoming when a "just and practical settlement [of the] Dutch-Republican dispute" had been reached. On the same day he requested the Dutch government to support Hatta, "stressing the great importance which US attaches to bolstering Hatta Govt [at] this juncture."[41]

Hatta had not long to wait before Musso's revolutionary rhetoric sparked into revolt the underlying unrest and general dissatisfaction in Central Java. The mysterious disappearance of five left-wing army officers had heightened resentment against the government and there were accusations that the Siliwangi Division was the culprit. This event coincided with the commencement of a tour of the Republic by Musso, Amir Sjarifuddin, and Setiadjit. In Madiun, Musso delivered a challenging speech, admonishing Indonesian Communists for allowing the revolution to be led by the bourgeoisie and stating that "elements which opposed the

---

40 "Consul General at Batavia (Livengood) to Secretary of State (Marshall)," September 7, 1948 in *Foreign Relations of the United States, 1948* [hereafter *FRUS*], vol. 6 (Washington, D.C.: Department of State, 1974), p. 325.

41 "Secretary of State to Consulate General at Batavia," September 9, 1948, in ibid., p. 327; and "Secretary of State to Embassy in the Netherlands," September 9, 1948, in ibid., p. 328.

course of the revolution must be purged."[42]

On September 18, left-wing disgruntled army groups responded to Musso's challenge and took over the administration of Madiun, capturing or killing the government's administrative officers. Musso's immediate response was one of dismay, a realization that again a PKI revolt was being staged before the circumstances were right. He offered to settle the uprising peacefully if Hatta would include the PKI in his government.[43]

In an interview after his arrest, Amir Sjarifuddin denied that he had started a rebellion in September 1948, asserting that "even if it is assumed that there were preparations made for a coup, the time for such action was still premature, because it would not be possible to start the action with any chance of success if there were as yet no political unity, and our policy was to bring about this political unity first."[44] In Critchley's opinion, "the revolt was largely the work of people like Musso, and I am convinced that it took some of its supporters, such as Amir Sjarifuddin, by surprise."[45]

The uprising constituted a crisis for Hatta. Again Sukarno came to the fore, using his magnetism to draw the Javanese people to his side. On September 19 he appealed to them to choose between Musso and the *Dwi Tunggal*. Less than two hours later, Musso broadcast his reply, calling on the people to overthrow Sukarno and Hatta, contending that the revolution had been led by the national bourgeoisie, "uncertain and vague in its stand in facing the Imperialists in general and America in particular." He continued: "It is clear that in the past three years Soekarno-Hatta, the ex-*Romusha* dealers, the sworn Quislings, have executed a capitulation policy to the Dutch and the British, and at this very moment they are going to sell out Indonesia to the American imperialists."[46] There was no mention of Amir Sjarifuddin's acceptance of the Renville Agreement.

Hatta wasted no time. On September 19, PKI leaders in Yogyakarta

42 *Api Rakjat*, Madiun, September 9, 1948, as cited in Reid, *Indonesian National Revolution*, p. 142, n. 28.
43 Oey Hong Lee, *War and Diplomacy in Indonesia*, p. 190.
44 Tjekampa, "Interview dengan Bung Amir," in *Hidup* [Roman Catholic newspaper printed in Yogyakarta], December 18, 1948, in Kahin, *Nationalism and Revolution in Indonesia*, p. 285, n. 53.
45 Personal communication from T. K. Critchley.
46 *Front Nasional*, September 20, 1948, as cited in Kahin, *Nationalism and Revolution in Indonesia*, p. 293.

and other urban centers were taken into custody, including Tan Ling Djie and Abdul Madjid, several not even aware that a revolt had taken place. Hatta called an emergency session of KNIP's Working Body, and requested permission for "absolute authority" to be vested in the presidency and the proclamation of martial law. As defense minister, Hatta assigned to his most loyal unit, the Siliwangi Division, the task of quelling the PKI revolt. In this, he was not fully supported by General Sudirman, who preferred negotiation with the rebel forces.[47]

The original PKI plan was thought to be geared to an anticipated second military action by the Dutch, in which Sukarno and the Hatta government would be eliminated, allowing the PKI an opportunity to lead the final guerrilla struggle against the Dutch.[48] Hatta recalled in his memoirs that "about the end of September, I received a letter from Van Mook offering me assistance."[49] This Hatta rejected, determined not to present Van Mook with a *carte blanche* to enter Republican territory. Through Cochran, the new American representative on the Good Offices Committee, Hatta appealed for weapons and ammunition to fight the Communists,[50] but this was not agreed to.

Support for the PKI declined once people realized that this demanded a full commitment against Sukarno and Hatta. Yet the conflict was too heated for immediate settlement. Already savage killings and atrocities had been committed by both sides. The Republican forces quickly gained the upper hand. On October 31, 1948, Musso was killed in a skirmish, and at the end of November, while leading the PKI's main force, Amir Sjarifuddin was captured near the Van Mook line in the Purwodadi area.

According to Hatta, Gatot Subroto, the military governor of Surakarta, sought instructions on the treatment of captured leaders. "I said to detain all of them and bring them before the Court," Hatta recalled. Amir was

---

47 Lieut. Col. Suharto, later President of Indonesia, was despatched to Madiun to see whether compromise could be reached with the rebels. See Reid, *Indonesian National Revolution*, p. 143, n. 32.

48 See Kahin, *Nationalism and Revolution in Indonesia*, p. 284, n. 82, and Reid, *Indonesian National Revolution*, p. 141.

49 Hatta, *Memoir*, p. 531.

50 See "Consul General at Batavia to Secretary of State," September 20, 1948, in *FRUS 1948*, vol. 6, p. 382.

held prisoner until the Dutch began their second military offensive and then executed by firing squad. Hatta explained in an interview many years later: "Gatot Subroto said that, instead of taking the risk of their crossing over to the Dutch, 'it is better to finish them off.'"[51] Hatta may have been trying to clear his own name, for Gatot had claimed that he carried out the execution on Hatta's orders.[52]

In Critchley's opinion, "Amir Sjarifuddin became somewhat of a scapegoat."[53] Hatta acknowledged that Amir was an enigma. "He was an intellectual who believed in communism (atheist) and at the same time he was a Christian (theist). In confronting the Bible, he was a Christian, facing society and politics he was a communist." Hatta admitted: "I do not know how to analyze such a person; that is a job for a psychologist!"[54] Yet many of Hatta's fellow Minangkabau were both Communists and practicing Muslims. Hatta himself had, as a young nationalist, described the similarities between Marx and Islam, claiming both creeds were striving for social justice, but then Hatta did not regard communism as pure Marxism.

Overall, the Madiun revolt enhanced the status of Hatta's government. Coast noticed that "the general feeling in Yogya at the time was that the Communists were twice traitors: traitors to Hatta and his government: traitors to the nationalist struggle."[55] According to Roem, "Only Hatta could have coped with Madiun."[56] One positive result for the Republic was that the army on Java was much more integrated after the revolt. Also, internationally, Hatta's government was now seen by the Americans as responsible and moderate and, even more commendable in their view, anti-Communist. Although the United States did not immediately switch its support to the Republic, Washington was becoming convinced that the Hatta government could provide a bulwark against communism in

---

51 Hatta, *Bung Hatta's Answers*, p. 19.
52 D. C. Anderson in his study of the Madiun Affair suggests that Gatot Subroto carried out the execution on Hatta's orders as it was feared the Communist leaders might escape and rise to power after the second Dutch attack. See D. C. Anderson, "The Military Aspects of the Madiun Affair," in *Indonesia* 21 (April 1976): 48, n. 123.
53 Personal communication from T. K. Critchley.
54 Hatta, *Bung Hatta Menjawab*, p. 23.
55 Coast, *Recruit to Revolution*, p. 195.
56 Interview with M. Roem, February 2, 1982.

Indonesia.[57] The Dutch countered this American change of attitude by accusing Hatta of being Marxist. They drew attention to Hatta's release of Tan Malaka, which had permitted him to establish a new national Communist party, the Partai Murba, on October 3, 1948.[58]

There was little respite for Hatta. No sooner had the Madiun crisis been resolved than he was forced to return to Sumatra to settle a dispute between rival military commanders in Tapanuli. Situated so close to Dutch lines, such a clash could provide an excuse for the Dutch army to take over further Sumatran territory under the guise of restoring peace and order. Hatta had expected a parallel Communist upsurge in Sumatra, especially as Musso had spent several days in the Minangkabau on his way to Java, but the Minangkabau Communists remained loyal to Hatta's government.[59]

While in West Sumatra, Hatta began to make preparations for a transfer of Republican government to Bukit Tinggi in the event of a further Dutch offensive on Java, instructing his minister of economic affairs, Sjafruddin Prawiranegara, to remain in Bukit Tinggi. Hatta had already made arrangements with Nehru, through the Indian consul, for Sukarno and Sjahrir to be flown to India to plead the Republic's cause abroad and to protect Sukarno from the Dutch. He himself hoped to continue his prime ministership from Bukit Tinggi if Yogyakarta were seized. "I'm not sure how serious Hatta was about leading an emergency government in Sumatra," Critchley commented many years later, "but it would have been a realistic assessment of where such a revolutionary government would have had to be based."[60]

Hatta was summoned back to Java to resume negotiations with yet another delegation from the Netherlands government. His talks with

57 Elink Schuurman, a Dutch delegate in Jakarta, informed Foreign Minister Stikker on October 18 that "I receive lately the growingly strong impression from my contacts with British and American representatives and with the American delegation that these circles are planning to support the Hatta regime at any price," as cited in Oey Hong Lee, *War and Diplomacy in Indonesia*, p. 195.
58 Stikker suggested to Schuurman that he use the tactic of pointing out to the world that communism in Indonesia was not dead after the "Madiun Affair." See ibid.
59 While in West Sumatra Musso had spent a night at Nazir Pamontjak's house. After the Madiun revolt, several PKI leaders were detained in the Minangkabau but released on swearing loyalty to the *Dwi Tunggal*. Nazir Pamontjak himself was not arrested, and in October was sent abroad. In view of his close PI association with Hatta, Nazir Pamontjak may have been a restraining influence on PKI elements in West Sumatra. See A. Kahin, "Struggle for Independence," pp. 269-70.
60 Personal communication from T. K. Critchley.

Stikker, the Dutch foreign minister, were far from reassuring. "The general atmosphere was worse than in July 1947," Hatta acknowledged, "even the Good Offices Committee was concerned that the Dutch were bent on war."[61] Hatta still believed that it was to the Republic's advantage to continue to negotiate. As long as the Dutch were seen to be the aggressors, the Republic of Indonesia retained the goodwill of the Security Council, such sympathy being a powerful "psychological power factor."

On November 10, Hatta sent Stikker an *aide-memoire*, in which he agreed that, during the interim period before the establishment of the United States of Indonesia, "if the federal Indonesian government agreed that a state of insecurity existed, then the High Representative of the Crown might be permitted to use Netherlands troops to settle it."[62] Hatta conceded that the armed forces of the Republic would be partly incorporated into a federal army in the interim period, but with separate identity and answerable only to the interim federal government. Only in an emergency would the federal government ask for aid from Dutch troops and only in such an emergency would the High Representative of the Crown be in charge of all forces.[63] On returning to the Netherlands, Stikker ignored the subtleties of Hatta's note, indicating erroneously that Hatta was willing to allow Dutch troops entry anywhere in Indonesia.[64] The Republic was appalled. Mohamad Roem, representing Masjumi, wrote to Cochran, saying Hatta had gone too far, and asking him "to do whatever is possible to lead procedure back to its proper course under auspices of GOC [Good Offices Committee]."[65]

On November 26, the Dutch government had announced the appointment of a top-level delegation to Indonesia, in the hopes that direct talks "will yield results and will shortly lead to conclusion [of a] political agreement...."[66] In discussions with its chairman, Dutch Minister

---

61 As cited in Coast, *Recruit to Revolution*, p. 209.
62 See Oey Hong Lee, *War and Diplomacy in Indonesia*, p. 196, and Kahin, *Nationalism and Revolution in Indonesia*, pp. 323-24.
63 Kahin, *Nationalism and Revolution in Indonesia*, p. 324, n. 20.
64 Stikker interpreted the document as indicating Hatta's willingness to surrender key powers to the Dutch during the interim period. See ibid., p. 323.
65 "Consul General at Batavia (Livengood) to Secretary of State," December 1, 1948, in *FRUS 1948*, vol. 6, p. 503. Hatta had negotiated with Stikker against the wishes of Roem, then the head of the Indonesian delegation to negotiations with the Dutch.
66 Ibid.

for Overseas Territories Sassen, on December 2, Hatta made it clear that his *aide-memoire* had been misinterpreted. Unfortunately it had not only been misunderstood by the Dutch, but within the Republic a new left-wing protest front was being formed.[67] On December 4, Hatta conferred with Stikker and the delegation and, while saying he would adhere to his *aide-memoire* "in principle," asked for a "gentlemen's agreement... which would actually restrain high representative of Crown from using troops in Repub[lican] territory without concurrence [of the] interim government." Stikker recalled that Hatta was "quite tense" during the meeting, not surprising since he was treading a political tightrope.[68]

According to Hatta, Sassen insisted that the Indonesian army immediately be "converted into a 'gendarmerie,' so our discussions reached deadlock."[69] Hatta challenged Sassen, demanding to know if the Dutch intended to establish a federation of Indonesian states without including the Republic of Indonesia. Hatta recorded that Sassen assured him that the "Dutch government has no such intention."[70] yet, on December 13, Sassen persuaded the Dutch cabinet to authorize a full-scale military assault to destroy the Republic, which was to commence at midnight on December 18, the date Sukarno and his party were scheduled to fly to India.[71]

On December 7, the American government sent an *aide-memoire* to the Netherlands, threatening to cut off Marshall Aid if a military offensive was launched against Indonesia. Following Dutch protests, the note was reworded on December 9 and the threat of aid curtailment withdrawn. For the Dutch, this represented the green light for an attack on the Republic.[72] Hatta had previously warned Cochran that his own position with the Indonesian military and political parties was perilous,

---

67 The PNI, the Partai Murba, and the Partai Sarikat Islam Indonesia formed the Indonesian People's Congress with the prime objective of opposing Hatta's policy of negotiation. See Kahin, *Nationalism and Revolution in Indonesia*, p. 324, n. 20.

68 See "Consul General at Batavia (Livengood) to Secretary of State," December 5, 1948, in *FRUS 1948*, vol. 6, pp. 520-21.

69 Hatta, *Memoir*, p. 538.

70 Ibid., and Oey Hong Lee, *War and Diplomacy in Indonesia*, p. 199.

71 C. Smit, *De Liquidatie van een Imperium: Nederland en Indonesië 1945-1962* (Amsterdam: De Arbeiderspers, 1962), pp. 136-40. Kahin suggests that the timing of the Dutch attack was in part a result of their desire to keep Sukarno from reaching India. See Kahin, *Nationalism and Revolution in Indonesia*, p. 337, n. 13.

72 Oey Hong Lee, *War and Diplomacy in Indonesia*, pp. 200-201.

expressing the belief that it was reasonable for the Netherlands to make considerable concessions.[73] Critchley admitted, "There were times when I was unhappy about U.S. attitudes, but major power support was needed to bring about a settlement and we were fortunate that that power was the United States," adding: "Much of Australia's diplomatic effort, particularly in Indonesia, was directed to getting U.S. understanding and support."[74]

On Cochran's advice, Hatta made an attempt on December 13 to reopen negotiations. He sent a note to the Dutch which he knew would alienate him from practically every Republican, but which he needed as a trump card in his battle of wits with the Dutch. It read:

> We are fully prepared to recognize [that] the High Representative has the right of veto over acts of the various organs of the Federal Interim Government.... We are prepared further to concede that the High Representative be given emergency powers to act in a state of war, a state of siege or a state of insecurity. As part of an over-all agreement, we should be ready to stipulate that the High Representative himself be the ultimate judge of the necessity for the exercise of extraordinary powers under these circumstances.[75]

Hatta had now gone as far as he could possibly go. As far as his own political career was concerned, he had laid his neck on the block. Yet Hatta could read the mood of the Dutch because so many of their characteristics had rubbed off on him. He knew how difficult it would be for them to veer from their set course, seeing the weak and beleaguered Republic as the only obstacle in the path of repossession of the Indies. They were unable to accept that sympathy for the Republic of Indonesia, both externally and internally, could escalate into a force stronger than military might.

The reply Hatta had expected arrived on December 17, an insistence that the Republic accept all Dutch demands by 10 a.m., Jakarta time, on

---

73 Ibid., p. 199.
74 Personal communication from T. K. Critchley.
75 United Nations, S/1129, December 19, 1948, p. 3, as cited in Kahin, *Nationalism and Revolution in Indonesia*, pp. 334-35.

December 18.[76] This time even Cochran was enraged, protesting:

> You will agree, I am sure, that in such circumstances, I cannot in justice press Dr. Hatta for an immediate reply to a letter which calls not for a mere expression of willingness to resume negotiations but rather for surrender to the position of your Government on every material point.[77]

Hatta may have recalled his own words to the Netherlands court in February 1928: "Thus the Netherlands has it entirely within its own power to determine in what way Indonesia will become free, by violent means or by the path of peace."[78]

Hatta resignedly and heavy-heartedly instructed Commander-in-Chief Sudirman to prepare his troops to meet an imminent Dutch assault. He returned to Yogyakarta, spiritually drained, accepting his doctor's advice that he rest in the hills at Kaliurang, knowing that he would be in close touch with the Good Offices Committee, who were resident there. Coast remarked: "We were all quite sure that nothing on earth would ever stop Hatta's brain, but he had developed serious internal troubles, and by his consistent overwork was running down the whole mechanism of his body."[79] The cool air helped to revive him, and Critchley later remarked that he "did not seem seriously ill" and "as far as I was aware he was in Kaliurang primarily because the G.O.C. was there."[80]

Critchley had established a rapport with Hatta, a person he described as "friendly and pleasant, small in stature but big in intellect." According to Critchley, "Hatta was deeply religious, but this did not in any way alienate him from Australians," affirming: "Neither I nor the other Australians I knew at that time would have considered him a 'wowser.'"[81] He continued:

76 Oey Hong Lee, *War and Diplomacy in Indonesia*, p. 203.
77 See Woodman, *Republic of Indonesia*, p. 248.
78 Hatta, "Indonesia Free," in *Portrait of a Patriot*, p. 291.
79 Coast, *Recruit to Revolution*, p. 215.
80 Personal communication from T. K. Critchley.
81 Personal communication from T. K. Critchley. A "wowser" is defined as "fanatical puritan, spoilsport, killjoy, teetotaller." See *The Australian Pocket Oxford Dictionary*, p. 958.

I felt that Hatta accepted me as a close friend and I was not conscious of a cultural gap. I felt very comfortable in Hatta's presence. He had a sense of humour and we occasionally exchanged jokes. Although I do not remember actually discussing the opposite sex with him, I would not have felt inhibited about doing so.[82]

At midnight on December 18, Cochran, then in Jakarta, was handed a note stating that the Netherlands was terminating the Renville Agreement. Cochran tried to wire the message to his colleagues at Kaliurang, but the Dutch denied him access to telegraphic facilities. Nehru's plane, sent to collect Sukarno and Sjahrir, was refused landing rights, so it was forced to remain in Singapore.

For the Republic, the first direct intimations that the second military offensive had begun were the explosions from bombs dropped on Maguwo, Yogyakarta's airport, followed by rocket attacks on the city and parachute troop landings. Critchley came almost immediately to Hatta's bungalow to consult with him and took breakfast with him. Hatta later recorded that he informed Critchley that he would "discuss with the Cabinet what should be done and it would depend on its decision whether the government would join the guerrillas or stay in Yogya."[83]

On his drive to the capital from Kaliurang, Hatta was met by the Sultan of Yogyakarta, who had offered to fetch him despite the bombs and strafing. Ali Sastroamidjojo remarked that Hatta's arrival at the presidential palace had a calming effect; it enabled an emergency cabinet meeting to be held and decisions taken.[84] General Sudirman had already asked Sukarno to implement a previous promise that he would fight in the mountains with the people, although Simatupang believed that neither Sukarno nor Hatta were made of the stuff needed for guerrilla warfare.[85] Both Hatta and Sukarno were to suffer accusations of cowardice for deciding to remain in their offices in Yogyakarta. But Critchley has contended: "Their capture by the Dutch provided a focus for the G.O.C. and the Security Council

---

82 Personal communication from T. K. Critchley.
83 Hatta, *Memoir*, p. 540.
84 Sastroamidjojo, *Milestones on My Journey*, p. 169.
85 Interview with T. B. Simatupang, February 4, 1982. According to Des Alwi, "Oom Hatta was no coward but would have made a hopeless guerrilla as he had no stomach for bloodshed." Interview, Des Alwi, February 1982.

252 INDONESIA FREE: A POLITICAL BIOGRAPHY OF MOHAMMAD HATTA

to demand their release and their return to Yogyakarta. It was more in keeping with their status as national leaders to have been taken in their national capital than to have appeared as rebels fleeing into the jungle."[86]

According to Hatta, there were two good reasons why he and Sukarno could not escape into the hills at the conclusion of the emergency cabinet meeting. First, there were insufficient troops left in the city to cover their escape and, second, it was more advantageous from the point of view of the Good Offices Committee's report to the United Nations for them to be seen as victims of Dutch aggression.[87]

Before his arrest, Hatta managed to dictate a short speech for circulation throughout the Republic, which conferred full powers on Sjafruddin Prawiranegara, the economic affairs minister in Bukit Tinggi, to lead an emergency government and, should that government fall, authorizing his finance minister, Maramis, then in the United States, to establish a government in exile.[88]

On the morning of December 20, 1948, the Dutch commander on Java, Major General Meyer, requested Sukarno to declare a ceasefire. Sukarno refused. On December 28, Sukarno, Haji Agus Salim, and Sjahrir were flown via Brastagi to Prapat, a lakeside holiday resort in northeast Sumatra. Hatta, the Working Body chairman, Assaat, Gafar Pringgodigdo, Air Commodore Suryadarma, and, subsequently, Mohamad Roem and Ali Sastroamidjojo were detained in a small villa on the island of Bangka off the east coast of Central Sumatra. It was Hatta's third term of imprisonment at the hands of the Dutch.

The year 1948 ended uncomfortably for Hatta, sharing with his associates two rooms of the villa, encaged with barbed wire. Dutch methods had not changed from prewar days. Hatta and his colleagues were offered freedom of movement within the island of Bangka in return for a signed statement agreeing to refrain from political activity.

Hatta was determined that this time the Dutch must recognize that their captives were government leaders not native dissidents. He urged his fellow prisoners to observe a dignified stance. Ali Sastroamidjojo, in

---

86 Personal communication from T. K. Critchley.
87 Hatta, *Memoir*, p. 541.
88 Nalenan, *Arnold Mononutu*, p. 191, and M. Rasjid, *Rasjid -- 70*, Panitia Peringatan Ulang Tahun Mr. Rashid Ke-70, Jakarta, p. 85.

captivity with Hatta for the second time, humorously recounted Hatta's directives:

> He emphasized that even though we were in exile, we had to continue to regard ourselves as officials of the Republic of Indonesia.... He hoped that we would be neatly dressed whenever we left the bedroom; we should not wear pyjamas or a sarong. Apart from that, he emphasized that in our place of exile we must continue to hold fast to the principles of democracy. "For example," he said, "If we bathe, we must not use as much water as we please. I have measured the volume of the water for bathing and it turns out that there will be enough water if you use only ten dippers each time you bathe.[89]

Ali admitted that "Hatta's 'water regulation' made us laugh, but we obeyed it because he explained it so seriously."[90] Mohamad Roem recalled receiving a reprimand for leaving the bedroom not fully dressed. He defended himself by pointing out that Hatta had suggested that they maintain a homely atmosphere: "At home I wear pyjamas outside my bedroom," Roem protested. Hatta retorted teasingl'y: "At home does not mean as in Roem's house!" Roem did admit that Hatta's dominant personality and discipline in their situation of close confinement prevented the atmopshere from deteriorating into acrimony, as happened at Prapat.[91] Sukarno and Sjahrir, under any circumstances uneasy partners, became so hostile to one another that a rift developed which was never healed.[92]

Hatta's living conditions appalled Critchley on his first visit to the internees as a member of the Good Offices Committee. "He was startled seeing us in a cage," Hatta recalled, "this being contrary to the explanation given by the Dutch representative in the United Nations who said that we

---

89 Sastroamidjojo, *Milestones on My Journey*, p. 173.
90 Ibid.
91 M. Roem, "Bung Kecil yang Berbuat Besar," in *Mengenang Sjahrir*, pp. 141-42.
92 Haji Agus Salim, the third member at Prapat and Sjahrir's uncle, agreed that Sjahrir was undoubtedly rude to Sukarno, blaming him for talking too openly about the trip to India, criticizing him for begging favors of the guards at their bungalow, yelling peevishly at Sukarno to "Shut Your Mouth!" when Sukarno was singing in the bathroom.

were all free to move around Bangka."[93] This was the Dutch again playing into Hatta's hands; their deception merely added fuel to the international hostility created by their aggression.

Rahmi Hatta remembered that the letters she received from her husband in this period, "written neatly in pencil," expressed hope rather than despair. "He was very much convinced that the road of history was leading towards the aims of the Indonesian nation, that Indonesia would obtain its sovereignty." Hatta's letters were not just political, they showed his deep concern for his family:

> I felt relieved receiving your letter, having all along been convinced that you would be patient and withstand the trials. Trust in God Almighty, for He is our strength. Hopefully Meutia will calm down again. Environment has a big influence on a small child, so do try to surround her with rays of happiness to brighten up her spirits.[94]

After the removal of the government leadership, Tan Malaka on December 21 called for total war, declaring: "I shall lead the fight against the Dutch to the bitter end."[95] Using the Kediri area as a base, Tan Malaka began an intensive campaign of political indoctrination, assisted by Partai Murba leaders, including Rustam Effendi and his brother, pointing out the "mistakes and short-comings of the Sukarno-Hatta government."[96] Tan Malaka had the backing of an army battalion, but in a skirmish with the local military commander he and the other leaders were captured. His execution is believed to have taken place between February and May 1949, although mystery still surrounds the circumstances.[97]

The vacuum left by the capture of the Republic's top civilian leadership was filled on Java by the military commanders in liaison with the Sultan of Yogyakarta. From Bukit Tinggi, Sjafruddin Prawlranegara headed the

---

93 Hatta, *Memoir*, p. 545.
94 Ny. Rahmi Hatta, "Prinsip-Prinsip Bung Hatta Tak Pernah Luntur," in *Bung Hatta: Pribadinya dalam Kenangan*, pp. 41-42.
95 As cited in Reid, *Indonesian National Revolution*, p. 156.
96 See Oey Hong Lee, *War and Diplomacy in Indonesia*, p. 205.
97 In a meeting on June 8, 1949, the US State Department congratulated Indonesia's representatives to the UN when they reported that Tan Malaka had been executed. See "Acting Secretary of State to Consulate General in Batavia," in *FRUS 1949*, vol. 7, pt. 1, pp. 418-19.

Pemerintah Darurat Republik Indonesia [Emergency Government of the Republic of Indonesia], although his leadership activities were, through circumstances, mainly confined to Sumatra. The Dutch, the United Nations, and the BFO states persisted in treating the leaders in detention as the legitimate government. In his memoirs, Hatta was anxious to establish that he did not deliberately ignore the Bukit Tinggi government. He claimed that, when asked to confer with Dutch Prime Minister Drees at the end of January, he refused, telling Critchley that "Sukarno and I were no longer in control because from December 19, 1948 we handed over to Mr. Sjafruddin Prawlranegara in West Sumatra."[98]

The military leaders on Java and Sumatra, supported by the local people, undoubtedly played a major role in preventing the Dutch from gaining advantage from the removal of the Republican government. The ability of the regional commanders to continue guerrilla warfare against the Dutch forces on Java in particular was an essential component in convincing the Dutch that they could not win back the Indies by force.

The Dutch came under fire internationally after launching their second military offensive. On January 20, 1949, Nehru opened a special conference to discuss the Indonesian dilemma, held in New Delhi, which recommended to the Security Council that a firmer stand be taken against the Dutch. American disapproval was more punishing; on December 21, President Truman suspended Marshall Aid to the Netherlands. The United States also proposed that the Good Offices Committee become the United Nations Commission for Indonesia (UNCI), with powers to advise on what areas should be returned to the Republic.[99] The Security Council resolved on January 28, 1949 that the Republican leaders be restored to their government in Yogyakarta and that the United Nations, through its commission, supervise the formation of the proposed United States of Indonesia, with transfer of full sovereignty by July 1, 1950. This was a much stronger action than the Dutch had anticipated. Hatta commented with a hint of satisfaction: "It is not I who needs to talk to Prime Minister Drees but probably he who needs me."[100]

Sukarno and Haji Agus Salim were transferred to Bangka at the

98 Hatta, *Memoir*, p. 545.
99 See Kahin, *Nationalism and Revolution in Indonesia*, p. 400.
100 Hatta, *Bung Hatta Menjawab*, p. 57.

beginning of February 1949. When Hatta, backed by Sukarno, refused to negotiate while in captivity, the Dutch transferred Sjahrir to Jakarta, hoping to use him as an intermediary between the Dutch and Hatta. Sjahrir insisted that the political leaders must first be released and the Security Council's resolutions observed, assuring Hatta that he would make no commitment to the Dutch without cabinet's agreement.[101] Sjahrir was permitted to travel to Bangka to confer with Hatta, who suggested that Sjahrir go once more to the United Nations Security Council at Lake Success as a spokesman for the Republic. Again Sjahrir refused. He was still basically opposed to Hatta's policy of continued negotiation and reliance on the United States of America, disliking its tactics of forcing the Dutch to their knees by withdrawing aid.

On February 26, yielding to mounting pressures, the Dutch proposed that a Round Table Conference be held at The Hague on March 12, to which all Indonesian states, including the Republic, be invited to "discuss the conditions for and the ways along which the earliest possible transfer of sovereignty" could be effected.[102] The UNCI was still dissatisfied, reporting on March 1 that it considered that the Dutch statement was merely a "counterproposal" to the Security Council's resolution of January 28, nor did it sanction the return of the Republican leaders to Yogyakarta.[103]

A disquieting factor for the Dutch was the realization that their action had not only lost them international support but had turned the BFO states against them, inspiring an archipelago-wide spirit of Indonesian nationalism. Anak Agung Gde Agung, the Balinese prime minister of the Great Eastern Indonesia state, obtained permission to visit Bangka to confer with the political detainees. Anak Agung was impressed by Hatta; a strong and lasting friendship developed between the two men.

In the face of American pressure and with the realization that the majority of Indonesians were turning against them, the Dutch agreed to restore the Republican government to Yogyakarta on condition that

---

101 Roem, "Bung Kecil yang Berbuat Besar," pp. 152-53.

102 See Kahin, *Nationalism and Revolution in Indonesia*, p. 406.

103 According to Beel, Sukarno and Hatta would later be granted the same rights and duties as any other citizen but under the State of War and Siege which existed in Indonesia, they could not engage in political activity or return to Republican territory. See ibid., p. 407, n. 34.

informal discussions be held to draw up a basis for establishing the United States of Indonesia. Hatta admitted to Cochran that he had to be cautious "not to lose confidence of supporters through what might be considered weakness" in agreeing to negotiations with the Dutch. He feared that "Tan Malaka and others would attack him bitterly thereon."[104] This time Hatta rejected suggestions that Sjahrir act as an intermediary. "For a long time, since Renville, Sjahrir had not wanted to be included in delegations negotiating with the Dutch," he later explained.[105] Hatta instead appointed Mohamad Roem to be leader of the Indonesian delegation, asssisted by Ali Sastroamidjojo, but asked Sjahrir if he would assist Roem as an adviser. Although consenting to act in this capacity, Sjahrir consistently avoided the delegation's invitations to attend official discussions.[106]

In Critchley's opinion, "Hatta related better to and was more comfortable with Roem than he would have been with Sjahrir, but Sjahrir would also have been a valuable adviser and negotiator." Critchley defended Roem, asserting that his "qualities should not be underestimated; he was intelligent, honest, trustworthy, with considerable human understanding and sympathy."[107]

Sukarno was further irritated by Sjahrir's refusal to work with Roem. "Sukarno felt it to be a humiliation directed at him personally," recorded Hatta.[108] Sjafruddin Prawiranegara was also offended at being ignored when his government was officially the legal government of the Republic of Indonesia. Hatta tried to smooth Sjafruddin's hurt feelings by obtaining permission to fly to Aceh to confer with him. According to Hatta, he chose to go there as he believed it to be the only area of Sumatra outside Dutch control.[109] As Sjafruddin had decided to remain in West Sumatra, Hatta met only with Colonel Hidayat. One of the most sensitive issues to be raised in the forthcoming discussions was that guerrilla warfare

104 "Consul General at Batavia (Livengood) to Secretary of State," March 28, 1949, in *FRUS 1949*, vol. 7, pt. 1, p. 352.

105 Hatta, *Bung Hatta's Answers*, p. 35.

106 Roem, "Bung Kecil yang Berbuat Besar," p. 155. According to Hatta, when receiving his letter of appointment as adviser, Sjahrir queried Sukarno's signature on it, saying "What is he? Why should he appoint me? The one who should appoint me is Syafruddin (the head of the RI Emergency Government in Sumatra)." See Hatta, *Bung Hatta's Answers*, p. 36.

107 Personal communication from T. K. Critchley.

108 Hatta, *Bung Hatta's Answers*, p. 36.

109 Interview with Hatta, October 6, 1976, in A. Kahin, "Struggle for Independence," p. 351, n. 10.

should cease, both in Sumatra and Java. Sjafruddin Prawiranegara later exonerated Hatta from blame for by-passing his government, explaining that he "gained the conviction that he acted in all things according to a plan and purpose, which was honest and sincere."[110]

On June 14, Sjafruddin announced that the Emergency Government would support the agreement concluded between Roem and the Dutch representative, Van Royen. The main opposition to this agreement emanated from Sjahrir's PSI and the Partai Murba. It was also generally disliked in army circles, with army leaders disappointed that they had not been consulted. "Hatta could have communicated more with the people by radio while on Bangka," Nasution contended, "and also included the military leaders in consultations with the Dutch and UNCI."[111]

On July 6, the political prisoners were finally released, although they had been free to roam the island of Bangka since the end of January. Yogyakarta welcomed back Sukarno and Hatta with an air of warmth and festivity, special acclaim also going to General Sudirman, now so ill with tuberculosis that he had to be carried on a stretcher. Amid the welcome ceremonies, Sukarno and Hatta could sense the chill of army hostility. While they had lived in comparative safety and comfort in exile, many of those remaining on Java had died, including Urip, the former army chief. Sudirman was so antagonistic to the ceasefire order scheduled for August 1 that he wrote a letter of resignation, only retracting it when Sukarno countered by threatening to resign himself. A week following the *Dwi Tunggal's* release, Sjafruddin returned to Yogyakarta, formally returning his mandate to Hatta, thus allowing him to form a new cabinet.

A strategic move taken by the Republic was to invite the BFO states to an Inter-Indonesian Conference held in mid-July before the scheduled opening of the main Round Table Conference in the Netherlands in August. There was not complete unanimity among the BFO leaders about an absolute transfer of sovereignty to the United States of Indonesia. Anak Agung led a group which strongly supported the *Dwi Tunggal* and complete independence, while Sultan Hamid of West Borneo headed a group which preferred stronger ties with the Dutch. Most of the BFO

---

110 Sjafruddin Prawiranegara, "Bung Hatta Demokrat Sedjati dan Pemimpin jang Saja Hormati," p. 326.
111 Interview with A. H. Nasution, February 22, 1982.

states admired the Republic's refusal to accept defeat after the second Dutch military action, although there also still lingered resentment that the Republic had accepted the terms of the Linggajati Agreement which allowed the Dutch to continue in control of many of the Outer Islands.

One of the main topics discussed at the Inter-Indonesian Conference was the form of the Constitution for the proposed United States of Indonesia. This time there was no doubt that the voice of the Outer Islands was strong, showing preference for a federal state and knowing that the Dutch would insist on a federal parliamentary system. Hatta, in his opening address to the conference, stressed the need for unity, asserting somewhat inaccurately that the archipelago had been united both under the Majapahit empire and the Dutch colonial regime. He called to mind the oath taken by the youth at their historic conference in October 1928: "We are one nation, we have only one native land, we have one uniting language."[112]

Hatta once more asked Sjahrir to assist as an adviser at the all-important Round Table Conference commencing in The Hague on August 23, 1949. Again Sjahrir refused, worried by the dominating position of the United States representative, Cochran, and by statements made by Sukarno that "the solution of the Indonesian problem now rests solely with the United States," implying that, without American support, he and Hatta were finished and "chaos and Communism would be the inevitable result in Indonesia."[113]

Coast was disappointed that Sjahrir was not accompanying Hatta, recalling that "I rashly risked rebukes by trying to find out what really kept apart these two men, whom I so greatly liked and respected."[114] Sjahrir admitted that he had "little faith in the return of the Republican government to Yogya at the insistence of the United Nations," believing that "the Dutch were still not ready for serious negotiations." He preferred the "idea of the restoration of the Republican Government in unconquerable Achinese territory in North Sumatra."[115]

---

112 Hatta, "Pidato Pembukaan Konperensi Inter-Indonesia di Yogyakarta," in *Kumpulan Pidato*, p. 291.
113 As cited in Oey Hong Lee, *War and Diplomacy in Indonesia*, p. 235.
114 Coast, *Recruit to Revolution*, p. 292.
115 Ibid. Critchley was not impressed by this viewpoint, commenting: "To continue from Sumatra or elsewhere would have involved at best a long drawn-out struggle with all the suffering and

As prime minister, Hatta led the Republic of Indonesia's delegation to the Round Table Conference in The Hague, appointing Roem his deputy. Sukarno remained in Indonesia. Hatta called briefly to see Nehru on his way to the conference, receiving advice and, in return, expressing Indonesia's gratitude for India's solid support for the Republic. Then it was on to Europe. Hatta did not record his personal feelings on being back on Dutch soil after a lapse of seventeen years. He had left in July 1932, a recently graduated young nationalist. He returned a prime minister and head of government.[116]

Hatta began his stay on a hospitable note, holding a reception on August 17 to celebrate the fourth anniversary of the proclamation of Indonesian independence. His guests, he later recorded, included "Dutch Cabinet Ministers, members of the First and Second Chambers, party leaders and old acquaintances of mine from the time I was a student in Holland and a member of the PI."[117] Hatta, who only two months previously had been a reluctant "guest" of the Dutch government, obviously relished his role as host. Coast noticed how deferentially the BFO representatives looked to Hatta: "If a Federalist could sit down for a meal with Hatta, he was a conspicuously proud man for the rest of the day."[118]

The official opening of the Round Table Conference took place in the Knights' Hall in The Hague, at which Dutch Prime Minister Drees presided. In his speech to the assembly, Hatta pointed out that the Dutch had failed to appreciate how much the Indonesian people had changed under Japanese rule, strengthening the "will for freedom."[119] He averred: "The Indonesian Dutch conflict is mainly a psychological matter," without revealing that it was now his turn to practice psychological stratagems on the Dutch. Hatta assured the Dutch that "Netherlands capital and economic interest in Indonesia" would not be endangered, a promise which would be difficult to keep. In conclusion, Hatta called for a new understanding between his people and the Dutch:

uncertainties that this involved." Personal communication.
116 The Indonesian delegation was housed in the Palace Hotel in the seaside resort of Scheveningen.
117 Hatta, *Memoir*, p. 558.
118 Coast, *Recruit to Revolution*, p. 261.
119 Hatta, "On the Road to Transfer of Sovereignty," in *Portrait of a Patriot*, p. 513.

For four long years our two peoples have lived in mutual enmity and with feelings of resentment in their hearts. For four long years we have been fighting and killing each other, with vain sacrifice of property and blood. Let us now commence a new era, founded on peace and collaboration.[120]

The deliberations of the Round Table Conference continued until November 2, getting off to a slow start. Coast summed up the atmosphere: "The Dutch in their fear of becoming only a tiny West European state did all they could to bind Indonesia to them in what they termed a 'tight' union, while the Indonesians, who had accepted the principle of entering a Dutch-Indonesian Union symbolically headed by Queen Juliana and consisting of two equal and sovereign independent states, only wanted a 'loose' Union, with the flimsiest possible ties."[121] Three basic agreements were formulated: the transfer of sovereignty, the institution of the Union, and the Transitional Measures setting down the practical details involved in the transfer.

The three United Nations Commission members were present during the whole proceedings, Cochran and Critchley playing the major roles. Coast observed that the BFO delegates "were on the whole a dull and timid lot, showing an obvious inferiority complex in the presence of the Republic." The exception was Anak Agung, whom Coast described as the "second Indonesian power in the Conference," remarking that "perhaps Anak Agung did more than any one else to bring the Republicans and Federalists together."[122]

Coast noticed that Hatta was again suffering physical exhaustion, commenting that he was "losing weight visibly and looking terribly tired."[123] Roem was of the opinion that "Hatta did a fantastic job at the Round Table Conference,"[124] a view backed by Nasution, who acknowledged that "Hatta was clever at the Round Table Conference, he did not give too much away."[125]

---

120 Ibid., pp. 513-14.
121 Coast, *Recruit to Revolution*, p. 264.
122 Ibid., p. 260.
123 Ibid., p. 269.
124 Interview M. Roem, February 2, 1982.
125 Interview with Nasution, February 22, 1982.

One of the most contentious issues discussed was financial. The Dutch insisted that Indonesia accept an external debt of f 3,167 million and an internal debt of f 2,956 million, a large proportion of which covered the costs incurred by the Dutch army in fighting the Republic. Hatta was outraged, flatly refusing to accept any debts incurred after the Japanese Occupation. He called on the chairman of his Economic and Financial Subcommittee, Dr. Sumitro Djojohadikusumo, like himself a graduate of the Rotterdam Handelshogeschool, to present alternative figures. Hatta also wired Nehru, asking him to try to convince the Americans that the Dutch were asking too much.[126] Hatta himself took advantage of American "Cold War" nerves, reporting the "financial and monetary situation so bad" that, unless the Netherlands reduced their their demand he "might as well suggest sovereignty be transferred directly to Communists rather than first to his group."[127] Again in this statement was contained an uncanny foresight of future trends in Indonesia.

The Dutch were adamant that acceptance of their debt figure was a requirement for transfer of sovereignty. Cochran urged Hatta to accede to a reduction of f 2,000 million on the original Dutch figure, warning him that loss of sovereignty would not only entail renewed hostilities but would mean the loss of American sympathy.[128] Sumitro claimed that a serious difference of opinion arose between himself and Hatta when the latter finally accepted a figure of f 4,300 million on October 24.[129] Roem supported Hatta, reprimanding Sumitro for "taking such a hardline attitude."[130] At the same time, he praised Hatta's leadership, stating that achieving agreement between the BFO and the Republic at the conference was "in large part due to their trust in the Chairman of the Republic's delegation, Dr. Mohammad Hatta."[131] Sumitro conceded in retrospect

---

126 Oey Hong Lee, *War and Diplomacy in Indonesia*, p. 213.
127 "Chargé in the Netherlands to Secretary of State," October 8, 1949 in *FRUS 1949*, vol. 7, pt. 1, p. 510.
128 Oey Hong Lee, *War and Diplomacy in Indonesia*, pp. 243-44. In Subadio's opinion, Hatta was too naive in trusting Cochran at the Round Table Conference, allowing himself to be used. Interview, Subadio Sastrosatomo, February 22, 1982.
129 Sumitro Djojohadikusumo, "Bung Hatta Sebagai Manusia: Sekedar Kenangan Pribadi," in *Bung Hatta: Pribadinya dalam Kenangan*, pp. 424-25.
130 Ibid., and Roem, "Mohammad Hatta, Ketua Delegasi Republik," in *Bung Hatta Mengabdi pada Tjita-Tjita*, p. 386.
131 Roem, "Mohammad Hatta, Ketua Delegasi," p. 388.

that, although he still held fast to his own opinion, "I understood better how difficult was Bung Hatta's position and role while leading the Round Table Conference discussion."[132] Critchley admitted that "I was unhappy about the debt figure but it would have been hard to justify a break-down of the Conference on this alone."[133]

Another issue which almost deadlocked the conference was Dutch refusal to relinquish West New Guinea. Critchley knew that "Sukarno had instructed Hatta not to return without West New Guinea," observing that the attainment of the territory had become an emotive issue, backed by Anak Agung. Critchley also noticed that "Hatta was the one Indonesian whom I met at that time who did not seem emotionally concerned about the issue. He agreed with me that postponement was better than a breakdown of the Conference and that it was an issue that could be more readily and realistically solved after the Dutch had taken the major step of transferring sovereignty."[134]

The New Guinea issue was finally resolved at 5 a.m. on the morning of November 1, the deadline for discussions, with a compromise that the transfer of West New Guinea's sovereignty be settled within a year of the conference. Nasution expressed his satisfaction: "Hatta had to yield on West New Guinea but at least he got Surabaya Naval Base, which the Dutch hated giving up."[135] Hatta understood Dutch reluctance to part with West New Guinea: "For many Dutch people, who had grown grey in the colonial service, it was very hard to accept the loss of Indonesia." He explained: "Involved was a loss both of prestige and of what had long been called 'the cork supporting the welfare of the Netherlands.'" He added: "Memories of former 'colonial glory' could be kept alive only by retaining some part of the former Netherlands Indies under Dutch control. Hence the notion of excluding West Irian from the transfer of sovereignty."[136]

At the closing session on November 2, the formal records were signed. Coast noted that "on all sides there was a sort of guarded enthusiasm. No one could deny that Hatta, an Asian statesman, had shown to the world

---

132 Sumitro Djojohadikusumo, "Bung Hatta Sebagai Manusia," p. 425.
133 Personal communication from T. K. Critchley.
134 Personal communication from T. K. Critchley.
135 Interview with Nasution, February 22, 1982.
136 Hatta, "Colonialism and the Danger of War," in *Portrait of a Patriot*, p. 573. First published in *Asian Survey* 1, 9 (November 1961).

that, with the consistent, calm aid of the United Nations, it was possible, even in the year 1949 and after two military attacks, for a country to settle its urgent and all-pervading political problems with goodwill and patient, reasonable negotiation."[137]

In his address at the conclusion of the conference, Hatta admitted that "our job is somewhat tempered by the fact that not all problems at this Round Table Conference were able to be solved."[138] He also tried to make it clear that the new union differed from past association policies, that Indonesians were no longer younger brothers, as in the past, but that it was "on the basis of free will, equality and equal rights" that they continued their association with the Dutch.[139]

Hatta flew back to Indonesia immediately, aware that the terms he had accepted would evoke criticism, in particular the onerous debt and the failure to finalize the West New Guinea transfer. He defended his delegation's efforts, contending that "historically and internationally what we have achieved is the best that could be achieved at this time."[140]

Certainly it was difficult to believe that only one year previously the Republic of Indonesia had faced annihilation. Even more satisfying, victory had been achieved without the cost in human lives of a long-drawn-out war. Even Sjahrir admitted to Coast that "Hatta had achieved more than he had believed possible," qualifying his statement with the comment that, on the other hand, "it would now be impossible to carry out a socialist economic policy or a really free foreign policy."[141]

Hatta presented the Round Table Conference Agreement to the full session of KNIP on December 15. It was passed by 226 votes to 62.[142] For Hatta, perhaps the most hurtful aspect was that among those who voted against the Agreement were members of the PSI, the group which more than any other identified itself with the New PNI. Hatta could not prevent his resentment creeping into his memoirs, remarking with unusual pique: "What was manifest was that almost all the factions of the Partai Sosialis

137 Coast, *Recruit to Revolution*, p. 271.
138 M. Hatta, "Pidato Ketua Delegasi Republik Indonesia Pada Sidang Penutup Konperensi Meja Bundar," in *Kumpulan Pidato*, p. 318.
139 Ibid.
140 As cited in Woodman, *Republic of Indonesia*, p. 260.
141 Coast, *Recruit to Revolution*, p. 293.
142 Hatta, *Memoir*, p. 559.

Indonesia rejected the results of the negotiations. Many believed that they did this because it was not Sjahrir who successfully achieved the Round Table Conference Agreement."[143] This time Des Alwi supported Hatta, believing his view to be more sensible than that of Sjahrir, who was "too idealistic and inflexible."[144]

Abu Hanifah confirmed that the majority of people appreciated Hatta's achievements and were grateful to him. "Finally the period of fighting was over; the enthusiasm of the masses was overwhelming, refreshing and exciting."[145] But he noticed that Hatta's response was much less euphoric, carrying a note of warning: "Yes, we must hope that we will do better in the future in building up our nation. It is not enough to win the war, you must take care not to lose the peace."[146] Hatta was predicting that the social revolution which should follow national revolution might prove more difficult to achieve.

On December 16, 1949 in Yogyakarta, the BFO and Republican representatives met together to elect a President, the unopposed choice being Sukarno. The office of Vice-President had been discarded in the Draft Constitution of 1949. Hatta was unanimously elected prime minister, but this time leading a parliamentary rather than a presidential cabinet. The *Dwi Tunggal* now consisted of a constitutional head of state and a head of government responsible to parliament.

On December 23, Hatta and Sultan Hamid flew to the Netherlands to attend the official ceremonies for the transfer of sovereignty. Coast noticed that Hatta was "still terribly tired.... He looked drawn and pale, while even his hair seemed to be thinning."[147] The summer warmth which had greeted Hatta's return to Europe in August had become the chill of midwinter, as if the naked branches symbolized for the Dutch the stripping from them of their beloved Indies.

On December 27, in an impressive ceremony in the Royal Palace in Amsterdam, Hatta accepted the freedom of his country. He and the Dutch Prime Minister signed the Protocol transferring sovereignty, while

143 Ibid.
144 Interview with Des Alwi, February 6, 1982.
145 Hanifah, *Tales of a Revolution*, p. 329.
146 Ibid.
147 Coast, *Recruit to Revolution*, p. 279.

Queen Juliana read the Deed of Confirmation, stating:

> No longer do we stand partially opposed to one another. We have now taken our stations side by side, however much we may be bruised and torn, carrying the scars of rancour and regret.[148]

Having accepted the Charter of Sovereignty, Hatta made a brief speech in which he expressed his hopes for the future of Indonesia. Queen Juliana then shook his hand, while a carillon of palace bells rang out the *Wilhelmus*, the Dutch anthem, followed by *Indonesia Raya*. As Hatta stood quietly to attention, pale and drawn, exhausted after a year of imprisonment, negotiations, and bitter haggling, the words of the anthem may have formed in his mind:

> Indonesia is my country,
> It is the land of my birth,
> There I stand, guarding my motherland.

The dream of his boyhood had been accomplished; politically Indonesia was free and he had led the final negotiations which had achieved that freedom. It was undoubtedly for Hatta the crowning moment of his life, as confirmed by many of his friends and colleagues, and the pinnacle of his political career.

Hatta concluded his memoirs at this point, as if the years which followed faded into insignificance or were too painful to record. The struggle to achieve social revolution would never be quite as stimulating or satisfying as the struggle to oust the Dutch, nor would it meet with the same success. The Dutch had been physically removed but the system around which they had structured their colonial administration remained -- the traditional Javanese pattern of rule.

---

148 As cited in Woodman, *Republic of Indonesia*, p. 260.

CHAPTER ELEVEN

FROM DWITUNGGAL TO DWITANGGAL

When we abandoned the 1945 Constitution and replaced it with the 1950 Constitution, the meaning and position of the Dwitunggal began to change and decline. The PKI took advantage of this situation in its strategy and political struggle, speeding up the process of decline in the binding capacity and usefulness of the Dwitunggal. Misunderstandings between the two of us were often created, especially when the political parties began to fight among themselves, trying to overthrow one another.... The PKI succeeded in transforming the "Dwitunggal" [two-in-one] into "Dwitanggal" [doubly divided].[1]

Hatta, speaking in old age and once more playing with words, was describing his perception of the major factors which had shattered the *Dwi Tunggal*. His partnership with Sukarno had been consolidated in a period of struggle against foreign domination. Once the goal of independence was achieved, the latent conflict on how Indonesia should be governed once more assumed major proportions. Undoubtedly the schism between the two men was widened by the parties' exploitation of the *Dwi Tunggal* for their own interests. As in the closing months of 1949, Hatta's most consistent support came from the major Islamic party, Masjumi, a party ardently anti-Communist. His opposition came not just from the PKI but also from the left wing of the PNI and the Tan Malaka-inspired Partai Murba. Although the PSI was the party representative of *kedaulatan rakyat*, it looked to Sjahrir for direction, at times hindering rather than supporting Hatta.

---

1   Hatta, *Bung Hatta Menjawab*, p. 157.

The Masjumi, in spite of its loyalty to him, did not meet Hatta's requirement of a party dedicated to achieving social change. An unsigned article written in October 1954 pinpointed Hatta's dilemma, contending that while Sukarno and the PNI were compatible, "For Hatta there is not yet a party which really suits him."[2] The writer assessed that "the party which suits Hatta is an Islamic party with socialist aims because for Hatta socialism is a duty assigned to him by God."[3]

Hatta's task from now on was to imbue the elitist urban Masjumi with greater concern for the underprivileged masses, both rural and urban. Hatta's outlook was changing. He no longer insisted that political parties be religiously neutral, the stance he had taken in his polemics with Permi in the 1930s. From now on, he would stress that socialism was a basic tenet of Islam, maintaining that "it is the task of every Muslim to bring into being a society which will ensure to each of its members security and the good things of life."[4] "We have achieved an Indonesia which is independent and sovereign, but we must still achieve an Indonesia which is just and prosperous," he maintained.[5]

Hatta was to discover that instituting a system of parliamentary democracy did not guarantee the implementation of *kedaulatan rakyat*. The power of the ballot box was an alien concept, especially on Java. The implementation of local autonomy or village democracy was also very difficult to achieve. As Hatta pointed out: "A perfect system of democracy is to govern from below. The people must be able to feel that they govern themselves."[6] Hatta again refuted any suggestion that the masses were too stupid to participate in politics. "They must make more use of their intellect and take more initiative," he insisted.[7]

The 1949 Constitution, in theory, provided Hatta, as prime minister, with a stronger leadership position than Sukarno. In practice, Sukarno's prestige and magnetism assured him of the loyalty of the majority of Javanese, thus allowing him much greater power than a constitutional

---

2 *Pikiran Rakjat*, October 9, 1954.
3 Ibid.
4 Mohammad Hatta, "Islam, Knowledge and Society," in *Portrait of a Patriot*, p. 599. Speech delivered at Aligarh University, India, October 29, 1955.
5 Speech by Hatta in Solo, Central Java, reported in *Pikiran Rakjat*, July 24, 1957.
6 Mohammad Hatta, "Demokrasi dan Otonomi," in *Pikiran Rakjat*, April 27 and 29, 1957.
7 Ibid.

head of state usually enjoyed under a parliamentary system. Sukarno, his confidence restored, was advocating a return to unitary government. Federalism, in his opinion, encouraged regionalism. This became the focus of Sukarno's speeches during 1950 as he toured the archipelago, introducing himself to the Outer Islanders, who greeted him ecstatically in a wave of nationalistic euphoria. Thus Sukarno was, in essence, actively campaigning for the demise of the Republic of the United States of Indonesia, RUSI, Hatta's government.

It was not surprising that the RUSI should crumble. The puppet states, formulated according to the whim of Dutch strategists such as Van Mook, and based on the ability of the Dutch forces to reclaim territory, had become a symbol of intrigue and deliberate violation of the Linggajati Agreement. Hatta had actually surmised even before he left the Netherlands that the federal structure would disintegrate.[8] Yet, when reviewing his premiership in 1953, Hatta indicated that a unitary system per se did not necessarily prevent separatism, observing that "a federal system is in fact suitable for such a far-flung archipelago and might be expected to strengthen the feeling of unity."[9] The more decentralized the system of government, the more the people could control their own affairs rather than being at the mercy of a self-interested ruling elite.

Hatta returned to Indonesia on January 3, 1950. He realized that his government faced a daunting and chaotic internal situation which would tax his leadership and administrative skills to the full. He had chosen his cabinet mainly on the basis of expertise, a business-like cabinet. Hatta drew up a program based on seven main goals, among them repair of the shattered economy, creation of new defense forces, ensuring the protection of human rights, and setting in motion preparations for a general election to provide a parliament representative of the people and to elect a Constituent Assembly to frame a permanent Constitution. Education was also a priority in Hatta's program.

Although he assigned the defense ministry to the Sultan of Yogyakarta,

---

8 Interview with Nyonya Maria Ullfah Subadio, February 22, 1928; and Maria Ullfah Subadio, "Bung Hatta dan Saya," in *Bung Hatta: Pribadinya dalam Kenangan*, p. 264.
9 Hatta and Sukiman had been the more ardent advocates of a federal Indonesia many years before when the Perhimpunan Indonesia began to discuss the form of the independent state.

Hatta decided to take the foreign affairs portfolio himself.[10] He advocated non-alignment through an active and independent foreign policy. Two major international hurdles to be overcome were how to steer a middle course between the United States of America and the Soviet Union and how to persuade the Dutch to relinquish West New Guinea.

Hatta refused to be drawn into the Korean dispute. On June 30, 1950 his government issued a statement that "the so-called civil war in Korea is first and foremost a matter concerning the two major powers in the 'Cold War.'"[11] Hatta opposed the American policy of excluding the People's Republic of China from the United Nations,[12] and established diplomatic relations with the Mao Tse-tung regime. He delayed applying for Indonesia's admittance into the United Nations for fear that Chiang Kai-shek would retaliate by applying his power of veto. Hatta also rejected a proposal by the Philippines government for an anti-Communist Pacific Pact, and was also reluctant to recognize the French-backed Bao Dai regime in Vietnam. In response to criticisms that he had failed to establish relations with the Soviet Union, Hatta reiterated that, in his opinion, the Soviet Union wanted to dominate rather than work on a basis of "mutual esteem,"[13] He stressed that "we are neither following in the wake of Russia nor of the United States."[14]

Hatta defended the legality of the trend away from federalism; fobbing off Dutch protests by pointing out that "the transfer of sovereignty to Indonesia imposes no conditions, therefore the Indonesian people have the right to decide for themselves what constitutional form their state will take."[15] When in March 1950, a Dutch ministerial delegation arrived in Jakarta to participate in a Conference of Ministers of the Union Partners, Hatta noticed that the Dutch reaction to the unitary state was to adopt an

---

10 Coast, *Recruit to Revolution*, p. 289. According to Coast, who had worked in the foreign ministry, Hatta's decision was partly influenced by the fact that Sjahrir had refused to be foreign minister and partly because Hatta wanted to avoid embarrassing disputes between the nominees of the parties.

11 See J. M. van der Kroef, "Indonesia and the West," *Far Eastern Survey*, 20, 4 (February 21, 1952), p. 40.

12 See Michael Leifer, *Indonesia's Foreign Policy* (Sydney, Allen and Unwin, 1983), p. 27.

13 *Merdeka*, July 20, 1950.

14 See van der Kroef, "Indonesia and the West," p. 40.

15 *Merdeka*, June 5, 1950.

even more hard-line attitude to the release of West New Guinea.[16] With the election of the Liberal-Country Party in Australia in 1949, Australian sympathy for Indonesia was waning, an attitude Hatta criticized in an article written eight years later, averring: "For Australia, which supports the Dutch stand, the problem of West Irian is a tragedy also because its policy strengthens the very thing it so strongly opposes -- Communism in Indonesia."[17] The PKI, backed by Sukarno, was to use the West Irian question as a revolutionary theme, while the campaign to acquire the territory provided the army with added prestige and power.

Yet it was in domestic rather than foreign affairs that Hatta faced his greatest challenges. As he described the situation in 1950: "When the Kingdom of the Netherlands transferred sovereignty on December 27, 1949, the new régime inherited a devastated land."[18] Armed dissidents who refused to accept the new state under the transfer terms or who preferred to live as bandits rather than face civilian life, presented the most serious impediment to an orderly return to peacetime government.

West Java was a particularly volatile region. A pro-Dutch terrorist group, the Angkatan Perang Ratu Adil [Forces of the Just Prince], led by ex-KNIL officer Captain "Turk" Westerling, launched a challenge to Hatta's government on January 23, 1950. The timing was reminiscent of the second Dutch offensive, for Sukarno was about to depart for India. Hatta later discovered that Westerling was supported by Sultan Hamid of West Borneo, the leader of the BFO delegation to the Round Table Conference, whom Hatta had felt obliged to include in his cabinet. Both Sultan Hamid and Anak Agung Gde Agung were wary of the trend towards a unitary state, sensing that it ran contrary to the wishes of many of the Outer Islanders.[19]

Westerling's first assault was on Bandung. Since Dutch troops were involved, Hatta requested the Dutch High Commissioner to intervene.

---

16 The *New york Times*, March 6, 1950, commented on this conference: "The Dutch have not been acting like people who expect to be out of New Guinea by the end of the year."

17 Mohammad Hatta, "Indonesia between the Power Blocks," in *Portrait of a Patriot*, p. 567. First published in *Foreign Affairs*, April 1958.

18 Mohammad Hatta, "Indonesia's Foreign Policy," in *Portrait of a Patriot*, p. 554. First published in *Foreign Affairs*, April 1953.

19 Hatta had appointed Anak Agung Gde Agung his minister of the interior but later, to prevent a clash of loyalties, transferred him to a diplomatic post in Europe.

272 Indonesia Free: A Political Biography of Mohammad Hatta

Although the Dutch garrison in Bandung persuaded Westerling to leave the city, he was allowed to move on towards Jakarta. Later investigations revealed that his intent was to kidnap Hatta's cabinet while in session, and to kill the defense minister, the Sultan of Yogyakarta, and the acting chief of armed forces, Colonel Simatupang, who had taken over from the terminally ill Sudirman.[20] Hatta, forewarned of the coup, adjourned his cabinet meeting early, while the Siliwangi Division, now on its home territory, acted to counter Westerling's threat.

The attempted coup merely accelerated demands for a unitary state free of Dutch association, while Sultan Hamid's involvement, when revealed in April 1950, brought the BFO states into further disrepute. The States of East Indonesia and East Sumatra were among the most reluctant to change from a federal system, and a resistance force led by an ex-KNIL officer, Captain Andi Aziz, mounted a challenge to the proposed unitary state in Makassar in Sulawesi. On April 10, Hatta broadcast a speech to the people of Sulawesi, appealing to them to dissociate themselves from Aziz's action. Nevertheless, Hatta made it clear that there was a difference between Westerling's defiance and Captain Aziz's action: "Do not let us forget that the opponent is not an enemy but our own brother, our fellow national and fellow countryman. Therefore it is not right that the political struggle be accompanied by granite-fisted toughness or suchlike action."[21] Hatta pointed out that political opposition through correct channels was permissible but must not endanger security. "Democracy is not anarchy where anyone can take up arms as he pleases," he warned.[22] Aziz yielded. He was placed in military detention and later sentenced to a term of imprisonment.

Dutch influence was still strong in East Indonesia. Hatta's government faced a further challenge, this time from the East Indonesian minister of justice, Dr. Soumokil, who proclaimed a separatist State of the South Moluccas in Ambon. When negotiation failed, Hatta appealed to the people of the region: "If you truly love Bung Karno and me as your leaders, don't drag our names down by irregular action of an anarchical

---

20 Sultan Hamid, in his defense, told the court that he had warned Hatta that Westerling was dangerous. See *Times of Indonesia*, February 26, 1953.
21 *Merdeka*, April 11, 1950.
22 Ibid.

nature."[23] The South Moluccan region had a special place in Hatta's heart since his exile to Banda Neira; he understood the cultural dilemma in which the people were placed because they were different from the people of Java and Sumatra. While prime minister, he continued to use non-violent methods to settle the dispute, including a naval blockade, although the conflict was finally settled by military action. Hatta realized that strategically it was important to prevent the area from coming under Dutch control, as it was so close to West New Guinea.

In spite of the insurrection facing the government, Hatta still supported a thorough overhaul of the armed forces. Under the terms of the Round Table Conference Agreement, Indonesia had to accept ex-KNIL Indonesians into the army, a most difficult task in view of the animosities which had built up between Republican and KNIL troops during the independence struggle. Republican personnel expected to be accorded greater recognition, but there was also the practical consideration that KNIL personnel were better trained for modern warfare. Thus, as in the past, "rationalization" of the armed forces became a very emotive issue, in spite of Hatta's attempts to defuse tension by initiating rehabilitation programs.[24]

In regard to the civil service, Hatta faced problems of integrating the Republican and NICA administrations. Again, it was a task requiring sensitivity. Under the Round Table Conference agreement, the Republic had to retain 15,700 Dutch civil servants for at least two years.[25] The allocation of senior administrative posts to nationalists in preference to long-serving *pangreh praja* created tensions. Hatta again appealed to the old civil service corps to discard colonial attitudes, reminding them that they must show leadership but not play a political role: "What we desire are people who have sovereignty, not a state which has sovereignty.[26] It was a warning to change past patterns of considering the civil service bureaucracy as a ruling elite.

---

23 Ibid., May 9, 1950.
24 Hatta instituted training and education facilities, concentrating on craft skills. He also set up special transmigration schemes offering land in the Outer Islands to soldier settlers. See Herbert Feith, *The Decline of Constitutional Democracy in Indonesia* (Ithaca, N.Y.: Cornell University Press, 1964), p. 81.
25 See ibid., p. 82.
26 *Merdeka*, October 27, 1950.

To help formulate fiscal and economic policies, Hatta established an economic and finance council, made up of members of his ministry and chaired by himself. Certainly Hatta inherited a daunting economic situation. Three years later he described his cabinet's dilemma: "It found itself with an empty treasury; the budget for 1950 envisaged a deficit of f 1.5 billion, approximately 17% of the total -- a huge sum for a poor nation that had no facilities for raising capital within the country."[27] Inflation was rampant; much of the export trade was still being conducted through smuggling operations, which had become almost institutionalized. Estates were run down and independence had sparked off a wave of labor unrest, in which Hatta saw the renascent PKI's influence, contending: "In North Sumatra, the PKI incited the plantation workers to go on strike just at the time when the seedlings and young plants had to be transplanted."[28] yet Hatta refused to bear down on the unions; the right to strike was a principle which he had always respected.

Faced with a sizeable deficit and an enormous debt to the Netherlands government, on March 13 Hatta's government introduced an exchange certificate system which altered the 1:1 ratio of Dutch to Indonesian guilders to one of 1:3 as far as export, import, and other transactions were concerned.[29] Hatta's government also introduced another draconian measure. On March 19, currency notes of f 2.50 and above were cut in half and exchanged for new currency notes and government bonds. All bank deposits in excess of f 400 had to be halved, one half going to the government as a compulsory loan. This prevented the Dutch from converting Indonesian money into Dutch currency at a fictitious rate and encouraged export production. Fortunately the war in Korea had stimulated the demand for Indonesian products, with consequent above-average prices on the world market.[30] By the time Hatta's cabinet retired in August 1950, the economic crisis was greatly relieved and the position

27 Hatta, "Indonesia's Foreign Policy," p. 554.
28 Hatta, *Bung Hatta Menjawab*, p. 24.
29 Feith, *Decline of Constitutional Democracy*, p. 85. In September 1949, when the pound sterling was devalued, Indonesian currency had been adjusted to the dollar but not to Dutch currency. This move partly corrected this imbalance.
30 Ibid., p. 86. Hatta's wife remonstrated with him for not warning her of this move. Hatta's defense was: "Yuke, if I had told you in advance, you would have told your mother, and you both would have protected yourselves and possibly told other close friends." See Nyonya R. Hatta, "Prinsip-prinsip Bung Hatta," p. 43.

of foreign reserves improved, leaving an impression of strong, stable, if somewhat austere government.

The rapid demise of the federal states and the persistent demands for a unitary state from radical nationalist political groups, supported enthusiastically by Sukarno, forced Hatta to accelerate the dissolution of his government. His main concern was to make sure that the basic principles of *kedaulatan rakyat* be protected in the changeover and incorporated into the new Constitution.

Hatta and Halim, the acting prime minister of the Republic of Indonesia, on May 19 signed a charter of agreement setting in motion a return to a unitary state, a new Republic of Indonesia. A joint committee of RUSI and RI representatives was established to finalize the details, including once again a Draft Constitution to legalize the new state. The charter of agreement set down guidelines, suggesting that there be a "revision of the RUSI Provisional Constitution in such a manner that it shall contain the essentials of the Constitution of the Republic of Indonesia, including (a) Article 27; (b) Article 29; and (c) Article 33."[31] These were three articles in the 1945 Constitution which had been very close to Hatta's heart; the protection of the rights of the ordinary citizen, freedom to profess one's beliefs, and Hatta's own special economic clause safeguarding the economy from an overly liberalist approach. The agreement emphasized that "the unitary constitution will be provisional only."[32] As Hatta explained to the press, "it will be the Constituent Assembly which will decide the permanent Constitution."[33] As the years passed by, Hatta's hopes for implementing *kedaulatan rakyat* would rest increasingly on the deliberations of the Constituent Assembly.

In the discussions which followed, it became apparent that Hatta's position as prime minister was not a foregone conclusion as in December 1949. There were demands for the restoration of the *Dwi Tunggal*, with the inclusion of a Vice-Presidency in the new Constitution. The parties were also vying for power, promoting their own leaders as prime minister, such as Mohammad Natsir of Masjumi and Sjahrir of the PSI.[34] Hatta had

---

31 See Kahin, *Nationalism and Revolution in Indonesia*, p. 461.
32 *Merdeka*, June 5, 1950.
33 Ibid.
34 In regard to Sjahrir, there were doubts expressed about his support. *Merdeka* commented: "As

irritated the PNI by resisting the traditional patronage role of the ruler, refusing to accede to solicitations for bureaucratic and diplomatic posts and to requests for a share in the bounty of ex-Dutch colonial property which had been transferred to the new state.

Yet a commentary in the local newspaper *Merdeka*, whose editor, B. M. Diah, was not particularly close to Hatta, recognized that public opinion did not favor Hatta's immediate retirement from the premiership, claiming that "it is only someone like Hatta who can overcome party infighting."[35] Hatta recalled that in the joint RUSI/RI discussions, two viewpoints emerged:

> One line of thought, espoused by Masjumi supported the continuation of a Presidential Cabinet with me as Prime Minister while concurrently Vice-President, which clearly had been successful in safeguarding the nation in times of crisis. The alternative view, put forward by the PNI and supported by the PSI and others, was that I should choose to be Prime Minister or Vice-President in a unitary state.[36]

The dialogue on Hatta's future role was long and contentious. Hatta withdrew from it, agreeing that "whatever decision was reached, I would accept it."[37] The RUSI representation regarded Hatta's relegation to the Vice-Presidency as tantamount to being "kicked upstairs" and would only agree to it on condition that there was a legal way for him to be appointed prime minister in times of crisis. This legal loophole was termed an "escape clause."[38] The suggested "escape clause" was rejected by the PNI and several other parties, including the PSI.[39]

The PSI's vote against the "escape clause" was a bitter wound for Hatta

far as the PNI is concerned, it is certain that Sjahrir would not have backing, while in Masjumi this too is uncertain, taking into account opposition in certain Masjumi quarters to Sjahrir personally." See *Merdeka*, May 25, 1950. Sjahrir was regarded as an opponent also by the PKI and Partai Murba.

35 *Merdeka*, May 25, 1950.
36 Hatta, *Bung Hatta Menjawab*, p. 26.
37 Ibid., p. 27.
38 See *Merdeka*, July 4, 1950.
39 Feith maintains that the PSI hoped that Sjahrir could return to the prime ministership. See Feith, *Decline of Constitutional Democracy*, p. 96, n. 83.

since the party held the balance in the decision. The PSI claimed to be ardent advocates of parliamentary democracy but yet had insufficient foresight to understand that, if the system fell into disrepute through party deadlocks, as it had in Europe in the twenties and in the thirties, and as had happened closer to home during the struggle against the Dutch, the considerable forces preferring a return to more authoritarian government or to totalitarian one-party systems would gain credence. When Hatta in 1960 criticized the "ultra democracy" of the parties,[40] it was probable that he was including Sjahrir and the PSI, to him a group of intellectually brilliant people but yet immature and blind to the realities of Indonesia's domestic situation.

Hatta did not confine his criticisms to the parties. He indicated in an interview in his latter years that he believed Sukarno had misled those deliberating on the new unitary state when he remarked: "Bung Hatta will become a Vice President in a Parliamentary Cabinet. But when difficulties arise later on, *I know what I shall do.*"[41] Hatta recalled: "This was interpreted by all those present, that it would be the same as in Yogya before, namely, that when difficulties arose, Bung Hatta would be Vice President and concurrently Prime Minister."[42] By the time Hatta's name was suggested again as an emergency prime minister, Sukarno was too hostile to Hatta's promoters and too allied to their opposition groups to reinstate Hatta as head of government.

The new Republic of Indonesia came into being on August, 17, 1950, the fifth anniversary of the proclamation of Independence. Sukarno appointed Mohammad Natsir, the leader of Masjumi, formateur of a cabinet, a leader who was to become a thorn in Sukarno's flesh and almost as great a *bête noire* to him as was Sjahrir.[43] On October 14, 1950, the new parliament voted to recommend that Hatta be appointed Vice-President.[44] The PKI had tried to block Hatta's automatic selection but the

---

40 Mohammad Hatta, *Our Democracy*, trans. R. Cook (Brisbane: Griffith University School of Modern Asian Studies, Teaching Translation Series, Indonesian Series, No. 4, 1979), p. 7.

41 Hatta, *Bung Hatta's Answers*, p. 23. Italics in text.

42 Ibid.

43 Natsir's insistence that the President remain a figurehead irritated Sukarno. Natsir's developing rapport with the Sjahrir faction also alienated him from Sukarno.

44 The main contenders for office were Hatta and the veteran nationalist, Ki Hadjar Dewantoro, supported by the PKI. Hatta obtained a decisive victory with 113 votes to Ki Hadjar's 19. See *Merdeka*, October 16, 1950.

move was stalled by a majority decision to appoint a committee to draw up a list of names for submission to Sukarno, as stipulated by Article 45(4) of the new Constitution. Sukarno was left with little choice as only Hatta's name was submitted. The daily *Merdeka* expressed approval: "With the election of Hatta as Vice-President, our nation will be strengthened, both internally and externally. In the view of the people, Sukarno-Hatta are one."[45] How misled the people were.

From 1951 to 1956, his five-year term as Vice-President, Hatta tried to moderate his political comment, much as it went against the grain to do so. He could sympathize with Sukarno's frustration when the Natsir government requested the President to refrain from making political statements, although Hatta made efforts to support Natsir whose cabinet policies were almost identical with his own. The theme of "nation building" did not call for the same dramatic talent as hurling invective at the Dutch, nor were there clearly discernible feuding forces which were so much a part of past revolutionary rhetoric.

Yet both Hatta and Sukarno were called upon to play advisory roles, unable to avoid involvement in the incessant wrangling between political, religious, military, and regional groups during this period. Inter-party rivalry at the expense of stable government particularly irked Hatta. "Political parties are intended to be an orderly means of representing public opinion," he pointed out in 1951, "but in the development of our parties, the party is the goal and the State becomes its tool."[46] Nevertheless, Hatta never suggested that the party system be abandoned, merely trimmed and reformed. "Democracy cannot proceed without political parties," he insisted.[47]

A significant amount of Hatta's time over the next few years was spent touring the archipelago. He went out of his way to speak to young people wherever he traveled, seeing them in terms of Indonesia's future leadership, following the pattern of "caderization" set by the New PNI. He stressed: "It is no longer the time to play at being romantic heroes, we must get down to work."[48] He made clear to the illegal guerrilla bands still

---

45 Ibid.
46 *Pikiran Rakjat*, February 7, 1951.
47 Ibid., October 4, 1958.
48 *Merdeka*, February 14, 1951.

marauding the countryside that they should cease fighting: "Rebellion is no longer revolution, but counter-revolution, which must be wiped out. There must be no 'state within a state.'"[49] The "state within a state" was clearly an oblique reference to the groups fighting for an Islamic state.

Hatta still enjoyed close relationships with the army, especially with its current leaders Simatupang and Nasutlon, the Siliwangi Division officers who had played a decisive role in the Madiun Affair. He lectured to the Sekolah Staf Komando Angkatan Darat [Army Staff Command School] or SSKAD, trying to influence the middle-ranking officers who attended courses there to accept a professional military role rather than a political one. Hatta, although sympathetic to the army's frustration with the ineffectiveness of civilian government and the low caliber of many of the politicians, continued to emphasize that the country's armed forces should be depolitidzed, that "the Army is a national instrument."[50]

Regional dissatisfaction with the central government was provoked by inattention to the needs of the Outer Islands. A debacle over Government Regulation 39 of 1950 concerning regional elections finally toppled Natsir's government,[51] leaving the state's affairs in Umbo while parties wrangled and bargained with one another to try to form a new coalition cabinet. Sukarno ignored press comments that "community hopes are being expressed that... Hatta will be given the mandate to form a Cabinet,"[52] and instead appointed Sukiman, now a Masjumi leader but not in the Natsir faction, as cabinet leader. Sukiman was on amicable terms with the PNI through PI peer group ties and was liked by both Sukarno and Hatta. Certainly the *Dwi Tunggal* relationship improved during Sukiman's regime, Sukarno moderating his speeches, playing down the West Irian question and dwelling on nation building.

In return for Sukarno's support, Sukiman instituted a new interpretation of the roles of President and Vice-President, obtaining parliamentary

---

49 Ibid., September 20, 1951.
50 *Pikiran Rakjat*, July 26, 1955.
51 When acting as Prime Minister of the Republic of Indonesia, Halim had on August 15, 1950 issued Regulation 39 of 1950 concerning regional and municipal elections, which the Natsir government endorsed. Opposition to the regulation stemmed from a suspicion that it would favor the Islamic party, as the election system was based on established local organizations. See Feith, *Decline of Constitutional Democracy*, pp. 165-69.
52 See *Merdeka*, March 24, 1951.

consent for their wider involvement in state affairs, for which the cabinet was prepared to accept responsibility. As Karim Pringgodigdo analyzed the situation: "Considered politically, the government statement affirms that the Head of State remains unconditionally in office, whilst the activities of the President and Vice-President could possibly bring about the resignation of a Cabinet."[53]

Sukiman implemented an ardent anti-Communist program, supported by Sukarno, who advised the PKI not to "sell your national soul for a dish of international lentils."[54] When accused of harassing the PKI, Sukiman alleged that he was acting on rumors of Communist plans to murder both Sukarno and Hatta while they were en route to their weekend villas in the West Java mountains.[55]

Sukiman's leaning towards the United States of America was criticized by the PSI. Having spent the major part of 1951 overseas,[56] Sjahrir sought out Hatta on his return to Indonesia. "Sjahrir felt rebuffed by Hatta," recalled Subadio, "because he showed more interest in National Sports Week than in listening to what Sjahrir had to tell him."[57] This may have been Hatta's way of reminding Sjahrir that it was the PSI that had assisted in relegating him to the role of an impotent Vice-President, whose main function was to officiate at occasions such as National Sports Week. On the other hand, Hatta may also have been responding to an editorial in *Merdeka* which suggested that the English Labour Party was using Sjahrir and Nehru to form a "third power" in Southeast Asia.[58]

Since the Round Table Conference, Hatta had not only instituted but had tried to advocate an independent foreign policy. When writing on Indonesia's foreign policy a year later, he deplored the "bloc" mentality in international relations, declaring that Indonesia was "not prepared to

---

53 Pringgodigdo, *Office of President in Indonesia*, p. 49.
54 Feith, *Decline of Constitutional Democracy*, p. 216.
55 See ibid., p. 191.
56 While on this overseas trip, Sjahrir married in Cairo his former personal assistant, Siti Wahjunah, known as Poppy. Having looked at various socialist systems, including those of Poland and Yugoslavia, he came to the conclusion: "For all its shortcomings, democratic government is better than all other government systems." See *Merdeka*, September 13, 1951.
57 Interview with Subadio Sastrosatomo, February 22, 1982.
58 Editorial, *Merdeka*, October 3, 1951. Entitled "Quo Vadis, Sjahrir?" the editorial read: "Perfidious Albion, expert in diplomacy over the centuries... it wants to defend its position as a 'balancing power' in the East and West. The position in the West is achieved but in Asia it needs an Asian bloc with a basis of English socialism." British influence at this time was already on the wane.

participate in any third bloc designed to act as a counterpoise to the two giant blocs."[59] In rejecting the "third bloc" as a foreign policy strategy, Hatta was not just alienating himself from Sjahrir but also from Nehru. This viewpoint would also separate him from Sukarno, who in 1955 would see the potential of a third bloc for projecting himself as a Third World leader. Hatta pointed out that the "bloc" system violated the spirit of the United Nations.[60]

It was its deference to America which toppled the Sukiman cabinet, especially after Subardjo, as foreign minister, accepted mutual security aid which virtually committed Indonesia to sharing in the defense of American interests in Asia. While Indonesia wrestled with the problem of finding a new cabinet, Hatta prepared for what is the high point in a Muslim's life, his *haj* to Mecca.

Hatta combined state visits to Egypt and the Middle East with his religious pilgrimage, on which he was accompanied by his wife and her parents, Rusli and Anni Rachim. Hatta may have chosen to go to Mecca at this time for political reasons, as the religious affairs minister had been under attack for his mismanagement of transport arrangements for pilgrims in 1951.[61] Hatta has made scant reference to his *haj*, nor did he ever show the degree of affection for the Middle East which he expressed for Europe. His daughter Meutia recorded that he was irritated by the disorder which prevailed in Mecca, especially around the shrines, suggesting remedies to the Saudi Arabian government to correct weaknesses in the organization of pilgrims.[62]

Wilopo, a PNI leader and a keen socialist, had succeeded Sukiman as prime minister on Hatta's return to Indonesia. Hatta approved of Wilopo, who had served as labor minister in his own RUSI cabinet. However, Wilopo fell from favor with Sukarno for including in his cabinet people whom Sukarno disliked, men in the Natsir-Sjahrir groups such as Mohamad Roem, the Sultan of Yogyakarta, and the economist Sumitro.

---

59 Hatta, "Indonesia's Foreign Policy," p. 549.
60 Ibid., p. 550.
61 See Feith, *Decline of Constitutional Democracy*, p. 235.
62 According to Hatta, if the shops and hawkers in the vicinity of the Haram Mosque were removed and median strips provided on roads, there would be a more orderly flow of pilgrims, preventing people from colliding with one another. See M. F. Swasono, "Ayahanda: Pribadinya dalam Kenanganku," p. 56.

Perhaps even more worrying for Hatta was the realization that the PKI leader, D. N. Aidit, had begun to woo Sukarno and that the latter was responding. The PKI made a particularly vehement attack on Hatta and Sjafruddin Prawiranegara, accusing them of having accepted funds from the United States of America to liquidate Communists in the aftermath of the Madiun Affair.[63] Although taken to court for insulting the Vice-President, Aidit did not receive any significant sentence and the case dragged on over several years. From 1953 onwards, Masjumi and the PSI were to be the objects of constant abuse in the PKI press, Natsir, Sjahrir, and, after 1956, Hatta becoming prime targets for attack.

Army unrest escalated in 1952. The end of the Korean War in 1951 had broken the economic boom which had helped to ease the new Republic's first two years of independence. For the defense ministry, the need for tighter budget control provided a further rationale for the minister and his defense chiefs to implement policies which would rid the forces, the army in particular, of personnel who were inadequate in terms of educational standard and physical fitness. The army leaders had also tried to impose tighter control on regional commanders by transferring them away from their power bases, thus making them less independent and more subject to budgetary control. These policies disadvantaged the ex-Peta groups the most, many of which had political ties with the left wing of the PNI.

While Hatta was on close terms with the more professional group of army officers, Sukarno was building up a support group among those army officers disadvantaged by modernization programs, becoming the champion of the factions, mainly ex-Peta officers, most opposed to Nasution and Simatupang. Parliamentary supporters of the pro-Sukarno factions mounted criticism of Wilopo's defense policies, forcing the defense minister, the Sultan of Yogyakarta to resign. Nasution, disgruntled by government interference in military affairs, organized a demonstration which clamored for general elections to elect a new government. This minor coup, staged on October 17, 1952, included visits to the residences of Hatta and Sukarno. As Sukarno spoke to the crowd gathered outside his Palace, two tanks appeared, their guns trained on him. Sukarno agreed

63 See *Harian Rakjat*, February 5, 1955, where Aidit's statement on the Madiun Affair, first published in *Harian Rakjat* on September 14, 1953, is reviewed. It appeared, from the PKI accusations, that Hatta's government received a sum of $656,000 to wipe out the "Reds."

to receive a delegation of top-ranking officers, requesting that Hatta and Wilopo be present.

Since 1949, the army leadership had become increasingly disenchanted with civilian government, impatient with the left-wing elements in the parliament and their attitudes to defense policies. Military defiance was therefore not unexpected. Nasution had previously proposed that the parliamentary system be replaced, by means of a coup, with an oligarchy, a *Tritunggal* consisting of Sukarno, Hatta, and the Sultan of Yogyakarta. Hatta, although sympathetic, stressed that reform must take place through a properly elected government and Constituent Assembly. Nasution paid the price for his strong-arm tactics, being dismissed as chief of army staff. His successor was an ex-Peta officer, Colonel Sugeng, a friend of the President. His appointment was a temporary one.

Military defiance and economic decline combined to unseat the Wilopo government. The Masjumi called for a return to a Hatta cabinet, Natsir warning: "The State is in danger at this time, although this may not be evident on the surface."[64] This time the PSI strongly supported Hatta, aware that Sjahrir was increasingly withdrawing from direct participation in politics.[65] Again Sukarno acted quickly to deflect any proposals for Hatta's return to the prime ministership, declaring that he "still upheld the basis of our Constitution and parliamentary traditions," and adding: "So far there is unanimity between Vice-President Hatta and myself."[66] Sukarno's remark was significant in that it was an acknowledgment that the public was aware of strains in the *Dwi Tunggal*.

The cabinet crisis was finally resolved by recalling Ali Sastroamidjojo from his post as ambassador in Washington to become prime minister. As he could not reach agreement with Masjumi, Ali excluded the major Islamic party, although he included representatives from Nahdatul Ulama which had broken away to form a separate party.[67] His cabinet

---

64 Abadi, June 9, 1953, as cited in Feith, *Decline of Constitutional Democracy*, p. 332.

65 According to Natsir, "after Sjahrir was kicked out, he seemed to withdraw from government in terms of involvement, as if he were an onlooker. When I asked him to play a more significant role in government, Sjahrir's reply was: 'Do it yourself.'" Interview, February 1983.

66 See Feith, *Decline of Constitutional Democracy*, p. 336. Hatta stated that he would only act as formateur at Parliament's request.

67 See *Abadi*, March 10, 1952, in which Haji Wahab Chasbullah, an NU leader, after conferring with Sukarno, stated that unless Masjumi restored K. H. Wachid Hasjim to the Religious Affairs portfolio and appointed Sukiman as prime minister of its cabinet, the NU might break away from

was predominantly Javanese, and according to Mohamad Roem, it was dominated by Sukarno. In his view, Ali, in spite of his immense presence, was "a creature of Sukarno." As Roem portrayed the situation: "Ali's top priority was not to differ from Sukarno's wishes, thus Sukarno was behind the scenes manipulating Ali."[68]

The exclusion of the Masjumi from government incurred the wrath of strongly orthodox Muslim groups, especially those seeking an Islamic state. Regional unrest became particularly heated in Aceh.[69] Hatta, renowned as the Sumatran trouble-shooter, flew to this fanatically Muslim outpost to try to defuse the situation, directing attention to the need for stability and nation building.[70] His bid was unsuccessful as armed conflict erupted a few months later. A dilemma for Hatta was that, as far as the institution of an Islamic state was concerned, he was just as opposed to it as were Sukarno and the PKI and thus out of step with his most ardent Islamic supporters.

Patterns of traditional Javanese power relationships and elitist attitudes became more apparent during the Ali cabinet. By 1954, as if sensing that his goal of *kedaulatan rakyat* was losing ground, Hatta began to speak out more forcefully in defense of democracy. "There can only be justice in a state if the basic principles of the government have come from the people themselves," he stressed,[71] contending that an autocracy was "too dependent on the personality of one individual." Among the examples of dictators, he cited the name of Gadjah Mada, a strong man of Javanese imperialism. Hatta seemed to be warning the people that Sukarno and those who advocated more authoritarian rule were bent on destroying the present system of government. Hatta appealed to the parties to restore credibility to parliamentary democracy, suggesting that they play an

---

Masjumi. Masjumi did not include Wachid Hasjim's name on the list of persons recommended for the portfolio. On April 6, 1952, NU broke away from Masjumi. See also Feith, *Decline of Constitutional Democracy*, pp. 235-36.

68 Interview M. Roem, February 5, 1982. As Roem served as Ali's deputy in his second cabinet, his viewpoint carries some weight.

69 The military governor, Daud Beureueh, had close links with the outlawed Darul Islam movement in Java and with another extremist Islamic group in South Sulawesi.

70 *Times of Indonesia*, July 31, 1953, commented that Hatta was well received in Aceh. There were no posters setting out specific demands as was the case during Sukarno's visit a few months previously. Hatta's visit to Aceh was criticized by the PKI, which accused him of interference in government problems. See *Pedoman*, November 2, 1953, and *Harian Rakjat*, November 7, 1953.

71 *Times of Indonesia*, July 5, 1954.

educative role as teachers of sound government.[72]

The weakness of the successive cabinets directed public attention back to the *Dwi Tunggal*. The Bandung daily, *Pikiran Rakjat*, commented on the leadership abilities of both Sukarno and Hatta: "They have both high standing and are considered to have power by the people, but our Constitution fetters their actions and energies; they are not able to act according to their own concepts but are merely symbols." The article further commented:

> As far as we can see and hear, Hatta is able to control himself and remains within the constitutional boundaries; in other words, he does not interfere in executive affairs. But as far as we can gather, it is torture for Sukarno to remain within constitutional limits and not interfere in the executive and, because of his impulsiveness, he violates the limits of the Constitution.[73]

The writer had failed to discern that Hatta, too, was a tortured soul, but then Hatta's emotions were not easy to read because he had long ago trained himself to hide them. His pain at being excluded from power and of being unable to further his social goals was just as agonizing as Sukarno's, perhaps even more so since it could not find relief in open defiance.

"Hatta is too full of creativity to become a symbol without responsibility," asserted *Pikiran Rakjat*. The conclusion reached by the paper was significant in that it was one on which Hatta would act. It read: "It would be better if Sukarno and Hatta do not make themselves available to be reelected as President and Vice-President. It is better that they return to the people, putting forward their conceptions via party

---

72 An editorial in *Pikiran Rakjat* of October 25, 1954 followed up Hatta's remarks about the parties as educators, commenting: "Ah Hatta, we feel your suggestions will float in the air for a long time before finding fertile brains and hearts. Perhaps we should wait five more years! Aren't Easterners patient people? But if after five years the parties in our country are just as now, selling humbug and demagogy, grabbing seats and rank, riding on ignorant people made more befuddled by the parties, perhaps we should have a dictator! Would it be better to kill 'democracy' so that DEMOCRACY can live? Would it be better to follow Mustapha's example, whose actions you once praised?" Mustapha clearly refers to Kemal Pasha of Turkey.
73 *Pikiran Rakjat*, October 9, 1954.

politics."[74]

Hatta, like every other Indonesian, began to pin his hopes for clean and efficient government on the results of the general election, finally scheduled for late 1955. He was particularly concerned about the Ali government's fiscal policies. Hatta pointed out that, while the government enriched the elite, "there is considerable victimization of the people, especially by means of taxes" and that the people's economy had not been improved by giving priority to Indonesian businessmen because "many people who obtain licenses sell them to foreign enterprises."[75] Regional unrest was escalating because the government's economic policies worked to the advantage of importers on Java and against Outer Island exporters.

Ali's cabinet gained most renown in foreign affairs. It staged the first Conference of Asian-African nations in Bandung in April 1955, which was supported by Nehru and attended by the Chinese premier, Chou En-lai. The conference was enthusiastically espoused by Sukarno; Hatta played a much more low-key role, although the conference did allow him an opportunity to hold discussions with Nehru and to meet Chou En-lai. In spite of his criticism of the "third bloc" concept, Hatta admitted that "the Bandung Conference brought to birth a spirit of peace which we must try to fertilize."[76]

The prestige gained from staging the Bandung Conference did not save Ali's cabinet from mounting domestic disapproval of its policies. The greatest challenge came from the army, which had begun to patch up its own internal rifts in order to present an image of strength vis-à-vis civilian government. There was widespread disapproval of Iwa Kusuma Sumantri's performance as defense minister.

Ali returned his mandate to govern to Hatta on July 24, 1955, while Sukarno was overseas on his *haj* to Mecca. Since the general elections were scheduled to start in September, it was clear that the next cabinet must be of short duration. Both Masjumi and the PSI again proposed that the new cabinet be led by Hatta. In this they were supported by the daily *Pikiran Rakjat*, which reported: "Hatta is the only capable and honest

---

74 Ibid.
75 Ibid., November 26, 1954.
76 Ibid.

leader with sufficient authority to surmount the present emergency situation."[77] Hatta recalled that Subadio, then chairman of the PSI, urged him to take on the premiership. Resentfully Hatta retorted: "Why? It was you people who wanted a parliamentary cabinet so much! According to the 1950 Constitution, I cannot possibly hold office as Prime Minister again!" Subadio answered: "We never guessed that it would turn out like this!"[78]

Hatta insisted that the only legal way for him to accept the premiership would be for parliament to pass a resolution declaring him non-active as Vice-President while prime minister, in other words introducing an "escape clause." This the PNI would not accept, demanding that Hatta first resign as Vice-President. This proposal alarmed Masjumi, who suspected that the PNI and PKI wanted Hatta removed from the Vice-Presidency to suit Sukarno's purposes.

Hatta pursued the matter no further, and instead persuaded Burhanuddin Harahap, the parliamentary leader of Masjumi, to head the new government. As a relative of the acting chief of army staff, Colonel Zulkifli Lubis, a North Sumatran, he was a prime minister acceptable to the army leadership. Although Nahdatul Ulama agreed to join his cabinet, Burhanuddin could not persuade the PNI to work with him. This was not surprising since his main goals were to clean up the corruption and reverse the undesirable trends in government attributed to the previous PNI leadership.

On his return from overseas, Sukarno made it clear that the new cabinet did not meet with his approval. Even Hatta was disappointed with its performance, in particular its decision to ape PNI tactics of placing its own party members in senior civil service posts, a ploy redolent of the power politics it was supposed to rectify. Hatta realized that the Burhanuddin cabinet was too weak to restore faith in parliamentary democracy.

The final blow for Hatta was the general election result. No clear winner emerged. Masjumi and the PNI were tied with 57 seats each, although the PNI recorded more votes. Next came the Nahdatul Ulama with 45 seats,

---

77 Ibid., July 26, 1955.
78 Hatta, *Bung Hatta Menjawab*, p. 53.

followed closely by the PKI with 39 seats, having previously held only 17. The PSI polled extremely badly, gaining only 5 seats.[79]

One aspect of the electoral system which later drew criticism from Hatta was that the people voted for a party but the party chose the representatives. Thus, Hatta pointed out, the representative was not necessarily a person who had any direct association with the area where his party polled the votes.[80] Hatta also blamed the election system for the proliferation of minor parties, pointing to the example of the system in Britain, "where every area directly elects its representatives to Parliament" and the small parties are automatically eliminated.[81]

Hatta slipped away from Indonesia's post-election disillusionment to accept Nehru's long-standing invitation to revisit India. He returned to Indonesia in the New Year of 1956 to face what was to be a period of major decision in his life. The split in the *Dwi Tunggal* became a reality when Sukarno, for the first time in their partnership, refused to endorse a decree issued by Hatta while Sukarno was in Mecca.[82] Another development which must have chilled Hatta and made him realize that the balance of power was now in the hands of those advocating more authoritarian government was that there was a rapprochement between Sukarno and the recently reinstated army chief, Nasution.[83] It was apparent that Sukarno and Nasution were united in a common goal: to dismantle parliamentary democracy and restore presidential rule. It was the army's bid to gain political power by becoming the "powerhouse" behind Sukarno.[84]

The PNI, because of its larger vote in the general election, had the right to form a government, and it again called on Ali Sastroamidjojo to

---

79 For more comprehensive details of election results, see Feith, *Decline Of Constitutional Democracy*, pp. 435-36.
80 *Pikiran Rakjat*, July 24, 1957.
81 Ibid., September 2, 1957.
82 The decree in question had been issued by Hatta on the advice of Burhanuddin Harahap as defense minister, confirming the appointment of a new deputy air force chief of staff. The PKI was suspicious that the appointment was made to balance the influence of the left-wing air force chief of staff, Suryadarma.
83 Nasution had been reinstated in preference to Simbolon, the most senior officer, because the latter was regarded as a North Sumatran "warlord." It was expected that Sukarno would react unfavorably to Nasution's appointment as he was considered to be close to Hatta and Masjumi.
84 Nasution was prepared to retain Hatta in the *Dwi Tunggal*, recalling: "In the Army leadership, we all agreed that a *dwitanggal* would endanger national unity." See A. H. Nasution, "Bung Hatta Teladankan Konsistensi Pada Prinsip-Prinsip," in *Bung Hatta: Pribadinya dalam Kenangan*, p. 372.

become prime minister. This time Ali sensed that presidential support was nominal; in fact Sukarno had begun to drop hints that he was formulating a new conception of government for Indonesia. Sukarno was also reluctant to endorse Ali's choice of cabinet because it included Masjumi members whom Sukarno disliked, such as Mohamad Roem as deputy prime minister, a man close to Hatta.

Hatta was aware that Sukarno was on the attack and had acquired a formidable power base -- the Javanese people, the PNI, the PKI, Nahdatul Ulama, the Partai Murba, and now the powerful army chief, Nasution. Under the Constitution, Hatta was required to assist Sukarno in his duties. But Sukarno now considered it to be his "duty" to destroy the only type of democracy which accorded with Hatta's perception of "Indonesia Free." Hatta felt that, in order to defend his social revolution, he must place himself in a position of "opposition."

Hatta warned Natsir of his intention to resign, explaining: "I can't continue with Sukarno!"[85] Natsir and Halim appealed to him to reconsider his decision. He finally agreed to work with Sukarno for another six months.[86] Circumstances in the months from July to December 1956 tended to reinforce rather than weaken Hatta's resolve. Sukarno returned from overseas trips to the United States, the Soviet Union, and China more than ever determined to change the present system of government. In a speech on October 28, he suggested, "Let us now bury all parties,"[87] indicating that he had a new concept of democracy, which he termed *"demokrasi terpimpin"* [democracy with leadership].[88]

The Outer Islands, especially Sumatra and Sulawesi, reacted angrily to the trend away from parliamentary government. Power struggles were also taking place within the army, sparked to some extent by Nasution's alliance with Sukarno. Natsir recalled that Hatta came to see him, affirming: "This is it -- I can't go on!" Hatta was reluctant to denounce Sukarno openly, Natsir recalled, fearing that such a declaration might

---

85 As recalled by M. Natsir in interview, February 6, 1983.
86 Interview with M. Natsir, February 6, 1983. Hatta was particularly disgusted by Sukarno's granting a partial reprieve to the justice minister, Djody Gondokusumo, although he had been convicted of corruption in January 1956.
87 See Feith, *Decline of Constitutional Democracy*, p. 517.
88 Ibid., p. 515.

endanger Indonesia's unity.[89]

Hatta's speech to the University of Gadjah Mada in Yogyakarta on November 27, 1956, where an honorary doctorate was conferred upon him, revealed that the decision to leave the *Dwi Tunggal* had hurt. He began:

> Confronting realities -- particularly very bitter ones -- people often conceive of ideals as a cure for their wounded spirit, ideals that give them hope for the future.[90]

He reminded his audience that the nationalist struggle had not just been against the Dutch but also dedicated to freeing the Indonesian people from oppression and social injustice, an attempt to implement the Universal Declaration of Human Rights. He advocated that Indonesia's ideal should be social democracy, inspired by Western socialist thought, Islam, and Indonesian village democracy.

Defending the *Panca Sila* as a state philosophy, Hatta noted that it incorporated the elements of social justice and religion, and he believed that, in spite of its shortcomings, the 1950 Constitution contained all the ideals of the independence movement. In view of the fact that his resignation took effect as the newly elected Constituent Assembly was about to begin its deliberations, Hatta's speech was clearly intended to draw attention to the values which should be preserved in the permanent Constitution.

Hatta condemned the irresponsibility of the political parties and the "scramble for profits" which had caused so much dissatisfaction in the public generally.[91] He criticized the denial of autonomy to the regions. Hatta gave his opinion that since 1950 the type of government practiced had been "parliamentary democracy without democracy and without a parliament," resulting in political anarchy. "The authority of the government has further declined because party politics introduced

---

89 M. Natsir in interview, February 6, 1983.
90 Mohammad Hatta, *Past and Future*, an address delivered upon receiving the degree of *doctor honora causa* from Gadjah Mada University at Yogyakarta on November 27, 1956 (Ithaca: Cornell Modern Indonesia Project, 1960), p. 1.
91 Ibid., p. 12.

and maintained the peculiar custom that power is in fact not vested with the responsible government, but with the party councils which are not responsible."[92] Thus, claimed Hatta, there had been a distorted form of parliamentary democracy, a rule by the powers behind the throne.

In his official letter of resignation Hatta was restrained, giving little indication of his realization that without Sukarno's backing, he was facing an uphill task in achieving his goals. His comments were succinct but low-key: "After participating in the task of nation and community building from above for eleven years, I wish to contribute my strength from below as an ordinary person, free of any position."[93]

Hatta wrote Sukarno a personal letter which was much more condemnatory than his letter of resignation. Halim strongly advised him to publish the letter. "Do you want to risk the outbreak of civil war?" queried Hatta.[94] He was already anxious about the reaction to his resignation in the Outer Islands. "My letter is sufficiently rational and sufficiently pointed, even here and there accusing Sukarno of behaving like a dictator," he exclaimed, adding, as if to express a feeling of an unpleasant duty faithfully discharged. "By this letter, I have fulfilled my responsibility to history."[95]

Unless Sukarno were prepared to support him, Hatta knew that his position in the *Dwi Tunggal* was practically that of an impotent figurehead. Even more galling, he could be regarded as part of Sukarno's effort to dismantle parliamentary democracy, an essential component of *kedaulatan rakyat*. If he remained as Vice-President, he would be condoning the reintroductlon of authoritarian, centralized government, where the voice of the people could be overruled by the ultimate authority. The *Dwi Tunggal* would resemble the governor-generals of old, of whom Hatta had once been so scornful.

For Hatta, the roots of democracy had to be nurtured, not torn out before they could stabilize and grow to maturity. The civilian leaders and the people needed more time to gain experience about how a democratic

---

92 Ibid., p. 16.
93 Letter of resignation, in Anak Agung Gde Agung, *Twenty Years*, pp. 622-24.
94 A. Halim, "Gores-Gores tentang Bung Hatta," in *Bung Hatta: Pribadinya dalam Kenangan*, p. 692.
95 Ibid.

system should operate. Hatta agreed that the system needed modification in the transitional period, but not elimination. If Sukarno was determined to destroy democracy, he believed he had no alternative but to resign. As an ordinary citizen, he could voice his opposition, explaining how *kedaulatan rakyat* was endangered and putting forward suggestions to prevent its destruction.

For Hatta, it was back to square one. From now on to the end of his life, he would revert to the role of fighter for social justice, non-cooperator, and political critic, as if he were again proclaiming to the Dutch court: "Cooperation merely means that the stronger party bullies the weaker, using the latter as an instrument to support his own interests."[96] The *Dwi Tunggal* had become *dwitanggal.*

---

96 M. Hatta, "Indonesia Free," p. 246.

CHAPTER TWELVE
NON-COOPERATOR

If we truly love a Free Indonesia, which is united, indivisible,
sovereign, just and prosperous, let us reflect for a while on how to
return to those former ideals which were so pure, and bring back
honest leadershlp combined with a spirit which is prepared to make
sacrifices.... Our people are still poor, even poorer than formerly, in
the midst of abundant natural riches. It is best we contemplate the
present situation of our people, who truly are entitled to a better fate,
one which accords with our original aims.[1]

Hatta's resignation undoubtedly led to an escalation in regional
defiance. In the outcry there was an element of Sumatran loyalty to Hatta
personally which must have mollified his hurt feelings, while also alerting
him to the need to exercise a tight rein on his political behavior for the
sake of Indonesian unity. Hatta knew from his extensive tours of the
regions that central government economic policies had disadvantaged
the Outer Islands. The seeds of revolt were there ready to be fertilized.
Already there was speculation that the political situation must be critical
if Hatta retired from the apex of government. This was to some extent
true. Hatta did want to alert his people to the threat to legal government
and parliamentary democracy.

From November 20 to 24 there had been a reunion of the Banteng
Division, the main fighting unit in the Minangkabau during the
Revolution, which had subsequently been disbanded by Nasution. Before
the reunion ended, a decision was made to establish a Banteng Council

---

1 Mohammad Hatta, "Fifty Years of the National Movement," *Pikiran Rakjat*, May 19, 1958.

which would press for reforms, especially for improved state and army leadership.[2]

Following Hatta's retirement from the Vice-Presidency, the regional army commander, Lieutenant Colonel Ahmad Husein, acting as chairman of the Banteng Council, formally took temporary charge of government in Central Sumatra, the incumbent Javanese governor quietly surrendering his powers in face of Minangkabau militancy. Two days later, in North Sumatra, the army commander, Simbolon, declared a State of Siege and War in his area and assumed local leadership as military commander. Simbolon stressed that he did not favor separatism but wanted "to improve the situation of the nation and of the Indonesian people by handing over the reins of government to those national leaders, who with honesty and integrity can develop the nation, free from lust for power and self seeking."[3] Simbolon called for a restoration of the *Dwi Tunggal*, declaring: "It is our conviction... that the *Dwitunggal* may no longer serve merely as a symbol but must function as a moving force, with a careful division of duties."[4] The last phrase was significant, for it suggested that Hatta be accorded an office commensurate with Sukarno's new powers in order to restore reality to the concept of the *Dwi Tunggal*. The South Sumatrans followed the example of the other two provinces, army commander Barlian establishing the Garuda Council, forcing the Javanese governor to agree to regional self-government.

Defiance was not confined to Sumatra. On March 2, the commander of the South Sulawesi region, Sumual, proclaimed the *Piagam Perjuangan Semesta* [Charter of Common Struggle] or Permesta, a declaration of support for regional autonomy and an expression of disapproval of the Jakarta government. The Permesta declaration made clear that, if the proposed National Council and *Gotang-royong* cabinet were to gain support, they must be led jointly by Sukarno and Hatta. To absorb regional dissidence into national affairs, on March 14 Nasution declared a "state of siege and war," urging Sukarno to persuade Hatta to return to government, although not necessarily as prime minister. No direct government action was taken against the rebel regimes, although Nasution acted quietly to

---

2 See Feith, *Decline of Constitutional Democracy*, p. 523.
3 See ibid., p. 527.
4 Ibid.

undermine the power of the regional commanders.[5]

The PKI had seized upon a Masjumi representative's press comment that Hatta would consider the prime ministership if the parliament offered it to him and was prepared to back his program until the next general election. The PKI's reaction was to brand Hatta a "dictator" and an "American *djago* [champion],"[6] also pointing out that the other leading Islamic party, Nahdatul Ulama, considered Hatta to be *"kekurangan ajaran politik"* or politically insolent.[7]

On February 21, enthusiastically supported by the PKI, Sukarno announced the formation of the *Gotong-royong* cabinet, in which all parties, including the PKI, would be represented. "All members of a family should eat at a single table and work at a single workbench," he declared.[8] Hatta would have concurred with this conception in 1926 when he believed the PKI to be essentially a nationalist group. In 1957, however, he contended that "as the PKI is basically part of an international movement," Sukarno's blend of national, religious, and foreign-oriented parties into one cabinet was "like trying to mix oil and water."[9] Sukarno's *konsepsi* also included the establishment of a National Council which he himself would lead.[10] The National Council was reminiscent of two advisory bodies of the past, the Dutch Volksraad and the Japanese Central Advisory Council. The disturbing factor was that the National Council would take precedence over the popularly elected parliament.

Sukarno did not seek a replacement for Hatta as Vice-President. There was really no place for an institutionalized duumvirate in Sukarno's conception of "democracy with leadership," although in practice he relied heavily on having advisers and administrators by his side.

Sukarno's *konsepsi* drew its main support from the PKI and the

---

5 Nasution's strategy was to undermine Simbolon's position in North Sumatra by appointing to his command officers of different ethnic and religious persuasion. In the case of Husein, because of the homogeneity of the Minangkabau region and the high level of support for the Dewan Banteng, Nasution could only employ persuasion and negotiation.

6 See *Harian Rakjat*, January 5, 1957.

7 See ibid., December 3, 1956.

8 *Dewan Nasional* (Jakarta, 1957), p. 25.

9 Mohammad Hatta, "Assessing Bung Karno's *Konsepsi*," *Indonesia Raya*, March 5, 1957.

10 The National Council was to be a purely advisory body made up of representatives of the various streams and functional groups in Indonesia. The chiefs of the armed forces together with ministers would also be included. It was expected that membership would be nominated.

Partai Murba. Chaerul Saleh, now returned from studies in Europe, had become one of Sukarno's leading supporters, just as he had admired the more authoritarian form of government advocated by Tan Malaka. Indeed, according to Hatta, Sukarno had not coined the term "*demokrasi terpimpin.*" "As far as I know," said Hatta, "those who brought the concept to Indonesia were ex-Major Ahmad and Chaerul Saleh as a consensus of Indonesian students studying in Western Europe," adding: "This idea was born as a reaction to the crisis of democracy which has taken place in Indonesia."[11] Hatta pointed out that even the overseas students were vague about the meaning of guided democracy. "What is clear is that they do not want a dictatorship but feel the party way of implementing democracy is incorrect."[12]

Hatta accused Sukarno of failing to analyze his concept of "democracy with leadership"; that as a result, Sukarno "has only arrived at the bridge to be crossed... but what is its form and content has not yet been illustrated." Apart from its lack of constitutional basis, Hatta pointed out that the National Council membership "is not representative and has no authority at all." He added scathingly: "It is not surprising that this body is more like -- according to a term in Constitutional Law -- a *menagerie du roi* rather than a body which can uphold its own authority."[13]

Hatta defended the parliamentary democracy of the 1950 Constitution from Sukarno's accusations that it was "free fight democracy." He conceded that the proper implementation of such a system depended on "responsible leadership"; thus to correct its faults, "we should revive the feeling of moral responsibility in our leadership, and in political party leadership circles." In Hatta's view, Sukarno's chairmanship of the National Council was inappropriate in that "he is constitutionally not responsible," but "the leadership of a democracy -- even a guided democracy -- should be responsible."[14] Hatta was pointing out that under the Constitution in force Sukarno did not have to accept responsibility for his actions, this was the duty of the cabinet and parliament.

---

11 Mohammad Hatta, "Demokrasi Terpimpin atau Menyehatkan Demokrasi," *Pikiran Rakjat,* September 2, 1957.
12 Ibid.
13 Ibid.
14 Ibid.

Sukarno ignored the Masjumi's requests that it be given the mandate to form any new cabinet, aware that it would probably offer the prime ministership to Hatta. Instead Sukarno appointed himself "citizen Sukarno" in order to become the formateur of an "emergency extra-parliamentary-business cabinet" which would act "properly and firmly" and would establish the National Council.[15] Sukarno appointed Djuanda, a non-party man and a fellow graduate of the Bandung Institute of Technology, as prime minister. Hatta's reaction was swift. He pointed out the sections of the Constitution which Sukarno was violating by his actions and warned that they "will have major consequences for our country and for interpreting the rules of our Constitution."[16]

Hatta spent much of 1957 touring Sumatra, where he received an enthusiastic welcome as if he were a returning hero responding to his people's call. He emphasized that his intent was not to incite rebellion but to prevent it. The Sumatrans assured him that they wanted to remain part of Indonesia but were not prepared to accept the type of government being practiced in Jakarta. Anti-Java feeling was running high. In his press statements, Hatta denied that the regional rebellion was a Miningkabau affair. "In my estimation the movement which emerged on December 20, 1956 was not an *ethnic* but a *regional* movement, which demands improvement and development in areas which so far have been neglected."[17]

Hatta described the regional revolts as "explosions of dissatisfaction" and "a psychological conflict between the center and the regions," analyzing the attitudes of the regional leaders: "The dialectic which they frequently put forward is that they deliberately violate the law to negate the central government's present basis of illegality." Hatta cautiously commended the Minangkabau refusal to condone undemocratic central government, declaring that "providing the Banteng Council truly acted in the interests of the people, I am prepared to recognize it provisionally as a *fait accompli*."[18] Again Hatta was using the criteria of "people's welfare" and "social justice" as his measuring rod. The PKI's response was to

15 See Jhaveri, *Presidency in Indonesia*, p. 246.
16 Mohammad Hatta, "Pembentukan Kabinet dan Konstitusi," *Pikiran Rakjat*, April 17, 1957.
17 Mohammad Hatta, "Menindjau Sumatera-Tengah," *Pikiran Rakjat*, June 3, 1957.
18 Ibid.

lampoon Hatta in cartoons, criticizing his advice to the Garuda Council in South Sumatra that it seek overseas loans for regional development and suggesting that such action would "not result in improvement but anarchy."[19]

There was an unmistakable tone of ethnic pride as Hatta wrote about the achievements of the Banteng Council and the Minangkabau people. "Many kilometers of roads have been improved, roads which eight months ago were impassable," he reported. What impressed him even more was that this construction was carried out by *gotong-royong*, not *gotong-royong* which is forced but *gotong-royong* arising from a desire to improve the general welfare." This was a subtle dig at Sukarno's *konsepsi*. Hatta reveled in the spirit of dynamism in his home region, "as if the people have taken on new life,"[20] justifying what he had written about auto-activity and traditional democracy.

Hatta, at the same time, had to face up to the threat of separatism in any regional act of defiance. Underlying the positive and constructive regional actions were elements of personal revenge. The Sumatran army commanders, especially Lubis and Simbolon, were resentful of both Sukarno and Nasution, as were Masjumi and PSI leaders. Hatta knew that both Natsir and Sumitro were also in Sumatra seeking support. Hatta warned the Banteng Council to exercise restraint, knowing that the presence of the disgruntled Masjumi and PSI leaders might unbalance the region. "The spirit which is rampant at present must be nurtured and channeled into continuous nation-building," he stressed.[21] The PKI press was pointing out that Nazaruddin, the head of the security section of the Banteng Council, was in Singapore arranging the procurement of arms from the headquarters of the South East Asia Treaty Organization [SEATO].[22]

Hatta must have realized that his own presence in Sumatra was as unsettling an influence as those of other outraged politicians, heightening rather than calming the spirit of rebellion. He tried to avoid being treated like a conquering hero, even to the point of offending local dignitaries

19 See *Harian Rakjat*, July 1, 1957.
20 Hatta, "Menindjau Sumatera-Tengah."
21 As cited in *Pikiran Rakjat*, June 27, 1957.
22 See *Harian Rakjat*, May 29, 1957.

by refusing to be carried aloft in a special "Chair of Honor."[23] He was being pressured into becoming a leader of regional revolt, a position he would only accept in terms of social reform rather than armed uprising. Hatta emphasized that he was not in Sumatra as the leader of a breakaway movement. In South Sumatra he declared heatedly: "If it is the case that the movements in South Sumatra intend to separate themselves from the unitary state, then I will never again return to South Sumatra."[24]

Hatta directed his pen to the question of regional autonomy. He criticized civil servants who "feel suspicious about autonomy at the village or *desa* level" because "in their opinion the village is too lowly, too narrow-minded, politically and socially."[25] Hatta returned to his basic view that the various ethnic village structures contained the essence of Indonesian democracy, "units of society which were clearly democratic with meeting halls for sessions and deliberations on joint projects through *gotong-royong*." Although damaged by the colonial impact, Hatta believed that the roots of democracy were "still there and alive."[26]

While Hatta was touring Sumatra, Sukarno was expressing his dissatisfaction that the major parties had not been more supportive of his *konsepsi*, especially that they had rejected the PKI's inclusion in the new cabinet. He again attacked the party system. He pointed out that "it wasn't I who ordered the existence of parties," that "Thank God, it wasn't Sukarno who signed that decree!"[27] Of course, the signatory in November 1945 of the decree instituting the party system had been Hatta. It was noticeable that Sukarno did not attack *Maklumat x*, the decree by which Hatta had converted the National Committee into a parliament. Sukarno had already undone much of *Maklumat x* by forcing the elected parliament to take second place to a National Council, which had not been elected. Yet as the army encroached on his power domain in the years ahead, Sukarno would turn to the parties for support, becoming extraordinarily adept at the old ploy of *divide et Impere*, playing one force off against the other.

---

23 See *Pikiran Rakjat*, June 27, 1957.
24 See ibid.
25 Mohammad Hatta, "Demokrasl dan Otonomi," *Pikiran Rakjat*, April 29, 1957.
26 Ibid.
27 Cited in Daniel S. Lev, *The Transition to Guided Democracy: Indonesian Politics 1957-1959* (Ithaca: Cornell Modern Indonesia Project, 1966), p. 55.

Hatta retaliated against Sukarno's assaults in a speech delivered to the alumni of the University of Indonesia, which he entitled the "Moral Responsibility of the Intelligentsia," In the Minangkabau, the intelligentsia traditionally acted as a watchdog on the councils of *penghulu*.[28] Hatta dwelt on the subject of dictatorship, warning that historical example demonstrated that dictators were only effective if they were men of high moral standards, with courage to act and accept responsibility and with extraordinary ability to organize and administer.[29] Hatta was making it patently obvious that Sukarno did not possess the abilities and character of a responsible dictator. On the other hand, it was interesting to note that the attributes which Hatta ascribed to such a benevolent despot were those qualities for which he himself was most admired.

Hatta followed up the theme of this speech in his public addresses, pointing to the example of his archenemy, Stalin. "Stalin taught people to submit only to the leadership in the party hierarchy, teaching them to become machines with a soul which shows no mercy for their fellow men."[30] He drew attention to the fate of Stalin's former comrades, that "his opponents were cruelly removed without consideration for their past services." He was justifying his own determination to take no part in Sukarno's *konsepsi*. "Dictators have no place for dualism in leadership," he contended.[31] In other words, if Sukarno had ambitions for unquestioned authority, then it was unlikely he would encourage a restoration of the *Dwi Tunggal* as a leadership partnership.

Nevertheless, the disintegration of the *Dwi Tunggal* was increasingly a matter of public concern, not only in the Outer Islands. "Hatta was popular in Java as well as Sumatra right up to the time of his death," reminisced Natsir.[32] To try to defuse the *Dwi Tunggal* issue, in April 1957 Sukarno empowered Djuanda to offer Hatta the chairmanship of a national planning board. Hatta declined the offer, accusing Sukarno of

---

28 According to Taufik Abdullah, "Modernization in the Minangkabau World," p. 197, within the *nagari*, the village coffee house was nick named the *balai rendah* [lower council] as it was a meeting place for airing criticism of the ruling *penghulu* and did exert influence on decision making.

29 Mohammad Hatta, "Tanggung Jawab Moril Kaum Inteligensia," in *Bung Hatta Berpidato, Bung Hatta Menulis*, p. 82.

30 Mohammad Hatta, "Pimpinan didalam Diktatur," *Pikiran Rakjat*, August 1 and 2, 1957.

31 Ibid.

32 Interview with M. Natsir, February 6, 1983.

supporting the Western economic system, pointing out that "the policy of 'free exchange' in Indonesia's present economic climate bites deeper than the free exchange in the time of nineteenth-century liberalism."[33] It was a damning accusation. Hatta was implying that not only was Sukarno taking on the "exorbitant rights" of Dutch colonial rulers but condoning at the same time economic policies which were even more exploitive than those of the colonists.

The success of the PKI in the regional elections in 1957 heightened tensions both in Java and the regions, drawing together the three main non-Communist parties. On Prime Minister Djuanda's initiative, a Musyawarah Nasional [National Consultative Conference] was held in September 1957 in a further attempt to reunite Sukarno and Hatta presumably in the hope that Hatta would draw Sukarno away from the PKI. Civilian and military representatives from every region were invited, including the Sumatran and Sulawesi rebels. Prior to the conference, the dissidents gathered in South Sumatra to prepare their case, drawing up a document which they entitled the "Palembang Charter." It called for the restoration of the *Dwi Tunggal*, changes in the central army leadership, regional autonomy, and the conversion of the new National Council into a senate.[34]

Hatta agreed to attend the National Conference but made it clear that, unless Sukarno allowed him a position of real power within the Constitution, the *Dwi Tunggal* would remain a mere facade, unable to fulfill its function. In such circumstances, Hatta reiterated, he would rather "let Sukarno run things his own way."[35] At most, Hatta was prepared to sign a joint statement with Sukarno supporting nation building and the *Panca Sila*.

Although there was widespread disappointment that the *Dwi Tunggal* was not restored, no one in government took action to meet Hatta's requirement or to try to countermand Sukarno's unconstitutional behavior. Nasution did not respond to the dissident commanders' demands for changes in the central army leadership. Surrounded by mounting pressure to accommodate himself to the new regime, Hatta

---

33 Mohammad Hatta, "Diatas Djalan Jang Salah," *Pikiran Rakjat*, August 13, 1957.
34 See Lev, *Transition to Guided Democracy*, p. 37.
35 Ibid., p. 32.

was glad of an opportunity to escape from Indonesia, accepting Premier Chou En-Lai's invitation to visit the People's Republic of China.

Hatta was impressed with China's postrevolutionary achievements, so much so that the PSI's newspaper, *Pedoman*, expressed some concern at the warmth of his public statements.[36] Hatta's retort was that "any sane and objective person must admit that China has carried out massive nation building,"[37] He praised the role played by the People's Liberation Army under the direction of the civilian leaders, and expressed the opinion that such cooperation between people and army need not be confined to a Communist regime: "A democracy which is responsible and has moral discipline could do as much," he insisted. Hatta was pointing out to the regions that an army could work constructively alongside responsible civilian leaders; it did not need to take over command. He believed that China's success lay in "its tidy organization and strong discipline" and the "realistic outlook" of its people.[38] Rather pointedly he remarked: "Anyone who follows Mao Tse-tung's analyses carefully will find them to be *practical* and *realistic*," adding: "the people understand Mao Tse-tung's *konsepsi*."[39]

On his return from China, Hatta found that not only were the regions smoldering, but Indonesia's failure to obtain a two-thirds United Nations' endorsement of the return of West Irian had stirred up anti-Dutch feeling. The issues of his return to the *Dwi Tunggal* confronted him the moment he stepped off his plane, when he saw placards reading "Long live the *Dwitunggal* Sukarno-Hatta" being prominently displayed. Hatta was evasive about his future role in politics, his only concession being to participate with Sukarno in a special study of the economic situation.[40]

Hatta alone opened the economic study group commencing on November 26, 1957, because Sukarno had been shaken by an attempt on his life while he was attending a function at his children's school in Cikin1. It was suspected that this act of terrorism was the outcome of Colonel

36 See *Pedoman*, October 4, 1957.
37 *Pikiran Rakjat*, October 19, 1957. Hatta may have been trying to indicate that he was not an American "*djago*" but a neutral in bipolar politics.
38 Mohammad Hatta, "Pembangunan RRT," *Pikiran Rakjat*, November 20 and 21, 1957.
39 Mohammad Hatta, "Masalah Pembangunan dalam Republik Rakjat Tiongkok," *Pikiran Rakjat*, December 23 and 24, 1957.
40 The economic study group evolved from the National Conference.

Lubis's anti-Communist exhortations to extremist Muslim youth. Hatta condemned the assassination attempt, which took the lives of innocent bystanders. "In a country based on Belief in God and Humanity," he rebuked, the religious reference clearly directed to his fellow Muslims, "I regret that a despicable act like this can take place."[41]

The failed assassination attempt sparked off rumors in the Dutch press that Sukarno had been overthrown, which in turn provoked PNI and PKI union retaliation. Supported by Sukarno, although condemned by Hatta and Djuanda, employees in Dutch enterprises took control, ousting their employers. The army acted quickly, Nasution ordering his forces to take over from the unionists. The army never relinquished the Dutch properties it acquired. With the excuse that it was controlling radical unionism, the army became an economic force in Indonesian society while the Dutch sustained a major loss.

The general unrest in the wake of the takeover of Dutch enterprises, dissatisfaction with Nasution's army leadership, the assassination attempt on Sukarno's life, the failure of the National Conference to satisfy the demands set out in the Palembang Charter, and the disruption of inter-island shipping brought regional dlssidence to a head.[42] While Sukarno was away on an overseas tour, the Sumatran rebel commanders, together with Sumual from Sulawesi, met between January 9 and 13, 1958 with the political leaders Natsir, Sjafruddin Prawiranegara, Burhanuddin Harahap, and Sumitro at Sungai Daren, a small town near the West Sumatra-Jambi border.[43] They drew up plans to establish an alternative Indonesian government with headquarters at Bukit Tinggi. As in 1949 Sjafruddin would again act as prime minister as if he were determined to come once more to Indonesia's rescue as it faced a foreign threat, a danger which he this time perceived as international communism.

Rumors of the impending rebellion reached Jakarta. Both the Masjumi and PSI sent delegations to Sumatra to try to persuade the rebels to discard

---

41 As cited in *Pikiran Rakjat*, December 5, 1957. Colonel Lubis was believed to be in hiding in the Jakarta area. He had been evading detention since his attempted coup against Nasution in October 1956.

42 The captains of KPM ships on the seas were instructed to take their vessels to non-Indonesian ports. Interisland shipping lost 78 percent of its tonnage. See Feith, *Decline of Constitutional Democracy*, pp. 584-85.

43 Harvey, *Permesta: Half a Rebellion*, p. 86.

any plans to form an alternative government. Hatta too was appalled when he heard of the proposed challenge to the central government. He recalled that he sent an urgent message via the chief of police in Padang to cancel the plans, warning Husein, the Minangkabau commander, that rebellion would destroy his region.[44] The Javanese regional army commanders had been reluctant to take action against their brother officers in Sumatra and Sulawesi, but the establishment of a rebel government raised the level of dispute to an issue of treason and national security. Hatta's call for abandonment of the plan went unheeded, about which he later spoke with distinct annoyance, alleging that he "told Ahmad Husein not to rebel." "I told him three times," Hatta recalled, "but he still did it."[45]

On February 10, 1958, the Sumatran rebels delivered an ultimatum to Jakarta demanding that PM Djuanda's cabinet resign, that Hatta and the Sultan of Yogyakarta be appointed formateurs of a new cabinet, that parliament allow these formateurs to form a national business cabinet to operate until the next general elections, and that Sukarno resume a "constitutional" position. When the ultimatum expired on February 15 without any of the demands being met, the Pemerintah Revolusioner Republik Indonesia [Revolutionary Government of the Republic of Indonesia] or PRRI was formed. Sukarno returned hurriedly from his overseas trip the next day.

In spite of Hatta's rejection of the rebel government's action, the English reporter, James Mossman, in interviews with rebel leaders, found that they hoped that Hatta would join them once the government was established. According to Simbolon in North Sumatra: "If we waited for Hatta to act against Sukarno, we would wait a hundred years, but if we take the initiative ourselves, Hatta will follow."[46] Natsir was more skeptical about Hatta's participation, although he was of the opinion that Hatta would "be on the shelf for a long time, perhaps for the rest of his life,"[47] if he did not join the rebels. In an interview twenty-five years after the event, Natsir stressed that Hatta did aspire to return to power, but

44 See "Riwayat Singkat Bung Hatta," in *Membangun Kooperasi dan Kooperasi Membangun*, A Collection of Essays by Dr. Mohammad Hatta (Jakarta: Pusat Kooperasi Pegawai Negeri, 1971), p. xxxvii.
45 Hatta, *Bung Hatta's Answers*, p. 40.
46 James Mossman, *Rebels in Paradise* (London: Cape, 1961), p. 65.
47 Ibid.

through Sukarno's self-destruction rather than by illicit action.[48] Hatta had the patience to sit tight and wait; the rebels did not.

Apart from Hatta's repugnance for civil war, there was another disturbing element in the regional revolt: the rebels were seeking support from the Americans and British.[49] Although John Foster Dulles in March 1958 testified to Congress that the United States was not "intervening in the internal affairs" of Indonesia, there is evidence that many in the Central Intelligence Agency and the State Department saw merit in supporting the rebels, fearing Sukarno would fall under Communist domination.[50] The PKI press in March 1958 pointed to a statement made by the Council of SEATO ministers held in Manila on March 13 which read: "It is hoped in top circles here that the rebels will be able to... force a compromise which can place the former Vice-President Mohammad Hatta in power. This is the hope of the 'anti-communist' world!"[51] It is unlikely that Hatta wanted to return to power on the back of the CIA and SEATO, which would place him in the category of an American "puppet." He knew from the history of the archipelago that its unity had been shattered in the past by foreign exploitation of internecine war. Mossman also mentioned in his account that there were rumors that Sumatra might establish links to Malaya.[52] Hatta personally never supported such links, because of the problem of Chinese economic domination, a point he was to stress in the future when Indonesia and the new state of Malaysia were in confrontation.[53]

It was not easy for Hatta to ignore the call of his own people. As a distinguished fellow Minangkabau, Dr. Z. Zain, commented: "It

---

48 Interview with M. Natsir, February 6, 1983.
49 According to Mossman: "It is no secret that Britain and the United States keep in touch with the rebels. The British do so through agencies in Singapore and Malaya and the Americans through Formosa and Manila." See Mossman, *Rebels in Paradise*, p. 230.
50 See David Wise and T. B. Ross, *The Invisible Government*, 3rd ed. (New York: Random House, 1964), pp. 139-43.
51 *Harian Rakjat*, March 14, 1958.
52 Mossman states that "the argument used is that if Java should ever become Communist, it might be necessary to encourage the secession of Sumatra and the other main islands." See *Rebels in Paradise*, p. 230. This was Secretary of State Dulles's policy. Mossman also cited the opinion of the old-guard Sultan of Deli, who claimed that: "We Sumatrans would do better to leave the Republic altogether and join Malaya," accusing the Javanese of "colored colonization." See *Rebels in Paradise*, p. 75.
53 See Mohammad Hatta, "One Indonesian View of the Malaysia Issue," in *Portrait of a Patriot*, pp. 576-81. First published in *Asian Survey* 5, 3 (March 1965).

would have been sufficient for Hatta to cross the Sunda Straits for the Republic of Indonesia to exist no more."[54] Mossman reported an unnamed rebel's disappointment that Hatta had not supported the rebel government, saying: "He never let us down exactly, but he never lived up to our expectations either. He hasn't the imagination it takes to act unconstitutionally." Yet Hatta did have the imagination to foresee the effects of a secessionist movement sponsored by the United States and Britain. The rebel spokesman continued: "I used to tell him sometimes that he had been in Rotterdam too long and picked up the habits of mind of a Dutch grocer." He concluded: "Sukarno may have too much fantasy in his make-up, but Hatta has too little. At heart he's a bureaucrat not a leader."[55]

How short was the rebel's memory of Hatta's leadership of the struggle for sovereignty when in 1948 no party leader was prepared to take on the task. Hatta was then prepared to use foreign aid to obtain independence, but he would not use it to split the unity of Indonesia. He had been criticizing for years the unwieldly bureaucratic centralized government in Jakarta, stressing the need for the people to have a greater role in managing their own affairs. Bureaucracy and *kedaulatan rakyat* did not go hand in hand.

Yet how much were Hatta's criticisms to blame for regional insurrection? His detailed analyses of how extensively the regions were being disadvantaged had exacerbated latent feelings of grievance and anger. Hatta's warnings on what to expect from dictators like Stalin had alerted many Indonesians to the need to restrain Sukarno and had heightened fears about communism, especially after the results of the regional elections were announced. Indeed, the force of Hatta's political comment in 1957, curbed for five agonizing years while Vice-President, might have brought rebellion to boiling point, even if this had not been Hatta's deliberate intention. Hatta had been hurt and demoralized by Sukarno undermining his authority. He may have underestimated the accumulative effect of his outspoken protests, and not have realized how sensitive his own Sumatran people were to his personal slight.

---

54 See Rinto Alwi, "Bung Hatta, Pemimpin yang Berkarakter," in *Bung Hatta: Pribadinya dalam Kenangan*, p. 390.
55 Mossman, *Rebels in Paradise*, p. 99.

The American historian, Louis Fischer, recorded an interview with Hatta at this time when he suggested to him that he did have the authority to end the civil war. Hatta was scornful. "I can't do it by running a Planning Board,"[56] he retorted, the position offered to him by Djuanda in 1957. He pointed out that the rebels were demanding "a Cabinet with Hatta as prime minister and the Sultan as deputy prime minister." Hatta made it clear that it was up to Sukarno to end the debacle by forming "a responsible government." When Fischer hinted that Hatta was being overly "constitutional and legal," Hatta's anger erupted. "My way is political, not legalistic," he responded, "All sides must return to the Constitution. The Sumatran government must be scrapped and a Presidential Cabinet established in Jakarta."[57] Hatta's words sounded contradictory, an indication of his own distress and confusion.

Hatta admitted to Fischer that it would be pointless for him to join the Sukarno government in order to undermine it by "boring from within" because "the parties won't let me," meaning most of all the PKI. "The PNI wants me back," he conceded, "to use my prestige," but he refused to be part of unconstitutional action, stressing that he "must not pave the way to totalitarianism."[58] Caught off guard, Hatta let slip the depth of his distaste for Sukarno's dominance and his hypnotic power over people. "I don't wish to be the prisoner of other men's policies," Hatta declared hotly, averring: "I have known Sukarno for decades. He won't change."[59]

Sukarno returned prematurely from his overseas trip, visibly shaken that a revolutionary government had been established. He sought out Hatta, and prevailed on him to negotiate with the rebels on behalf of the central government. Hatta agreed to Sukarno's request, although refusing to join him in a public address on the emergency situation, merely urging him to "speak calmly."[60] Hatta suggested that Sukarno bargain with the dissidents: a return to the Constitution in return for a restitution of the pre-February 1 status quo, with a conversion of the National Council into a "pro-Senate," if approval for this were given by parliament.[61] Hatta

---

56 Louis Fischer, *The Story of Indonesia* (Westport, Conn.: Greenwood Press, 1959), p. 286.
57 Ibid., p. 286.
58 Ibid., p. 287.
59 Ibid., p. 287-88.
60 Hatta, *Bung Hatta's Answers*, p. 40.
61 See *Pikiran Rakjat*, March 4 and 5, 1958.

declared his willingness to be prime minister of a temporary presidential cabinet if Sukarno reverted to being a constitutional President.

Sukarno was reluctant to accede to what amounted to a reversal of his leadership ambitions. He knew he had the support of the air force chief, Suryadarma, and Nasution had also issued a warning that there would be no compromise with the rebels.[62] According to Mossman, Nasution and Suryadarma both ordered the first military actions against the revolutionary government.[63] Nasution made use of the defection of the rebel commander in South Sumatra, which enabled his troops to enter from the southern flank.

The unexpected use of force before he had been given an opportunity to negotiate infuriated Hatta. Mohamad Roem recalled that this time Hatta vowed that "he would never work with Sukarno again."[64] Hatta was also strongly critical of the Islamic party, Nahdatul Ulama, for supporting Sukarno against their anti-Communist brothers in Sumatra, declaring: "From the very beginning of this tense situation, the NU considered me as being on the side of the rebels. They were in favor of attacking the rebels."[65]

Hatta also lashed out at American interference in other nations' affairs to suit its own interests and denied American insinuations that "Indonesia has entered the Communist trap."[66] Hatta himself had been criticized in the pro-American Manila Times for his complimentary remarks about China, the paper suggesting that Hatta's thinking was turning left, which meant that he "no longer had an influence which could stabilize Indonesian politics."[67] At home he had acquired the reputation of having an American bias, the PKI seizing on the statement of a Masjumi member that "it seems that Bung Karno leans more towards

---

[62] Nasution was of the opinion that the type of government which Hatta was defending was suitable for a homogeneous society like Great Britain but not for Indonesia. Interview with A. H. Nasution, February 22, 1982.

[63] See Mossman, Rebels in Paradise, p. 102. The first government attack was a drop of 700 paratroopers over the Caltex oil depot at Pekan Baru in Central Sumatra, a strategic drop as it was also the site of a rebel arsenal.

[64] Interview with M. Roem, February 5, 1983.

[65] Hatta, Bung Hatta's Answers, p. 42.

[66] Hatta, "Indonesia between the Power Blocs," in Portrait of a Patriot, p. 563.

[67] Pikiran Rakjat, November 1, 1957.

Russia while Bung Hatta on the other hand, leans towards America."[68]
"Everything is measured by American axioms, the American view of life,"
he commented in exasperation.[69]

The failure of the regional challenge strengthened the position of
Sukarno and the PKI and also added to the prestige of the national armed
forces under Nasution. The regional failure meant further loss of support
for Hatta in his efforts to salvage parliamentary democracy. He was forced
to move further towards the position he had occupied in the colonial
period, a man building up opposition to the government in the shadows.
As in the 1930s, his task was made difficult by the secret agents assigned
to surveillance of his activities.

In 1959 Hatta intensified his role as political educator, concentrating
especially on university students and army officers undergoing training.
He did not incite them to violence against Sukarno, insisting that "there
is no aim to replace Bung Karno because he is a chosen person."[70] Instead
Hatta attacked the prevailing standards of political behavior, and appealed
to his audiences not to act as "goats," following the example set by their
parents, but rather to "choose to be 'herdsmen'... putting aside ambitions
for self-enrichment."[71]

The Constituent Assembly, on which Hatta in December 1956 had
pinned hopes of achieving constitutional reform, remained deadlocked
over the contentious issue of whether to give more recognition to Islam or
to retain the *Panca Sila* in its present form. The assembly was now expected
to incorporate Sukarno's "guided democracy" into its formulations.
When Hatta recalled this period in a speech he made in 1975, he was
sharply critical of the "Islamic State group, whose voice was only 48%,"
therefore below the required two-thirds majority,[72] for slowing up the
deliberations, giving a more valid reason for the assembly's dissolution.
He commented:

How much better it would have been if it had been more tolerant.

---

68 As cited in *Harian Rakjat*, September 29, 1958. The remark was attributed to Drs. A. Sigit.
69 Hatta, "Indonesia between the Power Blocs," p. 564.
70 *Pikiran Rakjat*, February 7, 1959.
71 Ibid.
72 Mohammad Hatta, *Menuju Negara Hukum* (Jakarta: Yayasan Idayu, 1975), p. 15.

Having earnestly struggled and been outvoted, it should not have continued but democratically accepted its defeat and reached a consensus on the *Panca Sila*, which was the original basis of the State.[73]

Nasution was again urging a return to the 1945 Constitution. Sukarno, while agreeing that his *konsepsi* could be accommodated within this Constitution, was now wary of Nasution, who had adopted threatening attitudes to civilian politicians while Sukarno was abroad. Nasution was undoubtedly ani-Communist and the trend towards military takeovers in postcolonial nations was too well-defined to be ignored.

The dissolution of the elected Constituent Assembly and the reversion to the 1945 Constitution not only brought protests from the Masjumi but also demands for Hatta's recall to the Vice-Presidency, which it pointed out was an intrinsic part of that Constitution. Sukarno ignored these; nor did Hatta have any intention of again working directly with Sukarno. Hatta's response to the dissolution of the Constituent Assembly was, nevertheless, surprisingly mild, although admittedly he was overseas at the time. He knew that he had included the principles of *kedaulatan rakyat* in the 1945 Constitution. He was also no doubt relieved that the state philosophy remained the *Panca Sila*, which for Hatta was the basis of religious socialism and, in contrast with communism, was avowedly "theistic."

Hatta again castigated the Islamic leaders for their lack of social concern, accusing them of allowing the Communists to gain influence among the people. As he pointed out:

As far as a just and prosperous society is concerned, Islam does not differ from Marx. But Islam is unable to provide a defense against the magnetism of Marxism, which is in opposition to Islam, because at present Islamic education stresses dogma and religious duty rather than the community. Social work is limited to formal almsgiving.[74]

---

73 Ibid.
74 *Pikiran Rakjat,* May 14, 1959.

As the Communists regained confidence under Sukarno's umbrella, Hatta increasingly became the target for abuse, directed through the media and in demonstrations. Now that he had to take into consideration the safety of a wife and three children, he had to be ever more cautious. Halida, his youngest daughter, recalled that the first time that she realized that her father was an important political figure was when, as a small child, she observed him being mobbed by jeering Communist youths at the airport, his Buick repeatedly blocked on the journey home.[75]

On Proclamation Day 1959, Sukarno issued his regime's political manifesto, like the *Panca Sila* based on five principles, which he referred to as Manipol-Usdek.[76] In spite of protests, in particular from academics, allegiance to its principles became compulsory.[77] Another matter of concern to Hatta was the announcement of a monetary purge, which vaguely resembled action taken in his own second prime ministership, except that Hatta's measures had been aimed at the Dutch while the new initiatives hit the Indonesians. Hatta was contemptuous and dismissed the policy as "nonsense," claiming that it would not overcome the huge budget deficit.[78] Prime Minister Djuanda was nettled. He accused Hatta of being "very shallow and insolent,"[79] claiming that his government's measures were not as stupid as Hatta had intimated. Hatta's response was terse: "*Tweede nonsens* [More nonsense]."[80]

When in March 1960, Sukarno dissolved Indonesia's only elected parliament because it had tried to exercise its prerogative under the 1945 Constitution and rejected the government's budget, protest against the erosion of democracy began to intensify. In April 1960, a Democratic League was formed, the main initiative coming from the Masjumi and the PSI, although the group also gained support from the army veterans'

---

75 See Halida Nuriah Hatta, "Mengenang Ayahanda," in *Bung Hatta: Pribadinya dalam Kenangan*, p. 84.

76 U = *Undang-undang Dasar 1945*, S = *Sosialisme Indonesia*, D = *Demokrasi Terpimpin*, E = *Ekonomi Terpimpin*, K = *Kepribadian Indonesia*.

77 Many academics, including Hatta, opposed Sukarno's Manipol-Usdek, and in 1963 tried to promulgate their own cultural manifesto. Those who refused to accept Sukarno's manifesto were denied teaching positions.

78 Rp. 500 and Rp. 1,000 notes were reduced to 10 percent of their face value and bank deposits over Rp. 25,000 were frozen.

79 See *Pikiran Rakjat*, October 9, 1959.

80 See Rinto Alwi, "Bung Hatta, Pemimpin yang Berkarakter," p. 392.

party, IPKI[81] and to a limited extent from Nahdatul Ulama and Christian party members. The league's aims were "to establish democratic life in Indonesia in the fields of politics, economics, and socialism," opposing "all fascism, totalitarianism, imperialism, feudalism, and bureaucracy, which all lower the status of man, making him a mere instrument of those in power."[82]

Hatta, although fully supportive of the league's intentions, was skeptical about its effectiveness. He saw weaknesses in its structure in that it was "built by parties who participate in the *Gotong-royong* Parliament."[83] To Hatta, Sukarno's new parliament was another toothless body, a *"dewan rajap."* Hatta had learned from the performance of the PPPKI in the early nationalist days that a democratic front must be completely non-cooperating, otherwise it became a *"per-saté-an,"* a hotchpotch.

Before leaving Indonesia to attend an International Cooperatives Alliance meeting in Lausanne in April 1960, Hatta wrote an article to support the Democratic League's intentions, which he entitled "Demokrasi Kita." At last he gave public airing to his personal criticism of Sukarno, pointing to his flagrant disregard for the Constitution and condemning his dissolution of the elected Constituent Assembly and parliament. Hatta gave as his opinion that democracy had been replaced by a dictatorship.

He reminded his readers that dictatorships tended to be short-lived, that when Sukarno disappeared from politics "his system will collapse by itself like a house of cards" because of the low caliber of those in authority around him.[84] Hatta compared Sukarno with Mephistopheles in Goethe's *Faust,* in that "Mephistopheles said that he was part of those powers that always want what is evil and yet always produce what is good." According to Hatta, "Sukarno is the opposite of this. His objectives are always good but the steps that he takes often lead him away from those objectives."[85] But Hatta laid equal blame on the unprincipled and self-interested political elite who had been in government since independence. He pointed out that "Indonesian history over the last ten years seems to reflect the picture

---

81 Ikatan Pendukung Kemerdekaan Indonesia [League of Upholders of Indonesian Independence].
82 See *Pikiran Rakjat,* June 7, 1960.
83 Ibid., May 2, 1960.
84 Hatta, "Our Democracy," p. 13.
85 Ibid., p. 14.

painted by Schiller," quoting the German poet's lines:

The century has given birth to a momentous epoch, But the momentous epoch is met by little people.[86]

Sukarno's reaction to the article was angry. From now on, Hatta would find it very difficult to publish within Indonesia. Even *Pikiran Rakjat*, the newspaper consistently loyal to Hatta, was forced to stop publication of his articles in order to remain in circulation.[87] The editor of the Muslim journal *Pandji Masyarakat*, Hatta's Minangkabau friend Hamka, who first published "Our Democracy," was arrested and his journal banned. 1960 saw the forced closure of many newspapers, including the PSI's *Pedoman*. In August 1960, both Masjumi and the PSI, which had refused to participate in the *Gotong-royong* parliament, were banned on charges of being involved in the PRRI/Permesta rebellion. For Hatta personally, this denial of a free press limited his scope for political criticism. He was forced to use personal correspondence as a means of protest and correction, from 1960 to 1965 criticizing Sukarno's policies through private letters, including letters to his former partner.[88]

Hatta's secluded villa at Megamendung from now on became a base from which to organize opposition to governments which violated the principles of *kedaulatan rakyat*. According to journalist Rosihan Anwar, a leading PSI member, Hatta suggested the formation of a Partai Daulat Rakyat which he hoped would be able to function in the open once Sukarno's regime had collapsed. He envisaged that the new party would include Islamic groups but have as an ideological basis the *Panca Sila*, with a stress on democracy.[89] Hatta proposed that the party be built up by the formation of cells of four or five people, the methodology of the New PNI, aiming in particular at Muslim youth.[90] Hatta was clearly trying to

---

86 Ibid., p. 25.
87 This information was passed on to the writer by the former Indonesian journalist, Tom Solomon.
88 The writer sought access to copies of Hatta's letters to Sukarno but Pak Wangsa Widjaja was unable to grant this request.
89 Rosihan Anwar, *Sebelum Prahara: Pergolakan Politik Indonesia 1961-1965* (Jakarta: Sinar Harapan, 1981), p. 159.
90 Ibid., p. 160.

woo Muslims away from their preoccupation with doctrinal issues, in particular with the concept of an Islamic state, using the common ground of *kedaulatan rakyat* and theism with an emphasis on social justice as the bonding material for struggle against autocratic government and atheistic communism.

The year 1962 opened in an atmosphere of war tension, as on December 19, 1961 Sukarno had ordered mass mobilization for an invasion of West Irian. On January 4, while seeking support for the struggle in Sulawesi, Sukarno was the target of another assassination attempt as a hand grenade was hurled at his car, but he escaped uninjured.[91] Following this incident, Sukarno suffered the humiliation of learning that two Indonesian naval boats had been sunk by a Dutch frigate off Aru Island. His response was to arrest the strongest opponents of his policies. On January 16, 1962, Sjahrir and his close associate, Subadio, were detained on the orders of the Supreme War Command, of which Sukarno was head,[92] although the order was signed by Nasution and the minister of foreign affairs, Subandrio, a politician now working very closely with Sukarno.[93]

Sjahrir and Subadio were joined in detention by Mohamad Roem, Anak Agung Gde Agung, and Sultan Hamid, along with several other prominent non-cooperators.[94] Hatta was not detained, but an even closer surveillance was maintained on his movements, including strict measures to prevent him from having direct communication with the detainees. Hatta was an old hand at circumventing prison regulations. Anak Agung's wife, Vera, became his messenger, concealing Hatta's communications in

---

91 It was suspected that the culprits were followers of the fanatical Darul Islam supporter, Kahar Muzakar.

92 The charge was that they were involved in the assassination attempt on Sukarno's life in South Sulawesi.

93 In Subadio's opinion, Sukarno and Nasution were most to blame for the trumped-up charge against himself and Sjahrir. (Interview, Subadio Sastrosatomo, February 22, 1982.) Sol Tas believed that Subandrio had had a grudge against Sjahrir because of the latter's off-hand treatment of him. (See Tas, "Souvenirs of Sjahrir," p. 151.) Nasution claimed that he had no alternative but to sign the detention order as there was a signed document implicating Sjahrir in the attempt on Sukarno's life, although this accusation was later proved to be false. (Interview, A. H. Nasution, February 22, 1982.) Nyonya Sjahrir states with absolute conviction that Sjahrir was not involved in any assassination attempt on Sukarno's life. (Interview, February 1982.)

94 Anak Agung had been holding the traditional Balinese funeral ceremony for his father, to which he had invited close friends such as Mohamad Roem, Hatta, and the recently released Sultan Hamid. Sukarno may have suspected that the funeral ceremony was used as a trysting place for those plotting his overthrow.

the hem of her skirt.[95]

Hatta was shocked and sickened by the arrest of his friends, and in particular of Sjahrir. As Des Alwi had maintained: "No matter what their differences, there remained a very special bond between Hatta and Sjahrir which was never broken; they were closer than many people realized."[96] Des Alwi had participated in the Permesta resistance in Sulawesi and was thus more involved in rebellion than his foster father.

In a letter to Sukarno, Hatta pleaded for Sjahrir's release, trying to restrain his comments to prevent further antagonism:

> I think that a sane person would condemn an act of terrorism such as took place in Makassar, and I am convinced that Sjahrir and other principled people would oppose any kind of terrorism in politics because it is contrary to socialism and humanity.... They would not hesitate to carry out determined opposition in politics, as they did in the time of the nationalist movement, but it would never enter their heads to participate in acts of terrorism.[97]

Sukarno ignored Hatta's letter. When his associates suggested that he speak directly with Sukarno, Hatta was of the opinion that "it was not yet the right moment."[98] He also warned that Nasution's influence over Sukarno was waning, as evidenced by Sukarno's deliberate attempts to bring Javanese generals to the fore, that "the President was emerging as the one with the most power, as an all-out dictator."[99]

Sjahrir had always been more adversely affected by isolation than Hatta. This time the consequences were grave. In November 1962, he suffered a stroke, necessitating his removal from Madiun jail to Jakarta's main hospital. Through the cooperation of friends among the medical staff, Hatta managed to be included in a routine visit to Sjahrir's room,

95 See Anak Agung Gde Agung, "Bung Hatta jang Saja Kenal," in *Bang Hatta Mengabdi pada Tjita-Tjita*, pp. 72-73.
96 Interview Des Alwi, February 6, 1982.
97 As cited in Ny. Siti Wahjunah Sjahrir, "Bung Hatta: Beberapa Catatan," in *Bung Hatta: Pribadinya dalam Kenangan*, p. 480.
98 Rosihan Anwar, *Sebelum Prahara*, p. 159.
99 Ibid., p. 160. Nasution had been relieved of his post of chief of army staff and made chief of armed services. His place was taken by General Yani, a Central Javanese.

but his surreptitious visit did not go undetected. On December 11, an order was issued that Sjahrir be transferred to a military hospital.

The strain was also taking its toll on Hatta; he suffered a stroke himself six months later. This time Sjahrir tried to visit his friend. "I am really loath to ask the government for any concessions," he admitted to his wife Poppy, "but because Hatta is acutely ill and we do not know what will happen tomorrow, I want to ask permission to see him a while."[100] Poppy begged the attorney-general to convey Sjahrir's request to Sukarno, stressing that "this is not a matter of politics but of humanity; Sjahrir and Hatta have been fellow strugglers since colonial times." When Hatta was out of danger and still no permission to visit him had been received, Sjahrir suggested that his wife cancel the request. "I was not asking for a social call," he remarked bitterly, "but when Hatta's condition was acute and causing concern, then I wanted very much to see him again."[101] They were never to have a reunion.

Instead Sukarno himself visited Hatta in hospital, insisting that he be sent to Sweden for treatment at state expense, accompanied by his personal doctor, Professor Mahar Mardjono. Hatta's secretary noticed the look of compassion on Sukarno's face when Hatta climbed weakly from his car to visit Sukarno at the Palace before his departure. Sukarno's parting words were: "Wangsa, look after Bung Hatta well!"[102]

Before Hatta's departure for Sweden, Sukarno relaxed the ban on his speeches, allowing him to make a radio address on August 25 to celebrate the eighteenth anniversary of the proclamation of independence. Hatta's speech called for a proper implementation of the *Panca Sila*, the *Indonesian Herald* commenting that, in spite of their differences, "Dr. Hatta has always stood by President Sukarno as a staunch exponent and defender of *Pantjasila*."[103] But Hatta was not just supporting Sukarno, he was recalling the colonial period and the Japanese Occupation when "many freedom fighters languished in jail." Without drawing direct parallels with the present time, he also pointed to the "determination of

---

100 Ny. Siti Wahjunah Sjahrir, "Bung Hatta: Beberapa Catatan," p. 481.
101 Ibid.
102 I. Wangsa Widjaja, "Mengenang Bung Karno," in *Bung Karno dalam Kenangan*, ed. Solichim Salam, p. 115.
103 See *Indonesian Herald*, August 26, 1963.

the youth and people to struggle to defend Free Indonesia with the motto 'once Free, always Free.'"[104] He begged the youth not to use the *Panca Sila* "for lip service only," continuing:

> "Belief in God" does not just mean respecting each person's religion but is a basis which leads towards truth, justice, goodness, honesty, and brotherhood. According to this basis... the nation's government must not deviate from the straight path towards the people's well-being and the security of the community, peace and national brotherhood.... Hopefully these aims will come alive in the spirit of young people today and in the future so that they can truly carry out their historical duties to the archipelago and the nation.[105]

Dr. Mardjono observed that Hatta's health improved amazingly in Europe once Indonesia's tense and stressful atmosphere was left behind.[106] From Sweden, they moved on to West Germany and the Netherlands. In Holland Hatta's reception was unusually warm. He was no longer viewed as a traitor but as someone who had had the courage to stand up to Sukarno. It was a strange situation for Hatta, but Dr. Mardjono noticed that he gained immense personal satisfaction from being hailed as a defender of democracy.[107]

Hatta nevertheless was careful not to condemn Sukarno publicly when abroad. When studying at the University of California's Berkeley campus, economics student Emil Salim, later a government minister, recorded how Hatta responded to a question concerning Sukarno when he was addressing a meeting in 1960:

> In many matters I disagree with Bung Karno but he is the President

---

104 *Data Masjarakat*, August 26, 1963.
105 Ibid.
106 Interview with Dr. Mahar Mardjono, January 13, 1982.
107 Interview with Dr. Mahar Mardjono, January 13, 1982. The Americans had prevailed on the Dutch to transfer West Irian to Indonesia by May 1, 1963. For details of American involvement in the West Irian issue, see F. P. Bunnell, "The Central Intelligence Agency -- Deputy Directorate for Plans, 1961, Secret Memorandum on Indonesia: A Study in the Politics of Policy Formation in the Kennedy Administration," in *Indonesia* 22 (October 1976): 131-55.

of the Republic of Indonesia, the country for whose independence I struggled for years.... Right or wrong, he is my President.[108]

On any of his trips abroad, Hatta went out of his way to maintain contacts with Indonesian students. They were the people he must fire with his ideals while they were living in a free society, just as the Perhimpunan Indonesia had awakened under the influence of veteran nationalists like Dr. Tjipto Mangunkusumo and Douwes Dekker. The University of California's Berkeley campus had become the new training ground for many of Indonesia's future economists, replacing Rotterdam.

Having helped to defuse the West Irian question, the Americans were pressing Sukarno to concentrate on Indonesia's economic problems. Sukarno's national planning council, chaired by Muhammad Yamin, had produced an Eight Year Overall Plan with a strong nationalist orientation.[109] The plan, in theory, incorporated many of Hatta's ideas and suggestions, while Sukarno's supportive slogan of "*Berdikari*" [*Berdiri atas Kaki Sendiri* -- Stand on your own feet] was a reiteration of Hatta's theme of autoactivity. Hatta had set out details of how a village unit could be self-supporting, and his ideas seemed to have been enlarged to national proportions in Yamin's plan.[110] At the national level, the problem was how to finance development projects when most of the nation's resources, including foreign aid, were being used to purchase military equipment or to erect ostentatious national buildings and monuments.

In 1964, the economic situation was so critical in Indonesia that Sukarno sought Hatta's help. This immediately raised speculation that Hatta might at least be appointed a deputy prime minister,[111] which brought angry rebuttals from both the PKI and the Partai Murba, especially the latter's leaders, Chaerul Saleh and Adam Malik. Hatta scotched the rumors, making it clear that he would act as an adviser only. "Our State is not a

---

108 Emil Salim, "Manusia Bung Hatta," in *Bung Hatta: Pribadinya dalam Kenangan*, p. 637.

109 The Eight Year Overall Plan was designed around the proclamation date with 17 volumes, 8 parts and 1945 clauses. See Herbert Feith, "Dynamics of Guided Democracy," in *Indonesia*, ed. Ruth T. McVey (New Haven, Yale University, 1963), p. 384.

110 For further details of Hatta's plans, see M. Hatta, "Autonomi dan Auto-Aktivitet," *Pikiran Rakjat*, May 14, 1957.

111 See Rosihan Anwar, *Sebelum Prahara*, p. 449. Djuanda, who had died in office, had been replaced as first minister by a triumvirate of Subandrio, Chaerul Saleh, and Dr. Leimena.

legal state, so it is very difficult for me to occupy an official office, although I will be an unofficial adviser."[112]

Perhaps because of Sukarno's softened attitude to him, Hatta was permitted to return to Sumatra in 1964, the first time since the eruption of the PRRI revolt in 1958. Hatta deplored the deterioration in services and infrastructure in Sumatra. "Transportation by land, sea and air at that time was terrible," he recalled many years later, "the state budget was spent on politics and glory."[113] In spite of his age and indifferent health, Hatta was determined to travel by jeep from Medan to Bukit Tinggi, noting that the road was "indeed appalling," one twenty-four kilometer stretch taking five hours to traverse. In interviews with his own people, Hatta recorded that there were complaints that "although many new mosques had been built in West Sumatra, nevertheless the whole situation in the Minangkabau was dominated by the PKI."[114] Even the red and white flags brought out to greet Hatta had been confiscated. In spite of his refusal to join the rebels, Hatta was still popular. His parting words to his people were to be patient and to prepare themselves for whatever possibilities the future had to offer.[115]

The year 1965 opened in an atmosphere of gathering crisis, related not merely to Sukarno's new campaign to "Crush Malaysia." Just as in early 1945, Indonesian society was in turmoil, seeking an outlet for pent-up emotions and inner hostilities. Sukarno leaned even more heavily to the side of the PKI, as if aware that the military were closing in on him. The PKI had succeeded in gaining entry to a new "Nasakom" cabinet which Sukarno had established in spite of Army protests.[116] Since 1963, Aidit had been trying to give his party a more nationalist image, claiming that the PKI rejected "the baton of any other Communist party,"[117] as if

---

112 Ibid., p. 416.
113 Hatta, *Bung Hatta's Answers*, p. 39.
114 Ibid.
115 See Deliar Noer, "Bung Hatta yang Taqwa," in *Bung Hatta: Pribadinya dalam Kenangan*, p. 620.
116 "Nasakom" represented Nationalism, Religion (*Agama*), and Communism. Hatta later wrote that "Sukarno had meant well in creating Nasakom, its purpose being to eliminate the system of 'free fight democracy' and replace it with mutual cooperation between the four most influential groups in the community: the nationalists, religious groups, communists and functional groups." See M. Hatta, "Panca Sila Jalan Lurus," in *Bung Hatta Berpidato, Bung Hatta Menulis*, p. 102.
117 See Arnold C. Brackman, *Indonesia: The Gestapu Affair* (New York: American-Asian Education Exchange, 1969), p. 13. In January 1965, Sukarno yielded to PKI demands and banned the Partai Murba, although not insisting on its disbandment until September. The Partai Murba had tried

responding to Hatta's accusations that the party was dominated by the Soviet Union.

At Megamendung, discussions continued on Indonesia's political future. Hatta considered that three main parties would be sufficient: an Islam-*Panca Sila* group, a Nationalist party, and the Communists.[118] Although Hatta disliked the Communists, he still believed that they played an important role as an opposition group. Hatta's colleagues noticed that Hatta did not include a military party, an indication that he was still holding to his principle of the army serving the state rather than governing it. When asked his opinion about "the military groups who now play a major role in our national life," Hatta answered that it would be best to return to the original idea of a militia-type army. "But can that be done remembering the number of vested interests in the armed forces?" queried his colleagues. Hatta was optimistic, mentioning the names of several officers whom he considered to be still uncorrupted.[119]

Not only had Sukarno weakened Nasution's power by his appointment as chief of armed services, but he was promoting another Javanese general, Suharto, by appointing him head of a new Army Strategic Reserve Command [Komando Cadangan Strategis Angkatan Darat -- Kostrad], an appointment which was to have great significance both for Indonesia and for Sukarno himself, in that he had unwittingly promoted his own successor. Sukarno also began to bestow on his top civilian advisers, such as Subandrio, military ranks, giving a military look to government which was to continue into the future.

In April 1965, Sukarno organized a Bandung Conference Reunion, the main guest being Chou En-lai. Aidit, now turning to China for guidance rather than to the Soviet Union, sought the Chinese premier's advice. In spite of the PKI's considerable following in Indonesia, the Communists lacked fire-power. The party's infiltration into the armed forces was insufficient to ensure victory in a showdown with Generals Nasution and Yani. In discussion with Sukarno, Chou En-lai suggested the formation

---

to woo Sukarno away from the PKI in August 1964 by founding a Body for the Promotion of Sukarnoism.

118 Rosihan Anwar, *Sebelum Prahara*, p. 415.

119 Ibid. According to Nasution, "Our Constitution, our State philosophy, the *Panca Sila*, and the direction of Manipol-Usdek give sufficient guarantee that we are not heading towards militarism." See *Duta Masjarakat*, September 29, 1962.

of a "Fifth Force," a people's army of peasants and workers, offering to supply arms.[120] Hatta tried to obtain an interview with Chou En-lai but was not permitted access to him.[121] "Fortunately the Fifth Force was never formed," Hatta commented in later years, "But Aidit's efforts to seize power were accelerated from the beginning of 1965."[122]

Rumors had been rife since February that there was a top army leadership plan to oust Sukarno. The atmosphere grew more heated when Sukarno publicly revealed the contents of a telegram allegedly sent by the British ambassador in Jakarta hinting that an army plot was afoot. Yet Hatta was of the opinion that, in the event of a showdown between the army and the PKI, "if the PKI had really won, Sukarno would have been eliminated."[123]

On May 26, Sukarno convened a conference of military leaders, including Nasution and Yani, and informed them that the military forces must adopt Nasakom and be prepared to have political commissars to "nasakomize" their servicemen. Sukarno's directive was received coolly, the army leaders being particularly hostile when on May 31 Sukarno requested the four armed services to assist in the establishment of a militia, a "fifth force." Only Air Marshal Omar Dhani offered to conduct citizen training. Hatta recalled that he advised Yani to pay close attention to what was happening, commenting: "I saw that the army was the only force capable of facing up to the PKI."[124] Hatta seemed to have made a choice. If totalitarianism were unavoidable, he preferred the Indonesian army to be at the helm. He had a long-standing special relationship with prominent officers, especially those from the Siliwangi Division in West Java, and many "cadres" among the army command from his association with the Staff College at Bandung.

Life was particularly insecure for Hatta in 1965 as the PKI sought out targets for condemnation and attack. Sukarno did not fully support PKI

---

120 See Harold Crouch, *The Army and Politics in Indonesia* (Ithaca and London: Cornell University Press, 1978), pp. 89-90; B. Dahm, *History of Indonesia in the Twentieth Century* (London: Pall Mall Press, 1971), p. 224; and A. C. A. Dake, *In the Spirit of the Red Banteng: Indonesian Communists between Moscow and Peking* (The Hague: Mouton, 1973), pp. 331-32.

121 Personal communication from Ny. Meutia Swasono.

122 Hatta, *Bung Hatta's Answers*, p. 37.

123 Ibid.

124 Ibid., p. 38.

322 INDONESIA FREE: A POLITICAL BIOGRAPHY OF MOHAMMAD HATTA

assaults on Hatta, and reacted strongly when the party cited Sukarno as the sole proclamator of independence. Guntur recalled his father's anger. "I myself am sometimes fed up with Hatta's policies," Sukarno admitted, "Hatta and I sometimes bug each other! But omitting Hatta from the Proclamation Text... that is the action of a coward!"[125] The bonds of comradeship may have been frayed but were not completely severed.

In July 1965, Sukarno gave permission for Sjahrir to be flown to Zurich for medical treatment as he had suffered a second stroke in January which had robbed him of his speech. No sooner had Sjahrir left than Sukarno himself became seriously ill, a team of Chinese doctors warning that his condition was grave. This medical bulletin seemed to bring to a head PKI-army confrontation.

Sukarno recovered sufficiently to deliver his proclamation day speech on August 17, warning against military leaders who regard themselves as "directors of the Republic."[126] With an obvious dig at Nasution, he declared: "Even though a man was a brave general in 1945, if he now starts to destroy revolutionary national unity, to stir up trouble in the Nasakom front, and to oppose the principles of the revolution, he is nothing but a champion of reaction."[127]

On the night of September 30, 1965, the PKI-army showdown took place, an event referred to in later years as Gestapu [*Gerakan September Tiga Puluh* -- the September 30 Movement]. The coup aimed to annihilate those army leaders who had most resisted Sukarno's "nasakomization" program, especially the council of generals suspected of plotting to overthrow Sukarno, including Nasution and Yani.

Hatta was in Bali at the time of Gestapu, having been advised to holiday there for health reasons,[128] perhaps an indication that those who suspected that a coup was imminent were concerned for his safety. He recalled that "I heard the first news about the kidnapping and murder of the leadership of the Army from Simatupang on the morning of October 1st 1965," adding: "Further reports revealed that Nasution, after having

---

125 Guntur Soekarnoputra, "Orang Besar, Jiwa Besar," in *Bung Hatta: Pribadinya dalam Kenangan*, p. 625.
126 See Dahm, *History of Indonesia*, p. 229.
127 Ibid.
128 See Hatta, *Bung Hatta's Answers*, p. 48.

left his hiding-place, went straight to Kostrad. He found that Suharto had already taken action."[129] The coup was to bring the Javanese General Suharto to the fore, forcing Nasution into second place.

How deeply Sukarno was involved in Gestapu has never been fully explained. Certainly Hatta considered that Sukarno was culpable, stating: "I presumed that the happening was at least carried out with the knowledge of Bung Karno, that very probably he was even backing it." Hatta added firmly: "Without Bung Karno's consent, I do not think all this would have possibly happened."[130]

It was a strong judgment, for the aftermath of the Gestapu coup produced one of the most horrific and murderous episodes in Indonesia's history. Anti-PKI action became the release valve for years of bottled-up resentment and incitement to revolutionary action. In 1945 the targets had been the foreigners: the Japanese, the British, and the Dutch. In 1965, it was brother against brother. By the end of 1965, the rivers of Indonesia were literally running with blood.

Hatta admitted in retrospect, although cautiously, that "from the Moslems, the reaction was very strong, especially from those who at that time felt the worst pressure," that Nahdatul Ulama leaders were prepared to "take revenge by killing at least ten PKI people for every Moslem scholar they had killed."[131] Hatta could not conceal his repugnance for this kind of Islamic justice, especially from an Islamic group which had been prepared to work alongside the Communists for the sake of retaining Sukarno's patronage.[132]

From the PKI point of view, Hatta assessed that "the actions of the people who were under pressure and who afterwards took revenge showed that Aidit had miscalculated." He considered that Aidit's campaign was "based on the mobilization of masses of people, accompanied by agitation and mental terror, so that people went along for their own safety." In Hatta's opinion, Aidit had not paid enough attention to "factors of education." Hatta could not refrain from correcting Aidit's methodology

---

129 Ibid.
130 Ibid., p. 49.
131 Ibid.
132 According to Minister of Religion Wahib Wahab, "cooperation between the three groups -- Islamic, Nationalist, and Communist -- had been going on since the beginning and did not pose any problem." *Harian Rakjat*, August 19, 1960.

as if presenting a lesson for all socialists to learn. "Cadres who truly understood and who were really convinced should have been built up first, until they had reached an adequate number to give support to the mobilized masses."[133] The PKI had used methods espoused by Sukarno and the Japanese Propaganda Department, methods which Hatta had denounced nearly forty years earlier.

When in March 1967, Sukarno was finally replaced by Suharto, Hatta was free to attack the man who had perhaps done most to destroy his democratic ideal and his career. Hatta had already censured Sukarno at Sjahrir's funeral in April 1966, following his death in Zurich at the age of 57 years. Hatta's graveside address included a bitter condemnation of the persecutors of his former associate:

> Sutan Sjahrir, who carried in his heart great aims, led a life of continual struggle, suffering and sacrifice for them. He died without achieving them.
>
> He struggled for a free Indonesia, endured exile for a free Indonesia, participated in building a free Indonesia, but he became ill and died in detention in the free Republic of Indonesia.
>
> Isn't that a tragedy? Sutan Sjahrir suffered more within the Republic of Indonesia itself, which is based on the *Panca Sila*, than in the colonial Dutch Indies, which he opposed.
>
> Sjahrir is now buried in a state ceremony. Is this not a sign that the Government acknowledges the mistake it made in the past in regard to Sjahrir? If this is true, then all those who were arrested at the same time as Sjahrir should be released, those others who were arrested on a mere rumor. Hopefully justice will prevail.[134]

---

133 Hatta, *Bung Hatta's Answers*, p. 50.
134 As cited in Leon Salim, *Bung Sjahrir: Pahlawan Nasional* (Medan: Masadepan, 1966), pp. 62-63.

Hatta concluded on a note of personal farewell:

> My brother Sutan Sjahrir, up till now we have accompanied you on
> your last journey.... Rest in peace.[135]

---

135 Ibid., p. 63.

CHAPTER THIRTEEN
THE UNACHIEVED FREEDOM

Hopefully the spirit of the Panca Sila which is alive again and seethes in the hearts of the Indonesian people, can restore the political movement of the Indonesian nation to a straight course towards implementation of the aims of the Indonesian Revolution, which were ignored by the Proclamation of August 17, 1945.

Young Indonesians, both now and in the future, must be aware of their obligations to understand in as great depth as possible the basis of the nation so that they can truly fulfill their historical task to their homeland.[1]

As one of the few civilian leaders with sufficient prestige to challenge the military's assumption of power, Hatta in 1966 expressed his willingness to stand as President for a limited period.[2] His offer was ignored, proof that the downfall of Sukarno symbolized the passing of the 1928 Generation and that the political ambitions of the military, which had been present since the Revolution, had been fulfilled. Yet the offer did indicate that Hatta never intended to retire permanently from government.

For Hatta, a return to the apex of power would not only have presented him with an opportunity to try to restore creditability to civilian government but, indirectly, would have enabled him to prove himself as a leader in his own right without Sukarno. Hatta had lived with recriminations that he had failed Indonesia by refusing to accept a position in Sukarno's regime, being categorized as an academic who

---

1 Hatta, "Panca Sila Jalan Lurus," in *Bung Hatta Berpidato, Bung Hatta Menulis*, pp. 163-64.
2 See *Merdeka*, June 2, 1966.

preferred to formulate and criticize policies rather than exert influence within government. Although his forebodings on the dire consequences of unlawful government had been vindicated, he still had to face up to murmurings that his country had been sacrificed for his moral purity.[3] Hatta reiterated that he could not have restrained Sukarno: "In the 'guided democracy' system, everything was decided by President Sukarno himself. He was the dictator above the name 'guided democracy'; dissent was not allowed."[4]

A second option open to Hatta was to return to government as a party leader. The civilian forces clamoring most forcefully for a genuine democracy were Modernist Muslim students and academics. Hatta was close enough to the ex-Masjuml leaders to harness this Modernist dynamism. While he had admitted the need to make use of the ardor of Muslim youth at the clandestine gatherings at his villa in Megamendung in 1962, Hatta had not specifically advocated forming an Islamic party. The overriding consideration for Hatta now was the institution of a party prepared to continue the struggle for social democracy. 1966 was a year when socialism was in disrepute. Although several former PSI members were accepted into positions of influence in the New Order because of their expertise, such as the economist Sumitro, neither the PSI nor Masjumi, the two main exponents of parliamentary democracy, was permitted to re-form. For the Modernists, who had been so supportive of the military action against Sukarno and the PKI, this rejection came as a blow. As a sop, the Suharto government conceded that an alternative Islamic party could be established.

Hatta must have realized that, if the PSI were debarred from politics, a party with similar roots and overtly advocating parliamentary democracy and social reform such as the proposed Partai Daulat Rakyat would never gain acceptance. The New Order, following Sukarno's example, preferred to appoint the majority of representatives to the MPR and would also

---

3 This view came through in my interview with Subadio Sastrosatomo, February 22, 1982. The opinion that Hatta had failed as a leader by his withdrawal from direct involvement in politics during the Guided Democracy period was particularly evident in my interview with T. B. Simatupang on February 4. 1982.

4 Mohammad Hatta, "Pengantar, Rencana Dasar, Program dan Struktur Partai Demokrasi Islam Indonesia," March 17, 1967, in H. Oemar Bakry, *Bung Hatta Selamat Jalan, Cita-Citamu Kami Teruskan* (Jakarta: Mutiara, 1980), p. 168.

screen future election candidates for the DPR. A party drawing attention to *kedaulatan rakyat* would have appeared hopelessly Utopian, almost verging on the anarchical, in the prevailing political climate.

Hatta now hoped to blend Modernists and displaced socialists, presumably including former Communists, into a Partai Demokrasl Islam Indonesia. When introducing his new party, he claimed that it would correct inadequacies in past Islamic parties, stating:

> In the past, people often used Islam as a "name" only. The Indonesian Islamic Democratic Movement seeks to practice what it preaches about the welfare of society. The basis of "Belief in God" will be implemented, along with religious duties, within the framework of the *Panca Sila*....[5]

Hatta's task from now on would be to convince his supporters that the *Panca Sila* was the most appropriate ideology for Indonesia, particularly as, not only was it associated with Sukarno and the PKI, but it had been adopted as the principal maxim of the New Order.

Hatta discovered that his new party was causing Muslim disquiet. "Some people say that the newly created Partai Demokrasi Islam Indonesia is not an Islamic party but a *Panca Sila* party," Hatta admitted. He queried with barely concealed irritation: "Can the basis of 'Belief in God,' which permeates the whole *Panca Sila*, not be put into practice according to Islamic concepts?" He accused his fellow Muslims of inflexibility, questioning: "If Protestant and Catholic churches can accept the *Panca Sila* according to their religious tenets, why can't Muslims?" Hatta defended the new party from accusations that sufficient Islamic parties were already in existence. He stressed that the party would be different from other Islamic parties because it would be based on "socialism which is sanctioned by God," a party for "Islamic youth of the 1966 Generation."[6]

Certainly the party platform gave as much weight to socialism as to Islam. The first aim of the Partai Demokrasi Islam Indonesia was

---

5 Hatta, "Pengantar, Rencana Dasar," p. 165.
6 Ibid., pp. 168-69.

to implement "Indonesian Socialism,"[7] an indication that Sukarno's "Socialism à la Indonesia" was perfectly acceptable if practiced correctly. The role of Islam in character training was acknowledged but coupled with Hatta's usual stress on political education. Hatta still intended to use the cell system, and urged party branches to establish Islamic Political Education Clubs "to teach prospective members the aims of the party and to educate party cadres."[8]

In launching a new party so similar in aims and format to the New PNI, Hatta was treading a tightrope. He was using a strategy which had split asunder Sarikat Islam in the past, although to Hatta his brand of socialism was eminently compatible with Islam because it was not atheistic. Hatta recognized that Indonesia needed a socialist party in order to keep in focus the dire needs of the masses. Certainly the events of 1966 were hardly conducive to attracting ex-PKI members to an Islamic party. Members of Ansor, the youth wing of Nahdatul Ulama, had played a very active part in purging suspected Communists and settling old scores.

Hatta contended that Marx "never clarified socialism positively," that it was "his disciples who gave it positive form by converting Marx's theories into an ism, creating an atheistic Marxism."[9] He reiterated the statement he had made in 1938: "Marx stressed that he was not a Marxist." To satisfy the Muslims, Hatta was attacking Marxism; to appeal to the left-wing, Hatta was exonerating Marx. "Marxism is socialism which is Anti-God," he affirmed.[10] Yet in mentioning Marx even so delicately, Hatta was in danger of creating doubts in the minds of his Islamic following. Marx and Islam were uneasy bedfellows and Hatta and the New PNI were often perceived in the past to have had a Marxist slant.

In 1962, Hatta had accorded the PKI the democratic right to remain in existence as a party drawing attention to misgovernment and corruption. In 1966, without fully supporting the inhumane assault on the PKI, Hatta alleged that the party had sealed its own doom. "By its

---

7 Ibid., p. 172.
8 Ibid., p. 179. According to M. Natsir, in the PDII Hatta hoped "to work through private Islamic educational institutions. Hatta was very interested in supporting wide political education." Interview M. Natsir, February 6, 1983.
9 See *Merdeka*, June 3, 1966. An address by Hatta to the Angkatan Muda Islam [Islamic Youth Force] in Bandung.
10 Ibid.

brutal action in trying to seize power, which was by the grace of God foiled by the Army, the PKI revived its fierce opponents."[11] Hatta did not, in 1966, speak out hotly against the arbitrary slaughter of thousands of Indonesians who had followed the PKI, a party openly advocating social revolution. As in Madiun, Hatta viewed the PKI coup as endangering Indonesia's Independence from foreign domination. As he commented in his introduction to the new Islamic Democratic party, there were fears whether "Indonesia would become a colony of Peking."[12] Hatta always perceived communism as a type of social revolution which opposed *kedaulatan rakyat.*

Certainly so ardent was the anti-Communist sentiment in 1966 that it would have been tantamount to political suicide for Hatta to defend the PKI's democratic right to a continuing voice in politics. From late 1965 onwards, Indonesia entered an era of institutionalized anticommunism which far exceeded that of McCarthy's era in the United States. Nor had Hatta any personal reason to defend the PKI. The New Order had dawned in an orgy of revenge. Hatta had suffered indignities, abuse, and harassment at Communist hands since the Second Congress of the League against Colonialism in 1928. He knew from the past, that whenever he took any initiative to promote his brand of socialism, the Communists did their best to undermine his esteem. Hatta carried too many PKI scars to endanger the delicate balance in his new party by defending the PKI's right to exist.

The New Order had an important redeeming feature for Hatta. Suharto had promised to make a determined assault on the economic chaos which he had inherited and had also adopted *pembangunan* as the watch cry for the future. Any dedication to economic betterment and nation building sounded sweet in Hatta's ears. He had in the past commented that increased prosperity not only relieved poverty but engendered the conditions for a return to more liberal government.

Suharto was not a charismatic leader like Sukarno, nor was his oratory more than mediocre. He appeared basically quiet and unassuming, presenting an image of affability in spite of the toughness of his regime.

---

11 Hatta, "Panca Sila Jalan Lurus," p. 163.
12 Hatta, "Pengantar, Rencana Dasar," p. 165.

On the surface, he was more like Hatta than Sukarno, calm and self-contained. Suharto had distinct advantages which Hatta did not. He was Javanese and a generation younger; and supporting him was a formidable military machine.

Hatta was aware that his age would prevent him from remaining a party leader for long. When writing about the Partai Demokrasi Islam Indonesia, he commented: "The prime task of a democratic leader is to look for his replacement, and the quicker he is replaced the better."[13] Although the statement applied to himself, it could also have been directed to Sukarno, a hint to him to step down gracefully.

Hatta admitted that the new party would have a marathon task ahead of it, that "returning to a correct path will require moral courage."[14] Now that he was identifying openly with an Islamic party, Hatta used the concept of the "correct path" more frequently, as if returning to the thought world of the *tarekat*, the Sufist way. In leading an Islamic party, Hatta seemed to be looking back to Batu Hampar, to the social inspiration he claimed to have attained from Syech Arsyad, stressing that social concern was an essential part of the Muslim's religion.

In view of the party's social democratic flavor and its methodology, it was not really surprising that Suharto refused to sanction it. Islamic socialism combined with Leninist practices constituted a volatile mixture, presenting much too dangerous an opposition. Instead Suharto appointed a conservative Muhammadiyah leader to form a Partai Muslimin Indonesia. To ensure that the new Islamic party was relatively acquiescent, former Masjumi leaders were excluded from its leadership. Hatta bowed to *force majeure* with his customary stoicism, concealing his disappointment and frustration from the public eye, admitting: "For me, there was nothing else but to accept the decision, and so the Partai Demokrasi Islam Indonesia never materialized."[15]

Hatta later defended the proposed party, claiming that "it would have been a fresh and refreshing antidote to the extremely confused situation of the period."[16] To him, a swing to the far right had always

---

13 Ibid., p. 169.
14 Ibid., p. 166.
15 Hatta, *Bung Hatta's Answers*, p. 161.
16 Ibid., p. 159.

had associations with fascism, which he rejected on both humanitarian and socioeconomic grounds. But it was not just the Suharto regime with which he was disappointed, but also his fellow Muslims. In one of his last interviews he commented: "One of the things to be taught to the Islamic communities is that they should apply the science of salt, which is felt but not seen, rather than the science of lipstick, which is seen but not felt."[17] Now that his brief courtship with a new-look Islamic party had ended, he would have to fight for *kedaulatan rakyat* from the shadows rather than in the open. It was a situation with which he was all too familiar.

On March 27, 1968, Suharto was sworn in as President for a five-year term, the office of Vice-President remaining vacant. In the same month, Hatta published a booklet entitled simply *Pendidikan Nasional Indonesia*, in which he recounted the history of the New PNI from its inception to the present time, stressing that the party must continue to operate in some form until its aims were achieved and contending that the "Pendidikan Nasional Indonesia had never been dissolved nor dissolved itself,"[18] in other words the groups which had espoused the New PNI's aims had never ceased to struggle for them.

Hatta admitted that he must surrender the struggle to present and future generations of socially concerned youth, optimistically predicting that "our children and grandchildren will fight for Free Indonesia with an organization and spirit which we have set alight."[19] He still urged the use of non-cooperation as a useful weapon, because it "encourages a responsible feeling in the breasts of young Indonesians, *awakening the manhood* in their bodies and showing them the way back to their own people." Hatta warned the younger generations that they must be "prepared to make sacrifices and not live in ease, trying seriously and with all their strength to create a new situation rather than cooperate like robots as in the old system."[20] This was again an echo of his defense speech, his call to sons of the elite not to ape their parents' comfortable but subservient lifestyle.

In spite of his assertion that he did not want to "rehash the quarrels and conflicts of the past," Hatta was on the attack again, determined to

---

17 Ibid., p. 161.
18 Mohammad Hatta, *Pendidikan Nasional Indonesia* (Bogor: Melati, 1968), pp. 5 and 8.
19 Ibid., p. 6.
20 Ibid., p. 12.

warn future generations to be cautious of leaders like Sukarno:

> As a skilled speaker who became more spirited on hearing the claps and tumultuous responses of the people, he believed he was an actor who played a role on the podium, with the masses his audience. He did not teach them to be fellow strugglers, only to be followers. According to his ideals, only *one party* should pioneer the independence struggle, all others should trail behind. That one party should be his party; it would be he who would mobilize it, he who would lead it and he who would steer it.[21]

Hatta was back in spirit in the New PNI polemics of the thirties. Although he acknowledged that "Sukarno, besides his faults, gave great service in developing a spirit of Indonesian freedom," he refuted the claims of overseas writers that Sukarno engendered unity. According to Hatta, Indonesian unity was first nurtured by the Perhimpunan Indonesia in the Netherlands. This was a subtle way of claiming that he personally had done more for Indonesia's unity than Sukarno, and he wished Western writers could overcome their fascination for Sukarno and recognize the real situation. "Sukarno merely strengthened the existing aims with his sonorous voice," Hatta contended. In other words, Sukarno was the *pembeo* [parroter] of ideas already formulated by Hatta and others, rather than an original thinker. Hatta went even further, claiming that Sukarno actually endangered unity. "It was Sukarno who broke the aims of Indonesian unity when he deviated from the basis of the state with his policy of Nasakom." This, according to Hatta, had sparked off the PRRI and Permesta rebellions. "The civil war which ensued considerably damaged Indonesian unity and the aims of a just and prosperous Indonesia." Hatta allowed the resentment welling up inside him to erupt on the surface, accusing the former President: "Having participated in nation building, Sukarno destroyed it!"[22] Hatta's indignation contained an element of pique, as if adding: he also destroyed my political career and my plans for Indonesia.

---

21 Ibid., pp. 13-14.
22 Ibid., pp. 31-32.

Hatta lashed out at Sukarno's egomania, his desire to be the "center of everything." He denounced Sukarno's regime as being more dastardly than any of its predecessors, a very strong condemnation. "For a long time, Indonesia lived in the shade of feudalism, but Sukarno's neo-feudalism was more evil and more vicious," he contended. Hatta pointed out that most feudal rulers "understood their responsibilities as well as their rights," even though "those rights were almost unlimited." Hatta scornfully gibed: "the neo-feudal big shot, who has no tradition, only knows his rights, not his responsibilites." He concluded hotly: "We do not want either feudalism or neo-feudalism, we want *Kedaulatan Rakyat* as created and propagated in the past by the Pendidikan Nasional Indonesia, which is now rooted in our Constitution. This we must defend!"[23]

Recalling informal discussions with Hatta in 1968, Professor Kahin of Cornell University commented that "certainly he was disappointed because his hopes had not been realized." Kahin remarked that Hatta never lost his conviction that "Islam could play a progressive socio-economic role, which would present Indonesia with a superior social justice."[24] Kahin noticed Hatta's hurt. "I could sympathize with his disappointment and dejection at that time and in future discussions," he said, "because the government had rejected his desire to establish and lead a political party to achieve these aims." Kahin personally deplored the situation, remarking: "The reality that one of the two people who had established a nation was not allowed an opportunity like that certainly constituted a tragedy in the history of that nation."[25]

Hatta managed to escape from the frustrations of Indonesia for six months in 1968 when he accepted an invitation from the University of Hawaii to be a Special Visitor to its East-West Center to allow him an opportunity to record his struggle for independence. His eldest daughter, Meutia, accompanied him, enrolling as a student in an anthropology degree course.

---

23 Ibid., pp. 32-33.
24 George McT. Kahin, "Mohammad Hatta Sebagai Pemikir Bebas, in *Bung Hatta: Pribadinya dalam Kenangan*, p. 459. According to Natsir, Hatta saw Islam chiefly at the individual and community level, therefore Hatta was not emphatic that everything had to follow Islam. Although Hatta's motivation was religious, Natsir thought that Hatta did not consciously use Islamic ideas in terms of state and nation in the way Masjumi did. Interview, M. Natsir, February 6, 1983.
25 Kahin, "Mohammad Hatta Sebagai Pemikir Bebas," p. 459.

On his return from Honolulu, Hatta received a firm offer of leadership of a party which was permitted to operate, the Partai Nasional Indonesia. The news first broke in the press on June 23, 1969. The response from Hatta's secretary, Wangsa Widjaja, was that "Bung Hatta knows nothing about his nomination as chairman of the Partai Nasional Indonesia [PNI]" and that he was engaged in writing his memoirs. A press report alleged that "almost all the leaders of the PNI, old and new, support Hatta as chairman of PNI."[26] Hatta did not accept the offer, whether on ideological grounds, for fear of endangering the party's existence, or because of his past relationships with the party is unclear. The PNI had always been closer to Sukarno than Hatta.

Nevertheless, for Hatta existence in the New Order was not as uncomfortable as for his fellow Proclamator. Sukarno, now condemned for involvement in the Gestapu coup and stripped of his "Presidency for life," was confined within his Jakarta home, the only companionship permitted him being occasional family visitors. Like Sjahrir, Sukarno suffered greatly if cut off from social intercourse. His isolation further aggravated his already serious health problems.

Sukarno's son, Guntur, recalled his own dilemma in 1970 when his father was not granted permission to attend his wedding in Bandung. To Guntur's surprise, Sukarno suggested that he ask Hatta to deputize for him. Guntur was reluctant to approach Hatta, querying his father: "Are you sure that Pak Hatta will want to?"[27] Sukarno knew Hatta. Hatta might attack and revile him for his policies and political behavior, but in their private lives, the bonds of comradeship forged in the independence struggle bound them like blood brothers. When Guntur's mother telephoned Sukarno's request to Hatta, the answer was spontaneous and in the affirmative.

In June that year, Sukarno's health deteriorated, and he had to be admitted to the military hospital. When it was evident that he was near death, Hatta applied for permission to visit him. Their last meeting took place on Friday, June 19. Hatta's secretary, Wangsa Widjaja, who accompanied Hatta and his family to the hospital, recalled that Sukarno

---

26 See *Harian Abadi*, June 25, 1969.
27 Guntur Soekarnoputra, "Orang Besar, Jiwa Besar," p. 626.

was comatose, indeed Hatta wondered if he would regain consciousness. The once handsome face was swollen and moonshaped, disfigured by disease. Suddenly Sukarno's eyes opened and he exclaimed in surprise: "Hatta, you're here!"[28] Meutia remembered that her father greeted Sukarno by the special affectionate shortening of his name: "Ah, how are you, No?" The reply came weakly in Dutch: "*Hoe gaat het met jou?*"[29] Hatta sat quietly holding Sukarno's hand while the tears streamed down the dying man's cheeks, his hand groping for his spectacles so that he could see Hatta more clearly. Speech was too great an effort for Sukarno, so Hatta remained silent. Meutia recalled: "Although there was no further conversation it seemed as if they were speaking to each other with their hearts, as if the two of them were remembering their ups and downs in the struggle together in past years, in the period when they worked with one another, possibly asking each other for forgiveness."[30] Hatta had difficulty in disengaging his hand when finally it was time to leave. Sukarno died two days later.

Although forced to accept the constraints imposed by the new regime, Hatta continued to propagate his ideals, traveling widely around the archipelago. He had to be circumspect to avoid house detention, yet it was basically against Hatta's carping nature for him to observe undemocratic government and economic mismanagement without voicing critical comment. It was part of his role as a political educator and social reformer. From time to time, he would throw discretion to the winds, allowing his thoughts free expression. The technique of the "hidden message" wrapped up in protective layers of verbiage was brought to perfection by many Indonesian academics and journalists in the New Order. If dissidents became too skilled or too daring in their word games, they simply lost their jobs or were restrained in some way. Hatta was fortunate; his prestige acted as a safeguard.

Hatta sought out opportunities to address students, taking advantage of appointments he held as an emeritus professor up until 1971. In a speech at Syiah Kuala Darussalam University in Banda Aceh on September 2, 1970, Hatta pointed out that poverty had not been eliminated within

---

28 Wangsa Widjaja, "Mengenang Bung Karno," p. 115.
29 Swasono, "Ayahanda: Pribadinya dalam Kenangan," p. 58.
30 Ibid.

338 INDONESIA FREE: A POLITICAL BIOGRAPHY OF MOHAMMAD HATTA

the first quarter century after independence, as he had planned as prime minister, but had "even worsened," although there were "many Indonesian millionaires" with domestic and overseas business interests.[31] By 1970, the extent to which army generals and their families, including Suharto's, had enriched themselves was gaining public attention and was being highlighted in the more daring newspapers such as Mochtar Lubis's *Indonesia Raya*. In 1969, Hatta had agreed to act as an adviser to a special commission set up by the government to investigate corruption, chaired by former Prime Minister Wllopo. Mochtar Lubis recalled showing Hatta documents he had acquired indicating large-scale manipulation of funds in Pertamina, the government oil company. "At first Bung Hatta just shook his head as if he could not believe what he was reading," Lubis recalled.[32]

Hatta also criticized the dual function or *dwifungsi* theories espoused by the New Order to rationalize the civilian role played by the military. Hatta observed that, unless "there is an insufficiency of civil servants," a military civil service was undesirable.[33] It was a remark loaded with sarcasm for Indonesia had suffered from an oversupply of civil servants for years.

Hatta was also concerned about the military regime's strategies to ensure that no viable opposition could emerge in the already limited section of government scheduled for election in 1971. The Golongan Karya [Functional Groups] or Golkar, formed in 1964 under army initiative to counter the PKI's proliferation of organizations, had by 1969 become an instrument for vitiating the existing political parties. Hatta appealed to his audience to choose responsible leaders, using the past "as a lesson to pioneer a new way."[34] Hatta again suggested that electors look to Great Britain as a model of democratic government.

In May and June 1971, immediately prior to the general elections, an Indonesian Committee to Uphold Democracy was established by a group of university students, who appealed to Hatta for support. Hatta praised their spirit, advising them not to be "afraid to take risks." He reminded

---

31 Mohammad Hatta, *Sesudah 25 Tahun*, pp. 7-8.
32 Mochtar Lubis, "Bung Hatta, Manusia Berdisiplin," in *Bung Hatta: Pribadinya dalam Kenangan*, p. 581.
33 Hatta, *Sesudah 25 Tahun*, p. 18.
34 Ibid., p. 20.

them that "I myself took risks and was even betrayed by friends,"[35] no doubt a reference to his expulsion from the Perhimpunan Indonesia. Although he encouraged the student protest, Hatta was not prepared to join the young people on the streets. His days of student activism were over.

Hatta's association with young dissidents did not go unnoticed, and he received a summons to the President's palace, together with his wife. Mrs. Suharto, a figure of power and wealth behind the President, announced that it would be best if Hatta leave for Europe for medical treatment, which journalist Brian May interpreted as a presidential command to Hatta to absent himself from Indonesia during the elections.[36]

It was not a harsh exile for Hatta. He had many sympathizers among the overseas embassy staffs and valued contacts with Indonesians studying abroad. It was now common practice to dispatch prestigious "thorns-in-the-flesh" to countries far removed from Indonesia. Hatta traveled via the United States of America, spending most of his time in Austria and Rome. His old friend, Anak Agung Gde Agung, was now the Indonesian ambassador in Vienna. Anak Agung noticed that Hatta "was physically very tired, that his health was genuinely troubling him."[37]

Golkar's decisive win in the 1971 elections gave the government added confidence. To Hatta, the poll was a meaningless exercise because of the factor of intimidation,[38] and he lent his support to a group of abstentionists, known as the Golongan Putin [Blank Group]. He sympathized with their refusal to cooperate in elections to a body which was not fully democratic. 1971 was a year of disillusionment and cynicism. The corruption commission's report did result in an anticorruption bill being passed in parliament but this was neutralized by the government's refusal to bring the worst offenders to trial.[39]

Hatta was certainly free of the taint of profiteering; indeed, there were times when he found it difficult to meet his household expenses.[40]

---

35 Brian May, *The Indonesian Tragedy* (London: Routledge and Kegan Paul, 1978), p. 265.
36 Ibid.
37 Anak Agung Gde Agung, "Bung Hatta jang Saja Kenal," p. 74.
38 See May, *Indonesian Tragedy*, p. 265.
39 In cases involving members of the armed forces, all criminal charges were referred to military courts, and thus remained an internal army affair.
40 Ny. H. S. S. A. Rachim, "Pribadi Bung Hatta yang Saya Kenal," p. 32, in which it is suggested that

Although his income, acquired from his writings, a government pension, and family property, was above that of the average Indonesian, it was below that of the governing elite. Ironically in the last two years of his life, Hatta's pecuniary predicament was drastically remedied. The Sultan of Yogyakarta had accepted the MPR's offer of the Vice-Presidency in 1973 but, on leaving office in 1978, he received a much higher pension than Hatta's. As a result, Hatta's pension had to be raised in line with the Sultan's.

For Hatta personally, one of his official visits around the archipelago had special significance. In April 1973, he was invited back to Banda Neira, accompanied by his wife and two younger daughters and also by Sjahrir's widow and Des Alwi. Poppy Sjahrir noticed that aboard the naval ship which carried them from Ambon to Banda Neira, Hatta seemed "unusually relaxed and happy."[41] On approaching the harbor, their ship was welcomed by gaily decorated boats from the kampungs, while on the shore schoolchildren greeted them in song. The names of Hatta and Sjahrir were now a part of the islands, a mosque being named after them as well as two offshore islands.

In spite of the warm welcome which he received, Hatta seemed disappointed as he observed the neglect and deterioration of the Island.[42] The fine old colonial buildings were decaying, and the standard of living generally had declined. Poppy Sjahrir too noticed Hatta's concern at the "rundown plantations and dilapidated houses, the poverty of the inhabitants and the number of children who did not go to school because they had no money."[43] was Hatta experiencing a pang of guilt for having assured the prosperous Moluccan Islanders that Independence would be to their advantage?

Protests escalated in January 1974 against the New Order's neglect of the Indonesian small businessman while encouraging foreign enterprise. Certainly Hatta had seen evidence of indigenous decline in Banda Neira. A student demonstration coinciding with the visit of the Japanese Prime

---

even providing refreshments for Hatta's frequent visitors was a strain. When Hatta was made a Special Citizen of the Greater Jakarta Region in 1972, the governor, Ali Sadikin, helped by absorbing Hatta's electricity and water charges.

41 Ny. Siti Wahjunah Sjahrir, "Bung Hatta: Beberapa Catatan," p. 484.

42 Interview Des Alwi, February 6, 1982.

43 Ny. Siti Wahjunah Sjahrir, "Bung Hatta: Beberapa Catatan," p. 484.

Minister Tanaka deteriorated into a mass riot, known afterwards by the acronym Malari, signifying the January 15 Disaster. There were claims that the Malari violence was deliberately provoked by the government to allow Suharto an excuse to dismiss his security chief, whom he suspected of plotting against him.

Yet in some ways Hatta, too, had provided fuel for the Malari outburst. A month previously, in an article entitled "Foreign Capital" written for the student paper *Mahasiswa Indonesia* [Indonesian student], Hatta had pointed out that Article 33 of the Constitution concerning a cooperatively organized economy, based on the situation in Scandinavian countries, had been disregarded.[44] He argued that the government's American-trained economists had "turned around the economic policy of Indonesia from a guided economy along the lines of the 1945 Constitution into one which goes in the direction of economic liberalism." He alleged that "what is being emphasized is private enterprise" but that Indonesia's entrepreneurs were not yet ready "to confront a period of economic liberalism." Hatta pointed to the damage being caused by foreign exploitation, especially Japanese, and by the inability of the Indonesian businessman to compete with the Chinese, claiming that "new citizens of Chinese origin" had profited most from foreign loans. Again Hatta could not conceal his innate dislike of the Chinese businessman, refraining from mentioning that there were many Indonesians, too, especially in the top levels of government, who were receiving benefits from foreign business enterprises. Hatta gave his opinion that the "consequences of this new economic policy is that the gap between the social classes has increased tremendously and the difference between the rich and poor has become glaringly evident."[45] Despite expressions of derision emanating from the New Order's economic experts, Hatta refused to alter his emphasis on cooperatives being best for the welfare of the weakest economic groups.

But not only Hatta and the students were protesting. Islamic opposition to the military regime was becoming more fanatical and fundamentalist. The Acehnese rebel, Daud Beureueh, echoing Hatta, was also advising Suharto "to return to the real and correct path,"[46] dubbing Golkar the

---

44 See Oey Hong Lee, *Indonesia Facing the 1980s* (Hull: Europres, 1980), pp. 249-50.
45 Ibid.
46 See ibid., p. 231. Beureueh's letter to Suharto was reproduced in *Impact International* [London],

Golkur [Golongan Kuraish], the aristocrats in Mecca against whom the Prophet Mohammad had waged his *Jihad*. Daud Beureueh supported the formation of a new Islamic State movement, the Komando Jihad, reminiscent of Darul Islam.

Hatta moved to offset the "Islamic State" trend in opposition to the government and agreed to chair a Committee of Five set up to reinterpret the *Panca Sila*. In supporting the state ideology, he needed to make public that his opposition to the New Order was as strong as ever. This point Hatta clarified in August 1975 when, on the thirtieth anniversary of Indonesia's proclamation of independence, he was awarded his third honorary doctorate, this time in Constitutional Law by the University of Indonesia. He entitled his address "Towards a State based on the Rule of Law," an indication that he did not consider that the present regime behaved as a government conforming to the Constitution should. His speech resembled a new manifesto, running hand in hand with "Towards Free Indonesia," the political statement Hatta drafted for the New PNI in 1932. Both discourses set down the goals which must be achieved before Indonesia could be considered "free." The first manifesto charted the reader through the dangers of a colonial regime, the second through the equally hazardous waters of autocratic Indonesian military rule.

Having issued a plea to his Islamic associates to accept the *Panca Sila* Hatta went on to indicate the ways in which the Suharto regime was not living up to its state ideology. He hit out at the government's handling of public monies. One of the difficulties which the corruption commission had faced was the lack of detailed accounting in state agencies. He expressed his disapproval of such methods, stating: "There still exists a custom which does not accord with the 1945 Constitution, which is called 'non-budgetary' expenditure," adding peremptorily: "Hopefully this custom will be abandoned."[47]

Hatta next turned to the human rights clauses in the 1945 Constitution, his criticism of the military regime sharpening as he accused it of "having done very little up to now" for the poverty-stricken and their children. He alleged that the social welfare proposed during the struggle for

---

May 9-22, 1975.
47 Hatta, *Menuju Negara Hukum*, p. 12.

independence thirty years ago was "still mainly drifting along."[48]

Hatta's old fire began to engulf the initial veil of caution. "The democracy of the *Panca Sila* can only come into being when Indonesia becomes a state based on the rule of law," he declared bluntly, "and so far a state based on the rule of law has not yet been achieved." As if his audience were his cadres in training, he exhorted: "Therefore every one of us must try to accelerate the implementation of this state based on the rule of law," continuing:

> Since establishing the Republic of Indonesia, it is this kind of legal state which we aimed for and immediately set the course towards achieving. But because of misconceptions about the *Panca Sila* and impatience among our freedom fighters at that time, people forgot to differentiate between *ideals* and reality. The reality was that the 1945 Constitution was right at that time.[49]

This time Hatta's criticism was aimed at Sjahrir for his denigration of the 1945 Constitution in his booklet *Our Struggle*, and his inability to understand that Hatta had managed to include the major aims of the New PNI in the 1945 Constitution. It had been a more suitable document for Indonesia than Sjahrir had surmised once the transitional clauses were discarded.

Hatta reminded his audience of the Dutch and Outer Island influences in the 1950 Constitution, with its parliamentary cabinet and its relegation of the *Dwi Tunggal* to the sidelines. Certainly Hatta would have benefited from the 1950 Constitution if he had remained prime minister. He did not mention this fact, but rather maintained that "because of that change of governmental system, the *Dwitunggal* became a *dwi tanggal* and presented opportunities for disruptive groups."[50] In regard to the Constituent Assembly, he reiterated that the lack of an "attitude of tolerance" on the part of those supporting an Islamic State had allowed Sukarno to dissolve the assembly. Because of Sukarno's illegal action, the 1945 Constitution, which was basically sound, was thrown into disrepute,

---

48 Ibid., p. 13.
49 Ibid., p. 14.
50 Ibid., p. 15.

Hatta had been unusually quiet about Indonesia's takeover of East Timor at this time, as if undecided which side to support. He was suspicious of the Communist element in Fretlin, alleging that there were foreign influences, "people calling themselves representatives of East Timor, who were in fact among persons from Africa and other countries (who *nota bene* had been said to represent other countries)." Hatta suggested that "the economic situation and the people's livelihood should be restored immediately... through proper planning."[51] As an economist, Hatta believed that East Timor would benefit more from integration with Indonesia. As a nationalist, he found it difficult to condemn his country's action.

By the mid-seventies, Hatta was becoming noticeably more frail. He was now too infirm for the bicycling, mountain climbing, and golf which had kept him fit in middle age. Following the example of many of his contemporaries, Hatta turned to a new fitness program, a type of Yoga known as the *Olahraga Hidup Baru* [Sports for a New Life] or Orhiba, to offset the immobility of aging. Orhiba combined gentle exercise with a state of tranquility. Orhiba also provided an admirable screen for intrigue.

The organizer of the Orhiba Movement was Said Sukanto, who had been chief of police in Hatta's government in 1950. Sukanto was a devotee of Javanese mysticism, *kebatinan*, as was also President Suharto. Through Sukanto, Hatta in 1972 first met Sawito Kartowibowo, a former civil servant.[52] A distant relative of Sukarno, Sawito had established a reputation as a mystic and there had been speculation that he was a *Ratu Adil* sent to unseat the Suharto regime which had lost its moral right to rule because of the extent of corruption and social injustice it had perpetrated. It was remarked that Sawito and Hatta fraternized easily,[53] and Sawito became a member of the group which met regularly at Hatta's villa at Megamendung. Perhaps Hatta saw Sawito as a potential mouthpiece for the group.

There was clearly a political element in Sawito's writings on Javanese

---

51 Hatta, *Bung Hatta's Answers*, pp. 140-41.
52 David Bourchier, *Dynamics of Dissent in Indonesia: Sawito and the Phantom Coup* (Ithaca: Cornell Modern Indonesia Project, 1984), p. 51.
53 Ibid.

mysticism, which were frequently published in the journal *Mawas Diri* [Introspection] established by Dra. Trimurti, the left-wing nationalist who had worked in Hatta's office during the Japanese Occupation. What Sawito was writing had strong echoes of what Hatta himself was saying to the orthodox Muslims: "It is clear that the *Pancasila* is not a creation of man, but a way of life created and offered by our Creator for the needs of mankind."[54] Sawito called for the "leaders of religious and mystical groups to come forward and set an example for the rest of the community,"[55] an appeal Hatta had made to Muslims when trying to establish the Partai Demokrasi Islam Indonesia. The New Order regime had divided the two opposition parties roughly along religious lines, Islam versus *abangan* and Christian. Hatta's tactics were reminiscent of the nationalists in the 1920s, when they resisted Dutch "divide and rule" policies by uniting the ethnic groups. Like the Theosophists, Hatta and Sawito were proposing the elimination of religious barriers, creating *le desir d'etre ensemble* in the fight against unjust and dishonest government.

At Hatta's seventy-second birthday party in August 1974, the suggestion that Hatta replace Suharto for a transitional period was first openly discussed among the group. General Ishak Juarsa, a former military commander in both Aceh and South Sumatra, had urged Hatta in 1970 to accept the Presidency as an interim measure.[56] Hatta, at his birthday party, signified his willingness to act as President, provided the transfer of power was effected constitutionally and without violence. It was a role which Hatta had played most successfully in the past, taking over the reins of government in times of crisis. He pragmatically pointed out that he would also require the backing of a leading military figure.[57] This was to be Domo Pranoto, a former police chief in Central Java and once a close friend of Suharto. Domo Pranoto held the important position of vice chairman of the MPR/DPR, representing the armed forces faction in the consultative assembly.[58]

The group continued to make careful preparations to stage a bloodless

54 See G. J. O'Rourke, "Between Dreams and Reality: The Sawito Affair" (MA Thesis, University of Melbourne, February 21, 1980).
55 *Mawas Diri*, October 1975, p. 13.
56 Bourchier, *Dynamics of Dissent*, p. 74.
57 See O'Rourke, "Between Dreams and Reality," p. 26.
58 Bourchier, *Dynamics of Dissent*, p. 84.

coup against Suharto, challenging his rule on the basis of morality, an important factor in the Javanese concept of power since the ruler is expected to reflect a godlike image. Three of the early nationalists, Iskaq Tjrokrohadisurjo, the joint founder of the original PNI, and two other former Perhimpunan Indnesia members of Hatta's generation, Singgih and Sudjono, were now participating in the deliberations. To add credence to the religious and moral theme of the challenge to Suharto, Domo Pranoto suggested that the backing of four prominent religious figures be sought.[59] This was not an easy task as many such men were in their positions of leadership because of their loyalty to the Suharto government. However, four prestigious religious leaders were prepared to support the challenge. These were Cardinal Darmoyuwono, the highest ranking prelate in the Indonesian Catholic church; former armed forces chief, Simatupang, representing the Indonesian Council of Churches; Hatta's Minangkabau friend Hamka, representing the Council of Islamic Scholars; and Said Sukanto, who held the post of head of the Secretariat for Cooperation among Mystical Sects.

As Singgih had received an invitation from Suharto to visit him in the Presidential Palace in September, he was assigned the task of handing over the documents which the group had prepared. Singgih visited Hatta at Megamendung on September 7 to make sure he understood the likely repercussions.[60] Politically it was an opportune time to act, as most Indonesians were appalled at the news of Pertamina's collapse and at the huge debt and misappropriation of public money involved.

Before Singgih had time to present his documents to the President at the palace, he was arrested. On September 22, 1976, Suharto summoned the leaders of the MPR, DPR, Supreme Advisory Council, several Supreme Court judges, the attorney-general, and the head of the intelligence body, Bakin. Following discussions, the government made a public announcement that "there had been an illegal attempt to replace President Suharto by unconstitutional means."[61] It was further reported that leading religious and political figures had been deceived into signing a document entitled "Menuju Keselamatan" or "Towards Salvation,"

---

59 Ibid.
60 Ibid., p. 73.
61 *Kompas*, September 23, 1976.

dated July 17, 1976. It was later disclosed that the signatories were Hatta, Cardinal Darmoyuwono, Simatupang, Hamka, Sukanto, and Sawito Kartowibowo.[62] The term *"Menuju"* was in itself suggestive of Hatta's influence, one he had used in previous manifestoes which mapped out the path towards *kedaulatan rakyat.*

The document "Towards Salvation" had strong overtones of people's sovereignty running through it. It stressed that the "leadership of the Indonesian people is not restricted to those who run the State or who take an active role in the government leadership."[63] The document further made the accusation that "if the current progress in national development is evaluated in the context of the way it has really benefitted the Indonesian people as a whole, "it is clear that... it has brought about an obvious deterioration in the standard of human dignity."[64]

Sawito denied at his trial that he had masterminded the coup. He also denied that he had drafted "Towards Salvation," testifying that "Bung Hatta was the source of this affair."[65] Sawito explained that "Towards Salvation" was based on Parliamentary Decision No. X/MPR/1973, which enabled the President to transfer responsibility to someone else when "the unity of the nation and the success of national development were threatened."[66] It was hoped that Suharto would transfer his powers to Hatta, who would then request the MPR to elect a new President. A "savior team" would assist Hatta in the interim period.

"Towards Salvation" was not the only document which the government seized. There were supposed to be eleven in all, although only five were specifically mentioned.[67] The final, and perhaps the most intriguing of them, was a "Statement Forgiving Bung Karno" signed by Hatta and Sawito, in which Sukarno's part in propagating the *Panca Sila* and in proclaiming independence was recalled. The paper ended with the words, "we the undersigned... do officially PARDON... all the mistakes and shortcomings of the late DR. Ir. Haji SOEKARNO/Bung Karno."[68]

---

62 Bourchier, *Dynamics of Dissent,* p. 22.
63 Ibid., p. 23.
64 Ibid.
65 Ibid., p. 86.
66 Ibid., p. 79.
67 For a listing and analysis of these, see ibid., pp. 22-31.
68 Ibid., p. 29.

Whether Hatta was prepared to regard Sukarno in a warmer light for the sake of unity and to gain Sawito's cooperation is difficult to judge. At his trial Sawito was adamant that this was the only document for which he was completely responsible, an indication that he was anxious to clear Sukarno's name. Certainly Hatta was still criticizing Sukarno two years later in interviews, but by then the Sawito case was over and lost. Hatta tended to be most ambivalent when Sukarno was involved, torn by the events and frustrations of the past.

What was totally out of character for Hatta was that, together with all the other signatories, he signed a statement to the effect that the documents had been read hurriedly and he had not known the use to which they would be put.[69] The government obtained Hatta's repudiation before making their seizure of the documents public. There is evidence that considerable pressure was exerted on Hatta before he complied with the government's request, and that the statement the government published was the third he wrote for them, dated September 20, 1976. The most he had been willing to concede in his first statement dated September 16, following a visit by two leading government figures, Adam Malik and Emil Salim, was that he had signed the documents "because they defended the *Pancasila*."[70] Many of those involved in the coup signed statements under duress which they later rescinded during the trial proceedings. The problem for Hatta was that he was never called as a witness.

Sawito's trial opened on October 6, 1977, the charge being subversion and intent to overthrow the President. It was assumed that all the signatories would be called as witnesses, including Hatta. One of the judges, John Loedoe, later removed from his position on corruption charges, informed the press that "if the accused summons Bung Hatta as a witness 'a de charge' and the judges considered it important that his testimony be heard in the interests of the inquiry, then he may indeed be called to testify."[71] Yet Hatta was never called to give evidence. As Sawito himself informed the court, "It is very clear that the judges and

---

69 Titania, *Sawito: Siapa, Mengapa dan Bagaimana?* (Solo: Sasongko, 1978), p. 58.
70 Bourchier, *Dynamics of Dissent*, p. 91.
71 Titania, *Sawito*, p. 35.

prosecutors are afraid of hearing Bung Hatta's testimony."[72] It was no doubt a disappointment to Hatta, remembering how his heated appeal on behalf of the Indonesian people had undermined the prosecution's case in the Netherlands.

The trial dragged on until May 1978, its most important contribution being the opportunity it afforded Sawito for revealing actual instances of political opportunism, corruption, and illegal practices which had greatly enriched the President's family and the governing elite. The prosecution accused Sawito of manipulating mysticism for his own ends and of deceiving important people such as Hatta. Sawito was found guilty and sentenced to eight years' imprisonment plus the costs of the trial.

Hatta had been too prestigious a person to arrest but the government employed subtle methods to damage his standing and reduce the impact of his revolt. He was cited as being a senile old man, the victim of manipulation, while his failure to support Sawito as a witness left an impression that he had not supported his fellow conspirators as loyally as he might. Hatta's family and associates strongly denied that his mind was impaired at the time of the coup, a statement supported by his closest medical advisers. Certainly Hatta had been in poor health in 1976, having suffered a slight stroke in the aftermath of two major operations in March of that year.[73] But by August, he was in command again, leaving not only his signature but his stamp on the incriminating documents.

In August 1976 Hatta had also been sufficiently fit to make a tour of West Sumatra, invited by the governor to celebrate the thirty-first anniversary of the proclamation of independence in Bukit Tinggi. As usual, Hatta included the Batu *Hampar surau* in his itinerary, his particular concern being the health of his eldest stepsister Halimah, a child of his father's first marriage and now ninety-two years of age. He confidently promised Halimah that he would return in 1980 to celebrate his seventy-eighth birthday with her. It was a promise he could not keep; Halimah outlived

---

72 Bourchier, *Dynamics of Dissent*, p. 86.
73 According to Dr. Mahar Mardjono, there were fears that this stroke, in the aftermath of operations for a prostate gland and hemorrhoids and complicated by diabetes, might impair Hatta's faculties. When Hatta regained consciousness, the medical team anxiously tested his responses, Dr. Mardjono enquiring: "Who am I?" Hatta's testy reply, "What game are you playing now, Mahar?" assured the team that Hatta was still mentally alert. Interview Prof. Dr. Mahar Mardjono, January 1982.

350 INDONESIA FREE: A POLITICAL BIOGRAPHY OF MOHAMMAD HATTA

him. Hatta was never to set foot in the *Alam Minangkabau* again.

In spite of his frailty and diminishing eyesight, Hatta continued to attend meetings of the Committee of Five set up to promote the *Panca Sila*. On June 1, 1977, the thirty-second anniversary of the acceptance of Sukarno's *Panca Sila*, a special remembrance ceremony was arranged in Jakarta at which Hatta insisted on delivering the major speech. He was realistic enough to recognize that he might not have the strength to complete the address, deputizing his youngest daughter, Halidah, to take over from him when his strength ran out.

Having dwelt again on the origins of the state ideology, complaining that it was now only given "lip service," Hatta concluded on a note of concern for the general lack of humanity in Indonesian society: "Look how easily people kill each other!" he exclaimed.[74] Hatta deplored the widespread indifference to human suffering and the lack of justice, giving the example of detainees who had starved to death because the prison officers neglected to feed them. Such cold indifference, Hatta pointed out, was "completely contrary to the basis of the nation, to the basis of humanity and social justice." He concluded: "Note carefully, the Republic of Indonesia is not yet based on the *Panca Sila*."[75]

By 1979, Hatta was forced by ill-health to curb his activities and restrict his travel. He was suffering frequent blackouts and his heart was weakening. His mobility was hampered by swollen legs, which entailed rest with his feet raised. 1979 became a year of loneliness and accentuated frustration, and even worse, a consciousness of approaching senility and loss of his mental powers. Hatta began to turn his attention to the Islamic scriptures, as if preparing himself for the last stage of his *tarekat*.[76] He was particularly irate when advised to stop attending the mosque, snapping peevishly: "Why can't I attend the Friday prayers, I can still walk?"[77] As he had already fallen and wounded his head through sudden loss of consciousness, it was risky for him to venture out in public.

Because of his condition, it was not expected that he would attend the

---

74 Mohammad Hatta, *Pengertian Panca Sila* (Jakarta: Yayasan Idayu, 1981), pp. 20-21.
75 Ibid., p. 21.
76 See "Bung Hatta, Pancasilais yang Saleh," in K. H. Saifuddin Zuhri, *Kaleidoskop Politik di Indonesia*, vol. 2 (Jakarta: Gunung Agung, 1981), p. 116.
77 See Wangsa Widjaja, "Mengenang Bung Hatta," p. 160.

1979 Congress of the Association of Indonesian Economics Graduates to be held in Bogor in June. But as if realizing that this would be his last chance to meet with Indonesian economists, on whom he depended so much for the improvement of the people's welfare, Hatta not only insisted on attending, but declared that he would make a speech. He had difficulty reading in the poor light but struggled on until his strength failed, when he handed over the script to his son-in-law, Edi Swasono, also an economist, to continue on his behalf. Not unexpectedly his speech once more pressed home the importance of cooperatives for the advancement of the underprivileged. The audience, many of them Hatta's former students but also graduates of the University of California, greeted his comments with a round of applause, in spite of his rebuke that they, the technocrats, had "deviated" from the 1945 Constitution.[78] Seeing Hatta's physical condition they probably realized that it was his economic swan song.

Hatta's last political act in 1980 was to lend his patronage to a Committee of Fifty led by Nasution, who intended to present a petition to the DPR pointing out the New Order's disregard for the *Panca Sila* and the 1945 Constitution. It was to be his final participation in a challenge to the Suharto government. He did not live to savor the repercussions which followed in the wake of the Committee of Fifty's presentation of the petition on May 13, 1980.

On March 3, Hatta left home for the last time, entering a private hospital for medical treatment. When his condition worsened on March 13, he was transferred to the intensive care unit of Jakarta's main hospital. His family and friends maintained a vigil by his bedside, hoping that, as in the past crises, he would rally and pull through. This time there were no reserves of strength to call on. On March 14, 1980, Hatta died.

The state funeral accorded him drew a huge following. As one press report read: "In their thousands ordinary folk flocked to Jakarta's Tanah Kusir public cemetery for the funeral of former Vice-President Mohammad Hatta."[79] Hatta's final instructions were that he wanted to be buried in an ordinary cemetery among the people. An elderly mourner commented to a reporter: "It was Bung Hatta's honesty that made me come." A

---

78 See Sri Edi Swasono, "Bung Hatta Tokohku, Bung Hatta Mertuaku," in *Bung Hatta: Pribadinya dalam Kenangan*, p. 97.
79 *Asia Week*, March 28, 1980.

student leader remarked: "He was integrity personified, everything that a modern Muslim should be," adding: "He set a superb example." Perhaps the most enigmatic remark came from President Suharto: "For those of us left behind, the greatest tribute we can pay is to struggle to realize Mohammad Hatta's dreams."[80]

Although Hatta had many critics while alive, in death the voices of condemnation were hushed. "The Guardian of the Nation's Conscience" was one of the epithets given to him as a tribute.[81] From Indira Gandhi came a letter portraying him as "one of the pioneering giants, who along with my father took a leading role in their countries' fight for independence." On a more personal level, she added: "To us who had the privilege of knowing him, Dr. Hatta was a warm human being, deeply concerned with the problems which your country and ours have in common."[82]

According to a Rotterdam newspaper: "Many people are of the opinion that Hatta was not a leader but an idealistic theoretician, he can perhaps be called 'naive.'"[83] It was a strange remark to make about a man who more than any other Indonesian had finalized the transfer of sovereignty. Perhaps Hatta was idealistic, but he also desperately wanted to be a leader as well as a theoretician. The problem of being an advocate of the type of democracy practiced in Western Europe and in Minangkabau traditional society is that one cannot grasp power, one must be placed in power, if one is to play by the rules.

The Minangkabau scholar, Taufik Abdullah wrote: "One thing is sure, expressed by others also, I feel a sense of very great loss now that he is gone."[84] The mourning of the nation and his family was expressed in a poem by Anni Rachim, written in the Dutch language in which she and Hatta had received their schooling:

80 See *Bung Hatta Kita*, pp. 138-39.
81 See *Kompas*, March 15, 1980.
82 Letter from Prime Minister Indira Gandhi to Mrs. Mohammad Hatta, March 17, 1980, as cited in *Bung Hatta Kita*, p. 94.
83 *Nieuwe Rotterdamsche Courant*, March 15, 1980. Critchley did not support this view, stating: "I never considered Hatta to be 'naive.'" Personal communication from T. K. Critchley.
84 Taufik Abdullah, "Ataukah Dialog Antara Gambaran dan Kesan?" in *Bung Hatta: Pribadinya dalam Kenangan*, p. 543.

A miracle has taken place!
After the grave is filled
Ah! See! a gentle rain falls!
Nature's farewell to a great man!
Afterwards...
A dark cloud
Spreads over the ground below
Like an umbrella's shade
Giving shelter to those who need it.
Gone five o'clock
The sky has shed its tears
In a heavy shower.[85]

---

85 Ny. H. S. S. A. Rachim, "Pribadi Bung Hatta yang Saya Kenal," p. 34.

INDEX

Indonesia Free: A Political Biography of Mohammad Hatta
is indexed by Google Books.
Kindly visit http://books.google.com to search the full text.